THE
GREAT
EXPLORERS

THE
GREAT
EXPLORERS

Piers Pennington

Facts On File  **New York**

Editorial Coordinator: John Mason
Art Editor: Grahame Dudley
Design: Ann Dunn
Editor: Mitzi Bales
Research: Sara Butler

Library of Congress Cataloging in Publication Data
Pennington, Piers
Great explorers
Includes index
1. Explorers – biography. 1. Title
G.200.P36   1979   910'.92'2   79-15413
ISBN 0-87196-411-2

Printed and bound in Hong Kong by
Leefung-Asco.

Introduction

This book tells the story of the world's great adventures
into the unknown through the lives of the explorers
themselves – their personalities, achievements, goals, and
disasters. Each chapter deals with an age or area of discovery,
from the early Egyptians about whom little is known to the
much publicized race for the Poles in the recent past.
Da Gama and Columbus, Magellan and Hudson, Bering and
Cook, Livingstone and Amundsen – these are just some of
the most famous of over 50 explorers described. Theirs are
now classic tales of sheer courage, strong convictions,
personal hardship, and sometimes death. These are the men
who filled in the map of the known world, first by outlining
the coasts and then by penetrating the interiors of Asia, the
Americas, Africa, Australasia, and the North and South
polar regions. Among the numerous illustrations are old
maps that show the world as it was thought to be at the time
that various expeditions of exploration were setting out. In
all, the book offers an unusual and interesting approach
to one of the most fascinating of all human endeavors – the
journey into the unknown.

Contents

Chapter 1

The Ancient World

Man has been an explorer since the early days of his existence on earth. Prehistoric men probably first ventured into the unknown seeking food and shelter, or fleeing from danger. Today, their wanderings have been traced by archaeological researches, but no information about earlier journeys was available to the travelers themselves. They had no means of recording their expeditions, and each migrant had to forge his way anew. It is therefore only with the invention of writing and the beginning of recorded history that the story of exploration becomes clear. It tells of man's gradually increasing knowledge of the world he lives in, a knowledge acquired slowly and with difficulty, often in the face of hardship and danger and with only primitive equipment as an aid. The first recorded journeys were made more than 4000 years ago, from the lands at the eastern end of the Mediterranean. There, less than 1000 years earlier, civilization had first emerged.

Left: written travel records began with the Egyptians, who braved the unknown to search for goods they lacked in their own land. One of the most famous journeys was made to Punt in 1493 BC at the behest of Queen Hatshepsut to obtain myrrh trees, but trade with Punt had probably been established before. This ancient colonnade in Dayr al-Bahrī commemorates the seamen who voyaged to Punt.

The First Explorers

The world's first civilizations were born in the so-called Fertile Crescent of the Middle East, an arc of rich land curving from the Persian Gulf, through the valleys of the Tigris and Euphrates rivers and the coastlands of the eastern Mediterranean, to the valley of the Nile River. The highly developed and organized societies which emerged in this region between 5000 and 6000 years ago shared certain common characteristics: towns and cities, laws enforced by a central authority, and a developed technology and expert craftsmen to exploit it. Each accorded importance to religion, learning, and the arts, and each possessed a system of writing, enabling records to be kept.

In Mesopotamia, the land between the Tigris and Euphrates rivers, civilization first emerged around 3500 BC. Before 2400 BC, a king called Sargon established an empire which eventually extended from the Persian Gulf north to the upper Tigris and west to the Mediterranean. The Akkadian Empire – as Sargon's dominions were known – had by 2100 BC been replaced by a smaller empire centered on Ur but within 100 years this had been overthrown by Amorite invaders from the western desert. From the chaos which followed, the Babylonian Empire emerged. Babylonia reached its zenith in the

Right: a depiction of an Egyptian boat on one of the voyages to Punt, decorating the temple of Thebes. These journeys were part of the explorations undertaken by the ancients, usually for trading.

Below left: an Akkadian seal of about 2300 BC. The Akkadians pushed their empire's boundaries to the Persian Gulf in the south, the Mediterranean in the west, and the Upper Tigris in the north.

Below: a fresco from Knossos, capital of Minoan Crete. The Minoans were the first serious explorers of the Mediterranean Sea.

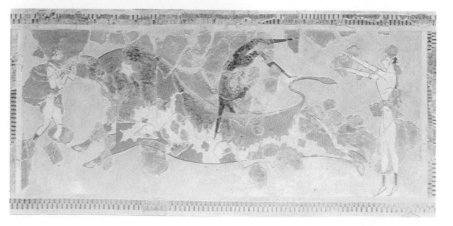

first half of the 18th century, during the reign of Hammurabi, but it survived until 1595 BC when the Hittites of Asia Minor attacked. When the Hittite army withdrew, Kassite tribesmen from the hills northeast of Babylon swept down on the country, establishing a control which was to last for 500 years.

Civilization emerged in Egypt, in the valley of the lower Nile, within 500 years of its appearance in Mesopotamia, and the Egyptian civilization was not only among the most distinctive, but also the longest-lived of ancient times. Egypt's life and its prosperity were based on the Nile River and, like the Mesopotamians on the Tigris and Euphrates, the Egyptians built boats to sail the Nile in very early times. Later, the need for raw materials unobtainable at home drove Egyptians and Mesopotamians to look for them abroad, and as civilization developed, so too did trade. In 2600 BC, the Egyptians made the first seagoing voyage ever recorded, when 40 Egyptian ships sailed to Byblos in Phoenicia for cedarwood from the Mountains of Lebanon. Besides western Asia, the Egyptians traded with Nubia, Ethiopia, and Crete, while by 2000 BC Mesopotamian trading links stretched as far east as India.

Most journeys of exploration in ancient times were made, like the Egyptian voyage to Byblos, in pursuit of material ends. In those days, there was little incentive to travel for the sake of discovery. Ships were small and lacked accurate timekeeping and navigational devices, and while direction-finding was possible with the help of sun and stars, these were of no use if the sky were overcast. Land travelers with no familiar landmark to guide them were equally likely to lose their way. They also faced attack by those through whose lands they passed. Keeping food and water fresh was difficult, and death an ever-present danger should supplies run out.

Despite the hazards of their journeys, however, explorers from the early civilizations gradually pushed back the boundaries of the known world. Egyptian travelers made their way south down the Nile and there are records of several Egyptian voyages down the Red Sea to a land they called *Punt*, (probably present-day Somaliland), where they obtained incense for their religious ceremonies. The most famous expedition to Punt was commissioned in 1493 BC by Queen Hatshepsut, to obtain myrrh trees for her temple in Thebes.

Generally however the Egyptians preferred to leave sea voyaging to other nations and it was the Minoans of Crete who were the true pioneers of exploration in the Mediterranean Sea. The Minoan civilization dates from before 2000 BC, when the great palace of Knossos was built, and at its height, from around 1700 to 1450 BC, there are indications that it ranked with the civilizations of Mesopotamia and Egypt. Crete is ideally situated as a trading center, and Minoan trade routes linked the island not only with Egypt, Cyprus, and the eastern Mediterranean coastlands, but perhaps also with the hitherto unknown western end of the Mediterranean.

After 1450 BC however the Minoan civilization declined. For a short time Minoan trading interests were taken up by the Mycenaeans of

Above: a Phoenician glass bead. Glass products were among the main exports of this ancient nation that pushed out into unknown waters to increase its trade, establishing colonies along the way.

Above right: a Phoenician round ship of the kind used by these hardy seafarers for their trading trips.

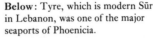

Below: Tyre, which is modern Sūr in Lebanon, was one of the major seaports of Phoenicia.

mainland Greece but from around 1100 BC it was the Phoenicians who dominated the Mediterranean. Phoenicia was a narrow land, bordered on the west by the Mediterranean and on the east by the mountains of Lebanon. The sea coast provided fine harbors, and the mountains timber valuable for ship building, and the Phoenicians became the foremost sea traders of the Mediterranean, carrying cargoes for other nations as well as Phoenician-produced goods. Their ships ranged the Mediterranean from end to end, even sailing through the Strait of Gibraltar into the unknown Atlantic Ocean. Phoenician colonies, strategically placed throughout the Mediterranean, included Carthage which later became a great power in its own right. Among the other places colonized by the Phoenicians were the Aegean islands on the threshold of mainland Greece.

The Greek Spirit of Inquiry

Above: a wall painting found in Paestum, Italy, of Mycenaean Greek soldiers. Paestum was the farthest north that these early Greeks reached and settled.

While the ships of Minoan Crete dominated the Mediterranean seaways, the Mycenaean civilization was developing in mainland Greece. It was the Mycenaeans who inherited Minoan trading interests after the collapse of Crete around 1450 BC but within 300 years Mycenae itself had been overthrown. The centuries that followed are often called the "Dark Age" of Greek history. Not until the 8th century BC was Greek civilization reborn.

The civilization which flourished in Greece after the founding of the first city-states in the years after 800 BC was in sharp contrast to the first civilizations of the Middle East. The Greeks valued their personal and political freedom highly and placed great emphasis on the importance of the individual, rather than solely on the state. They were also intensely curious about the world they lived in, not only geographically, although they were the first to create the science of geography, but in other fields as well.

The first Greek voyages of discovery took place soon after the founding of the city-states and they soon led to the establishment of numerous Greek colonies overseas. Greek settlers made their homes on the shores of the Aegean and the Black seas, on the north coast of Africa, in Sicily, Italy, and in France. In the second half of the 7th century BC, the Strait of Gibraltar –

already known to the Phoenicians – was discovered by a Samian merchant called Colaeus. He returned to Samos with a cargo of silver from Spain.

The Greek world was first mapped by geographers from the colony of Miletus in Asia Minor, Anaximander and Hecataeus, and, following Hecataeus' example, most Greek works on geography were thereafter accompanied by maps. A more vivid picture of the Greek world than any map is, however, given by Herodotus in his *Histories*, written in the 5th century BC. Herodotus traveled widely for his studies and in his work he included everything he had been able to find out about the world. A map reconstructed from his descriptions shows how much geographical knowledge had been acquired by the Greeks.

Herodotus' world was centered on the Mediterranean, bordered by the continents of Europa, Libya (Africa), and Asia. He described accurately how the continents were surrounded to the west and south by ocean, but he knew little of the Atlantic coast of Europe, mentioning neither Britain nor Scandinavia. As evidence that Africa was surrounded by sea, he cited a Phoenician voyage commissioned by Necho in around 600 BC, but his is the only record of such a circumnavigation and many authorities doubt its truth. He described Asia as much smaller than it is in reality, and India to him was simply the region

Below left: a bust of Herodotus, known as the Father of History. He wrote the earliest history that has survived, and in it he recounts the great voyage allegedly made by the Phoenicians around Africa.

ΗΡΟΔΟΤΟΣ

Below: a map showing Greek and Phoenician colonies on the Mediterranean. Larger symbols indicate the mother cities of the colonies.

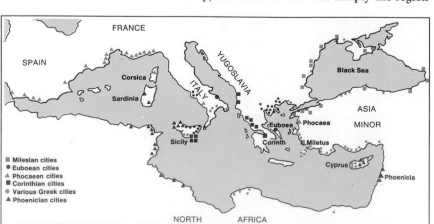

FRANCE
SPAIN
Corsica
Sardinia
ITALY
YUGOSLAVIA
Black Sea
ASIA MINOR
Euboea
Phocaea
Sicily
Corinth
Miletus
Cyprus
Phoenicia
NORTH AFRICA

■ Milesian cities
● Euboean cities
▲ Phocaean cities
■ Corinthian cities
● Various Greek cities
▲ Phoenician cities

of the Indus River, and not a subcontinental peninsula. Herodotus was greatly mistaken both in the course of the Indus and in that of the Nile – according to him, the Indus flowed southeast, while the Nile rose south of the Atlas Mountains and flowed across Africa, before turning north to the Mediterranean.

It is surprising that Herodotus mistook the course of the Indus, because, when he wrote, the river had already been explored by a Greek. Between 510 and 507 BC, Scylax had sailed down the river, then coasted Arabia to the Red Sea. It was after the writing of the *Histories*, however, that another Greek expedition began the exploration of Armenia and Asia Minor. In 401 BC, Prince Cyrus of Persia attempted to overthrow the Persian King Artaxerxes with the help of a Greek mercenary force. When Cyrus' army was defeated and he himself killed, the Greeks found themselves stranded deep within the Persian Empire. Among those they elected to lead them back to Greece was the historian Xenophon who wrote a vivid account of their journey north to the Black Sea. The way led through mountainous country which they crossed in the depths of winter, suffering greatly from frostbite and snow blindness, as well as exhaustion, from which many died. So rugged was the territory they traveled through that it remained almost unknown until modern times.

More than a century passed after Herodotus wrote his *Histories* before his picture of the Atlantic coast of Europe was set right. Then, late in the 4th century BC, a native of Massalia (present-day Marseille) called Pytheas made a pioneering voyage north. Pytheas was a skilled astronomer – before his voyage he had determined the latitude of Marseille very nearly correctly – and during his voyage into the Atlantic he made observations of latitude besides studying the tides. There is however some dispute about his landfalls because the book he wrote about his voyage has been lost. He certainly sailed north to Britain, probably circumnavigating the island, and made several expeditions into the interior. On one of these, he

Right: Xenophon leading his troops back to Greece from Turkey after his Persian ally was defeated. He broke new ground in the route he chose for the return, and wrote up these travels.

Below left: a woodcut of a man with huge ears, published in 1544 but based on the tales of the ancient Greek Scylax. He was the first Westerner to travel down the Indus and across the sea to Arabia.

Below: a map showing Thule, which was described by Pytheas in one of the first recorded journeys north by a Greek. Some think that Thule was present-day Iceland and others say that it was Norway.

appears to have heard of an island called *Thule*, six days' sail to the north. Pytheas visited Thule, – variously identified as Iceland and Norway – then he returned to the European mainland. Some authorities believe he reached the Baltic, but he may have only explored the European coast north to the Elbe River before turning back to Marseille.

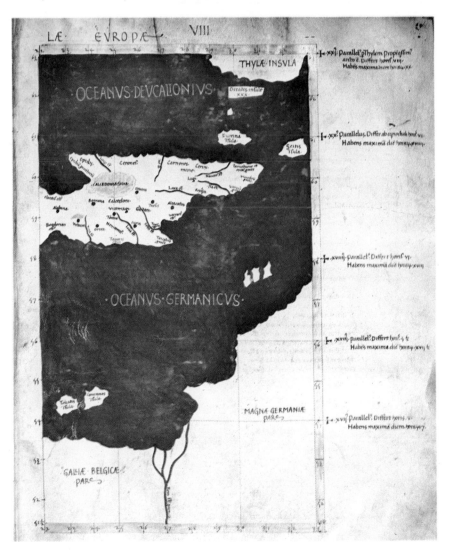

Alexander the Great 356-323 BC

In 334 BC Alexander of Macedonia crossed the Hellespont into Asia with an army of 35,000 men. When he died 11 years later, he ruled the greatest empire the world then knew. His conquest of the Persian Empire involved the exploration of Asia east to the Indus River, including many lands previously unknown to Europeans. His expedition can be said to have opened a whole new world to the Greeks.

Alexander was born in 356 BC and between the ages of 13 and 16 he was educated by the Greek philosopher Aristotle, who fostered his interest in philosophy and scientific investigation. His father, King Philip II of Macedonia, united the Greek city-states under Macedonian rule, and was planning the conquest of Persia when he was assassinated in 336. Alexander succeeded not only to the throne of Macedonia but also to his father's ambitious plan. After Philip's death he first secured his rule in Greece and then led his army east.

Alexander's army crossed the Hellespont – now called the Dardanelles – in the spring of 334 and on the Granicus River, which flows into the Sea of Marmara, it met the Persians in battle for the first time, inflicting a heavy defeat. Alexander then pressed on through Asia Minor. He was at Myriandrus (near present-day Iskenderun) when he learned that King Darius III of Persia and his army were at Issus, to his north.

The story goes that, while Alexander was in

Above: stonework decoration showing the Persian king fighting a lion on one of the few gateways left in Persepolis. This royal Persian city was burned by Alexander the Great on his journey of conquest across Asia Minor and Asia.

Asia Minor, he had succeeded in loosing the famous Gordian knot which, according to legend, could only be untied by the man who was to rule Asia – the usual name for the Persian Empire at that time. Certainly his victory over Darius at Issus must have indicated that the legend was to be fulfilled. The Persians were routed and Darius put to flight.

From Issus, Alexander turned south down the Mediterranean coast, intending to capture the ports from which the Persian fleet was refitted and supplied, and thus render the fleet ineffective. Byblos and Sidon were taken, but Tyre only fell to Alexander after a seven-month siege. The conquest of the city in July 332 was accompanied by terrible cruelty; many Tyrians were massacred, and women and children sold as slaves. During the siege, Alexander received a second offer of peace from Darius. The terms were so favorable that Alexander's second-in-command, Parmenio, is said to have commented that he should accept, were he Alexander. "That," replied Alexander, "is what·I should do were I Parmenio," and he again refused to consider Darius' terms.

Alexander's campaign then led south via Gaza into Egypt, where he was welcomed as a liberator. He visited the oracle at Siwah and founded the city of Alexandria, one of some 70 cities he established before his expedition came to an end.

The pursuit of Darius led Alexander back from Egypt and into Mesopotamia where at Gaugamela, east of the Tigris River, he met the Persian king once more. Alexander's victory put Darius to flight again, and effectively won the war, although much more fighting was necessary before the Persian Empire could truly be said to be his. He entered Babylon, however, without battle, then continued to the great treasure-houses of Persia, Susa, Persepolis, and Pasargadae. At Persepolis he burned down the palace of Xerxes, either as retribution for Persian atrocities in Greece, or as a symbol that his war with Persia was at an end.

By this time, Alexander's army had passed into country unmapped by and virtually unknown to the Greeks – indeed, the route he followed from Susa to Persepolis remained little known until recent times. From Persepolis, he turned northwest for Ecbatana (modern Hamadan) then northeast for Rhagae (near Teheran), always in pursuit of the retreating Persian king. Soon, however, he learned that Darius had been murdered by Bessus, Persian satrap or provincial governor of Bactria. In accordance with his chivalrous treatment of Darius' wife and children, who had been left in his charge after Issus, Alexander sent Darius' body to Persepolis, to be buried in the royal tombs. The Persian king's death did, however, leave Alexander free to confirm his conquest of Persia by styling himself Lord of Asia – as the ruler of the Persian Empire was then known.

It still remained to bring Bessus to justice, and

Left: a portrayal of the birth of Alexander the Great from a 16th-century manuscript.

Above: section of a Roman mosaic showing the Persian King Darius III at the point of retreat in the Battle of Issus. He was defeated by Alexander the Great.

Left: another part of the mosaic depicting Alexander. His pursuit of the Persians took him and his army into lands previously little known to the Greeks.

when Alexander heard that he had usurped Darius' title of Great King and was fomenting revolt in the eastern provinces of the empire, Alexander led his army toward Bactria. The Hindu Kush mountains north of Kabul were crossed by the Khawak Pass, which lies more than 11,500 feet above sea level, then the army descended into Bactria to find Bessus had laid the province waste and fled north beyond the Oxus River (Amu Darya). By the time Alexander's men overtook him, he had already been overthrown. To punish his revolt, he was flogged and had his nose and ears cut off before being sent to Ecbatana where he was publicly put to death.

Alexander had now accomplished his principal aims – the Persian Empire was his and the rebellious Bessus had been captured and punished – but he was unwilling to abandon his expedition yet. He spent the year 328 in the subjugation of Bactria and in early summer 327 recrossed the Hindu Kush to the south. Sending half of the army ahead by way of the Khyber Pass to build a boat bridge across the Indus River, Alexander himself fought his way to the river through the hills north of the pass. On this journey he achieved one of his most impressive successes in a siege with the conquest of the reputedly impregnable Mount Aornos (Pir-Sar). But simply to have led such an army through that rugged mountain territory would have been a magnificent feat.

Crossing the Indus by means of the boat bridge his men had constructed, Alexander continued to the Hydaspes (Jhelum), where he met and defeated the king of the region in what was to be his last great battle. He then pushed on east, but on the banks of the Hyphasis – probably the Beas River – his men mutinied. Alexander's greatest eloquence could not persuade them to continue into the unknown. They were weary with the long years of war, and anxious to see their homes and families again. At last, Alexander submitted to their will and consented to return.

At that time, Alexander believed that the Indus was probably the source of the Nile, known under a different name, and he determined to sail down the river to test his theory. On the Hydaspes River, he assembled a large fleet in which he embarked part of his force. The remainder of his men were divided into three groups and made the journey down river by land. In November 326 they set off. The mouths of the Indus were reached the following summer, and after thoroughly exploring both arms of the river and sailing out to sea, Alexander conclusively proved that it was not connected to the Nile.

Right: a statue of Bucephalus, the horse that Alexander rode on his long journey to India.

Below: Alexander's army caught in the tide at the mouth of the Indus River. Tidal waters were a new experience for the Greeks, who did not encounter changing currents in the almost tideless Mediterranean.

Even before the expedition reached the mouths of the Indus, Alexander dispatched Craterus, one of his senior officers, back to Persia together with most of the army. The fleet, under the command of Nearchus, was then instructed to sail along the coast to the Persian Gulf to open a sea route to the Euphrates. Alexander himself, with his remaining men, made his way along the unexplored Makrān coast. He intended to establish supply depots for the fleet but the Taloi Mountains forced him to turn inland, leaving his fleet to forage for itself. Alexander's journey was among the hardest he had undertaken. For 200 miles his followers, who included women and children, trudged through waterless desert, marching at night to avoid the intense heat. Food and fuel were in short supply, and many of the marchers died before a more hospitable region was reached.

Meanwhile, Alexander's failure to provision the fleet from the shore caused the sailors nearly as much hardship as the marchers overland. Nearchus' men were forced to land and fight for food and in time conditions on the ships became so bad that Nearchus was afraid to land in case his men deserted. It was six months before he and Alexander were reunited near Hormuz, and the great expedition to the east could be said to be over.

Alexander's army reached Susa in the spring of 324 BC. In June 323, at the age of 32, he died. During the year that remained to him after his return from the East, his interest appears to have turned increasingly to exploration. Heraclides was sent to explore the Caspian Sea, and in particular to find out whether it was connected to the ocean then supposed to bound the world to the north, and Alexander also sent ships to

Above: a Greek vase decorated with ships. Vessels similar to these were probably used by Nearchus to sail from India to the Persian Gulf while Alexander was traversing the terrible Makran Desert overland.

sail around Arabia, hoping to discover a sea link between India and the Red Sea. Both these projects were however abandoned when Alexander died.

The last year of Alexander's life was marked by an ever-increasing belief in his own power and infallibility, which culminated in the demand that his dominions should recognize him as a god. Not all were wholehearted in their acceptance – Sparta's proclamation of divinity read "Since Alexander wishes to be a god, let him be a god" – and Alexander's decree emphasized the growing discontent of the Macedonians and Greeks. They believed that Alexander intended to become an absolute monarch in the Persian manner, and perhaps to transfer the capital of his empire to Asia. With such divisions among his subjects, and no strong heir to succeed him, it is not surprising that Alexander's empire did not long survive his death. His conquests had, however, moved the focus of the world eastward, spreading Greek civilization deep into Asia. Similarly, he had drawn a fuller and more accurate picture of Asia for the Greeks.

Below: a map of Alexander's empire at its height. In the brief period from 334 to 323 BC, the Greeks went as far east as the Indus River and as far west as the desert of what is now Libya.

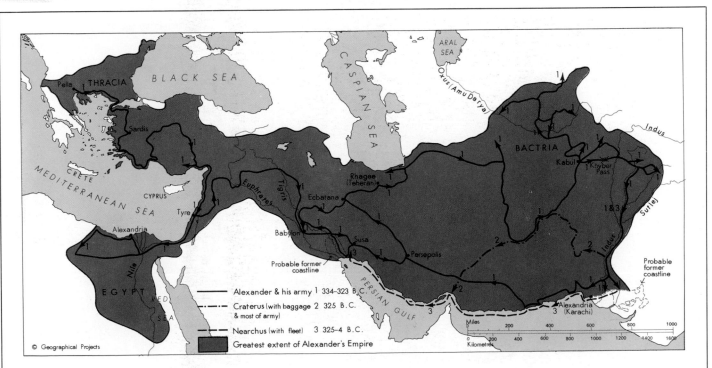

Alexander & his army 1 334–323 B.C.
Craterus (with baggage 2 325 B.C. & most of army)
Nearchus (with fleet) 3 325–4 B.C.
Greatest extent of Alexander's Empire

© Geographical Projects

The Roman Achievement

At the time of Alexander the Great Rome was an independent republic ruling a small area of western Italy. In the following centuries it built up an empire far greater than Alexander's had been. By the second century AD Roman rule extended from northern Britain southeast through Europe to the Persian Gulf and Egypt, and along the north coast of Africa, and the Romans were in contact with lands much farther afield.

Throughout the Roman dominions the benefits of Roman civilization were felt. This originally owed much to that of Greece but the Roman world was both more highly organized and more materialistic than the Greek. Fine roads linked the outermost provinces with the hub of the empire, Rome; each province was in charge of a governor responsible to Rome; and in each Roman law operated – for Roman citizens at least – and Roman coinage, Roman weights and measures and the Latin language were used.

From the point of view of discovery, Roman travels within the empire were perhaps even more important than the journeys they undertook outside. The Romans were responsible for the detailed exploration of much of Europe, for little was yet known about the interior of most

Right: a 15th-century map of eastern Africa carries on the tradition of depicting Ptolemy's Mountains of the Moon as the source of the Nile River. This misleading information may have come to Ptolemy from a Greek merchant who, it is said, traveled in this region.

Below: a battle between troops of Julius Caesar and a Germanic tribe. The Romans explored much of Europe as they extended their empire north and west.

European countries. Roman soldiers bent on conquest tramped the length and breadth of Spain, Gaul (France), and Britain. They forged and surveyed routes over the Alps to link their conquests with Rome, and pushed the empire's frontiers north to the Danube and the Rhine and, for a brief period, to the Elbe. In Africa, in the first century AD, several expeditions were made from the north coast into the interior; in 42 AD Suetonius Paulinus crossed the Atlas Mountains and later the Emperor Nero sent a party to discover the sources of the Nile. While his explorers failed in their main object, they penetrated farther south than any travelers had before. It is

also reported that a trader named Diogenes traveled inland from the east coast of Africa and discovered two lakes fed by melting snows from a range of mountains. These lakes Diogenes believed to be the sources of the Nile.

Vast as the Roman dominions were, they could not satisfy the demand for luxuries in imperial Rome, and many of the most sought-after goods came to Rome from the East. Often, they were brought by Arab traders, and it was in an attempt to break the commercial monopoly of the Arabs that the Emperor Augustus sent Aelius Gallus into Arabia in 25 BC. Although Gallus appears to have reached the borders of the Hadhramaut and Yemen, his expedition was a failure. It was however the only attempt to explore Arabia made in ancient times.

In the first century AD trade with India was facilitated by a Greek mariner called Hippalus who discovered that the seasonal monsoon winds could be used to cross the Arabian Sea. In summer, the monsoons blow across the Arabian Sea from the southwest and in winter from the northeast, and with the southwest summer monsoon Hippalus sailed from the coast of Arabia to the Indus River. Later voyagers used the southwest monsoon to reach the southern coast of India; they rounded the subcontinent and sailed across the Bay of Bengal to the Malay Peninsula. By the second century AD, European travelers had reached China by sea.

The sea route to China was however so long and perilous that it appears to have been seldom used. Silk – the most important European import from China – and other Eastern luxuries were usually brought to Europe overland. Each section of the so-called silk routes was controlled by different people, and the silk appears to have changed hands several times, rather than remaining the property of any one trader. It was therefore some time after the appearance of Chinese goods in Rome before journeys were under-

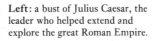

Above: a mosaic of a small Roman boat and its crew. The Romans had to be good navigators because they often had to cross the seas to reach new lands to conquer.

taken between east and west. In 97 AD Chinese travelers visited Antioch and subsequently the Romans used the silk routes to journey into central Asia. It is said that in the sixth century AD two monks made their way overland to China, smuggling out the silkworms' eggs which made it possible to produce silk in the west.

By that time, however, the Roman Empire was effectively at an end. At the end of the third century AD, it had been divided into two, and although the East and West Roman Empires were later briefly reunited, by 400 AD they had been divided for good. Already the barbarians were pressing on the empire's frontiers. In 406 AD, the Rhine was abandoned; three years later, Britain was left undefended and in 410 AD Rome itself was sacked. The West Roman Empire struggled on until 476 AD, when the last emperor was deposed and Rome fell to the barbarians. Only the East Roman Empire, from its capital of Constantinople, remained to keep the memory of Roman civilization alive in the medieval world.

Left: a bust of Julius Caesar, the leader who helped extend and explore the great Roman Empire.

Right: a coin with the head of Attila the Hun. Attila's troops swept over Europe in a campaign of conquest that meant the end of the already dying Roman Empire.

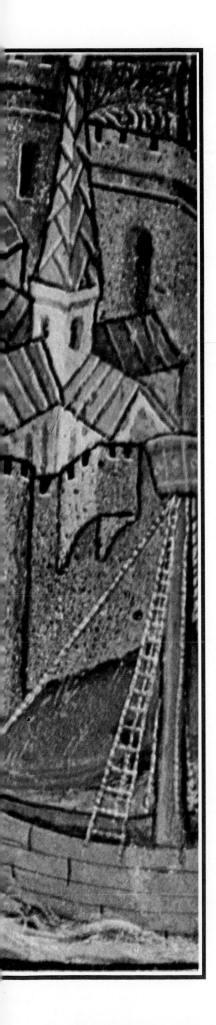

Chapter 2

The
Middle Ages

The fall of the Roman Empire involved far more than the loss of a unifying government that had brought peace and civilization to much of the known world. Long before the 5th century AD, the Romans had largely lost interest in exploration, but after the fall of Rome the spirit of scientific inquiry that had been so marked a feature of classical culture also completely disappeared. The only unifying force in medieval Europe was the Church, but although missionaries were sent into the unknown to convert non-Christians, the Church tended to hinder rather than advance the progress of geographical knowledge. Ecclesiastical ideas about the world were strictly based on the Bible, and discoveries were unwelcome in case they disproved accepted belief. However the urge to discovery never completely died in Europe, although its first manifestation was characteristically in a non-Christian country.

Left: Marco Polo made one of the best-known, and certainly the most important overland journeys of medieval times, traveling from the city of Venice to what is now China. Welcomed in the court of the enlightened Kublai Khan, he spent 24 years exploring the Far East – and left a book that records his adventures for following generations. This early 15th-century manuscript shows the Bridge of Sindufu in Tibet, which Polo visited.

The Irish and The Vikings

Toward 800 AD, the Viking ships first nosed their way out of the sheltered fjords of Norway and turned their bows south toward the English coast. For more than 150 years afterward, Europe was seldom free from the menace of these ruthless raiders – "no haven, no landing-place, no stronghold, no fort, no castle might be found, but it was submerged by waves of Vikings and pirates" wrote an Irish chronicler some 30 years after the Vikings made their first raid. The appearance of the Vikings, however, heralded one of the few spurts of exploration which took place from medieval Europe. Pursuing their three-fold aims of land, wealth, and fame, the Vikings set sail west into the Atlantic, reaching Iceland, Greenland and eventually discovering the New World nearly 500 years before Christopher Columbus made his first landfall there.

The Viking homelands in Scandinavia, in the very northernmost regions of Europe, possessed insufficient agricultural land to support their ever-increasing population, and as the centuries passed it became necessary for the Vikings to seek their living elsewhere. The Swedish Vikings, who were principally traders, looked across the Baltic to the lands of eastern Europe. By 700 and probably even earlier, the Swedes were established on the eastern shores of the Baltic, and from their bases there they made their way along the great Vistula and Dnepr rivers to the Black Sea and eventually to Constantinople and along the Volga to the Caspian. It was Swedish Vikings

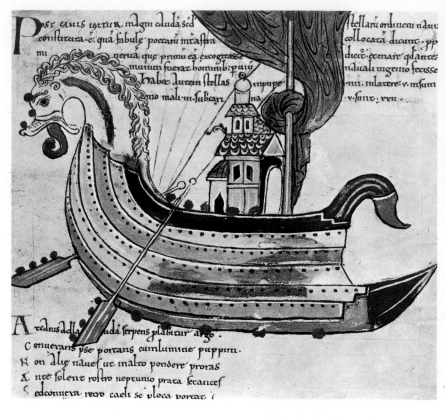

Above: a Norse dragon ship used by the Vikings for their terrifying lightning raids throughout western Europe. It was many years before they settled any of the places that they plundered regularly.

who founded the city-states of Novgorod and Kiev in the country to which one Swedish tribe, the Rus, gave its name.

The land-hungry Vikings of Norway and Denmark, however, looked almost exclusively south and west toward the coasts of Europe and the Atlantic Ocean. As befits the people of sea-girt countries they had from early times been seafarers, but Viking mariners were limited to coasting voyages until they developed a ship capable of withstanding long periods at sea. Around the middle of the 8th century, they developed such a vessel – the *knörr*.

The Viking knörr of the 9th century was eminently seaworthy, first and foremost a sailing ship, but possessing oars as an auxiliary means of power. The ship was clinker-built – that is, with planks overlapping – principally from oak, although the oars were usually pine. The single mast carried a big square sail. Several of them have been excavated in good condition. One of them, the Gokstad ship, built around 850, is some 76 feet long and 17.5 feet in beam, but only 6.5 feet deep from gunwhale to keel. With such a shallow draft, the knörr could be sailed up-river deep into the heart of the countryside, or run ashore on a shelving beach.

In 793, Viking raiders reached the monastery of Lindisfarne, off the northeast English coast, and within a few years southern England, Wales, and Ireland had all been subjected to Viking attacks. The European mainland was the next object of Norse attentions; in 842 Nantes on France's Atlantic coast suffered a raid of terrible brutality, Paris was plundered in 845, and by 862 Viking ships had sailed through the Strait of

Left: a map showing how the Vikings fanned out from Scandinavia on their many expeditions for booty. The orange areas indicate their original homelands and the farflung regions that they invaded or influenced.

Left: St. Brendan and his missionaries in a small boat encircled by a huge fish, an illustration of one of the somewhat fantastic tales in the book describing his travels. There is evidence, however, that this Irish abbot undertook real voyages of great distances.

Below: the coast of Iceland, which Irish monks probably first reached in about 770. A hundred years later, adventurous Vikings settled this harsh island believed by some to be the Thule of ancient Greek writings.

Bottom: a reconstruction of a knörr, the sturdy Viking ship used by merchants and settlers because of the good storage capacity and landing ability.

then climbed Reydarfjall before sailing for home. Naddod named the island Snaeland (Snowland) because a snow storm enveloped Reydarfjall as he left. It was Iceland's third Norse visitor, Floki Vilgerdason, who gave the island the name by which it is known today. It seems that Floki intended to settle in Iceland, for he took livestock on his voyage, but although he over-wintered in the region of Breidhafjördhur he returned home disenchanted the following year.

The first settler to remain in Iceland was a Norwegian Viking, Ingolf, who made his home where the Icelandic capital Reykjavik now stands. Others soon followed him for most Norsemen, unlike Floki, saw Iceland as an earthly paradise. The pastureland was rich, and there was sufficient timber for building, fish abounded in the island's streams and rivers, while offshore swam fish, seals, and whales. The pace of Norwegian emigration to Iceland quickened toward the end of the 9th century, when King Harold Fairhair attempted to unify Norway under his rule. By about 930, all the habitable land had been settled, and Iceland's civilization was almost exclusively Norse.

In the meantime, what had become of the Irish who had first settled Iceland? The Norse

Gibraltar bringing rapine and slaughter to North Africa and the Balearics and east to the Italian coast. Although at first the Vikings came merely to raid, returning each winter to their northern homelands, in time they began to settle these lands that were so much richer than theirs.

The peoples of the European mainland could, and no doubt did, flee inland from the Viking onslaught, but for the inhabitants of the offshore islands there was no such easy escape. Their only route to safety lay across the hostile, almost unknown sea. The first travelers to venture far on the waters of the Atlantic were Irish monks, seeking religious retreats. Soon after 700, the Irish reached the Faeroes, and by the end of the 8th century they were in Iceland.

Although the Faeroes were among the first landfalls of Viking raiders, more than 50 years passed before Vikings first reached the Iceland coast. Even then, the Norse discovery of Iceland appears to have been accidental. The first Viking to sight Iceland was probably Gardar Svarsson, who around 860 was driven off course to the island. He wintered at Húsavik, then circum-navigated his discovery, which he named Gardarsholm. Naddod, the second Norse visitor, likewise arrived in Iceland unintentionally. Storm-driven, he made land at Reydarfjord,

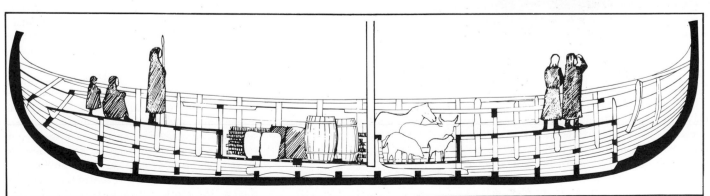

found only a few solitary monks when they reached the island, but it appears that other settlers had fled farther west to Greenland where, on the southwest coast, there was land suitable for settlement and reasonably secure from the Norse. The Viking discovery of Greenland, like that of Iceland, appears to have been accidental. Perhaps around 930, a Norwegian sailor named Gunnbjorn was blown by storms to the Greenland coast.

Fifty years passed after Gunnbjorn's discovery before the Vikings made any attempt to follow it up. In 982, however, as punishment for manslaughter, an Icelandic settler was exiled from his country for three years – the usual sentence for a crime common in a land whose inhabitants regarded killing as a sign of manhood and where blood feuds were rife. This particular exile is however of special importance to the story of Norse exploration, for he and his family played a prominent part in future Norse voyages west. His name was Eric Thorwaldsson, but he is usually known as Eric the Red.

When Eric received his sentence of exile, he decided that, rather than spending its term in raiding, as was then usual, he would investigate the land Gunnbjorn had sighted long before. Rounding Cape Farewell at the southern tip of Greenland, he passed the first winter on the island of Eriksey, then in spring continued into Eriksfjord. No doubt to his surprise he could see no sign of any inhabitants. The fate of the Irish settlers, whose presence is indicated by archaeological findings, as well as by tradition, remains a mystery. Eric must, however, have been impressed by the country, for it appears that he marked out the site of a settlement for himself before continuing his travels. Some scholars believe that these led him across the Davis Strait to Baffin Island, but it seems more likely that he spent the following years exploring the west coast of Greenland before returning to Iceland in 985. The following year he led a colonizing expedition west.

Eric made his home at Brattahlid on Eriks-

fjord in what became known as the Eastern Settlement of Greenland. Later colonists settled around what is now Ivigtut and some 10 years after Eric's expedition the Western Settlement was founded in the region of present-day Godthaab. Probably as many as 3000 people lived in the Norse colonies of Greenland at their height. Although the colonists possessed pastureland and fish in abundance, they would have been unable to survive without trade, particularly for timber – Greenland is almost treeless – and corn. These and other necessaries were imported, usually from Norway, and in exchange the Greenlanders supplied furs, oil, and other natural products of their land.

In 986, an Icelandic trader named Bjarni Herjulfsson returned from a winter's trading in Norway to stay with his father, only to find that his father had sailed for Greenland with Eric the Red. No doubt sure that the Greenland colonists would be glad to purchase his cargo, Bjarni set sail for Greenland himself. Soon however his ship was caught in northerly gales and driven south. Fog closed in and Bjarni and his men were totally lost. When at last the sun reappeared, they attempted to establish their position, but sailed for two more days without reaching land. The country that then came into sight was hilly and heavily wooded – quite unlike the descriptions Bjarni had heard of Greenland – and so he

Above: a double-ended vessel of the type used by Bjarni Herjulfsson when, in searching for Greenland, he got lost and made the first sighting by a European of the coast of North America.

continued north. After sighting two more lands, neither of which was the one he aimed for, he turned his ship east, and after four days' sailing reached Greenland's southwestern tip.

It thus appears that Bjarni Herjulfsson was the first European to discover America, but although he sighted the continent, he never went ashore. Some years after his voyage, however, there seems to have been much talk of discovery in Greenland – perhaps because the Greenland settlements in their turn were becoming overcrowded – and around the year 1000 Leif Ericson, son of Eric the Red, bought Bjarni's ship and fitted it out for a voyage west. He seems to have traced Bjarni's route in reverse, making three landfalls on the American mainland. The first of these he called *Helluland,* or Flat-stone Land, and from the descriptions of it in the Norse sagas most scholars have identified it with the southern part of Baffin Island. Leif's second landfall was named *Markland* or Wood Land, and this appears to have been Labrador, but there is no such agreement about *Vinland* (Wine Land), the third land visited by Leif. This has been situated at various points on the American mainland from northern Newfoundland south to Cape Cod and even beyond.

Leif's men wintered in Vinland, at a site they called *Leifsbudir* or Leif's Booths, then returned to Greenland, perhaps with a cargo of timber which would have been invaluable in that treeless land. They were full of praise for their new discovery but, curiously enough, Leif never returned there himself. His brother Thorwald did, however, sail to Vinland, probably in 1002, the year after Leif's return.

From Leifsbudir, Thorwald sailed north, then west into a great inlet where, according to the sagas, he saw a wooded headland where he would have liked to make his home. On this headland, the Norsemen had their first encounter with the natives of the American mainland – they found three skin boats, with three natives under each.

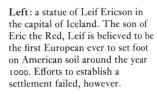

Eight of them were captured and killed by Thorwald's men, but one escaped to raise the alarm. His tale brought a native force down upon the Norsemen, and in the ensuing clash Thorwald was killed. His men buried him on the headland he had admired, then returned to Leifsbudir, where they spent the winter before sailing for Greenland with their sad news.

The next Norse voyage to Vinland failed, like Thorwald's, because of friction between the Vikings and the natives. It was led by an Icelander, Thorfinn Karlsefni, who was married to Eric the Red's daughter-in-law Gudrid, and it appears that his intention was to settle in the New World. While they were there, Gudrid bore Thorfinn a son, whom they named Snorri, and who has been called the first North American of wholly European descent. Accounts of Thorfinn's expedition vary – according to *Eric the Red's Saga,* he actually sailed in company with Thorwald – but he seems to have reached Leifsbudir, to have founded his colony and begun trading with the natives. Although this was carried on peaceably at first, hostilities did break out, and the Norsemen were eventually forced to abandon their settlement and return to the safety of Greenland. The sagas do tell of another expedition to Vinland, led by Freydis, Eric the Red's illegitimate daughter, but this seems to have been notable principally for the bloodthirsty way in which Freydis murdered her companions. After these voyages, Norse attempts to settle Vinland came to an end.

Voyagers from the Greenland colonies seem, however, to have continued visiting Vinland, presumably in search of wood and furs, and it was only in the middle of the 14th century that these sporadic expeditions ceased. By that time, the Greenland colonies themselves were in decline. The climate of the northern regions was becoming progressively colder; regular contact with Europe, always difficult but vital to the survival of the colonies, died out; and Eskimos settled in Greenland in increasing numbers. It is not known exactly what happened to the Greenland settlements, but by about 1500, the Norse colonies which had been the springboard for the first European discovery of North America had completely disappeared.

25

The Beatus Map

Cartography in the Middle Ages was profoundly affected by the Church's desire for religious conformity, for the map makers were usually monks who drew their maps according to accepted ecclesiastical ideas. Had the Bible conformed to geographical reality, accurate maps might have been possible, but because the two differed Christian maps were a strange blend of geographical fact and Biblical fantasy. Only in the Islamic Empire was the spirit of the classical geographers kept alive, partly through the translation into Arabic of one of the most influential classical works on geography, the *Geography* written by Ptolemy of Alexandria in the second century AD.

It was also in Alexandria that one of the most notorious medieval works on geography was written, the *Christian Topography* compiled by a merchant turned monk called Cosmas in the mid-6th century AD. Cosmas drew on the Bible to support his theory of a flat earth, with Jerusalem in the center, and boxed in by the heavens. Less preposterous, but still far from reality, are the so-called "Beatus" maps, drawn between the 10th and 13th centuries and copied from a map used by a Spanish monk, Beatus of Valcavado, to illustrate his *Commentary on the Apocalypse* of 776. Beatus maps are oriented not to the north, but to the sacred East, where Palestine, the birthplace of Christianity, lies. They are therefore easier to read if given a quarter turn to the right, so that the position of the continents corresponds to a modern map of the world.

According to an inscription on this map, nothing is known of the land called the "fourth part of the world" because of the heat of the sun. Of the rest, Beatus' world is roughly circular, surrounded by an ocean studded with islands. Although off the western coast of Britain the ocean is named "Britannicus," none of the islands is identified as Britain, but off the coast of Libya (Africa) the Insulae Fortunatarum – a former name for the Canary Islands – are shown. Within the encircling ocean, the continents are depicted in their correct positions in relation to each other and careful study of the map reveals a number of real, if hard to recognize, geographical features. The distortions of shape, distance, and scale are, however, so great that a Beatus map would have been of little value to a medieval traveler setting out into the unknown.

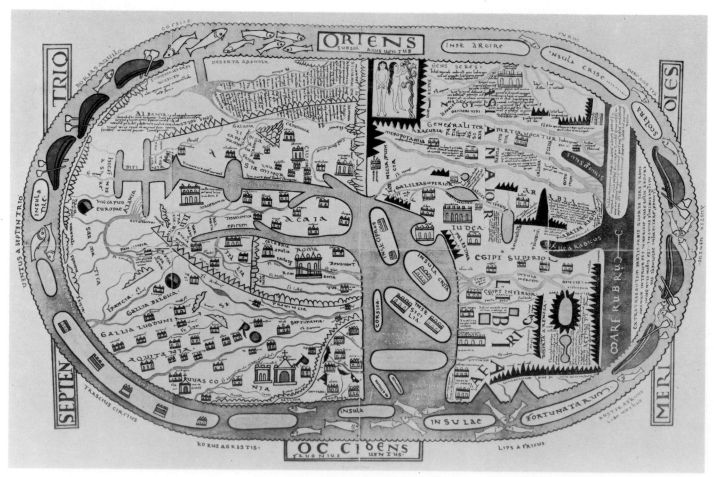

The Mongol Expansion

At the dawn of the 13th century, Europeans knew very little about Asia, apart from the Levant, where the Crusades to rescue Palestine from the Muslims had been in progress for more than 100 years. Their reawakening, when it came, was as sudden and painful as their subjection to the Viking onslaught centuries before. Out of the East swept the armies of the Mongols, fresh from victories in China and western Asia, and poised for further conquests. It was the threat of the Mongol invasion that prompted European diplomatic missions to the Mongol capital, and it was the final consolidation of the Mongol empire that once more opened trade between east and west.

The homeland of the Mongols is the huge plateau of Mongolia, today divided between China and the Mongolian People's Republic. The natives of this region, traditionally nomad herdsmen, evolved a hierarchical society based

Right: a portrait of the great Mongol ruler Genghis Khan in later life. It is taken from a Chinese album of emperors that dates from the 13th century.

on the clan, the tribe – or group of clans – and the people or state – or group of tribes. The first tribal empire in the region dates back to the 4th century BC and in the succeeding centuries shifts in power secured the dominance of first one group of tribes, then another. Then around 1162 AD Temujin was born. From the nomad peoples of Mongolia had sprung a world conqueror in the tradition of Alexander, and the campaigns that he initiated spread Mongol rule across Asia from east to west.

By 1206 Temujin had effectively made himself master of Mongolia and was proclaimed ruler of all the Mongols, with the title of Genghis Khan. The new Mongol leader was no simple tribal chieftain, but a skilled general, politician, and administrator. He converted the Mongols' traditionally hierarchical society into a new feudal order superseding all existing tribal ties, and binding his men both in war and in peace; existing laws were codified and added to in the *yasa*, a system of legislation governing every

Left: detail from a painting of two travelers in conversation. Travel to the East increased after the death of Genghis Khan, and Europeans began to learn about the advanced civilizations of the eastern lands.

Below: a 14th-century Chinese painting of a Mongolian caravan.

aspect of Mongol life, from personal behavior to criminal penalties, taxation, and foreign relations; and the army was so organized and disciplined that it became one of the most efficient fighting forces the world has known.

The first campaigns of Genghis Khan's remodeled army had as their object the security of Mongolia. With that assured Genghis was ready to lead his men farther afield. In 1211, he crossed the Gobi desert into China and after four years' campaigning, in 1215 he took and sacked the Chin capital Chung-tu (Peking). Then, leaving the Mongols in control of China north of the Hwang Ho River, Genghis Khan himself turned west, to Karakhitai, in the region of Lake Balkhash. Subjugating Karakhitai, he pushed west into the Islamic empire of Khwarazm. By the time he set out for Mongolia again in 1223, the great cities of Khwarazm – including Balkh and Samarkand – had fallen to the Mongols, thousands of their inhabitants had been massacred, and their Islamic culture destroyed.

Genghis Khan died in 1227, while campaigning in China and, following Mongol tradition, his empire was divided between his four sons. His third son, Ögödei, succeeded Genghis as Great Khan, or supreme ruler of the whole. Under Ögödei, the Mongols turned their attention to

Above: Genghis Khan (with the scepter) outside his luxurious tent.

Below: Batu, grandson of Genghis Khan and leader of the Golden Horde. He ruled the part of the Mongol Empire lying in present-day Russia and Kazakhstan.

the administration of their empire, which stretched from the Yellow Sea in the east to the Caspian in the west. The imperial post, or *yam*, with post stations at regular intervals, carried orders and reports throughout this vast empire and, if they had the necessary authority, officials and ambassadors too. During this calm period, conquest was not forgotten. Ögödei continued his father's campaigns in China and on the western front the Mongols invaded Russia, where Genghis' grandson Batu established the Golden Horde. In 1240, they took Kiev – one of the city-states founded by the Swedish Vikings – then they advanced into Poland and Hungary. By 1241, Austria and Bohemia were threatened. Suddenly however the Mongol advance westward stopped. Ögödei was dead, and the Mongol leaders had to return to Mongolia to attend the election of a new Great Khan.

As the Mongols thrust westward, the leaders of Christian Europe looked on in fear, appalled both by the invaders' methods and by the speed of their advance. During the regency which followed Ögödei's death Mongol troops reached southern Asia Minor and the shores of the Mediterranean Sea. In June 1245, the Council of Lyons met to consider how Christian Europe should deal with the Mongol terror and sub-

sequently the Pope, Innocent IV, sent four missions east. One of these, led by Giovanni di Piano Carpini, reached the Mongol capital Karakoram in time for the enthronement of Ögödei's successor Güyük in 1246. Carpini carried a letter from the pope, reproaching the Great Khan for Mongol atrocities, threatening him with Heavenly vengeance – and asking what his future intentions were. The reply was hardly promising. "If you . . . run counter to our orders," wrote Güyük, "we shall know that you are our foe. [Then] how can we forsee what will happen to you? Heaven alone knows."

Unknown either to Güyük or Pope Innocent, however, the Mongols had already reached the westernmost limit of their advance. Güyük's successor, Möngke, turned his attention to the Middle East, where his forces subdued the heretical Ismaili Muslim sect, the Assassins. They took Baghdad and Syria, and were preparing an attack on Egypt when news came of Möngke's death. Möngke brought a measure of civilization to the Mongol court, surrounding himself with scholars, foreign ambassadors, and representatives of all known religions. Among the latter was William of Rubruck, a missionary sent to the Mongols in 1253 by King Louis IX of France. Rubruck's journey was valuable for his account of Karakoram, at that time still the Mongol capital, although it was Möngke who first proposed moving his capital to Peking. Louis must have felt, however, that Rubruck's description of his journey was small compensation for the letter he brought Louis from Möngke which ended as threateningly as Güyük's letter to Pope Innocent had done.

In 1259, however, Möngke died of a fever and the struggle for the throne which followed appears to have saved Europe yet again. It was five years before Kublai, Genghis' grandson, was unchallenged as Great Khan. Kublai carried out Möngke's plan to move the capital east to Peking, which the Mongols named Khanbalik or Cambaluc – the Lord's City. His court there, and the vast empire he ruled from it, were to be described by one of the greatest travelers of medieval times.

Marco Polo 1254?-1324

Kublai Khan was already supreme ruler of the Mongols when around 1265 two Venetian merchants arrived at the Mongol court. The Venetians were brothers named Nicolò and Maffeo Polo, and they were the first European travelers to reach China. In 1271, two years after their return to Europe, they set out again for the East, taking with them Nicolò's son Marco. "No man," the prologue to the book describing Marco's travels later confidently asserted, "Christian or Pagan, Tartar or Indian, or of any race whatsoever . . . has known or explored so many of the various parts of the world," and this proud boast is literally true. Marco Polo not only undertook the long overland journey to China, and returned to Europe by the sea route around the Malay Peninsula and India, but during his 17-year stay at the Mongol court he traveled widely within the Mongol domains. Moreover, the book about his travels which appeared after his return to Europe opened an entirely new world to the Europeans of the day. Europe, long cut off from Asia by the formidable barrier of the Muslim Empire, was for the first time for centuries brought into contact with the civilization of the East.

That the story of Marco's journey became widely known in Europe within years of his return from China owes much to a fortunate coincidence. In 1298 Marco was taken prisoner by the Genoese during a sea battle between Genoa and Venice. In prison in Genoa, he met a Pisan writer named Rustichello, a well-known author of romances, who collaborated with

Right: Marco Polo relating his story while in prison in Genoa. He told it to the writer Rusticello.

Below: scenes of the Polos' adventures from a mid-14th century French manuscript. In the upper left are Nicolò and Maffeo Polo being received by Emperor Baldwin, last Latin ruler of Constantinople. Next to it the brothers are shown in the presence of the patriarch, chief religious leader of the East. Below they are seen embarking for their next goal, the Black Sea port of Sudak.

Below left: detail from a portrait of Marco Polo. Marco's father and uncle stayed at or near the khan's court most of the time, but the younger man traveled widely.

Marco in writing a book about the latter's travels. It appears that Marco provided the information, and Rustichello the literary skill. The resulting work is so fascinating that many of Marco's contemporaries read it purely as fiction, disregarding its documentary importance. Today however it is clear that Marco was an acute and accurate observer, who described factually what he saw and reported faithfully what he heard. However, because the information Marco obtained from other people was not always accurate, he has always been open to accusations of romancing. Some stories he included are

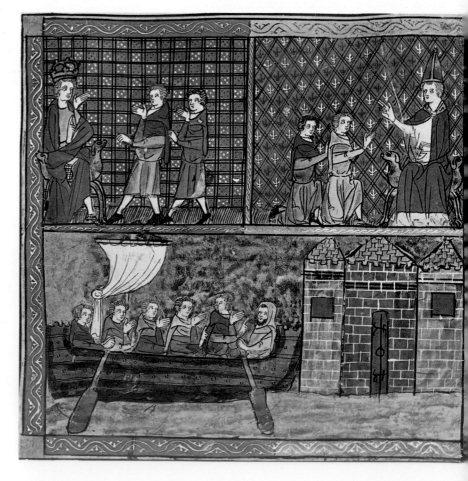

aquesta carahanaes partidade liupi
de barrapauar adlcatayo

simply fabulous while others – among them his account of the rise of the Mongol Empire – are not historically true. This does not alter the fact that his is one of the most absorbing travel books ever written, and one whose geographical value was recognized increasingly widely in the years after it appeared.

Marco Polo was born in Venice in about 1254, and nothing is known about his early life. When he was still a child his father, Nicolò Polo, and his uncle, Maffeo, while on a trading expedition to Constantinople decided to continue to the Black Sea port of Sudak. At Sudak, there was already a Venetian colony, but when the Polos left Sudak for Sarai, the Mongol leader Barka Khan's capital on the Volga River, they were breaking new ground. While they were at Sarai, war broke out between Barka and another of the Mongol leaders and their route back to Venice was closed. Instead, they resolved to return by a roundabout way, first traveling east to Bukhara. While they were there, an envoy passed through

Above: the camel caravan of the Polos on their travels in Asia. It is a detail from the famous Catalan map of the world made in 1375 for the king of France.

Below: Kublai Khan, who welcomed Europeans more than any Mongol ruler before him, handing the golden seal to the Polo brothers on their visit to his new capital city. (Bodleian Library, Oxford. MS. Bodley 264,fol.219.)

the city bound for the Mongol capital Cambaluc and he invited Nicolò and Maffeo Polo to accompany him to the court of the Great Khan.

Kublai, Great Khan to the Mongols, was a very different ruler from his predecessors. He had been educated by a Confucian scholar, and had absorbed many of the best elements of Chinese culture. By moving his court to Cambaluc (present-day Peking) he had exposed the barbarous Mongols to the ancient civilization of the land. He received the Polos courteously and when they left his court he gave them messages for the Pope, bidding him send "up to a hundred men learned in the Christian religion" besides "oil from the lamp that burns above the sepulchre of God in Jerusalem." Kublai also presented the Polos with a gold tablet entitling them to lodging and transport anywhere within his domains.

Aided by Kublai's safe conduct, the Polos reached Venice in 1269, only to find that the Pope had died the previous year. When, two years later, a new Pope had still not been elected, they decided to go back without further delay. This time, they took with them Nicolò's son Marco, who was about 15 years old. At Acre in Palestine, the papal legate, Tedaldo of Piacenza, gave the Polos letters for the Mongol emperor. But they were no sooner on the road than they heard that Tedaldo had been elected Pope. Back in Acre, the new Pope gave them his blessing, and answered Kublai's request for a hundred learned men by sending with them two friars. Neither of the priests completed the journey to Cambaluc, but the Polos were able to take Kublai the holy oil.

From Acre, the Polos first made their way to Hormuz on the Persian Gulf, where they intended to take a ship for the east but once there they decided to make the journey overland instead. Marco's book describes in detail each region they passed through, beside others a little

31

way off the route, of which he had only heard. His accounts contain such details as the natural products of the area, the source of the livelihood of its inhabitants, their religion and their customs, and the book is thus far more truly the description of the world which a 13th-century prologue called it than an account of the Polos' journey – of which in fact little mention is made. It does appear, however, that in Badakhshān, in what is now Afghanistan, one or more members of the party fell ill for Marco confirms "from his own experience" how the pure air of the mountains there in a few days restored the sick to health.

After leaving Badakhshān, the Polos began the ascent into the Pamirs, "climbing so high that this is said to be the highest place in the world." Marco remarks that because of the great cold in the mountains food did not cook as well there as elsewhere. This has now been scientifically proved. With increased altitude and lower atmospheric pressure, water boils at a lower temperature and food therefore takes longer to cook. Descending from the Pamirs, the Polos skirted the Taklamakan desert, passing through Yarkand, Khotan, and Charchan to a city Polo called Lop, on the edge of the Desert of Lop – the Gobi. There, he records, travelers rested for a week to refresh themselves and their beasts before setting out across the desert. A month's provisions were necessary for the journey, for there was no food in the desert, although there were water holes 24 hours' journey apart.

Most fearful of all however were the spirit voices of the desert which, Marco recounts, lured many travelers to their deaths. Not only voices but "the strains of many instruments, especially drums, and the clash of arms" could be heard by the lonely traveler, so that those journeying across the desert kept close together and fastened little bells around the necks of their animals "so that by listening to the sound they may prevent them from straying off the path."

The Polos achieved the crossing of the desert safely, then made their way through Suchow and Kanchow toward the Mongols' summer capital, Shang-tu. They were still 40 days' journey from the city when they were met by the Great Khan's couriers, sent to escort the travelers safely to his court. Curiously enough, although their route must have crossed, if not actually followed, the Great Wall of China, built to keep out barbarian invaders more than 1500 years earlier, Marco does not mention it at all.

Kublai received the returning travelers warmly, entertaining them "with good cheer" and with "mirth and merrymaking" and giving them a place of honor at his court. He was delighted with the messages the Polos brought him from the Pope, with the holy oil from Jerusalem – and with Nicolò's son Marco, whom his father presented to Kublai as "my son, and your liege man." This was, perhaps, a prophetic introduction, for Marco, according to his own account, remained fully 17 years at the Mongol court and became a faithful servant of Kublai, for whom he entertained a great respect. "All the emperors of the world," he wrote "and all the kings of Christians and of Saracens combined would not possess such power or be able to accomplish so much as this same Kublai, the Great Khan."

Shang-tu, the city where Kublai was holding

court when the Polos reached China, was the site of the Mongol capital from June until August each year. There, Kublai had built a great palace of marble and ornamental stones, adjacent to a private park filled with game which, for recreation, he would hunt with hawk or leopard. The hunt that took place each winter was however a far more serious affair. From December to February, when the Mongol court was at Cambaluc, all those living within 60 days' journey of the capital had to devote themselves to the chase. Those living nearer the city sent the carcasses of the animals they killed to the Great Khan, but those who lived farther away sent only the dressed and tanned hides which were used to make equipment for the army. It was possible for this great slaughter to take place year after year because of the foresight of the Great Khan. He forbade the hunting of game animals from March to October to enable the beasts to breed, and so tame did they become during those months that Marco records that they would often come right up to a man – who would still do them no harm.

Marco's account of the Mongol capital shows that the Great Khan supervised the lives of his subjects as closely as he did the hunt. In Cambaluc, even the prostitutes were organized along military lines. The farther from the capital

Right: the splendid city of Hang-chow in Marco Polo's time. It was a thriving and busy market center. (Bodleian Library, Oxford. MS.Bodley 264, fol.257.)

Below: the Great Khan on a hunt. Marco Polo reported that such hunting parties took place during the three months of the year that the royal court was in the capital of Cambaluc. (Bodleian Library, Oxford. MS.Bodley 264, fol.240v.)

Marco traveled, however, the more unique and varied were the customs he saw. The Mongols were generally tolerant of the traditional way of life of the peoples they conquered, and Marco had ample opportunity to observe these peoples for himself. He undertook lengthy journeys throughout the Mongol Empire, probably on

lovers his bride had had, the better he would be pleased. "A fine [country] to visit," remarks Marco, "for a lad from 16 to 24!"

As the years passed, the Polos began to feel a longing to see Europe again. Nicolò and Maffeo were by this time elderly men and must have felt that if they delayed their return too long, they might not live to see their native city. But Kublai Khan was reluctant to let his European courtiers go. "He was so fond of them," records Marco, "and so much enjoyed their company that nothing would induce him to give them leave." Around 1292, however, the Mongol princess Kokachin was to be sent as bride to a Mongol ruler in the Middle East, and the Polos managed to obtain permission to join her escort on the journey west. It was to be made by sea, not by the overland route, and it gave Marco the opportunity to visit and describe many countries he had not seen before. At last, armed with the usual safe conduct from Kublai, and with messages for the pope and the Christian kings of Europe, the travelers were on their way. They took leave of the princess Kokachin in Persia, then rode north to Trabzon whence they returned to Venice by sea. They reached their native city in 1295, having been absent 24 years.

Marco's book ends with the travelers' arrival in Venice. Later he married, had three daughters, and became a merchant, as his father and uncle had been. Little is known about this period in his

special missions on behalf of Kublai Khan. His travels took him south through the coastlands of China to Hangchow and beyond and inland perhaps as far south as Burma. He also states that he visited India and there is no reason to doubt his word.

Hangchow according to Marco was "the finest and most splendid city in the world," and a thriving center in whose food market was sold "everything that could be desired to sustain life." Maabar, a kingdom on the Coromandel Coast of India, was the home of the religious order of *Yogi* who "fast all the year round and never drink anything but water" and who carried abstinence to such extremes that they slept naked on the ground, with no covering at all. In Tibet, travelers used the huge local canes as fuel because the popping and banging they made while burning scared wild animals away. In that area there existed a custom by which no man would take a virgin as his wife – indeed, the more

Above: a detail of a map showing the city of Zaitun, now Ch'üanchou. The Polos embarked from this port to make their return home.

Right: an engraving of Marco Polo in old age, taken from a painting of the 17th century.

life. But for the accident of his imprisonment in Genoa with Rustichello, his great journey might have remained as obscure. The book Marco wrote with Rustichello, however, became an instant success and for a time other travelers – merchants and missionaries – made their way along the road he had forged. But with the break-up of the Mongol empire in the 14th century the door to the East swung closed, and Europe was once more cut off from the lands where Marco had lived so long. His descriptions, however, inspired Christopher Columbus to try to reach those lands by sailing west. Columbus discovered, not Asia, but an entirely New World.

Right: Marco Polo refused admission to his home on his return from his travels in the orient. Polo was away from Venice for 24 years, which made him a stranger to his own people.

Below: a view of Venice, Marco Polo's hometown, about 12 years after his death. (Bodleian Library, Oxford.MS.Bodley 264,fol.218.)

Chapter 3

The Great Age

In the 15th century the invisible frontiers that had so long surrounded Europe at last disappeared. A new spirit of inquiry was abroad, fostered by the Renaissance, a great revival of art and learning based on classical models. This brought with it an awareness of the outside world. Trade with the East had long been reestablished, but in the 15th century Eastern goods reached Europe overland through the Middle East, and the Eastern trade was entirely in Muslim Arab hands. Eastern goods were excessively expensive when they reached Europe and besides, Christian Europe resented the Muslims, Christianity's traditional enemies, having a trade monopoly. By the 15th century Europeans were seeking a new route to Asia so that they could trade directly with producers themselves, cutting out the Muslim middlemen. From such practical beginnings was the Great Age of Discovery born.

Left: it was the small country of Portugal that launched the great burst of exploration in the 15th century – and it was in ships like the one pictured that they set sail into totally strange waters. These sturdy vessels proved to be up to the test of storms and waves, and enabled the Portuguese to round the tip of Africa before the century was out. The two main motives for taking the risks of travel were to get a share of Far East trade and to gain more converts for Christianity.

The Ptolemy Map

In the Dark Ages which followed the fall of Rome in 476 AD, the geographical knowledge of classical times was forgotten, and for hundreds of years the works of classical geographers almost completely disappeared. It was not until the Renaissance of the 14th and 15th centuries that classical works on geography were rediscovered and translated into Latin. They profoundly affected European knowledge of the world.

No classical work was received by 15th-century Europe with greater attention than the *Guide to Geography* written at Alexandria by Claudius Ptolemaeus, known as Ptolemy, in the middle of the second century AD. Ptolemy's *Geography* had been familiar to the Arabs since early in the 9th century, when it was translated into Arabic, but it was unknown in Europe until 1410, when the first Latin translation appeared. The *Geography*, in eight books, consists of two main parts. One concerns the construction of maps and map projections and the other is a list of places arranged according to latitude and longitude. Although the work as a whole contains many inaccuracies, the information on cartography provided a starting point for the production of reliable and consistent maps.

This map was drawn in the 15th century on the basis of Ptolemy's *Geography*, and it demonstrates clearly the immense value of his work – particularly when compared with the Beatus maps being produced up to 200 years before. It also reveals the areas where his knowledge was weak. First, he depicts Africa merely as a great peninsula of an unknown southland, Terra Incognita, and by the extension of Terra Incognita east and north to join the coast of China, the Indian Ocean is transformed into a vast inland sea. This supposition could hardly have been encouraging for Europeans attempting to reach India by sea. Less than a century passed after the appearance of the *Geography* in Europe before Portuguese ships proved Ptolemy wrong by sailing around Africa to India, but the possible existence of a southern continent based on Ptolemy's Terra Incognita was to perplex explorers for several hundred years more. More immediate was the effect of Ptolemy's view of Asia as stretching indefinitely eastward, and his underestimate of the earth's circumference. From these, explorers deduced that only a short sea passage separated Europe from eastern Asia, and that they could therefore easily reach China by sailing west.

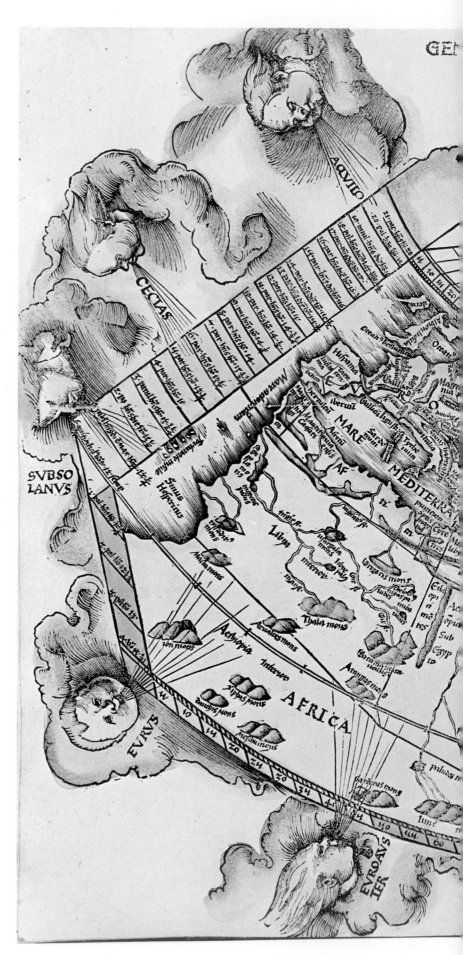

Henry's Explorers

Portugal is a small country which lies on the westernmost fringes of Europe bordering the Atlantic Ocean. There early in the 15th century the Great Age of Discovery can be said to have begun. At that time the country's geographical position was not the only circumstance favoring exploration, though it was naturally responsible for the maritime outlook of the Portuguese. Portugal in the 15th century was relatively stable politically, unlike many other European countries, and its explorers had the advantage of the support of the crown or of those near the throne. Improvements in ship design led to the development of the *caravel,* a light vessel so rigged that it could sail close to the wind, and navigation was made easier by improvements in the compass. The Renaissance was felt in Portugal as in other European countries, and there it showed itself most markedly in a new interest in the world.

The man who inspired the first Portuguese journeys of exploration was born at Oporto in 1394, third son of Portugal's King John I and his English queen Philippa. Prince Henry was to devote his life to discovery and although the area opened up by his mariners was comparatively small, his men took the first and most difficult steps into the unknown. Even though Henry himself never sailed on any of the voyages he organized, his pioneering work earned him the title "the Navigator," and he can be regarded as the initiator of discovery's greatest age.

In 1415, the Portuguese crown organized an expedition against the Muslim stronghold of Ceuta in Morocco, and following the capture of the city Prince Henry was appointed its governor.

Above: the wedding ceremony of Henry the Navigator's parents, King John I of Portugal and his English bride, Philippa of Lancaster.

Left: this illustration from the Nuremburg Chronicles shows how boats were built in the 15th century. The typical Portuguese ship of the period was the caravel.

The post did not involve him in living permanently at Ceuta but it did mean that he always had ships at his command. By 1418 he and perhaps others had begun to sponsor voyages into the unknown. The following year he was appointed governor of the Algarve, Portugal's southern province, and he set up his court in or near Lagos, near Portugal's southwestern extremity, Cape St. Vincent.

Tradition has it that Prince Henry founded a school of navigation and cartography at Sagres on Cape St. Vincent, but this story is probably exaggerated, although the prince no doubt attracted to his court anyone who could help further his aims – seamen, shipbuilders, instrument makers, cartographers, and astronomers probably all found their way there. Soon Prince Henry was sending yearly expeditions to explore the African coast, and his sailors were also responsible for the rediscovery of the Azores, which were probably reached around 1427.

Before Prince Henry's expeditions the southern limit of Portuguese knowledge was Cape Bojador and beyond this point many mariners feared to sail. Gil Eannes, sent out in 1433 to round Cape Bojador, turned back in the Canaries, but on a second voyage, in 1433–4, he succeeded in rounding the cape. The following

year, with Afonso Gonçalves Baldaya, he sailed beyond Bojador and into a seal colony. Sealskins would be marketable in Portugal, and this indicated the trading possibilities of the African coast.

In 1436 Baldaya reached Rio do Ouro and there for some years the Portuguese push southward ceased. Prince Henry was occupied first with a disastrous expedition against Tangier and then with problems over the regency which followed the succession of his young nephew Afonso to the Portuguese throne. In 1441 however he sent two ships to the Rio do Ouro. Antã Gonçalves was to collect sealskins, but Nuno Tristão's expedition was intended purely as one of exploration. The two men joined forces however in capturing some natives to take back to Portugal, probably thus initiating Portuguese slaving on the west African coast.

The next landmark reached by the Portuguese was Cape Blanc, sighted in 1442–3 by Nuno Tristão and others. In a few years, the first Portuguese overseas trading post was founded on Arguin Island, beyond the cape. From Arguin Portuguese ships pushed on to the Senegal River, and thence to Cape Verde, the most westerly point of Africa which was sighted by Dinis Dias in 1444. Two years after the discovery of Cape Verde Nuno Tristão reached the

mouth of the Gambia River. The natives resisted the entry of the expedition into the river, and Tristão and most of his men were killed.

In 1446, King Afonso V came legally of age and assumed the government of Portugal and in the power struggle that followed exploration was again abandoned for a time. It was 1455 before a Venetian nobleman and merchant, Alvise da Cadamosto, made his first voyage to west Africa. In 1455 Da Cadamosto only reached the Gambia River, but the following year he pushed south to the Bissagos Islands and the Geba River. Da Cadamosto sailed some way up the Gambia River and he may have discovered the Cape Verde Islands, although this claim is disputed. The chief importance of his voyages however lies in his lively account of the lands he visited, and of the African peoples and wildlife which he was the first European explorer to describe.

In 1460 Prince Henry of Portugal died. It is generally accepted that by the time of his death his mariners had reached Sierra Leone and for

Above left: the North African port of Ceuta, taken from the Muslims by the Portuguese in 1414. Fighting in this battle, Prince Henry realized the importance of sea power in trying to seize the Far East trade from the Muslims.

Above: Prince Henry the Navigator. In spite of his pioneering work in the exploration of sea routes to India, Henry never sailed on any of the voyages he sponsored.

Right: on landing on the west coast of Africa, Prince Henry's explorers found a thriving slave trade. Later expeditions from Portugal themselves turned to slave trafficking.

Below: a map of 1489 shows how much more was known of the world because of Portuguese exploration.

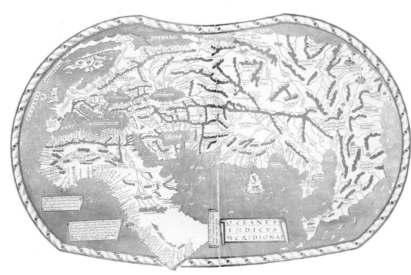

Left: Afonso V, King of Portugal after 1448. He was not interested in exploration as a government aim.

Below: King John II, son of Afonso, was as enthusiastic about exploration as Prince Henry had been. During his reign, Bartolomeu Dias sailed around the Cape of Good Hope.

some years this was to be the limit of Portuguese exploration south. The Portuguese crown temporarily lost interest in discovery and in fact in 1469 Afonso leased the rights in exploration to Fernão Gomes who paid an annual rent in return for an undertaking to explore 100 leagues (between 300 and 400 miles) of coast annually, starting from Sierra Leone. The arrangement was a conspicuous success. By 1474 or 1475, around when Gomes' lease expired, his men had reached Cape St. Catherine, 2° south of the

Below: a picture of Goa drawn 20 years after Pero da Covilhã reached it by traveling overland.

Equator, having explored some 2000 miles of coast in six years, more than Prince Henry's sailors had in 40. Gomes had also amassed a considerable fortune for himself.

When Gomes' lease expired, rights in exploration reverted to the crown, and Afonso entrusted discovery to his son John, who in 1481 succeeded to the throne as King John II. John's enthusiasm for discovery was equal to Prince Henry's, and he sent his first exploratory voyage south down the African coast the year after his accession, 1482. It was led by Diogo Cão who seems to have been charged specifically with finding a passage to the Indian Ocean and establishing the Portuguese right to it. Cão took with him on his voyage carved and dated stone columns, called *padrões*, which he was to erect in prominent positions to mark the progress of his voyage. Passing Cape St. Catherine, still the most southerly point known, Cão discovered the mouth of the Congo River, where he set up his first *padrão*, then continued to Cape St. Mary, 13°S, where he set up a second *padrão* to mark the furthest point south he had reached. In 1485, Cão made a second voyage, this time pushing south as far as Cape Cross, 22°S, and setting up *padrões* on Monte Negro and Cape Cross. It is not certain what happened to Cão after he reached Cape Cross – some accounts indicate that he may have died before reaching home.

After Cão's voyages King John began collecting all the information he could about the Indian Ocean – his ultimate goal was now obviously to find a sea route to the East. In 1487 he sent out two separate expeditions, one led by Pêro da Covilhã and the other by Bartolomeu Dias. Covilhã was to travel overland to India, and after many adventures he succeeded in reaching Calicut, one of the most important spice ports of India. In 1490, from Cairo, Covilhã sent King John a report on India and the then unknown east African coast. The aim of Dias' expedition was to open the sea route around Africa's southern tip.

To avoid the notorious calms of the Gulf of Guinea, Dias set his course directly from Cape Palmas to the mouth of the Congo. Then he

GOA fortissima Indiæ vrbs in Christianorum potestatem anno Salutis 1509 diuenit.

began a coasting voyage south. Like Cão before him he was troubled by the adverse southerly winds and the north-flowing Benguela Current and, probably off Cabo da Volta, he stood out to sea, perhaps intentionally, but perhaps blown off course by a storm. Whichever is the case, he did not turn east until he had passed Africa's southernmost point. When Dias made land again he was some 250 miles along the south African coast and he sailed east, probably as far as the Great Fish River, before turning for home. On his return voyage, he sighted the great cape that marks the most southerly point of Africa and it is said that he named it Cabo Tormentoso – the Cape of Storms – because bad storms had hidden it on his voyage out. King John, however, changed its name to Good Hope, for the promise its discovery conveyed.

Right: a compass dating from about 1500. It is possible that this kind of instrument was used by Portuguese expeditions of exploration.

Below: the Cape of Good Hope at the southernmost tip of Africa. Dias, who first rounded it, called it the Cape of Storms.

Vasco da Gama 1469?-1524

The four ships lay at anchor in the Tagus River. They were prepared for a long and important voyage, for they carried stores for three years and they had been provided with the most up-to-date equipment available. As they lay there, the fleet's commander, Vasco da Gama, was taking solemn leave of his monarch, Manuel of Portugal, swearing fealty to the king, and asserting his intention to uphold and defend the consecrated banner which Manuel had given him. When Da Gama returned from the court he and his three captains spent the night before sailing in vigil at the chapel which Prince Henry had built for his sailors on the bank of the Tagus, then the following day, walked in procession to the place where they were to embark. The mariners carried lighted candles, and were followed by a vast crowd of people who gave the responses in a litany chanted by accompanying priests. It was the morning of July 8, 1497, and the expedition

Above: ships built for Vasco da Gama's expedition to India, from a manuscript of 1497.

Below: Da Gama being blessed by the king before leaving on his voyage to India.

whose departure was attended with such ceremony was to attempt – and attempt successfully – to reach India by sea.

Little is known of the early life of Vasco da Gama, who led this history-making expedition to India. He was born around 1460 at the Portuguese seaport of Sines, where his father, Estêvão da Gama, was civil governor, and he probably received the usual upbringing of a young nobleman of his time, concentrating on military and courtly accomplishments. He also appears to have studied mathematics and navigation and must have had some seagoing experience, although there is no record of his commanding a ship before becoming leader of King Manuel's expedition to the East.

Two of the four ships prepared for Da Gama's expedition had been specially built for the enterprise under the supervision of Bartolomeu Dias. They were the *São Gabriel*, Da Gama's flagship, and the *São Rafael*, of which his brother Paolo had command. These two vessels were supported by a caravel, the *Berrio*, under the captaincy of Nicolau Coelho, and a storeship. Estimates of the fleet's complement vary in different accounts of the voyage between 118 and 170 men. Of these a number were convicts, who were regarded as expendable, and used to perform particularly dangerous tasks. When the four ships sailed from the Tagus on that July day, they were accompanied by a fifth under Bartolomeu Dias who

was on his way to take over command of the Portuguese fortress of Elmina on the Gulf of Guinea coast.

From the Tagus, Da Gama's ships sailed to the Cape Verde Islands, where they remained eight days. Then they continued south until they stood off Sierra Leone. There they parted company with Dias, and their voyage into the unknown began. Rather than creeping south down the coast of Africa, Da Gama steered his fleet west-southwest into the open sea. From August 3, when the ships left the Cape Verde Islands, they saw no land until November 4, when they reached the southwest coast of Africa. This great sweep west into the Atlantic enabled Da Gama to avoid the contrary winds and currents of the Gulf of Guinea and to take advantage of the favorable winds prevailing at sea. His exact

Left: Da Gama made the successful sea voyage to India from Portugal in 1498, opening up the trading route that his country dominated for some years.

Below: a map showing the lines of Da Gama's journey to India after rounding Africa. The solid line is the outgoing voyage.

Below left: Da Gama's three ships, the *Berrio*, the *St. Raphael*, and the *St. Gabriel*. The burning boat at bottom is the storeship.

course is unknown but at its farthest point west the fleet may have been within 600 miles of the coast of South America. Certainly his strategy was effective, for later mariners followed his example and Da Gama's sweep into the Atlantic became the normal course for ships making for the Cape of Good Hope.

On November 7, the Portuguese reached Saint Helena Bay and there they remained until November 16, taking on wood and water, and making their first contact with the Hottentot people of South Africa. Adverse winds prevented their rounding the Cape of Good Hope until November 22, but by November 25 they were at Mossel Bay, where they met more Hottentots and were able to trade some of the baubles they carried for an ox which they found "as toothsome as the beef of Portugal."

While his ships were at Mossel Bay, Da Gama erected a *padrão* to mark the progress of the expedition and he also ordered the breaking-up of the storeship and the redistribution of the stores among the three remaining ships. They set sail on December 8, and eight days later passed the last *padrão* set up by Dias, and the farthest point reached by the Portuguese up to that time. On December 25, they named the land they were coasting Natal, because they had sighted it on the day Christ was born, and the river they reached on January 11 they called the Copper river because of the quantity of that metal the natives possessed. Two weeks later

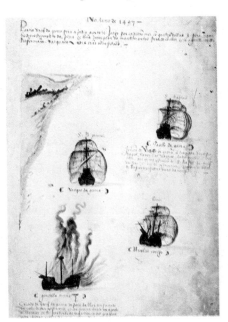

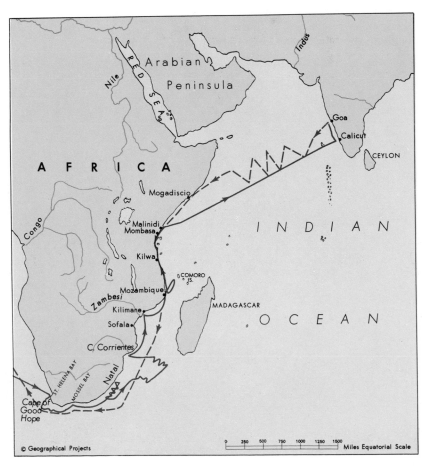

© Geographical Projects

0 250 500 750 1000 1250 1500   Miles Equatorial Scale

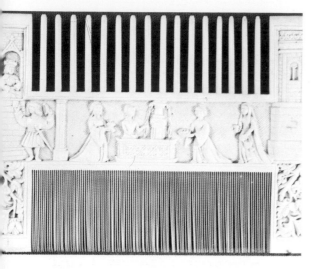

Left: a medieval comb carved from ivory. Such luxury items of Indian and African ivory were much sought after in medieval Europe, prompting more trade with the East.

they arrived at the Kilimane River, where they set up another *padrão*, and rested for a month, taking on water, and repairing the ships. While the fleet lay at Kilimane, scurvy broke out among the men. The disease, caused by a lack of vitamin C, brought about the deaths of a large number of the crew before the expedition's end.

Da Gama named the Kilimane River the Rio dos Bons Sinais, or River of Good Omens, because while he was there he saw the first signs that the Portuguese were nearing civilization again. The waters they were now sailing, although unknown to Europeans, were constantly traversed by merchant vessels making their way to and from the important ports of east Africa. From these commercial centers, grain, ivory, gold and other products of Africa were shipped throughout the Indian Ocean and to them were

Right: Calicut, Hormuz, and Cannanore in the late 15th century. The three ports were crucial to Muslim trading, Calicut being the most important port on the Malabar coast. Da Gama reached Calicut about 10 months after he left Rome in 1497.

Below: Arab dhows being unloaded in present-day Goa. Arabs have used dhows for centuries, and probably crossed the path of the Portuguese ships sailing on the Indian Ocean.

brought cargoes of textiles, metals, porcelain, and spices. The merchants who handled this trade were principally Arabs, and the region Da Gama was now entering a thriving center of Islamic culture. Not surprisingly, the welcome received by the Portuguese, traditional enemies of the Muslims, was hardly a warm one. The Sultan of Mozambique provided two pilots to guide Da Gama on his way, but one deserted when he found that his new employers were Christians and the other could be kept on board only by force. At Mozambique, however, Da Gama had his first sight of the thriving trade of the area, four Arab vessels "laden with gold, silver, cloves, pepper, ginger, pearls, and rubies."

At Mombasa, one of the most important towns on the coast, an attempt was made to seize the Portuguese fleet but at his next port of call, Malindi, Da Gama was better received. The ruler of Malindi was on poor terms with the sultan of his more powerful and prosperous neighbor and, thinking Da Gama might be an ally against Mombasa, he provided the Portuguese commander with a pilot to guide him across the Indian Ocean. The monsoon winds were favorable for a northeast crossing of the Indian Ocean and the pilot must have known his business for, on May 20, after sailing only 23 days out of sight of land, Calicut was reached.

Da Gama had needed great skill in seamanship and force and perseverance as a leader to

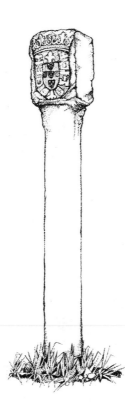

accomplish the voyage to India successfully. It had lasted something over 10 months, and of these three had been passed on the open sea. However the diplomatic side of his mission was far less successful, first because the only trading goods carried in his ships were the cheap cloth and baubles used to barter with natives on the Guinea coast of Africa. They were quite unsuitable for sale in sophisticated societies like those of India, and still less as presents, such as were made by visitors to the local king. Besides, although the Zamorin, the ruler of Calicut, and most of his subjects were Hindus, the trade of the city was dominated by Muslims, who were naturally hostile to the Portuguese. Although Da Gama had hoped that it might be possible to make some kind of commercial treaty in India, no such formal arrangement could be negotiated, and even though the goods Da Gama brought on this voyage were eventually sold, it was at a loss, and simply in order to obtain samples of the products of India to take back to Portugal.

The *Roteiro*, a journal of Da Gama's voyage probably written by Alvaro Velho, gives an account of the trade of Calicut, which was not only in spices from the surrounding countryside, but in those of superior quality imported from farther east. It also includes information collected by the Portuguese about other Asian countries. With this information, supplemented by the descriptions given by several Hindus who

Above: the stone pillar erected by Diogo Cão on Santo Agostinho, now Cape St. Mary, in 1482. It bears the arms of Portugal.

Above right: spices from the Far East. It was partly to break the hold of the Arabs on the spice trade overland that Portugal embarked on its great sea voyages.

Below: Da Gama's meeting with the ruler of Calicut. The early Portuguese explorers made a bad impression on eastern leaders by offering them the cheapest gifts and goods.

accompanied Da Gama on his return voyage, and with the samples of spices that had been obtained, King Manuel had to be content. As the months passed, relations between the Portuguese and their hosts steadily deteriorated and on August 29 Da Gama began his journey home. Despite the hostility between them, he left a *padrão* with the Zamorin to be erected to mark his visit, and he carried with him a letter to the King of Portugal in which the Zamorin promised spices and precious stones in return for silver, coral, and scarlet cloth.

Da Gama steered his ships up the coast of India to the Anjediva Islands, where the Portuguese remained for some weeks repairing their ships. Then they set sail across the Indian Ocean on the first leg of their voyage home. Now the winds were against them and it was three months before, early in January 1499, they sighted Malindi again. By that time, their numbers were so reduced by scurvy that Da Gama ordered the burning of the *São Rafael* and

47

the redistribution of her crew between the two remaining ships. From Malindi the *São Gabriel* and the *Berrio* sailed south. They rounded the Cape of Good Hope on March 20, but a month later were separated by a storm. On July 10 the *Berrio* reached the Tagus River, but Da Gama, on board the *São Gabriel*, went first to the Azores, where his brother Paolo died. It was September 9 before Vasco da Gama reached Lisbon, and nine days later when he made his triumphal entry to the city.

Da Gama's welcome in Portugal was tumultuous. Manuel rewarded him for his great achievement with a title, a generous annual income, and the town of Sines with which, however, the Order of Santiago, to whom the town belonged, refused to part. In 1502 he was also created Admiral of the Indian Seas and in 1519 Count of Vidigueira, and was awarded Vidigueira in place of Sines. Amid the general rejoicing at the discovery of a sea route to India

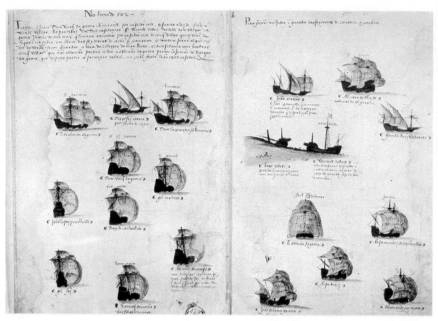

Above: Da Gama's second expedition fleet of 1502 was large enough to subdue the port of Calicut by force.

Left: King Manuel welcoming Da Gama on his return from his first voyage in 1499.

Below: the ruler of Cochin. He welcomed Pedro Álvares Cabral after the Portuguese captain had bombarded the city of Calicut.

however the cost of the voyage was partly forgotten. Not only was it expensive to outfit and provision such a lengthy expedition but of four ships, two had been lost and between a third and a half of the crew members had died. The spices bought in India had indeed cost a fraction of the price they would have commanded in Europe, but when the expenses of obtaining them were taken into account they no longer looked so cheap. And any Portuguese expedition that followed Da Gama would be operating in seas controlled by a hostile power. But Da Gama had proved that the Cape route to India was navigable and that spices could be obtained cheaply in India, and he had given Portugal a substantial lead over the other countries of Europe in the race to be first in the East. After his voyage, King Manuel took a new title, it would seem somewhat prematurely. Now he styled himself "Lord of the conquest, navigation, and commerce of Ethiopia, Arabia, Persia, and India."

Above: the Arabs attacked the Portuguese in Calicut to prevent them from trading. It was in retaliation for this ambush that Cabral fired on the port, though the Indians were innocent.

In February 1502, Da Gama sailed again for India, this time with a squadron of 15 ships which were joined later by another five. The Portuguese had good reason to send out so strong a fleet. Since Da Gama's pioneering voyage, a second Portuguese expedition, commanded by Pedro Alvares Cabral, had visited Calicut and established a trading post there, but a rioting mob had massacred more than 50 people in the trading post and Cabral in retaliation had bombarded the town. All Da Gama's actions on his second voyage seem to have been intended to impress the world with Portuguese power. At Kilwa he forced the ruler to pay tribute to the King of Portugal and off the coast of India he took personal revenge on the Muslims by the most frightful act of his career. His fleet overtook a ship returning from Mecca laden with pilgrims – men, women, and children – and, after seizing the treasure it carried, Da Gama set it on fire and allowed it to burn with all its passengers still aboard. In Calicut the terrified Zamorin sued for peace but Da Gama rejected his overtures and again bombarded the town. At other ports on the Indian coast he loaded his ships with spices then, leaving behind him a trail of blood and destruction, in February 1503 he set sail again for home.

For more than 20 years after his second return from India Vasco da Gama lived a comparatively retired life. In 1524 however, he was appointed viceroy to Portuguese India. In the years since the Portuguese had reached the country, cor-ruption had already crept into their administration, and it was in a vain attempt to restore good and honest government that Da Gama spent the last months of his life. On December 24, 1524, he died at Cochin in the country he had linked with Europe by sea.

Right: Vasco da Gama in the last year of his life. He died in India where he was serving as viceroy.

49

Christopher Columbus 1451-1506

On the morning of October 12, 1492 Christopher Columbus landed on Guanahaní in the Bahamas and took possession of the island for Spain. He believed that he was in Asia, for his dream was to open a westward route to the East. Today however his actual achievement appears greater than the one he so ardently wanted. He had rediscovered the forgotten Americas, had set a western limit to the Atlantic Ocean, and had proved that it was possible to sail across that ocean and return.

Columbus is a fascinating personality, for his voyage west was entirely his own conception. That it took place at all was due to his persistence and persuasive power. He was born in about 1451 in Genoa, the son of a weaver, and little is known of his early life. He himself recalled that he first went to sea at 14 and he seems to have arrived in Portugal 11 years later. There for some years he made his home. In 1478 he married a Portuguese noblewoman, Felipa Perestrelo e Moniz, and soon after they had a son, Diego. For

Right: Christopher Columbus, the explorer who defied all seafaring conventions to sail west as a way of reaching the East. He opened the New World to European colonization which, in historical perspective, was of much greater consequence than the achievement of his goal would have been.

Left: a sugar plantation in Haiti. The settlers who followed in the wake of Columbus started sugar cultivation in Haiti, which is on the island that Columbus sighted on his first trip to the New World.

a time Columbus lived on the Portuguese island of Porto Santo, Madeira, where his wife's family had interests, and while he was there he probably made at least one voyage south down the African coast.

The last quarter of the 15th century was an exciting time in Portugal for anyone interested in discovery because Portuguese exploration of west Africa was at its height and Lisbon the center from which the voyages were planned. It was in Portugal that Columbus heard of the Florentine cosmographer Paolo Toscanelli's theory that it was possible to reach Asia by sailing west across

the Atlantic ocean. This theory took a strong hold of Columbus. He read widely on cosmography and travel – including Marco Polo's story of his adventures – everywhere seeking support for Toscanelli's idea. The theory he eventually elaborated was based on a round earth, with a circumference of 360° of longitude, but he greatly overestimated the distance between western Europe and eastern Asia, and also underestimated the length of a degree. The distance he would have to sail west from Portugal to reach Asia was therefore reduced dramatically. His calculations placed Asia at approximately

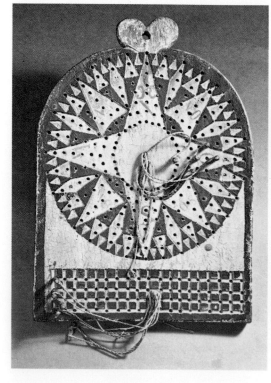

Right: a wooden traverse and wind rose used in Columbus' time to record changes in direction and speed during watches on ships.

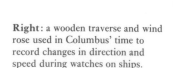

the same distance from Portugal as America actually lies.

In 1484, Columbus took his proposal for a westward voyage across the Atlantic to King John II of Portugal but although he was treated seriously his plan was turned down. King John himself was enthusiastic about discovery but Portugal was heavily involved in the search for a sea route to India. There may have seemed no material advantage in backing the expedition Columbus proposed. Soon after King John's rejection Columbus set off for Spain to try again.

By the spring of 1486 Columbus had managed to gain an audience with King Ferdinand and Queen Isabella of Castile and a special commission was appointed to study his proposals. It took four years to make its report and during that time Columbus also took his plan to England and back to Portugal, but without success. When at last the findings of the Spanish commission appeared in 1490 they too condemned the proposed expedition as impracticable. Although Ferdinand and Isabella were less discouraging they were involved in the conquest of the Muslim kingdom of Granada and had no time to spare for voyages into the unknown. In 1492 however the conquest of Granada was completed and the Muslims driven from Spain and Columbus was recalled to court. His terms were high, and it was some time before Ferdinand and Isabella would agree to them. But in that same year of 1492 the expedition got underway.

Columbus was provided with three ships for his voyage into the unknown, with a complement in all of some 90 men. His flagship was the *Santa María*, whose master was the cartographer Juan de la Cosa, and it was accompanied by two

Above: Queen Isabella and King Ferdinand of Spain. They sponsored Columbus in his venturous voyage.

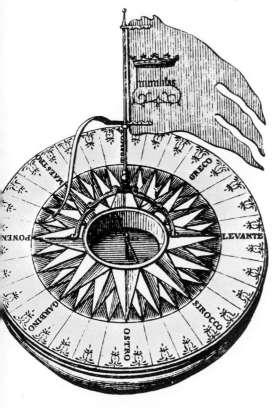

Left: a compass of the kind that Columbus would have used, dating from the 15th century.

caravels, the *Pinta* and the *Niña*, commanded respectively by Martin Pinzón and his brother Vicente. Beside stores, the ships carried cheap merchandise of the type used by the Portuguese to trade with natives on the coast of Africa and also letters of introduction in case they met Marco Polo's Great Khan. They sailed from Palos on August 3 and made first for the Canary Islands, always a vital stopping point for Spanish ships on expeditions westward, enabling them to take on wood and water and to refit.

Charts contemporary with Columbus' voyage show Japan and Hangchow, China, on the same

51

latitude as the Canaries, and Columbus must have seen such maps when making his sailing plans. When the fleet left the Canaries on September 6 it set its course almost due west. The winds were mainly fair, but even so there was discontent among the crew. The men feared sailing so far into the unknown, even though Columbus had ordered that after 700 leagues (some 2400 miles) there would be no night sailing as land would certainly be near.

By the beginning of October Columbus himself was somewhat concerned that no land had been sighted. But on October 7, at around longitude 68° west, flights of birds were sighted passing over toward the southwest and Columbus altered course in their wake. Two hours after midnight on October 12, a lookout on the *Pinta* sighted land.

At dawn the following morning the Spaniards found themselves lying off a small island. Columbus, the Pinzóns, and the officials accompanying the expedition went ashore to take possession in the name of Spain. The island, which they called San Salvador, has been identified almost certainly as Guanahaní or Watling Island in the Bahama group. Columbus, however, despite the primitive and naked people who inhabited his new discovery, was convinced that he had reached the islands he believed to lie off the easternmost shore of Asia, and he left quickly in search of Japan. For two weeks, he cruised among the Bahamas before reaching Cuba on October 28. There the Spaniards became the first Europeans to see tobacco, and to eat cassava, maize, and sweet potatoes, foods indigenous to the New World.

While Columbus' ships were off the coast of Cuba, the *Pinta* was parted from the *Niña* and *Santa María*, disappearing before a strong easterly wind. In search of the missing ship, Colum-

Above: San Salvador, the island on which Columbus landed in October 1492. One of the Bahama Islands, it was called Guanahani by the original inhabitants there.

Right: a map of Hispaniola, which Columbus had named La Española. He established the city of Isabela on the island, but it did not last.

bus set his course east, reaching Hispaniola which he named La Española – "the Spanish island" – because it was so beautiful. There, during the night of Christmas Eve, 1492, the *Santa María* ran aground and because action to save her was not taken quickly enough, it became a total loss. The *Pinta* had not reappeared, and there was no way that the *Niña* could take her own crew and that of the *Santa María* back to Europe, so Columbus decided to leave some of his men as colonists on Española. A cabin was built from timber from the *Santa María* and

there some 40 men were left with food and ammunition for a year. Columbus called his settlement Navidad, and it was the first Spanish colony in the New World.

Early in January 1493, Columbus set sail for Spain in the *Niña*. Within two days, he had been rejoined by the *Pinta* and, after a 10-day pause to make good the ships, the Atlantic crossing began. Although the weather was at first fair, in the middle of February the two ships were caught in storms so violent that Columbus, fearing shipwreck, wrote out the story of his discovery and put it in a cask which he threw into the sea. Neither ship foundered however and within a few days Columbus reached the Portuguese Azores. Although the Spaniards, as maritime rivals of the Portuguese, were received with some suspicion, on February 24 they were able to sail for Spain. Again they met storms, and unable to make Castile, were forced to enter the Tagus River. King John of Portugal received Columbus courteously. The Spanish ships were supplied from the royal Portuguese shipyards

Top: a woodcut in the 1502 edition of the journals of Christopher Columbus. It shows the presentation of a book to Isabella and Ferdinand.

Above left: the coat of arms of Columbus, which became his under a royal grant in May 1493 in recognition of his discoveries.

Above: two woodcuts from the 1493 edition of Columbus' journals. The one on the left shows some of the islands he sighted, San Salvador – the first – being in green. The one on the right depicts the fort he built on La Española.

and then allowed to proceed. On March 15 the *Niña* arrived in Palos. Martin Pinzón in the *Pinta* reached port soon after but, worn out by the voyage, on March 20 he died.

Ferdinand and Isabella were delighted by the success of Columbus' voyage although he had found neither gold nor spices. They immediately put preparations in hand for another expedition west. At the same time, to prevent Portugal taking advantage of Columbus' discovery, they obtained from Pope Alexander VI two decrees regulating discovery. The first, *Inter caetera*, divided the world from north to south by an imaginary line 100 leagues west of the Azores and Cape Verde Islands, and granted Spain the seas and lands west of that line, and Portugal those to the east. The second decree, *Dudum siquidem*, extended the Spanish grant by giving

53

Spain all lands and islands to the west and south "whether they be in regions occidental or meridional and oriental and of India."

With the Portuguese search for a sea route to India already nearing fruition, King John of Portugal was necessarily somewhat alarmed by the wording of this second decree. Representations to Pope Alexander were unsuccessful, and King John therefore entered into direct negotiations with Castile. In 1494, the Treaty of Tordesillas was signed, moving the boundary line specified in *Inter caetera* 270 leagues farther west. This left Spain in possession of central America – or, as the Spanish believed, the westward route to Asia – but gave Portugal the sea route to India – and then undiscovered Brazil.

Columbus' second voyage was obviously planned as a colonizing expedition. He carried some 1200 people aboard his 17 ships. The fleet left Cádiz in September 1493 and followed a more southerly course than that of Columbus' first voyage. Land was reached at Dominica in the Lesser Antilles, then the ships continued

Below: this world map of 1502 shows the line of demarcation agreed upon by the kings of Spain and Portugal in the Treaty of Tordesillas in 1494. Under the treaty, Spain kept all the possessions it already had, but could claim no others east of the demarcation line.

toward Española discovering Guadeloupe and Puerto Rico on their way. At Española the colony of Navidad was found to have been wiped out by the natives and Columbus sailed around the island seeking a better site. He found it, so he believed, at Isabela on the north coast of Española and there his colony was established. But the site was unprotected and unhealthy, the Spanish settlers undisciplined, and the colony never thrived.

In April 1494 Columbus left Isabela to explore Cuba and discover whether it was part of the mainland. Although he did not circumnavigate the island he remained convinced that he had reached a continental shore. All the members of his squadron were forced to swear agreement with him on pain of having their tongues torn out. On this voyage Columbus also discovered Jamaica, which he named Santiago. When he returned to Isabela, he put his brother Bartolomeo in charge of the colony with the title of governor, in direct infringement of Ferdinand and Isabella's royal prerogative. After Columbus'

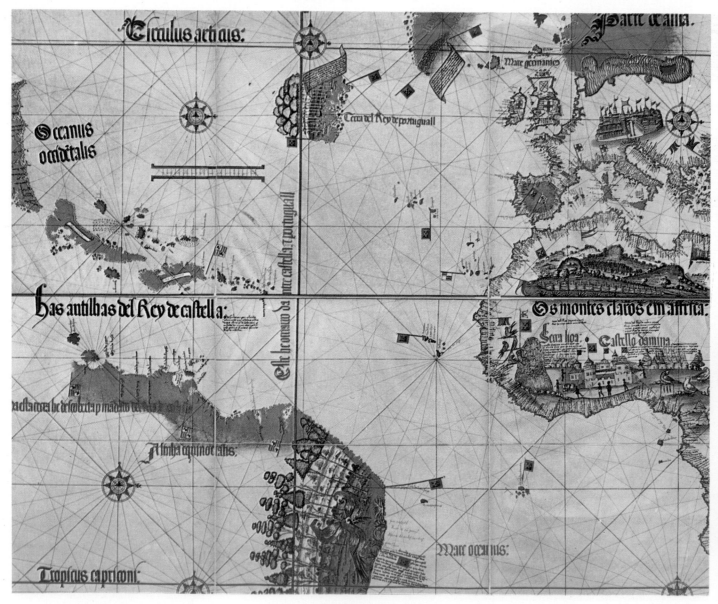

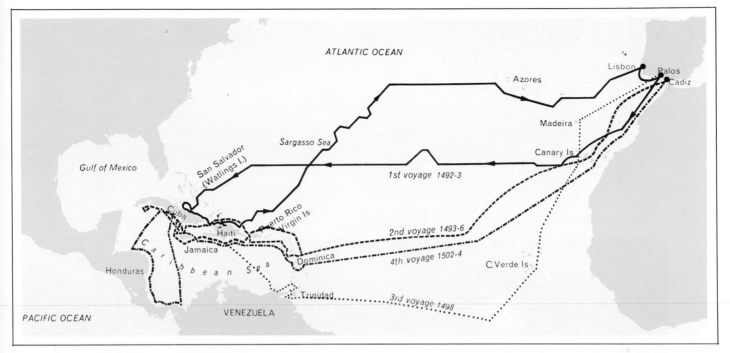

ATLANTIC OCEAN

Lisbon

Palos

Cadiz

Azores

Madeira

Canary Is

Sargasso Sea

San Salvador
(Watlings I.)

Gulf of Mexico

1st voyage 1492-3

Cuba

Haiti

Puerto Rico
Virgin Is

Jamaica

C a r i b b e a n   S e a

Dominica

Honduras

2nd voyage 1493-6

4th voyage 1502-4

C.Verde Is

Trinidad

3rd voyage 1498

VENEZUELA

PACIFIC OCEAN

Above: a route map of the four voyages made by Columbus to the New World. He died not knowing that the Americas and the Pacific Ocean lay between Europe and the Far East.

Left: pearl divers off the coast of what is now Venezuela. Columbus touched on the mainland of South America on his third voyage in 1498 but he never had the chance to exploit the wealth it promised.

departure for Spain in the spring of 1496, Bartolomeo began to move the colony from Isabela to a better site on the south coast.

Columbus' reception in Spain after his second voyage was noticeably cooler than the enthusiastic welcome he had received earlier. No material benefit had accrued from his expeditions and it was already clear that the Española colony was being seriously mismanaged. Nevertheless he received permission to sail west again. This time

he really did discover the American mainland, in the summer of 1498 reaching South America at the mouths of the Orinoco River and discovering the Paria peninsula, and he then sailed for Española. There he found part of the colony in revolt. News of his inept handling of the affair soon reached Ferdinand and Isabella and in 1499 they appointed Francisco de Bobadilla governor and chief magistrate to replace Columbus. Bobadilla arrived in the new Española colony of Santo Domingo in August 1500. Columbus, who regarded the islands he had discovered as his personal property, refused to acknowledge Bobadilla's appointment. Bobadilla had him arrested and sent back to Spain in chains.

Although the Spanish king and queen were sympathetic to Columbus, and restored him to his title and revenues, they were adamant in refusing to allow him to visit Española again. They did however grant him permission to make another westward expedition, provided he did not land on Española, and in May 1502 he sailed again from Cádiz. During the summer he reached the coast of central America on the Gulf of Honduras, and followed it south and east as far as the Isthmus of Panama. Despite the lack of evidence to support him, he still believed that he was in Asia and in fact continued to believe that he had reached Asia until he died.

In November 1504, Columbus reached Spain at the end of what was to be his last voyage. He was crippled by arthritis and although he managed to get to Seville he could travel no farther. On November 26 Queen Isabella died. It was not until the following May that Columbus was received by King Ferdinand who persisted in his refusal to reappoint him governor of Española. Eighteen months later, on May 20, 1506, Christopher Columbus died an unhappy and disappointed man.

De La Cosa's Map–1500

In the 10 short years between 1490 and 1500 the world changed radically for Europeans. Christopher Columbus found land by sailing west across the Atlantic Ocean, and Vasco da Gama demonstrated that it was possible to reach India by sea. The results of these two voyages were shown on a world map made in 1500 by Juan de la Cosa who had himself taken part in a number of Spanish expeditions to the west.

Juan de la Cosa was a native of Santoña in northern Spain. We first hear of him in 1492 as master of the *Santa María* on Columbus' first voyage west. His ability as a seaman is, however, open to question, because during the voyage the *Santa María* went aground, broke up, and had

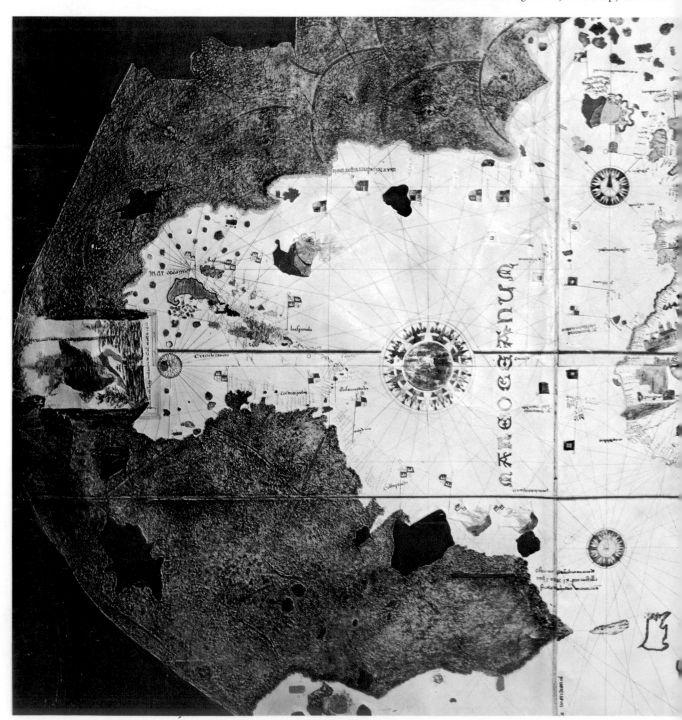

to be abandoned. This did not prevent La Cosa sailing, as either pilot or draftsman, on several more voyages to the Americas before 1500, when his map was drawn, or taking part in other expeditions in the early years of the 16th century. On the last of these in 1509 he was killed by a poisoned arrow during a battle for an Amerindian town in what is now Columbia.

The map La Cosa made in 1500 is probably the earliest chart in existence to show the Americas. The land mass is depicted as two curving coastlines, one going northeast, the other southeast from Central America, and although the northerly portion is described as "coast discovered by the English," the map does not take into account

that Brazil was discovered in the year it was made. It is also interesting that La Cosa shows Cuba as an island, although this was not proved until eight years after he made his map.

Besides the Americas La Cosa also shows Da Gama's fleet arriving in India. But he seems to have known nothing of the subcontinent apart from the mere fact of its existence for his picture of India is no more accurate than that of a Ptolemy map. Similarly his portrayal of the east coast of Africa, first navigated by Da Gama only two years previously, is merely an approximation of reality. The west coast, however, discovered in degrees by the Portuguese during the preceding century, is essentially correct.

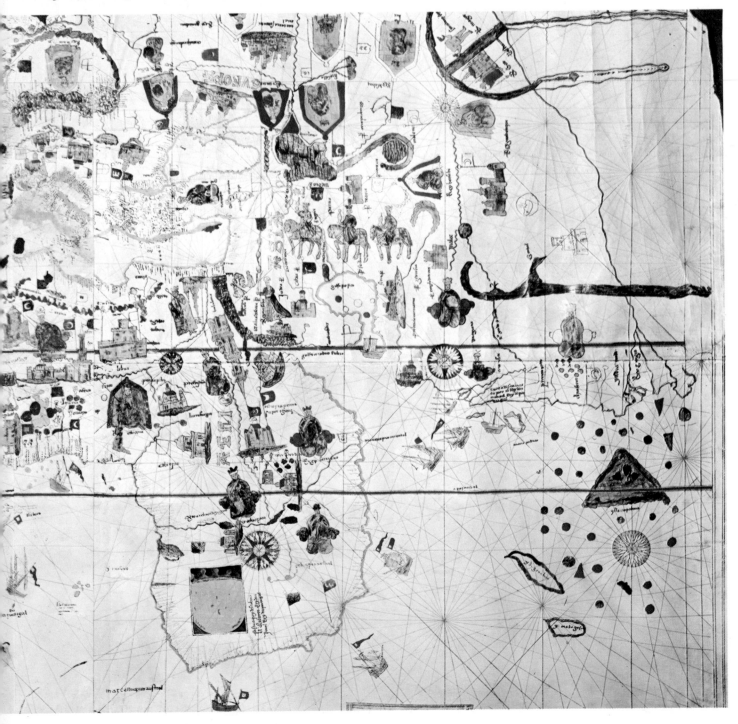

Ferdinand Magellan 1480?-1521

Ferdinand Magellan was killed on the Pacific island of Mactan on April 27, 1521. His fleet had reached Mactan from the east, discovering the long-sought strait through the Americas, and making the first European voyage across the Pacific Ocean. But Magellan did not live to see the greatest achievement of the expedition he had inspired and which owed its success to his determination. Sixteen months after his death one of his ships reached Spain, completing the first circumnavigation of the earth.

Magellan was born around 1480, probably in Oporto, Portugal. Little is known of his early years, but when he was about 12 years old, like the sons of many of the less wealthy Portuguese nobles, he became a page at the Portuguese court. Here he met for the first time Francisco Serrão, who was to be a lifelong friend of Magellan and who himself became an explorer. In due course, both Magellan and Serrão were promoted to the rank of squire and began service in the Marine Department at Lisbon. The great age of Portuguese exploration was at its height. The young Magellan would not only have been inspired by the magnificent discoveries of his countrymen but from his work he would also have learned something about the practical problems of exploration. He was responsible for providing supplies for Portuguese ships and he probably also acquired a theoretical knowledge of the science of navigation.

In 1505 Magellan was appointed supernumer-

Right: Dom Francisco de Almeida, first viceroy of Portuguese India. Ferdinand Magellan was aboard one of the ships taking Almeida's retinue to his post in 1505.

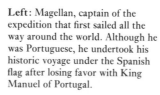

Left: Magellan, captain of the expedition that first sailed all the way around the world. Although he was Portuguese, he undertook his historic voyage under the Spanish flag after losing favor with King Manuel of Portugal.

ary aboard one of the ships of Francisco de Almeida, first Portuguese viceroy in the East. There is no detailed record of his Eastern service, though we know that in 1509 he was wounded at the great naval battle of Diu when the Portuguese won control of the Indian Ocean by defeating Indian and Egyptian fleets. Later that year Magellan sailed for Malacca with the first Portuguese fleet to visit this important trading port on the Malay peninsula. Some two years later he was back in Malacca, this time serving under Afonso d'Albuquerque who had replaced Almeida as viceroy. After a six-week-long bombardment Malacca fell to the Portuguese. With the city, they gained not only control of the wealth that passed through its markets, but also supremacy on the seas farther east.

Magellan's friend Serrão, who had also served with d'Albuquerque's expedition, was one of those selected to reconnoiter to the east. He succeeded in reaching the Moluccas – the fabled Spice Islands – but he never returned, choosing to settle on Ternate as adviser to the ruler there. From Ternate, he wrote to Magellan, instructing him how to reach the islands and no doubt telling him of their wealth. It has even been suggested that Magellan himself took part in the Portuguese exploration of the Moluccas, though no firm evidence for this supposition exists.

By 1513 however Magellan was back in Portugal and that same year he served with a punitive expedition sent by the Portuguese against the Moroccan stronghold of Azzemour. This venture was to lead to his break with

Portugal and thus, indirectly, to the great expedition made under the Spanish flag which gained him lasting fame. After the siege of Azzemour Magellan was unjustly accused of corruption in his dealings with the prisoners and booty of which he had charge. Because of this accusation the Portuguese king, Manuel, refused Magellan any reward for his long service to his country and although he was later acquitted of the charge against him, a renewed application for promotion was equally unsuccessful. Angered by this lack of recognition Magellan gained his monarch's permission to seek service elsewhere.

It may have been a rumor that a group of wealthy Spaniards proposed sending an expedition to find a westward route to the Moluccas that led Magellan to offer his services to Spain. The Treaty of Tordesillas of 1494 had divided the world between Portugal and Spain for purposes of exploration. Although the line of demarcation was clear in the Atlantic, no one was sure where it lay on the other side of the earth. Even the ownership of the Moluccas remained in dispute. Magellan proposed sailing west to the Moluccas, believing that by so doing he would prove that they came within the Spanish sphere. He was probably encouraged in this plan by the current cosmographical belief that the Pacific was narrower than it really is, and perhaps by letters he had received from Serrão, who seems

Right: Alfonso d'Albuquerque, the second Portuguese viceroy in India, laid the foundation for his country's Indian empire.

Below: King Charles V of Spain backed Magellan's expedition.

Below: a painting of Malacca after it had become a Portuguese colony. It was an important port on the sea route to the Spice Islands.

to have implied that the Moluccas were farther east than they are.

Be that as it may, Magellan's proposal fired the imagination of Charles, the 19-year-old king of Spain. On March 22, 1518, only two months after Magellan's arrival at the Spanish court, he gave his assent to the plan. Magellan and the Portuguese cosmographer Ruy Faleiro, who had

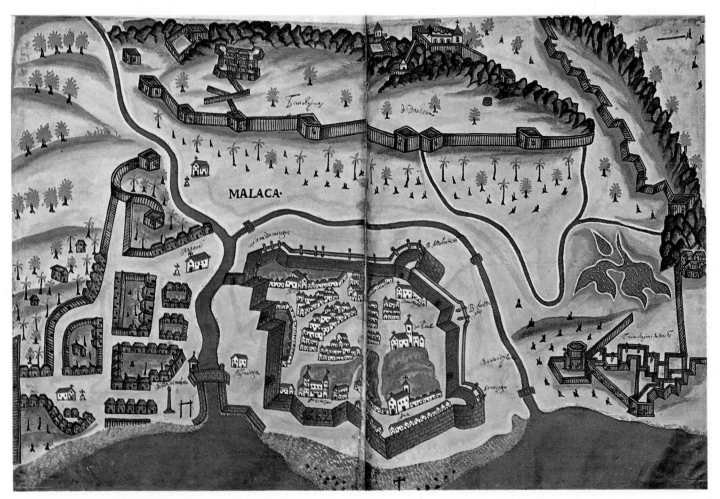

MALACA·

accompanied Magellan to the Spanish court, but who did not actually sail on the expedition, were appointed joint captains general of the fleet, promised a share of the profits and the government of any lands they might discover, and invested with the Order of Santiago, by which they became honorary members of the Spanish nobility and thus vassals of the King of Spain.

The Spanish officials in charge of East Indian affairs were instructed to prepare five ships for Magellan's expedition and by August 1519, despite Portuguese attempts to wreck the project, the ships were ready to leave Seville. Magellan's little fleet comprised the *Trinidad*, his flagship, the *San Antonio, Concepción, Victoria*

Above: scarlet cock-of-the-rock, one of the brilliant birds found around the Strait of Magellan.

Left: the island of Tierra del Fuego (Land of Fire) was so named by Magellan, who sighted it when the many fires of the inhabitants were lit for warmth.

and *Santiago*. The largest of the five, the *San Antonio*, displaced only some 145 tons – modern passenger liners can displace more than 65,000 tons – and all five were, according to an eyewitness, "very old and patched-up," but this description may have been prejudiced, for the writer was Portuguese. On August 10 the fleet left Seville for the port of Sanlúcar de Barrameda, farther downstream. On September 20, after each crew member had made his confession, it put to sea.

It is fortunate for us that with Magellan sailed as a volunteer a young Italian nobleman, Antonio Pigafetta, for Pigafetta kept a day-to-day account of the voyage, and his lively and enquiring mind delighted in the slightest detail about the lands that Magellan's men visited and the peoples they met. He also records the tensions and disputes between Magellan and his officers, which may have been inevitable as the captains of the other four ships were all Spaniards and Magellan Portuguese. Besides Magellan was wary about revealing his plans for the voyage, perhaps because of the distance to be covered and the hazards to be faced. Even before the ships had crossed the Atlantic, Magellan's orders were questioned, and the course he set disputed.

The expedition's first landfall was the Canary Islands, where the ships stopped for three days at Tenerife to take on wood and water, and then a further two days at nearby Monte Rosso to load pitch. On October 3 they left the Canaries for Brazil, rounding Cape St. Augustin on

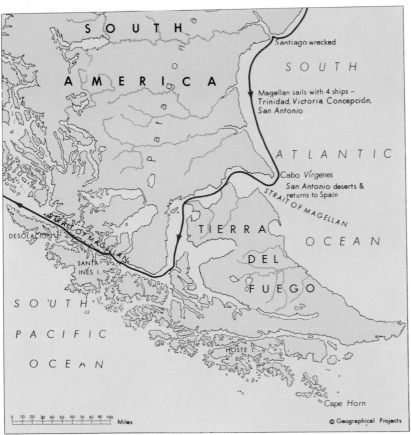

TIERRA DE PATAGONES

November 29 and entering the bay of Rio de Janeiro on December 13. Pigafetta records that they there laid in a "plentiful refreshment of fowls, [sweet] potatoes, many sweet pineapples – in truth the most delicious fruit that can be found – the flesh of the *anta* [tapir] which resembles beef, sugarcane, and innumerable other things. . . ." Thus provisioned they continued southward to the Rio de la Plata. This broad estuary had previously been believed to be the entrance to a strait, but Pigafetta describes it as a "freshwater river" and Magellan obviously realized that his strait must lie farther south.

Above: the *Victory*, the only one of Magellan's five ships to complete the around-the-world voyage.

Above right: the giants said by Antonio Pigafetta to live in Patagonia. Pigafetta sailed with Magellan and wrote an account of the trip.

Below: Magellan's route around the tip of South America. It shows how he had to weave through the strait that was named after him.

By this time, winter was approaching, and when Magellan's ships reached Port St. Julian, on the coast of what is now Patagonia, their commander decided that they should remain there until spring. Provisions were running low, for Magellan had counted on discovering the strait before the onset of winter, and he therefore ordered that the men's rations should be supplemented by hunting and fishing, while the amounts distributed from the stores should be reduced. Far from home, with little notion of where they were, and none of where they were going, the smoldering discontent of the Spaniards flared into open rebellion. They seized control of three of Magellan's ships, leaving the captain general in command of only the *Trinidad* and the tiny *Santiago*. Then they sent a messenger to make terms. Recognizing in this gesture a sign of weakness, Magellan dispatched an armed party to take over the *Victoria*, then blockaded the *San Antonio* and *Concepción* in the bay until they surrendered. Magellan dealt with the mutineers with a clemency remarkable for the time. Only one of some 40 men who took part in the rising was executed and two more were marooned ashore, to survive as best they might in the unknown wilderness.

According to Pigafetta, Magellan's men stayed at Port St. Julian for two months without seeing a single human being. Then one day a huge man appeared on the shore, singing, dancing and sprinkling dust on his head. He was "of such immense stature that our heads scarcely reached to his waist" and either because of the huge height of these natives, or because the skin shoes they wore made their feet look enormous, Magellan named them *Patagonians*, from Portuguese slang words meaning "big feet." Magellan's men captured two of the Patagonians to take back to Europe but both died before reaching Spain.

During the winter, Magellan occasionally sent one of his ships to reconnoiter further south. On one such expedition, the *Santiago* was wrecked and although according to Pigafetta her crew did not even get wet, two men had to make the 100-mile journey overland through difficult country to inform Magellan of the disaster. He sent food to the scene of the wreck, and there the *Santiago's* men stayed for two months while they salvaged the cargo. At last, on August 24, Magellan's fleet – now only four ships strong – left Port St. Julian for the Rio Santa Cruz. Here it spent a further two months before, on October 18, setting sail for the south. Three days later Magellan discovered the strait he sought.

Although Magellan's strait is only 320 miles long it took his ships 38 days to complete the passage through it. On sighting the broad ocean at its western end Magellan is said to have broken down and wept for joy. By that time his fleet was reduced to three ships – the *San Antonio*, sent out to reconnoiter soon after entering the strait, had turned tail and fled back to Spain. As the *Trinidad*, *Concepción*, and *Victoria* emerged into the calm waters of the ocean, Magellan named it "Pacific" in the hope that it would remain peaceful throughout their voyage. It is fortunate that it did, for had storms been added to the other hardships faced by the Spaniards, they might never have reached the western side.

Pigafetta records that for three months and 20 days after leaving the Strait of Magellan, the Spaniards were without fresh food. They "ate biscuit, which was no longer biscuit, but powder of biscuits swarming with worms, for they had eaten the good. It stank strongly of the urine of rats. We drank yellow water that had been putrid for many days. We also ate some ox hides that covered the top of the mainyard. . . . and often we ate sawdust from boards. Rats were sold

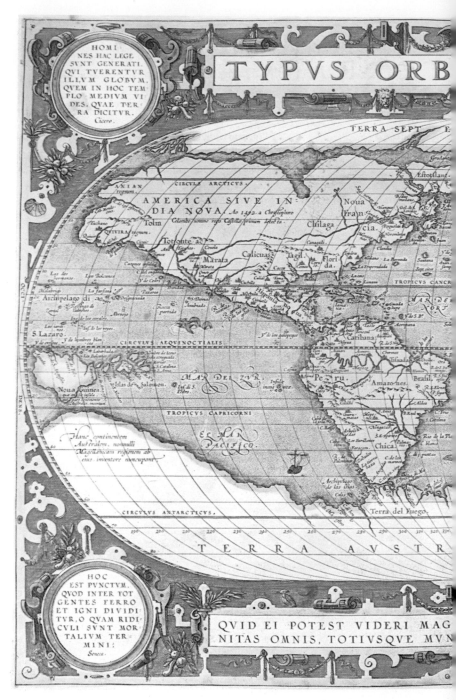

Above: an Ortelius map of 1570. It shows Tierra del Fuego attached to Terra Australis Incognita, the great unknown southern continent that many then believed existed.

Left: a painting on the ceiling of the church in Cebu, the Philippines. It depicts Magellan planting a cross to commemorate the first baptism on the islands.

for one-half ducado apiece, and even then we could not get them. . . ." They also suffered severely from scurvy, from which 21 men died, and many others fell sick from other diseases. "Of a verity" wrote Pigafetta "I believe no such voyage will ever be made [again]."

Although land was sighted toward the end of January 1521 it was early March before the ships made their first landfall at Guam in the Mariana Islands. It proved impossible to stay there long, or even to obtain fresh food, because the islanders were inveterate thieves, even stealing a ship's boat. Magellan actually named the island group the Ladrones, meaning the "islands of thieves."

On March 16 Magellan's fleet made land in the Philippines. Supplies were replenished, but rather than continue south to the Moluccas,

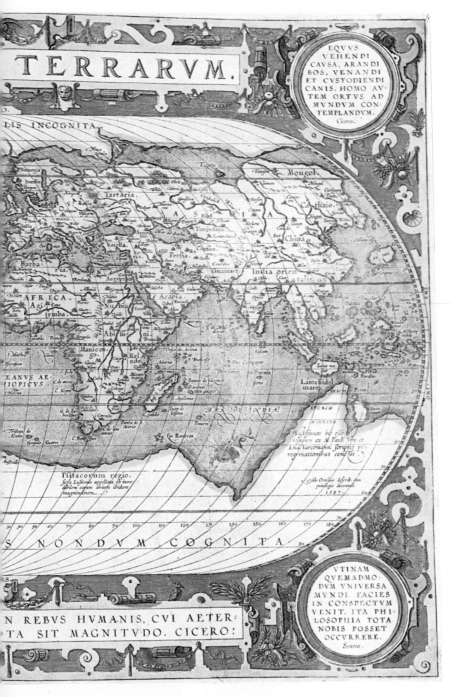

his perseverance in seeking it, and his strength of will, had brought within reach the first circumnavigation of the world. With him, the expedition lost its leader and for a time its aim. The *Concepción,* the least seaworthy of the remaining three ships, was abandoned, and the *Trinidad* and *Victoria* spent some months in piracy among the Pacific islands before making for the Moluccas where they loaded up with spices. The *Trinidad,* found to be unseaworthy, then attempted the calmer crossing of the Pacific Ocean, while the *Victoria,* under the command of Juan Sebastián del Cano, set sail for Europe by the Cape of Good Hope route. The *Trinidad* was forced to return to the Moluccas, but on September 6, 1522, after a voyage of hardship and privation, the *Victoria* reached Spain. It had at last provided practical proof that the world was round and had disproved the theory that only a few days' sailing from the Americas would bring ships to the East. The cost, however, had been immense. Four ships out of five had been lost, and of more than 230 men who had sailed from Spain, only 18 returned – but the cargo of spices they brought covered the costs of the entire expedition for three years and still left a profit. The Spanish were however never able to follow up the success of Magellan's expedition. The route he had discovered was too long and dangerous for regular use, and the Moluccas themselves were eventually proved to belong to the Portuguese.

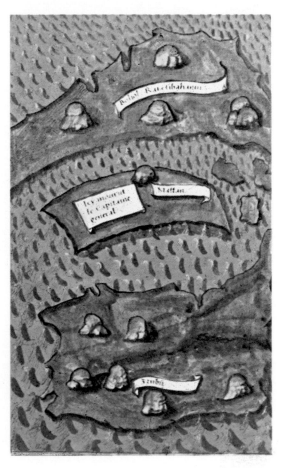

Magellan began a proselytizing campaign among the islands, converting the islanders to Christianity and securing their allegiance to the King of Spain. In Cebu, the most important port in the area, more than 800 people, including the king and queen, were baptized in a single day, and a peace treaty was concluded. While at Cebu, Magellan received a message from Zula, one of the two kings of the neighboring island of Mactan, saying that his fellow king Si Lapulapu would not recognize the King of Spain, but if he – Magellan – would send an armed force the following night Si Lapulapu could be forced to submit. Magellan, against all advice, decided to accompany the force himself and there, victim of a struggle between native rulers, he died.

It was Magellan who by his belief in his goal,

Right: a map drawn by Pigafetta showing the islands of Mactan, where Magellan was killed, Bohol, and Cebu in the Philippines. Pigafetta drew most of his maps with south at the bottom.

CONQVISTA DE MEXICO POR CORTES. N.7

Chapter 4

The Conquistadors

Christopher Columbus by sailing west had discovered a New World for Europe. He himself never acknowledged that he had reached a hitherto unknown continent, but within years of his voyage his discovery was recognized as such. From their first settlements on the island of the Caribbean, Spanish adventurers made their way west to explore. These adventurers earned themselves the name *conquistadors*, for they conquered where they explored. In a few short years they overthrew the rich and powerful civilizations they found on the American mainland, winning for Spain an empire, for the Church converts, and for themselves the wealth and glory that were their greatest desires. In their very success however they were doomed. The Spanish crown, fearing their power, did not allow them to enjoy it for long. Soon the lands the conquistadors had explored and conquered were ruled by bureaucrats from Spain.

Left: after Columbus had planted the flag of Spain in the New World, Spanish adventurers fired with ambition to acquire fame and wealth invaded it. They broke much new ground in Mexico, South America, and the southern part of North America – but they also destroyed whole empires as they went. This painting shows the conquest of what is now Mexico City by Hernando Cortés, who left the city in total ruin after a long siege.

The Realm of The Aztec

Some 150 miles west of Cuba lies the peninsula of Yucatan. Civilization existed there long before the Spanish reached the New World. The Maya people of the region built ceremonial cities containing stone temples in the form of step pyramids; they developed hieroglyphic writing, a numeral system, and a calendar. On these foundations the later Toltec civilization was built. The Toltec capital was Tula, northwest of Lake Texcoco, and from Tula the Toltec ruled much of central and southern Mexico between about 950 and 1150 AD. After the fall of the Toltec the Aztec appear among the succeeding tribes.

At that time the Aztec were seeking a land where they could settle. They found it, according to legend, in 1325 AD when the elders of the tribe spotted on a swampy island in Lake Texcoco an eagle, symbol of the sun and of Huitzilopochtli, the Aztec's greatest god, holding in its talons a snake. On that island the Aztec founded their capital Tenochtitlán and gradually they began to extend their power in the region around the lake. By the beginning of the 16th century, when the Spanish first reached Mexico, the Aztec ruled most of the central and southern

Right: a page from a Maya codex containing elaborate astronomical calculations. Unfortunately, most of the other books of the Maya were burned by the Spanish friars.

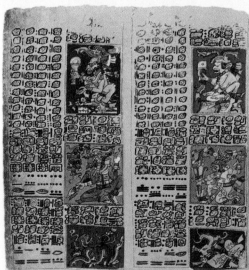

Left: a Maya bas-relief. The Maya built great palaces, pyramids, and temples to honor their gods. However, their empire was already in decay when the Europeans reached their homeland.

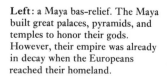

part of the country and their empire was at its height.

Aztec civilization owed much to that of the earlier Maya and Toltec peoples, not least its calendar which, like that of the Maya, recognized a solar year of 365 days. In addition the Aztec possessed a second, ritual calendar geared to a

Left: a human sacrifice by the Aztec, showing the removal of the victim's still beating heart.

point of honor with Aztec warriors to capture their enemies alive to preserve them for the sacrifice, and a soldier's bravery was judged by the number of his prisoners. Sacrificial victims were also demanded as tribute from nations conquered by the Aztec together with, as is more usual, all manner of precious goods.

The precious stones and metals, animal skins, and feathers of rare birds were used by Aztec craftsmen in the making of jewelry and ornaments of great beauty and originality for both everyday and ritual use in their capital, Tenochtitlán. The city itself, with its great temple-pyramids, palaces and well-built streets intersected by canals, was so lovely that the Spanish called it the "Venice of the New World." It was built on natural islands in Lake Texcoco, connected to the shores by three long causeways, besides aqueducts which brought fresh water

period of 260 days. The beginning of the solar year and the start of a new ritual period coincided only once every 52 years, and this was regarded as a time of crisis. The Aztec marked the event by a ceremony they called "tying up the years" in which, on the mountaintop of Huixachtécatl, priests lit the New Fire on a human victim's breast.

In the context of Aztec custom, this ceremony is less horrific than it might otherwise appear. Human sacrifice was the most notable feature of Aztec religious life. The Aztec believed that Huitzilopochtli, symbol of the sun, their war god and the chief deity of their panthenon, died each evening to be reborn the following day and that to do this he must be nourished by a constant supply of human blood. Each year thousands of victims perished on the altars of Huitzilopochtli, their breasts torn open by the obsidian knives of the priests and their hearts plucked out barehanded and offered to the sun. Certain rituals also demanded that the Aztec ate part of the victim's flesh.

The victims for sacrifice were sometimes slaves but more often they had been captured especially in the Aztec's ceaseless wars. It was a

Above: the Aztec god Quetzalcoatl. The Aztec believed that this god, who had been driven out of his empire, would one day return. They interpreted the arrival of Cortés and the Spanish as Quetzalcoatl's return and therefore showed no hostility at first.

from the hills of Chapúltepec some three miles away. As the islands became built over and the amount of productive land was reduced the Aztec built *chinampas* – artificial islands of matted reeds, surfaced with mud – which were used to grow vegetables and flowers for market in Tenochtitlán.

Agriculture, the Aztec believed, had been taught them by Quetzalcóatl, their god of learning and the priesthood, during a former "Golden Age" when he had lived among them on earth. The Golden Age had ended when Quetzalcóatl, offending a superior deity, had been driven from Mexico, but as he left he had promised his people that he would visit them again. When the Spanish arrived in Mexico the Aztec still awaited Quetzalcóatl's return

Hernando Cortés 1485-1547

Above: a contemporary drawing of Cortés by Franz Weiditz. It is believed to be the most authentic likeness of the Spanish adventurer.

Hernando Cortés, discoverer of the Aztec civilization and conqueror of Mexico, was born in the Spanish town of Medillín in 1485. His family was an ancient one, but had little money, and Cortés was educated to be a lawyer. His studies were however ill suited to his romantic, adventurous temperament and by the time he was 16 he seemed inclined to a military career. In 1501 he intended to join Nicolás de Ovando's expedition to the Spanish West Indies but was prevented from sailing by an accident. He at last made his way to the colony of Española, now Hispaniola, in 1504 when he was 19.

On Española, Cortés became a farmer but during his years there he also took part in a number of expeditions to quell native uprisings and the experience he gained proved invaluable in his later career. He had spent some seven years on the island when in 1511 Diego Velázquez led an expedition to conquer Cuba. Cortés joined him, and became an important member of the new colony. He seems to have been Velázquez' secretary and also served as mayor of the new capital, Santiago; he married, acquired land and slaves, and became a rich man.

From Cuba Velázquez sent several expeditions to investigate the nearby coast of mainland America. The first of these in 1517 was led by Francisco de Córdoba. He coasted the Yucatan

Below: Francisco de Córdoba's expedition, seen near the coast of Yucatán. Córdoba saw traces of the Maya's great past when he landed on the Yucatán Peninsula.

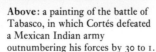

Above: a painting of the battle of Tabasco, in which Cortés defeated a Mexican Indian army outnumbering his forces by 30 to 1.

Left: a detail from a painting depicting the sinking of his fleet by Cortés. The expedition leader scuttled the ships on the coast of Mexico, showing his determination to conquer the interior.

peninsula and reported that the natives there were more civilized than those encountered elsewhere in the New World and that they possessed gold. His impressions were confirmed the following year by Juan de Grijalva, Velázquez' nephew, who sailed around the Bay of Campeche, went ashore, and met the natives. On the strength of these expeditions Velázquez proposed sending another west. Cortés was appointed captain general and put up some of the money.

In less than a month Cortés had acquired six ships for his expedition and 300 men had volunteered to join him. But his success aroused Velázquez' jealousy and the governor of Cuba resolved to deprive Cortés of his command. Determined to continue the expedition in which he had invested most of his money, Cortés put out to sea at once. Despite Velázquez' attempts to get him stopped and arrested, he was able to complete his preparations in other Cuban ports. On February 18, 1519 his expedition sailed for the mainland. He now commanded 11 ships, carrying some 500 soldiers and 100 seamen, as well as 16 horses and a number of heavy guns.

Cortés made his first landfall at Tabasco, near the mouth of the Grijalva River, and there he fought his first battle. He made his second landing farther west, near present-day Veracruz, and there he spent some months welding his volunteer army into a disciplined, cohesive force. He tried to build up good relations with the coastal peoples, which was not difficult for they had only recently been conquered by the Aztec and resented their new masters. They supplied the Spanish with food, porters, and information. It was there that Cortés first heard of the Aztec god Quetzalcóatl and of his expected return. He also received his first embassy from the Aztec war chief Montezuma who had watched the Spanish movements with foreboding. He identified the white man with Quetzalcóatl, but he also associated the invaders with recent grim omens which his astrologers had interpreted as foreshadowing the downfall of the Aztec, and he forbade them to visit his capital. Undeterred Cortés and his little force set out on their march inland. Before leaving the coast, Cortés wrote to the King of Spain, asking him to confirm his assumption of an independent command. He founded the municipality of Veracruz, then he destroyed the ships in which he had arrived. The act was symbolic – now he could not turn back.

When he reached the plateau of Mexico Cortés succeeded in forming an alliance with the independent state of Tlaxcala and 6000 Tlaxcalan volunteers accompanied him on his march toward Tenochtitlán. As he pushed on through Mexico, he received more embassies from Montezuma – they brought rich gifts, whetting the Spaniards' appetites for booty, but always sought to prevent Cortés from advancing. Now however he was all the more eager to press on. At Cholula, his force narrowly escaped a plot to annihilate them and, after leaving there, he sent a party up the volcano Popocatépetl, but they were unable to complete the ascent. At last, on November 8, 1519, Tenochtitlán was reached.

Although, contrary to their expectations, the Spanish were welcomed by Montezuma and the Aztec their position in Tenochtitlán seemed precarious, far as they were from support. Soon after their arrival Cortés resolved that only with Montezuma as hostage would his little army be safe. He managed to persuade the Aztec chieftain to take up residence in the Spanish quarters, where he was in effect made a prisoner. Soon Montezuma and his chiefs swore allegiance to the King of Spain and a collection of treasure was begun. Then, early in May 1520, Cortés heard that Pánfilo de Narváez had arrived at Veracruz, commissioned by Velázquez to arrest him. Leaving Pedro de Alvarado in charge at Tenochtitlán, he hurried to the coast.

When Cortés returned to the Aztec capital, having defeated Narváez and enlisted most of his troops under his own command, the Aztec were at war. Alvarado had attacked a peaceful religious gathering, entirely without provocation, and many of the natives had been killed. Cortés was able to induce Montezuma to try to pacify his followers, but they were so incensed that they stoned their former leader and soon afterward he died. Cortés was left with no alternative but to fight his way out of the city. With the battered remnants of his army, Cortés with-

Below: the epic meeting of Montezuma, supreme ruler of the Aztec, and Cortés, leader of the conquering Spanish expedition.

drew to the friendlier area of Tlaxcala.

Late in May 1521, Tenochtitlán was besieged by the Spanish. The aqueducts bringing water to the city were cut, food supplies were halted, and the buildings of the city were systematically destroyed. The Aztecs died in their thousands not only from hunger but from disease spread by the dead bodies putrefying in the rain and heat.

They held out, however, until August 15 when the city surrendered after nearly three months under siege. The beautiful capital of the Aztec had been almost entirely destroyed. On its site, however, Cortés built Mexico City as capital of New Spain.

In little more than two years, Cortés had destroyed the proud Aztec empire. The rest of his life, almost inevitably, seems an anticlimax. He occupied himself much with exploration, sending expeditions to all parts of his new domain and keeping up the search for the strait through America which would provide a westward route to Asia. Pedro de Alvarado was sent to Guatemala, which he partially conquered, and Cristóbal de Olid made an expedition to Honduras where he rebelled against Cortés and set up an independent command. After this, Cortés himself set out overland for Honduras on an arduous two-year-long expedition that tried his men's endurance to the limit and produced little useful result. In 1527, he sent a small fleet to the Moluccas and five years later patronized an expedition that reached the peninsula of Lower California, and made an unsuccessful attempt to found a colony there.

Cortés' successes in Mexico brought with them jealousy and slander and in 1528 he found it necessary to return to Spain to plead his cause with the Emperor Charles V himself. He was received with great honor, confirmed as captain general of New Spain and created Marquis of the Valley of the Oaxaca – where he held vast Mexican estates. By now however he was too powerful to be trusted to administer Spain's important new colony and in 1535 a Spanish Viceroy was appointed, holding both civil and military powers. Cortés occupied his final years in Mexico with the management of his estates and other businesses, but in 1540, disillusioned, he returned once more to Spain. He never again saw the country he had explored and conquered – on December 2, 1547 he died at his house near Seville. He was the supreme romantic adventurer, a subtle politician and a great military commander, popular with his soldiers, yet maintaining effective discipline, and if he was ruthless in the pursuit of his aims, he was not more so than was usual in his day.

The Inca of Peru

Far to the south of Mexico, on the west coast of South America, lies the land of Peru. At the beginning of the 16th century, when Aztec power was at its height in Mexico, Peru was ruled by the Inca. According to tribal mythology, the ancestors of the 16th-century Inca had emerged from caves to the south of Peru and made their way north seeking an empire. Their leader, Manco, carried a golden rod which the Inca believed would bury itself in the ground when they had reached their appointed homeland. At the place where the Inca later built their capital Cusco the prophecy was fulfilled.

Whatever the true origins of the Inca, it was not until the beginning of the 15th century that they emerged as a power in the Cusco region.

Left: the most famous of the Inca bridges, spanning the deep chasm of the Apurimac River. It continued in use until 1880.

Right: an Inca official holding a quipu, a device of cords used in counting and calculating.

Between 1438 and 1458, under the rule of Pachacutec Inca, they won control of a 600-mile stretch of the Peruvian highlands and in the 1460s Pachacutec's son Tupac conquered the coastal Chimú, the most powerful tribe in the area up to that time. By the beginning of the 16th century, the Inca empire stretched more than 2000 miles, from Ecuador in the north to Chile in the south.

and was walled at either side against the encroaching sand. At intervals along the road were post-stations, housing runners who carried messages throughout the empire – the Inca, like the Aztec, possessed neither the horse nor the wheel. These messages were probably recorded in *quipu*, a system of knotted cords which for the Inca replaced writing. The colors of the cords represented objects and ideas, and the knots numbers, and with the aid of the *quipu-camayoc* or official rememberers, the Inca even used *quipu* to keep archives.

The skill the Inca brought to road-building was also apparent in their cities, where temples and palaces were constructed of massive and accurately worked stone blocks. Even greater was the prowess of their craftsmen who fashioned delicate objects of gold and silver, shaped original

Unlike the Aztec, who sought tribute from the nations they conquered, the Inca welded their empire into a cohesive administrative whole. They divided their lands into provinces, and put each province in charge of a governor responsible to the central government at Cusco. This government controlled every aspect of Inca life, demanding from its citizens tax in the form of labor – on temple or state lands, in the army, the silver mines, or on the roads. So pervasive was state supervision that it was generally impossible for a man to change either the trade he was born to or the place where he lived. In return, however, the state provided for its people, irrigating arid regions, and working the land of those too old or ill to do so for themselves.

Communications throughout the empire were maintained through the magnificent road system, based on two principal north-south highways, linked by other east-west roads. The construction of these roads was in itself a great feat of engineering. The Royal Road, which ran 3200 miles from north to south through the mountains, spanned ravines and cut through mountains, while the coast road bridged wide rivers,

Above: an 18th-century genealogy showing the succession of Inca rulers and the Spanish who followed them. King Charles of Spain, at the end of the second row, succeeds Atahualpa, the last Inca emperor.

Above right: handle of a ceremonial knife. It depicts a demigod wearing a headdress, and is made of gold.

and ornamental pottery, and wove tapestries of surpassing beauty and splendor. Textiles for the use of the priests and the monarch were, however, woven especially in the temples.

The monarch was the hub of the Inca Empire, supreme and absolute, wielding a power greater than that of any European ruler of his day. By his people, he was regarded as a god on earth, the personification of the sun, supreme deity of the Inca people, and he played an important part in the ceremonial worship of the sun. The Inca monarchy was hereditary, and the legitimate heir born of the ruler by his sister. Around 1525 however there was a departure from this tradition. Huayna Inca on his death divided his kingdom between his legitimate heir, Huáscar, and his favorite son, Atahualpa, to whom he left the kingdom of Quito. For nearly five years the two monarchs coexisted peaceably, then hostilities broke out between them, caused perhaps by Atahualpa's ambition. In the ensuing war Huáscar was defeated and taken prisoner and Atahualpa assumed the title of his father. Only a few months later, the Spanish landed on the coast of Peru.

Francisco Pizarro 1475?-1541

The little band of ragged, famished men stood on the beach of the island of Gallo off the northwest coast of South America. They looked with longing at the ships which had come to take them back to Panama. Then their leader, Francisco Pizarro, drew his sword and traced a line from east to west across the sand. "On that side," he cried, pointing south, "are toil, hunger, nakedness, the drenching storm, desertion, and death; on this side, ease and pleasure. There lies Peru with its riches; here, Panama and its poverty. Choose, each man, what best becomes a brave Castilian. For my part, I go to the south." So saying, he stepped across the line, and 13 of his companions followed him. The enterprise to which they had committed themselves was the conquest of Peru.

Left: Francisco Pizarro, conqueror of Peru. He found and destroyed the thriving Inca civilization.

Below: a depiction of Pizarro's arrival on the coast of Peru, showing crowds of hostile Amerindians. In fact, Pizarro landed on almost uninhabited coast of harsh terrain.

Francisco Pizarro was already some 50 years of age when he embarked on his life's greatest adventure. He was an illegitimate child, and no record was kept of his birth, but it appears to have taken place around 1475, in Trujillo, Spain. In the early years of the 16th century he took ship for the Spanish Indies and eventually settled in Panama. There he participated in a number of expeditions of discovery. Since the arrival of the first Spanish settlers in Panama, there had been rumors in the colony of rich and civilized lands to the south. In 1523 Pizarro joined a three-man partnership to plan a voyage of discovery and conquest to South America. His companions in the enterprise were a soldier of fortune, Diego de Almagro, and a priest, Hernando de Luque, who provided most of the capital, but who did not sail on the expedition.

Pizarro's first expedition southward, which took place in 1524–5, was in itself unsuccessful. His men suffered badly from hunger and met great hostility from the natives they encountered. But they were able to collect a quantity of gold and learned that there were richer kingdoms farther south. On the basis of these reports, Pizarro decided to return to Panama to get backing for a second voyage. The governor of Panama reluctantly agreed to his request and on March 10, 1526 Pizarro signed his famous contract with Almagro and Luque. This bound the three men to divide all conquered lands equally between them, while Pizarro and Almagro, joint leaders of the expedition, undertook to continue their enterprise until it was accomplished on pain of reimbursing Luque with the monies he had advanced.

It must at first have seemed to Pizarro that he was pursuing a dream. That is certainly how his venture appeared to the governor of Panama. When Almagro returned to Panama for the second time seeking reinforcements the governor flatly refused to permit any further exploration. Almagro had brought back gold, it was true, besides further evidence of the existence of a wealthy civilization, but he had still not reached that civilization and many of his companions on the voyage had died. The governor sent ships to the island of Gallo to bring back Pizarro and the other members of the expedition. It was then that Pizarro declared his intention to continue, come what may, with those of his men who would join him. Leaving the 14 volunteers on

Gallo the ships returned to Panama.

Eventually Almagro managed to obtain permission to pick up Pizarro and continue the expedition southward. They visited Tumbes, finding it a beautiful and wealthy city, and continued south to the Santa Pau river. Everywhere they saw evidence that the people were civilized, and heard reports of the power of the Inca. Even so they were unable to get backing for an expedition of conquest when they got back to Panama. In 1528 therefore Pizarro returned to Spain to put his case to the emperor, Charles V. His

Above: a French map of 1550 of South America, Central America, and part of Mexico. The coasts in all cases are accurate for the most part, the interiors uncharted.

arrival in Spain coincided with Cortés' triumphant visit after his conquest of the Aztec and Pizarro's scheme for a similar expedition to Peru was consequently warmly received. In 1529 Pizarro was appointed governor and captain general of a province stretching 200 leagues south of Panama. Almagro also received a royal appointment, but in a subordinate position, which made him resentful of the man with whom he had been equal partners until that time.

Pizarro's expedition of conquest left Panama early in January 1531. The vanguard was made up of 180 men and 27 horses, and was to be followed later by Almagro when he had collected reinforcements. The first landfall was San Mateo Bay and Pizarro marched his men overland from there to Tumbes. He found that the city had been almost entirely destroyed since his previous visit, but while he was there he learned of the civil war among the Inca which had culminated in the capture of the legitimate heir, Huáscar, by the usurper, Atahualpa. Atahualpa was even then encamped at Cajamarca, which was much nearer to Tumbes than the Inca capital Cusco, far to the south.

Even before reaching Tumbes Pizarro had received some reinforcements and he founded San Miguel on the Chira River to act as a base for his forces before, on September 24, 1532, five months after landing at Tumbes, leading his little force inland. Their route lay across the high Andes, and was made difficult by the cold as well as by the mountainous country, but they eventually reached Cajamarca on November 15. Finding the Inca ruler encamped there with a large force Pizarro devised a scheme as audacious

Below: the beginning of the ruse by which Pizarro captured the Inca emperor Atahualpa, who had come unarmed to meet the Spaniards. The friar who greeted him distracted his attention and, at a signal from Pizarro, his attendants were massacred. He was taken prisoner.

as it was brutal. When Atahualpa visited the Spanish on the day following their arrival, his large retinue was massacred, and he himself taken prisoner. He offered to buy his release by filling a room 17 feet by 22 with gold to the highest point he could reach. The Spanish accepted greedily, but once the ransom was paid he was not set free. Instead, following rumors of an impending Inca rising, Pizarro had him tried and put to death.

By this time Almagro had arrived in Caja-

marca with reinforcements and together the conquistadors set out for Cusco, the Inca capital. On their way they were met by the Inca prince Manco, brother of Huáscar, who claimed the throne and Spanish protection. He was promised both, for Pizarro saw him as a possible puppet ruler who could be persuaded to cooperate with the Spanish, and after the Spanish arrival in Cusco Manco was officially enthroned. Up to this time, there had been no resistance from the Inca – at first they had welcomed the Spaniards kindly and later the capture and death of Atahualpa had left them leaderless and unable to act. Already, however, were felt the first stirrings of the struggles among the Spanish themselves which were to bedevil the early history of Peru.

In the spring of 1534 reports reached Cusco of a hostile landing north of Tumbes. Pedro de Alvarado, Cortés' lieutenant and now governor of Guatemala, had heard such rumors of the riches of Quito that he had resolved to capture the city himself. The strong force with which he

Left: a toucan made of gold, an example of the magnificent artifacts created by the Inca.

Left: the room that Atahualpa filled with treasure in a bid to get his freedom from Pizarro. The dark line marks the height to which the precious objects reached.

Below left: Diego de Almagro leads the force laying siege to the city of Cusco. This illustration from Gomara's *History of the New World* portrays the Inca city as a medieval European town.

Below right: the murder of Pizarro. Although Almagro is labeled as the murderer, he had already been dead for three years. It was his followers who avenged his death by killing Pizarro in the palace in Lima.

had landed was considerably weakened by the crossing of the Andes and when Alvarado was met by Almagro at Riobamba he was prepared to negotiate – particularly as a force from Cusco had already captured Quito and found no treasure there. In return for a cash payment and a meeting with Pizarro, Alvarado was persuaded to leave Peru.

Less easy to resolve was the defection of Almagro himself. After the conquest of Peru and the taking of the Inca capital, Almagro was empowered by Charles V to discover and occupy 200 leagues of country to the south of Pizarro's territory. Between 1535 and 1537 he led an expedition to his new domains. The country was harsh and difficult and he saw no trace of gold. Disappointed and jealous of Pizarro, Almagro returned to Cusco to find that the Inca had revolted and the city was besieged. He fought and defeated the Inca, then entered Cusco and claimed the city for himself.

The civil war which followed Almagro's rebellion ended officially with the defeat and beheading of Almagro. But the conquistador had many adherents among the Spanish soldiers and these men were resolved to revenge his death. Pizarro however made no attempt either to render them harmless or to win their friendship. He was much occupied with the construction of Lima – the new capital he had founded in 1535 in the Rimac Valley – and with attempting to restore order in the country where Manco Inca was still waging intermittent guerrilla war. The Spanish government was so concerned by the state of its new colony that in 1540 it sent Vaca de Castro to be Pizarro's adviser, and in the event of Pizarro's death to supercede him as governor. It was as well that that contingency had been provided for because on Sunday June 26, 1541 Almagro's followers murdered Pizarro, the conqueror of Peru.

Gold Seekers in the New World

The conquests of Mexico and Peru established the Spanish firmly in the Americas. The kingdoms yielded prodigious treasure, but did not satisfy the conquistadors' lust for gold. Rumors of new and richer countries were constantly heard in the Spanish colonies. Mexico had been rich, but Peru richer, reasoned the settlers. Why should there not be other unknown kingdoms whose riches might surpass theirs?

In the autumn of 1533 Francisco Pizarro sent

Left: a head that has been shrunk by the Jivaro Indians. Gaspar de Carvajal, a friar who accompanied Francisco de Orellana's expedition, described such trophies in his account of the journey.

Below: Orellana, the conquistador who followed the Amazon River to the Atlantic in his effort to find the fabled land of El Dorado.

Sebastián de Benalcázar to take charge of his supply port of San Miguel. But no sooner had Benalcázar reached there than he heard fabulous accounts of the wealth of Quito, farther north. He set off immediately, without orders, for Quito. His conquest of the city revealed none of the treasure he had hoped for, but he was subsequently appointed its governor. In 1539 however he was succeeded as governor by Pizarro's half-brother, Gonzalo, and with his followers Benalcázar thrust into the unknown north. Traveling through forest country inhabited only by primitive peoples he reached and conquered Popayán, southwest of the Nevado del Huila, then made his way through the high mountains of the Cordillera Oriental to the plateau of Bogotá. In this isolated spot, he met Gonzalo Jiménez de Quesada, who had reached Bogotá from the north.

Quesada and his followers had left Santa Marta, east of Barranquilla, in 1536 and had made their way south up the steep valley of the Magdalena river. Part of the force had traveled

on the river, the other section by land and the two, reunited near the junction of the Magdalena with the Cauca, had continued south through uninhabited and difficult country until they discovered indications that a civilized community was near. They had reached the kingdom of the Chibcha, on the plateau of Bogotá. When Benalcázar reached the land of the Chibcha and found it already conquered by Quesada the two men, rather than quarreling over the new-found territories, decided to refer the question of how they should be divided to Spain. Santa Fé de Bogotá, the city founded by Quesada, became the capital of a separate Spanish kingdom, New Granada, while Benalcázar was appointed governor of Popayán.

When Gonzalo Pizarro replaced Benalcázar as governor of Quito, he was instructed by his brother to explore the unknown country to the east. He was not seeking gold, but another treasure almost as valuable in Europe – *cinnamon!* Late in 1539, Gonzalo left Quito with a strong force of Spaniards, accompanied by some

Left: Gonzalo Pizarro's forces building a boat. It was used by Orellana to sail down the Napo River in search of food, but he went on to explore the Amazon.

Above: Orellana's capture of an Amerindian village for food and supplies. The inhabitants of the area around this village were not as friendly and helpful as others had been along Orellana's route.

4000 Indians. The crossing of the Andes was marked by intense cold, which caused the deaths of many of the natives, but the men found conditions still worse to the east of the mountains. For weeks they struggled through impenetrable rain forests, where the path had to be hacked out with axes. The rain fell without ceasing, the heat was intense, and although the expedition did discover the land of cinnamon, it was too far from the Spanish colonies to be worth exploiting. From natives, however, they learned of a populous land where gold abounded and to find it they made their way east.

By the time Gonzalo's men discovered the Napo River, one of the headwaters of the Amazon, they were lost, exhausted, and hungry. There, deep in the unknown, Gonzalo decided to build a boat to carry the weaker members of the party and to search for villages farther downstream. The work took two months. When the boat was complete it was launched on the Napo River and Francisco de Orellana put in command. He and his company set sail down the river to find pro-

visions and never returned. When at last it became clear that Gonzalo and his men were stranded, they had no alternative but to return to Quito. Hard as the outward journey had been, the return was worse, for the men were already tired, ill, and half-starving. It was more than a year when in June 1542, the survivors reached Quito, emaciated, barefoot, and wearing only skins.

Orellana, meanwhile, had sailed down the Napo to its confluence with the Amazon but there he found the current so strong that he could not return upstream. Rather than attempting to rejoin Pizarro, he decided to continue down the river, and although he was often in great danger of shipwreck in the turbulent waters of the Amazon, and suffered many attacks by the natives, he at last reached the Atlantic and made his way to Spain.

By this time the attention of the Spanish colonists in the Caribbean and central America had shifted to North America. In 1513 Juan Ponce de León had discovered Florida and 15 years later Pánfilo de Narváez made the peninsula the starting point of an expedition to conquer and colonize the Gulf Coast. Landing near Tampa Bay, he marched overland to Apalachee Bay where he built a small fleet of ships to transport his men around the gulf. The five ships were separated and three, including that of Narváez, disappeared completely. But eventually some 80 survivors of the 400-man-strong expedition were reunited on an island off the coast of Texas. By the end of the winter their number was reduced to 15.

One of these men, Álvar Núñez Cabeza de Vaca, reached the mainland and spent the next five years living with the Indians as a trader and healer. However he never abandoned hope of reaching Spanish civilization again. Gradually passing from tribe to tribe, he made his way west and south until in July 1536 he arrived in Mexico City. Later he returned to Spain and there he met Hernando de Soto, who had been created governor of Cuba and Florida and was engaged in organizing an expedition to the North American mainland. Despite the poverty and hardship of the years Vaca had spent with the Indians, his reports indicated that somewhere in North America was a wealthy country.

Below: a painting showing Cabeza de Vaca with his Amerindian captors in a barren region of what is now Texas. The Spaniard was held for nearly six years.

When De Soto landed in Florida in May 1539 his first enquiry was for gold.

It is not clear exactly where De Soto went in the course of his expeditions' wanderings, but he pursued his quest for riches over a great part of what is now the southern United States. He traveled through modern Georgia, pushing east nearly to the Atlantic, crossed the Appalachian Mountains, and trekked down the Alabama River before, in 1541, discovering the Mississippi River. He pushed far to the west of the Mississippi, hoping to find a way to the Pacific, but the country became so rough that he was forced to

turn back. In 1542, on the banks of the Mississippi, he died. The command of the expedition devolved on Luis de Moscoso who set out west, hoping to reach Mexico, but as the country became progressively more sterile and his men neared starvation he returned to the river where De Soto had died. There the Spanish built boats in which on July 2, 1543 they set sail down the river. Despite attacks by the Indians, they reached the mouth of the river safely and sailed around the Gulf of Mexico to the Spanish bases in New Spain. Of the 600-odd men who had landed, only 311 survived.

In 1539 a Franciscan friar, Marcos of Nice, traveled north into present-day Arizona and New Mexico and claimed to have seen a rich city named Cibola from afar. His report confirmed what Vaca had said of wealthy countries in the American interior and led to the dispatch in 1540 of a strong military expedition under Francisco Vázquez Coronado. Coronado was supported by a small fleet commanded by Hernando de Alarcón, which sailed up the Gulf of California in an attempt to find a water route to Cibola. He reached the head of the gulf, proving Lower California is a peninsula.

Coronado's land expedition was geographically of great importance, for he was traveling deep into a continent the interior of which was virtually unknown. His men marveled at the vast prairies and the great herds of "cows" – buffalo – that roamed across them, and they reported the dependence of the Indians on the buffalo and how they followed the migrating herds. One party of men, sent to visit a river reported to the

Right: a scene of torture in which Hernando de Soto commits atrocities on the Florida Amerindians. They suffered equally at telling the truth that there was no gold or lying to say that there was.

Below: drawing of a buffalo from a contemporary account of Francisco Vasquez de Coronado's expedition into the American southwest.

Left: an imaginary depiction of Coronado's search for Quivira, the kingdom of gold reported to him by a Plains Indian. The expedition traveled through what is now the state of Kansas on its search.

west, discovered the Grand Canyon. Coronado himself, in command of another small detachment, pushed far to the north and east, probably reaching the area where the Arkansas and Kansas Rivers approach close to one another. From the limited Spanish viewpoint however Coronado's expedition was not a success.

Friar Marcos' fabulous Cibola proved to be merely a Zuni Indian *pueblo* or village, and held neither gold nor riches. Quivira, a rich district of which Coronado was told by an Indian, and which he sought on his expedition northward, turned out to be an invention. "Neither gold nor silver nor any trace of either was found." In 1542 Coronado returned to Mexico in deep disgrace, and with his reputation damaged irreparably. The following year saw the resignation of Antonio de Mendoza, the Spanish viceroy, and the virtual end of the reign of the conquistadors.

The Gutiérrez Map–1562

The conquistadors not only won Spain an empire beyond the Atlantic; they were also the first Europeans to explore the lands they won. The first half of the 16th century witnessed an immense increase in knowledge of the Americas. In 1500, when Juan de la Cosa drew his world map, virtually nothing was known. By the middle of the century the rough outline of Central and South America was complete.

This map of the Americas in the years after the Spanish conquest was drawn by Diego Gutiérrez, until his death in 1554 a map maker to King Philip of Spain. It was engraved posthumously by Hieronymus Cock in 1562. The map is most detailed and accurate in its picture of the Caribbean region, Central America, and the

Mexico – had been extensively explored and colonized, and the knowledge acquired by Spanish expeditions is reflected in his map.

Pizarro's conquest of the Inca made known the northwest coast of South America. Gutiérrez was therefore able to draw a fairly accurate picture of Peru. He knew of the Amazon River from Orellana's voyage down it, and of the Rio de la Plata from Magellan's circumnavigation. But it is obvious that neither expedition furnished enough information to make his portrayal exact. The southern part of the continent had not been explored sufficiently thoroughly to make it possible for Gutiérrez to depict even the coastline accurately, although he had of course learned from Magellan's voyage that a strait divided southernmost South America from another land to the south. This southern land – Tierra del Fuego, which Gutiérrez calls Tierra de Magallanes – Gutiérrez extended south and eastward until it resembles the great land mass Ptolemy had depicted in the southern hemisphere.

Gutiérrez filled the sea with imaginary gods and monsters, with European ships in battle, or setting forth to explore. Pictures likewise enliven the barely known interiors of his continents – in Africa, he has drawn elephant, rhinoceros, and lions, while in Brazil cannibals carry out their horrible practices and in Patagonia he has drawn the giants that legend said lived there.

Gulf of Mexico, where the Spanish had made their first discoveries. Española, Cuba, and Jamaica are shown, besides Florida, which Ponce de León had discovered in 1513. By the time Gutiérrez was working New Spain –

Chapter 5

The New World

The great continent on whose threshold Columbus landed was indeed a "new world" for Europe – a land mass whose coast was unmapped, whose interior was unexplored, and whose possible extent was unknown. It was inhabited, it is true, but the Europeans disregarded the indigenous peoples in their struggle for possession of the rich new lands they had discovered, and as time passed, North America was divided among Europe's colonizing powers. The first settlements hugged the eastern coastline, but gradually explorers ventured into the interior. All North America was a frontier, a frontier that gradually crept west. Even in the first English settlements on the east coast there was a sense that the colonists rightfully owned all the lands to the west, and after 1783 when the United States came into being, this ambition took nationalistic form. Gradually pioneer traders and settlers pushed the frontier westward, and so North America was explored.

Left: the British settlers consolidated their colonies before they began any serious exploration into the interior of the vast North American continent. The French, bent more on increasing their fur trading, pushed up the St. Lawrence River, down the Mississippi River, and into the Great Lakes region. Robert Cavelier, Sieur de la Salle, was one of the most determined and successful of the early French explorers. This painting by George Catlin shows La Salle's party on a portage around Niagara Falls in 1679.

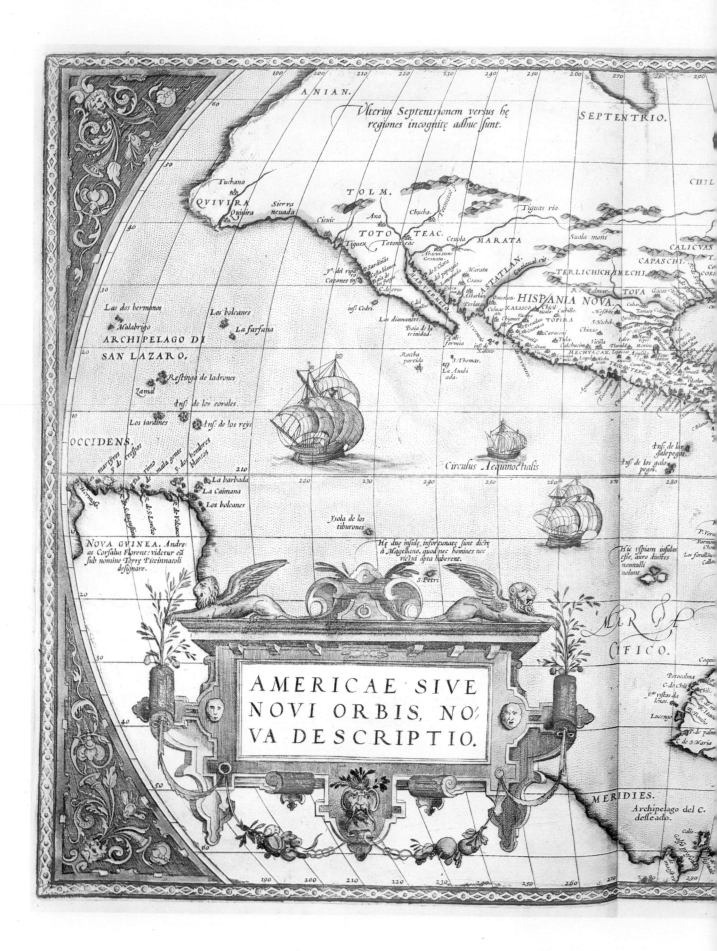

ANIAN.

Vlterius Septentrionem versus hę
regiones incognitę adhuc sunt.

SEPTENTRIO.

QVIVIRA
Tuchano
Quiuira
Sierra
neuada
Cicuic

TOLM.
Axa
Chucho.
Tiguas rio.

CHIL

TOTO TEAC.
Tiguex
Totonteac
Cenula
MARATA
Suala mons

CALICVAS
CAPASCHI.

MAR VERMEIO
Marata
Coana
ASTATLAN.
Cuinaual rio.
TERLICHICH IMECHI.

HISPANIA NOVA.
TOVA

Las dos hermanos
Malabrigo
ARCHIPELAGO DI
SAN LAZARO.

Los bolcanes
La farfana
insf. Cedri
Baia de la
trinidad.
Cali
fornia.
insf. de
Calico

Roccha
partida
S. Thomas.
La Anubi
ada.

OCCIDENS
Restinga de ladrones
Zamal
Insf. de los corales.
Los iardines
Insf. de los reys
I. de hombres
blancos

Circulus Aequinoctialis

Insf. de los
galepegos.
Insf. de los galo
pegos.

La barbada
La Caimana
Los bolcanes

Ysola de los
tiburones

Hic ysßiam insulas
esse, auro diuites
nonnulli
nolunt.

NOVA GVINEA, Andre:
as Corsalus Florent: videtur eā
sub nomine Terrę Piccinnacoli
designare.

Hę duę insidę, infortunatę sunt dictę
à Magellano, quod nec homines nec
vicīni opta haberent.

S. Petri

MAR PA
CIFICO.

AMERICAE SIVE
NOVI ORBIS, NO-
VA DESCRIPTIO.

MERIDIES.
Archipelago del C.
desseado.

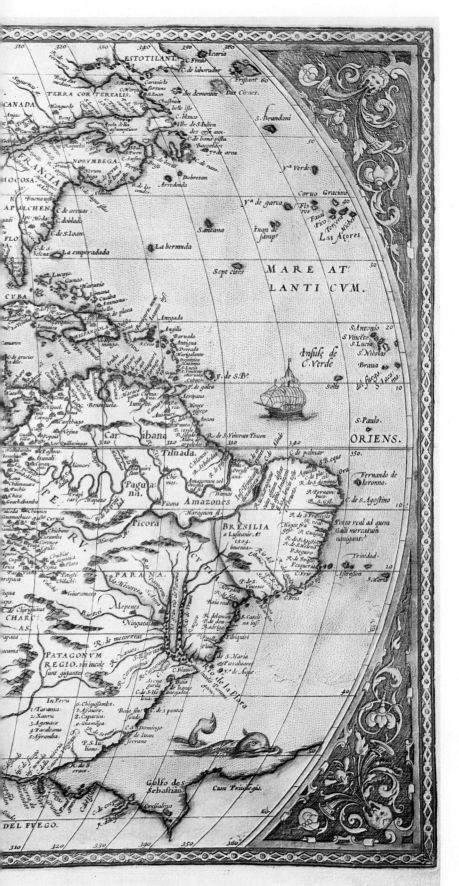

The Ortelius Map–1570

In 1570 Abraham Ortelius, a geographer and cartographer of Antwerp, published the first edition of his *Theatrum orbis terrarum (Theatre of the World)*. This work is generally considered to be the first modern atlas, for although collections of maps had been issued previously, they were made up of existing maps of varying sizes and by different cartographers. Most of the 70 maps in Ortelius' *Theatrum* were derived from, and acknowledged as, the work of other mapmakers, but they were all engraved in the same style especially for that edition.

The first *Theatrum* included only one map of the Americas, though others were added to later editions. This map – the "New Description of America, or the New World" – included both North and South America as well as a large part of the imaginary continent with which, following Ptolemy, mapmakers filled the southern part of the globe. Tierra del Fuego is depicted as part of this southern continent, as is New Guinea which the Portuguese had discovered in 1526.

Although Ortelius made his map some years after Gutiérrez, his outline of South America is less accurate than that of Gutiérrez. His North America, however, looks far more like the continent we know today. Ortelius mapped the west coast of North America as well as the east coast, and he even included what appears to be a great lake or gulf in the north, in the approximate position of Hudson Bay. His map was drawn 40 years before Henry Hudson reached the region and gave his name to it, so Ortelius probably learned of it from the Portuguese who seemed to have known about it at the time he was at work.

The voyages of the French navigator Jacques Cartier to the St. Lawrence estuary in the 1530s enabled Ortelius to chart that part of the North American coastline, but his estuary ends abruptly because he knew nothing of the Great Lakes. In mapping the coast, he underestimated the distance from the St. Lawrence to Florida and the length of the Gulf of Mexico coastline, but on the Pacific coast he showed Lower California correctly as a peninsula. Inland his map is almost totally blank – virgin country for European explorers and for Europe's colonizing powers.

Amerindians of the North

More than 12,000 years ago, and possibly much farther back in antiquity, the first people reached the Americas. As they and their descendants spread through the continents, they adapted themselves to its different environments, and they established numerous societies distinguished from one another by culture, language, and way of life. The members of these societies were the first Americans. The first Europeans to see them called them Indians, believing that their homelands were the East Indies.

Anthropologists studying the American Indians generally divide the tribes existing at the time of the European arrival in America into a number of cultural groups, based roughly on geographical areas. In the Arctic regions of North America lived the Eskimo, a hunting people whose culture, language, and origins differed from those of other New World peoples except perhaps the Aleut of western Alaska. They had adapted their way of life to make existence possible in the cold harsh lands of the

north. South of the Eskimo in a broad band stretching almost the entire width of North America were the homelands of the Subarctic Hunters, whose territory was hardly more hospitable than that of the Eskimo. The climate made agriculture impossible, so these Amerindians were hunters and fishers, living in family groups and not as a unified tribe. The rigors of their existence had led some tribes of the Subarctic Hunters to abandon or kill those too old or ill to keep up with the tribe.

Most of the northeastern Woodsmen, whose territory stretched inland from the coast of New England, subsisted from farming supplemented by hunting and fishing. In contrast with the cultural regions farther north, tribal ties were strong among the Northeastern Woodsmen. This led to frequent warfare between tribes, a warfare often conspicuous for its cruelty. Certain tribes of the Northeastern Woodsmen were the first people encountered by Europeans. Their

Below: Amerindians were ingenious fishers, as is illustrated in this 16th-century painting in Virginia.

League of Iroquois – an alliance of Mohawks, Oneidas, Onondagas, Cayugas, and Senecas – was the most powerful American Indian confederation of North America.

South of the Northeastern Woodsmen lived the Southeastern Farmers who had a village society and an economy based on an abundance

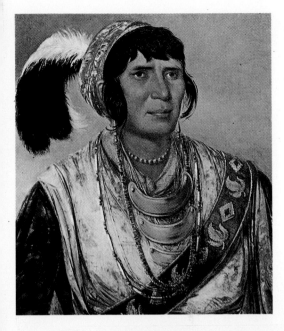

Left: a portrait of the Seminole leader Osceola as a young man, made by George Catlin in 1837-38.

Below: an earlier painting by Catlin shows a Sioux buffalo chase. The artist described the Sioux as "bold and desperate . . . horsemen."

many of the characteristics of their western neighbors. The nomadic western tribes were almost entirely dependent on buffalo meat and hides, and they followed buffalo migrations. Originally the nomadic Plains Indians traveled and hunted on foot, but after the arrival of Europeans they acquired horses and guns, which greatly increased both their mobility and hunting efficiency.

On the Pacific coast of North America from Alaska south to Oregon, the people belonged to the distinctive Northwest Coast cultural group. The Northwest Coast tribes lived principally from fishing and did not farm, but they evolved a stable society marked by clear class distinctions and an obsession with wealth and prestige. In contrast, the Seed Gatherers of the arid Great Basin lived very poorly, collecting roots, seeds, nuts and berries, and often verging on starvation. Those along the coast supplemented seed-gathering by fishing and hunting, which raised their economy above the subsistence level. Some of the inland tribes combined seed-gathering with fishing and, after acquiring horses from the Plains Indians, hunting.

Among the peoples of the southwest, the Apache had little in common with their neighbors. They were raiders, living from what they stole from other more peaceful tribes. The other tribes of Southwest Indians were mostly farmers, and in the case of the Hopi, Zuñi, and Pueblo, agriculture supported thriving village communities with a distinctive culture characterized by a communal lifestyle and an emphasis on religion. Like all American Indian cultures, however, that of the Southwest was doomed. As the Europeans, with their hunger for land and indifference to tribal values, spread over the Americas, the native inhabitants were dispossessed.

of crops. To the west, their territory abutted that of the Plains Indians, the ones whose culture became the stereotype of the American Indian as a hard rider and buffalo hunter. The easternmost tribes of Plains Indians were, however, primarily farming peoples. Only when they left their homes at intervals for the buffalo hunt did they adopt

Right: a Zuni jug in the shape of an owl. Such skillfully made pottery was disdained by the Spanish, who thought only of gold.

89

Henry Hudson ?-1611

In the service of his native land of England, the 17th-century navigator Henry Hudson made three attempts to discover a northern passage to Asia – and died while he was still seeking it. Previously, under Dutch colors, Hudson had coasted North America from New England south past Chesapeake Bay and had pushed far up the Hudson River, paving the way for settlement and colonization by the Dutch in what is now New York.

Nothing is known of the birth or early life of Hudson. He made his first voyage in 1607, commissioned by the English Muscovy Company to discover a northeast passage to China, but although he explored the coasts of Spitzbergen and rediscovered Jan Mayen Island east of Greenland, he found no sea passage to the Orient. Nevertheless, he was sent out again the following year, this time to seek the passage between Spitzbergen and Novaya Zemlya. When he found the way blocked by ice, he had to turn back.

Although Hudson's first two voyages were unsuccessful, he landed a commission from the Dutch East India Company in 1609 to search for the northeast passage again. He sailed in April in the *Half Moon*, manned by a mainly Dutch crew, but after rounding northern Norway it became clear that weather conditions would not permit

Journael van Herry Hutſon,

him to continue his voyage east. It appears that while he was in the Netherlands prior to his voyage, he had heard of two possible north*west* straits to the Pacific. When his voyage east became impossible, he made up his mind to seek the Orient via the west. In July he reached the North American mainland west of Nova Scotia and began a coasting voyage southward to beyond Chesapeake Bay. Returning north, he investigated Chesapeake Bay and made a brief survey of Delaware Bay before finding himself

Above: a depiction of Henry Hudson's arrival on Manhattan Island. His expedition got a friendly greeting from the Algonkian Indians.

Above left: the title page of Hudson's journal, published in Amsterdam in 1663. Although an Englishman, Hudson worked for the Dutch.

inside Sandy Hook at the entrance to what is now New York harbor.

Into the bay Hudson had happened upon flows one of the greatest rivers of North America, but the barriers of Sandy Hook and Long Island effectively hide it from the sea. Although Hudson sighted it, he was not the first European to see this river which now bears his name. Its mouth had been discovered in 1524, almost a century earlier, by Giovanni da Verrazano in the service of the king of France, and at the time of

Above: a bust of Giovanni da Verrazano, the Italian mariner who probably discovered the mouth of the Hudson river.

Below: a map of Manhattan drawn in about 1665. It shows part of Long Island as well.

apparent that Hudson was following a river and had not discovered a strait to the Pacific, but the country through which he passed seemed to offer many compensations. The land was rich, not only agriculturally to judge by the crops grown by the Amerinds, but also in fish, game birds, and furs. In exchange for beads, knives, and hatchets, the Dutch were able to get beaver skins and other hides from the American Indians with whom they were in constant contact. Some tribes they encountered were friendly, but others treated the European invaders with hostility from the first.

In November 1609 the *Half Moon* again reached Europe, making port at Dartmouth, England. There, Hudson and his English companions were detained while the Dutch crew members and the papers relating to the voyage were sent on to the Netherlands. Hudson and his fellow Englishmen were forbidden to explore for other powers again. When Hudson took sail for North America the following year, therefore, he flew the English flag. His plan was to seek the second of the two possible straits of which he had heard, the first having proven to be the Hudson River. It lay far to the north. Leaving England in the 55-ton *Discovery* in April 1510, he entered Hudson Strait on the night of June 24-25.

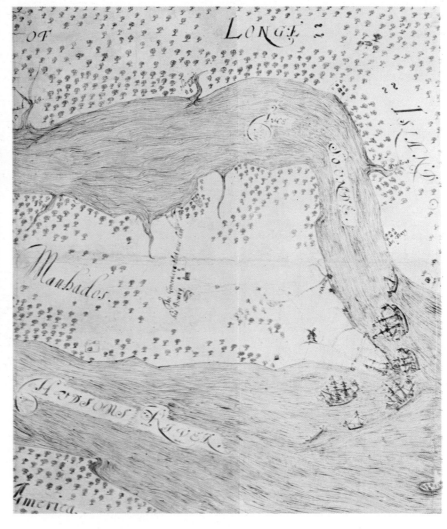

Hudson's voyage it was usually called the Grande Rivière. Hudson proposed naming it the Maurice after Prince Maurice, stadholder of the Netherlands, but it was soon generally known by Hudson's own name as the first European to explore it. The Dutch, however, often called it simply De Groote Rivier (the Great River).

The little *Half Moon* sailed some 150 miles up the Hudson to a point near present-day Albany, and some crew members went even farther north in the ship's boats. It had soon become boat and were never seen or heard of again.

The *Discovery* returned safely to England – though without the ringleaders of the mutiny, all of whom died on the voyage home. The expedition was a disaster in one way, but it laid the basis for subsequent English claims to Hudson Bay. Similarly, it was the voyage Hudson made for the Netherlands that gave rise to Dutch claims in the New World. The first of the Dutch to travel to the New World were attracted by the furs that Hudson had reported. Dutch traders reached the Hudson in 1610, the year after Hudson had explored it, and thereafter the Dutch were tireless in their pursuit of the rich fur trade.

In 1613 a Dutch trading post was established at the mouth of the Hudson River, and the following year a fort was built on Manhattan Island. The island was ideally situated as a base for Dutch operations in America. It lay both in a magnificent natural harbor and at the mouth of a great river up whose valley Dutch traders and settlers could travel far into the interior. Soon woodsmen were making their way up the valley of the Hudson and into that of its tributary, the Mohawk, to tap the fur supply at its source. These first explorers soon learned of the routes linking the Hudson valley with that of the St. Lawrence, and for a time they hoped that these might lead them to the Pacific Ocean. Their hopes proved unfounded, but they discovered another rich source of furs in the St. Lawrence valley. It was, however, already being intensively exploited by the French.

After rounding the Ungave Peninsula, Hudson decided to make his way slowly down the east coast of Hudson Bay rather than to strike boldly west across its mouth. When he reached James Bay at Hudson Bay's southernmost limit, it became clear that there was no way out to the west. On November 10 the *Discovery* became fast in the ice. The hardships of the Arctic winter appear to have been aggravated by Hudson's own behavior. He was accused of hoarding rations and of favoritism in distributing them, and discontent and resentment became general among the crew. Whatever the truth of the charges brought against Hudson, he had never been capable of inspiring loyalty or, in its place, of exacting unquestioning obedience. There had been murmurs of rebellion on his earlier voyages, and the mutiny that broke out soon after the *Discovery* was freed from the ice pack in June 1611 was simply a stronger expression of the same unease. Hudson, his son, and a handful of other men were cast adrift in an open

Above: *Hudson's Last Voyage*, a painting that shows the navigator and his son set adrift by his mutinous crew. No one will ever know exactly what happened on the ship in Hudson Bay because the only version of the events comes from the participants in the mutiny.

Right: the gulf of the St. Lawrence showing Percé Rock. Jacques Cartier's discovery of the St. Lawrence River gave the French an advantage in later territorial claims.

Left: Jacques Cartier. A skillful navigator who got his sailing experience fishing the North Atlantic, he explored about 800 miles of the St. Lawrence River.

Below: New Amsterdam in 1653. Behind the settlement were forests that covered the rest of Manhattan.

The French had gained a foothold in North America with Jacques Cartier's discovery of the St. Lawrence River. During the 17th century they pushed deep into the continent, discovering and exploring the Great Lakes and eventually sailing down the Mississippi River to the Gulf of Mexico. They planned to secure a monopoly of the North American fur trade by encircling the Dutch and English, who were by then also pushing inland from their colonies in New England and Virginia. Neither the Dutch nor the English was prepared to submit to this grand design without a struggle, and intensive trade wars ensued in which the European nations made alliances with the American Indians, playing on existing enmities between the tribes.

In 1614 the Dutch gained another base in North America when Adriaen Block discovered

the Connecticut River and a Dutch trading post was established near present-day Hartford to tap the fur supply of the Connecticut valley. Another Dutch settlement was founded on the site of Albany, New York, on the Hudson and a third near present-day Camden, New Jersey, on the Delaware River where, for a short time, there was a Swedish colony too. In 1622 the Dutch founded New Amsterdam on Manhattan Island as a center for their trading operations, and four years later they bought the island from the inhabitants. After 1638 the port of New Amsterdam was opened to ships of all nations to stimulate trade, and the city flourished.

Elsewhere, however, the position of the Dutch in North America looked less promising. Despite efforts to stimulate immigration, the population of New Netherland remained tiny, and that population was spread over a wide area of country which was also coveted by the English and the French. In 1633 William Holmes, an English settler from the Plymouth Bay colony, sailed up the Connecticut River past the Dutch settlement and established a rival trading post to intercept the furs on their way downstream. Gradually the Dutch were squeezed out of the Connecticut valley altogether. Although they managed to hold their other North American bases for longer, the colony known as New Netherland was on the wane.

Peter Stuyvesant 1592-1672

The armed trading post established by the Dutch in 1622 on Manhattan Island gradually grew into a thriving commercial center, a splendid testimony to Dutch enterprise and commercial skill. New Amsterdam, as it was known, was the center of Dutch operations in North America and the seat of the Dutch director general of New Netherland, which included all the Dutch possessions in North America and the Caribbean region. The most famous director general was Peter Stuyvesant. Stuyvesant did much to consolidate the prosperity of New Amsterdam, but in his attempt to strengthen the Dutch position

Above: Peter Stuyvesant, governor of New Netherland. He consolidated the Dutch position in the New World but later lost to the English.

New Amsterdam. He was welcomed warmly at first, but the approval of the Dutch burghers was soon turned to violent opposition by his arbitrary and despotic rule. He and the West India Company were opposed to representative government in the colony, and although in 1653 a municipal government was established in New Amsterdam modeled on that of a city in the home country, Stuyvesant continued to be the dominant figure. He also opposed religious freedom, though his persecution of Lutherans and Quakers was eventually stopped by the West India Company. On the other hand, he maintained friendly relations with the American Indians, also attempting to prevent the sale of alcohol and firearms to them. He tried to improve the defense of the colony and was always devoted to the interests of the company, working to increase its revenues.

In 1650 Stuyvesant reached agreement with the commissioners of New England on the boundary between New Netherland and Connecticut, but he yielded so much Dutch territory that he was highly criticized. He partly made up for this by a victory over the Swedes in Delaware. In 1654 the Swedes had taken the Dutch fort of Casimir on the Delaware River, which had been built only three years before. He led a strong force south, recaptured the fort, and ousted the Swedes from the Delaware valley. In contrast to his earlier dealings with the Indians, he ruth-

in North America, he ultimately failed in his aim.

Stuyvesant was born in 1592 in Scherpenzeel in the province of Friesland, the son of a Calvinist minister. At the age of 43, Stuyvesant joined the West India Company, which the Dutch had founded to challenge the Spanish power in the Caribbean region. He was subsequently appointed director of the company's colonies on the islands of Curaçao, Aruba, and Bonaire off the north coast of South America. In April 1644 during an attack on the Portuguese island of San Martin, he was so severely wounded in the right leg that he had to return home and have his leg amputated. Afterward he always wore a wooden leg decorated with silver bands.

In May 1645 the Dutch West India Company appointed Stuyvesant director general of New Netherland and, two years later, he arrived in

Above: ships leaving Amsterdam harbor and making for the Atlantic Ocean. Settler's in New Netherland were offered enormous grants of land by the Dutch West India Company as a way of strengthening Dutch claims in the New World.

lessly crushed their uprisings of 1655, 1658, and 1663.

Stuyvesant's rule in New Netherland ended without glory. In March 1664 King Charles II of England granted his brother the Duke of York all the land between the Connecticut and Delaware rivers, directly encroaching on the Dutch settlements there. Colonel Richard Nicolls was put in command of a fleet of four ships and between 300 and 400 men, and sent to take possession of the grant for the Duke. Stuyvesant, misled by instructions from the Netherlands into thinking that the fleet was bound for New England, made no preparations for defense until Nicolls' ships were nearly at New Amsterdam. The Dutch burghers, in revenge for Stuyvesant's unpopular policies, refused to support him and he was forced to surrender the town and fort. New Amsterdam became English, and was renamed New York.

The year after the surrender of New Amsterdam, Stuyvesant returned to the Netherlands. According to some historians, the Dutch West India Company made him a scapegoat for the

Above: a view of Stuyvesant from American eyes in an illustration for Washington Irving's book *Knickerbocker's History of New York.*

Left: a town plan of Manhattan drawn in 1664. It shows the English fleet in the harbor because that was the year in which the Dutch lost the city to England.

Right: an early Swedish settlement along the Delaware River. The Swedes were ousted by Stuyvesant.

New Amsterdam disaster, although it had been brought about as much by company policy as by Stuyvesant's personal rule. In 1667 he returned to the New World and settled on his farm "The Bouwerie," which has given its name to the Bowery district of present-day New York City. There, five years later in February 1672, he died. Peter Stuyvesant is remembered as a pioneer colonial administrator, the prototype of men sent to newly established colonies by the powers of Europe to consolidate the lands their explorers had won.

Samuel de Champlain 1567?-1635

Samuel de Champlain's work as an explorer and colonizer laid the foundations of France's empire in Canada and earned Champlain the title "Father of New France." From his first visit to the St. Lawrence region in 1603 until his death more than 30 years later, Champlain devoted himself to promoting French interests in Canada. He founded Quebec and worked ceaselessly to make the colony self-supporting. He and his followers opened up the interior for French fur traders to follow, using American Indian methods of travel to penetrate lands only the native inhabitants knew.

France's claim to Canada dated from the 1530s

Left: Samuel de Champlain, the man who was responsible for establishing the French in North America.

Below: European fur traders in the New World. Fur traders were often among the most enthusiastic and adventurous pathfinders in the unknown interior of North America.

a settlement in the country. Chauvin and François Pontgravé led a fur-trading expedition to the St. Lawrence, leaving 16 men to winter in Tadoussac east of Quebec. This first settlement was unsuccessful because some of the men died and others left the trading post for refuge with the Indians. Chauvin made a second voyage to Canada in 1602 and was preparing a third expedition at the time of his death the following year. Aymar de Chastes, governor of Dieppe, took his place as head of the venture in 1603. François Pontgravé was in charge of trading, and exploration and discovery were the concern of Samuel de Champlain.

Champlain was born in 1567 in the French port of Brouage on the Bay of Biscay. He was of bourgeois origin and Catholic by religion, but during the wars between Catholics and Protestants at the end of the 16th century, Champlain fought on the side of the Protestant Henry of Navarre, who became King Henry IV. When

when Jacques Cartier had discovered the St. Lawrence River and sailed up it to the Indian village of Hochelaga, on the site of present-day Montreal. After Cartier's voyage, however, little was done to exploit the lands he had discovered, although French fishermen did cross the Atlantic to fish on the Newfoundland banks. A hope still remained of finding a passage to Asia somewhere in the northern waters, and at the beginning of the 17th century France started to think about establishing colonies in the St. Lawrence area not only to exploit trading and fishing but also to occupy the area that might yield a way to the Far East for France. In 1600 a French shipowner, Pierre de Chauvin, was granted a monopoly of trade with Canada on condition that he establish

There he heard from local Indians of the Great Lakes that lay to the west. Lake Huron was described as being so large that they dared not venture on it and Champlain, who never lost sight of the quest for a westward route to Asia, wondered if it might be the southern part of the Pacific Ocean. Although the Lachine Rapids west of Montreal prevented him from traveling farther west to test his theory, he paved the way for later French successes in exploration when he observed that "he who would pass them [the rapids] must provide himself with the canoes of the savages. . . ." He set another important precedent by the formation of an alliance with the Algonkian Indians against their enemies, the powerful Iroquois.

De Chastes died in France while Champlain was in Canada, and the colonizing expedition that sailed from France in 1604 was commanded by Pierre du Guast, Sieur de Monts. The expedition landed at Nova Scotia and De Monts continued into the Bay of Fundy to found his settlement at the mouth of the St. Croix River on the west coast. It was a bad site for settlement and half the prospective settlers died of scurvy during the winter. The following year, in search of a more hospitable location, Champlain and De Monts examined the North American coast south below Cape Cod. In the end, they chose a site on the east coast of the Bay of Fundy. This colony had been in existence barely two years when the trade monopoly granted to De Monts was revoked and it was left without means of support. After Champlain and the colonists returned to France, however, De Monts managed to secure a new monopoly for one year only. He sent Champlain to Canada as his representative

the wars ended in 1598, Champlain visited Spain and was one of the few foreigners ever to take part in a Spanish expedition to Spain's American colonies. On Champlain's return, Henry was so impressed by his report that he appointed him royal geographer.

Pontgravé's 1603 expedition made its base in Tadoussac. From there Champlain went some 60 miles up the Saguenay River, more than half way to Lake St. Jean. He also traveled up the St. Lawrence as far as what is now Montreal.

Above: the city of Quebec in 1784. The Canadian city, now capital of Quebec province, had been founded by Champlain 76 years before this painting of it was made.

Below: Amerindians prepare for portage around the rapids of a river. Frequently the Canadian rivers were too fast and shallow for a canoe, and long distance travel meant a great many portages.

language and to find out more about the country. Champlain heard about a great lake west of the Huron River from Brulé in 1611, but could not follow up this lead at the time. On his return to Canada in 1613, he met up with a Frenchman who reported that the Ottawa River rose in a lake which emptied into the Northern Sea, and that the journey from the Lachine Rapids to the sea and back took only 17 days. Champlain acted on this information to try to find the Northern Sea.

When on the way Champlain reached the trading post he had established on the site of Montreal in 1611, he found that the Huron Indians had failed to come to meet him as arranged previously. He therefore resolved to go up the Ottawa River to visit them in their homes. With four Frenchmen, including his informant, an Indian guide, and two canoes, Champlain set off upstream. The river was so turbulent that Champlain was nearly drowned in one stretch of rapids before he reached his first destination. At last, however, the party arrived at the winter quarters of the Algonkians on Allumette Island, and there he discovered that the story about the route to the northern sea, on which he had banked so much, was unfounded.

Champlain's last great journey into the Canadian interior took place in 1615 and was made with a military expedition against the Iroquois. He joined the Hurons in their home-

Below: Champlain firing on the Iroquois to help his Huron allies. Champlain's alliance with the Hurons made the Iroquois join forces with the English in their later wars against the French.

with Pontgravé to oversee the fur trading which was to pay for the voyage. For this colony, the St. Lawrence was the chosen site.

In June 1608 Champlain and Pontgravé arrived in Tadoussac and, traveling up the St. Lawrence, founded their settlement in Quebec. In September Pontgravè returned to France, leaving Champlain to winter in Canada and, although 10 men died of scurvy, Champlain was ready to resume exploration in the west in 1609. The American Indians whom he had engaged to guide him told him that a party of Algonkian and Huron warriors several hundred men strong was on its way to meet him, having planned an expedition against the Iroquois and counting on Champlain's support. The war party was heading for the homeland of the Mohawk tribe of Iroquois between what is now Lake Champlain and the headwaters of the Hudson River, and on their journey Champlain became the first European to see and navigate the lake named after him. South of Lake Champlain, the Huron-Algonkian alliance met the Iroquois in battle and victory was theirs by the use of French firearms that the Iroquois had never seen before. Iroquois prisoners later told Champlain a great deal about the country to the south.

Champlain visited Canada again both in 1610 and 1611, but apart from a short journey up the Ottawa River, did not do much exploration. In 1610 he left Etienne Brulé, a youth of about 18, to live with the Algonkians to learn their

land east of Georgian Bay, the northern arm of Lake Huron, traveling there by way of the Ottawa River, Lake Nipissing, and the French River into the bay. Despite the numerous falls and rapids which meant that canoes had to be carried overland, this route remained the fur trader's highroad to the west for several hundred years.

From Georgian Bay, a small party under Brulé set off for the Susquehanna River to guide the Andastes, kinsmen and allies of the Hurons, to the scene of the attack. The main force, meanwhile, made its way via the lakes and rivers linking Georgian Bay with Lake Ontario to the stronghold of the Onondaga tribe of Iroquois southeast of that lake. Because there was no sign

Below: a view of Montreal in 1784 on the site of the former Amerindian village of Hochelaga. The name comes from Mont Réal, given to the mountain near it by Cartier.

Below right: David Kirke leading the English privateers who took Quebec after a siege lasting several months. Champlain was captured and exiled.

of Brulé and the Andastes, who arrived after the attack was over, the Hurons would not conform to Champlain's strategy and the attack was quickly repulsed. The Huron war party retreated to Lake Ontario but Champlain, instead of returning to Quebec as he wanted to, was forced to spend the winter with the Hurons. His enforced visit gave him the opportunity to visit tribes and explore country he would not otherwise have seen.

In 1616 Champlain returned to France and had his authority in Quebec confirmed. He spent the rest of his life trying to make the colony prosperous and self-supporting, but he had difficulty in attracting settlers to the colony and in 1629 Quebec fell to an English privateer-

ing fleet. Champlain was taken prisoner. Four years later he returned to his city, which had become French again. Two years afterward on December 25, 1635, the "Father of New France" died in Quebec. Though his last years were not greatly productive, his work of exploration was carried on by his followers who extended French knowledge and influence far west across the Great Lakes.

Robert Cavelier, Sieur de la Salle 1643-1687

On April 9, 1682 Robert Cavelier, Sieur de la Salle, stood at the mouth of the Mississippi River and claimed the river, all its tributaries, and all the country watered by them in the name of the king of France. His voyage down the Mississippi

was the first step toward the realization of a magnificent vision of French supremacy in North America. La Salle dreamed of linking the French settlements on the St. Lawrence with a new French colony on the Gulf of Mexico, and of establishing a great new empire for France in the Mississippi valley between them. His plan was too ambitious to be possible but it did lead to the first voyage to the mouth of the Mississippi and to France's claim of the Mississippi valley.

La Salle was born on November 22, 1643 in Rouen, France and was educated for the priesthood at a Jesuit college. He found that he was more attracted to a life of adventure, however, and in 1666 he went to Canada where his elder brother, a priest at the seminary of St. Sulpice,

Above: Louis Henri Buade, Comte de Frontenac, governor of New France. He encouraged La Salle.

Left: Robert Cavelier, Sieur de la Salle. He extended French dominion to the Gulf of Mexico.

Right: Henri de Tonti, friend and assistant to La Salle.

Below: Father Jacques Marquette and Louis Joliet made a point of building good relations with the Amerindians they met.

was already living. The seminary owned land in the Montreal neighborhood, and La Salle obtained a grant of territory west of Montreal at the head of the Lachine rapids. He became a farmer, but three years later he sold his land to start a life as an explorer. Amerinds had told him of a beautiful river to the west, which they called the Ohio, and in 1669 La Salle set out for that river. The course of his wanderings during the next two years is uncertain, and modern historians dispute whether he actually discovered the Ohio, but he appears to have reached the river and to have followed at least part of its course.

In 1672 the Comte de Frontenac became governor of New France. Frontenac shared with La Salle a desire to enhance French power and prestige in Canada, and in his first year as governor sent Louis Joliet to explore the Mississippi River – of which reports had been heard in Canada – and to follow it to its mouth. He also established Fort Frontenac at the site of present-day Kingston on Lake Ontario in an attempt to pacify the Iroquois and to intercept the fur trade between the Great Lakes and the English settlements on the coast.

La Salle had been placed in command of Fort Frontenac as soon as the post was built, and after a visit to France in 1675, his command was confirmed by King Louis XIV. Through control of a large part of the fur trade, he was able to build up capital, but he found the unclaimed lands of the Mississippi basin more attractive than commerce. So on a second visit to France in 1677 he obtained leave from the king to explore "the western parts of New France" and to build forts wherever he went to hold the country. He was also granted a monopoly of trade in buffalo hide. His projected explorations were, however, to be carried out at his own expense.

When La Salle returned to Canada in 1678, he was accompanied by Henri de Tonti, an Italian soldier of fortune who was to prove an invaluable lieutenant and La Salle's most loyal friend. On

Above: the conflict between de Tonti and the Iroquois ended with the capture of the Frenchman. Although wounded, he managed to escape and reach friendly territory.

Below: La Salle's party building the *Griffin* to transport furs around the Great Lakes.

his early explorations, La Salle was also accompanied by Louis Hennepin, a Franciscan friar who kept an account of the expedition and was the first European to describe Niagara Falls. Hennepin was, however, prone to exaggeration, particularly where his own exploits were concerned, and his report is unreliable.

Toward the end of 1678 La Salle's party started for Niagara. They established a fort there and the following year built a ship to carry the furs that were to pay for La Salle's expedition through the Great Lakes. The ship was named the *Griffin.* In August 1679 it sailed into the waters of Lake Erie, the first commercial sailing vessel to venture on the lake. From Lake Erie, the *Griffin* made its way through Lake Huron and into Lake Michigan, where a quantity of furs had been collected by an advance party sent out by La Salle. The furs were loaded on board the

Left: Louis XIV, the French king who was determined to keep his colonies in North America.

Right: La Salle meets Taensa Indians near present-day Natchez, Tennessee while sailing down the Mississippi in 1682.

and having succeeded in raising money to continue his expedition, he heard that many of the men he had left with Tonti had deserted.

When La Salle reached Fort Crèvecoeur, he found that it had been abandoned and learned that Tonti's men had mutinied and destroyed the fort, driving Tonti and the few who had remained loyal to him into the wilderness. La Salle traveled down the Illinois to the Mississippi in search of his trusted lieutenant, then returned to Fort Miami in what is now Michigan to spend the winter, reorganize his projected voyage down

Griffin, which was sent back to the Niagara River. Neither the *Griffin* nor her cargo was ever seen again.

La Salle, meanwhile, continued his journey to the southeast shore of Lake Michigan, where he established Fort Miami. In December 1679 he and Tonti set out for the Mississippi. They traveled along the St. Joseph River, then went overland with their canoes to the Kankakee, a tributary of the Illinois, and continued on the Kankakee and the Illinois. No word had been heard of the *Griffin* and La Salle, probably conscious that he had reached a low point in his fortunes, named the fort he built on the Illinois River *Fort Crèvecoeur* (Fort Heartbreak). In February 1680 Father Hennepin and two companions were sent to explore the Illinois River. They reached the Mississippi, but on the upper reaches of it, they were taken prisoner by Sioux Indians and never rejoined La Salle. Early in March 1680, leaving Tonti and his men to build another vessel at Fort Crèvecoeur, La Salle headed overland for New France.

The journey La Salle was undertaking has been called the most difficult made by Europeans in Canada up to that time. Winter was ending, and the previously frozen country had become a spongy mush of snow, melting ice, and mud. Even in those treacherous conditions, La Salle traveled on foot from the Illinois River to the St. Lawrence in little more than two months. His route lay along the Illinois River, around the head of Lake Michigan, and overland to Lake Erie, from which he continued to Niagara, Fort Frontenac, and Montreal. While in Montreal

Below: La Salle supervising the unloading of a supply ship.

Veue et Perspective de la nouvelle Orleans
1726

the Mississippi, and form an alliance of non-Iroquois tribes against the Iroquois. In the spring, he returned to Fort Frontenac to complete the arrangements for his journey. In the meantime, Tonti and his followers, having been captured by the hostile Iroquois, had managed to get away and make their way north to Wisconsin. There they had been helped by the friendly Ottawa, and afterward the two friends and associates were reunited.

On December 21, 1681 La Salle's expedition finally left Fort Miami for the Mississippi. The French canoes entered the great river on February 6 and two months later, on April 6, they reached the Mississippi Delta. The partysplit up to explore the three main channels into which the river divided, and the groups were reunited three days later at the sea. La Salle claimed the Mississippi and its valley for France, naming the region Louisiana in honor of King Louis XIV. The Frenchmen had been greatly impressed by Louisiana as they sailed through the country, and La Salle proposed founding two colonies to develop its resources, one on the Illinois River to exploit the fur trade and the other on the Gulf of Mexico. In 1683 Fort St. Louis was established on the Illinois, but La Salle was unable to obtain backing for the Gulf of Mexico project from Antoine de la Barre, who had succeeded Frontenac as governor of New France. He therefore sailed for Europe to appeal directly to the French king.

La Salle's last expedition left from France in July 1684 and was dogged by misfortune from the outset. The ships had been put in command of a naval officer and there was friction between him and La Salle for leadership; vessels were lost by piracy and shipwreck; and in the West Indies La Salle was for a time totally incapacitated by illness. Having no idea of the longitude of the Mississippi, La Salle's expedition later was unable to find the river's delta. Consequently, the party was put ashore west of present-day Galveston, Texas, hundreds of miles from where they wanted to be. A temporary colony was established, and after an unsuccessful attempt to reach the Mississippi, La Salle decided to leave a small party on the gulf and to lead the rest of

Above: New Orleans in 1726, only eight years after its establishment. This is the earliest known picture of the Louisiana capital.

Below: the murder of La Salle, from Father Hennepin's book. La Salle died without sighting the mighty river he had so long sought.

his men overland to Canada. The party had not even reached the Mississippi when La Salle's nephew and two other subordinates were murdered. Soon afterward, on March 19, 1687, he was killed as well. La Salle had a proud and reticent nature that kept him from being a popular leader, but he had pursued his dream of greatness for his country with all his energy and dedication. His dreams were, however, too ambitious to be realized.

103

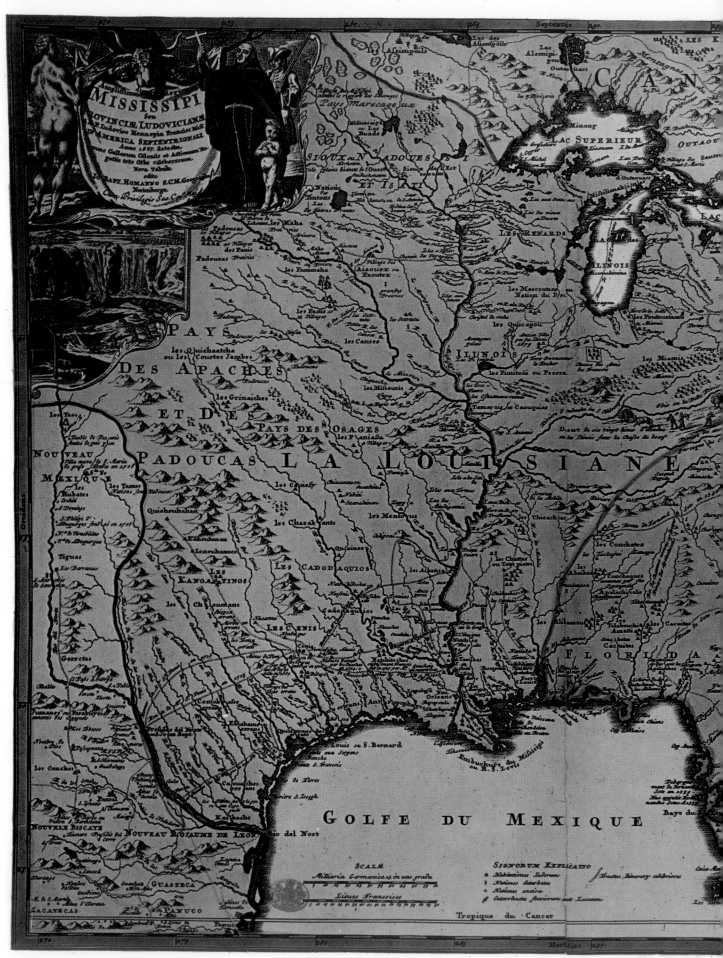

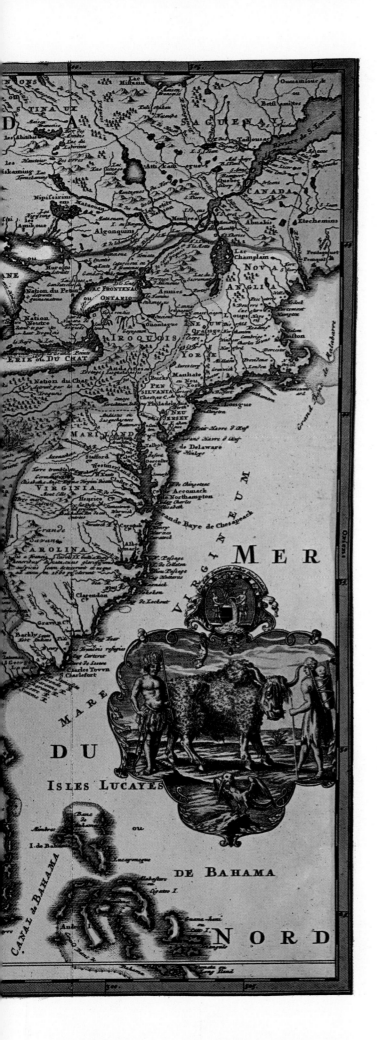

The French Map The New World

By the year 1700 French claims in the Americas extended from the St. Lawrence valley to Lake Superior and included the entire valley of the Mississippi, then known by the name of Louisiana as given to it by La Salle. This map of the French territories was made early in the 18th century and emphasizes the magnitude of the French achievement, particularly when it is compared with Ortelius' map made less than 150 years before. French explorers had discovered the five Great Lakes and charted them with great accuracy; they had sailed down the Mississippi River to the Gulf of Mexico and had discovered the Mississippi's principal tributaries. Ortelius' unknown continent had been transformed into a North America that could be recognized today.

Beside the main geographical features, this map also pinpoints the homelands of the various tribes of American Indians encountered by the explorers. A desert "extending six and twenty leagues" south of the Ohio River is even named as the site of the Illinois tribes' buffalo hunts. In addition, the map traces the routes of a number of the explorers of the Mississippi region and in particular those of Hernando de Soto, who discovered the river, and of Father Louis Hennepin. Hennepin accompanied La Salle on his early expeditions, was the first European to describe Niagara Falls, and later traveled extensively on the upper Mississippi as a prisoner of the Sioux Indians, but he greatly magnified his achievements in his own account of his explorations – and it is upon that account that this map seems to have been based. Hennepin appears to have been credited with the first voyage down the Mississippi, although he was already a prisoner of the Sioux when the voyage actually took place. La Salle, the true explorer of the river, is acknowledged only by his last disastrous expedition, from his ill-fated landing on the coast of Texas to the journey toward the Mississippi on which he met his death.

United States: Coast to Coast

The European explorers who first reached the Americas claimed the regions they discovered for the countries from which they came. As settlers followed discoverers, the European powers built up colonies in the New World. By 1700 England, France, and Spain had emerged as preeminent.

The principal English colonies lay on the eastern seaboard of North America, but the English also claimed the region around Hudson Bay. In the early years of English settlement on the east coast the southern – or Virginia – colonies had been divided from the New England settlements by the Dutch colony of New Netherland, but the two areas of English colonization were united in 1664 when the English captured what is now New York.

France's claims in North America were based on Cartier's discoveries and Champlain's explorations, and New France stretched from the mouth of the St. Lawrence River through the Great Lakes. After La Salle's voyage down the Mississippi in 1681–82, France also laid claim to Louisiana, which took in all of the Mississippi basin. Spain's New World empire was based on New Spain – present-day Mexico – which at the beginning of the 18th century included the territory between the Mississippi basin and the Pacific. Spain also claimed Florida.

No clear frontiers divided the English and French territories, and along the borders between their colonies were areas to which both countries laid claim. Both also sought control of

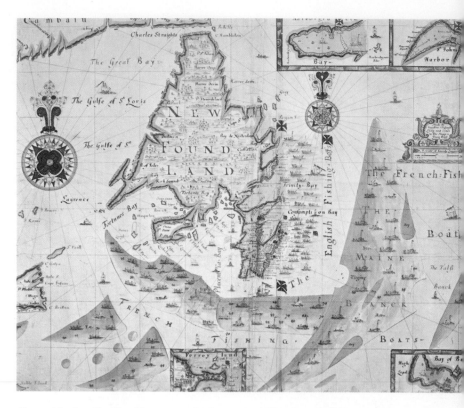

Above: Newfoundland in 1682 with the fishing districts marked out for the French, the English, and the American colony of Maine. The French and English were rivals for the sea as well as for the land.

the fur trade. When hostilities broke out between the two powers in Europe, it was inevitable that the fighting spread to North America for the purpose of gaining territorial or trading advantage there. King William's war from 1689 to 1697 resulted in the strengthening of France's claim to the fur-rich Hudson Bay territory, but the Peace of Utrecht of 1713, which ended the 11-year-long Queen Anne's War, gave Britain back the title to Hudson Bay and recognized its claim to Newfoundland and Nova Scotia.

King George's War of 1744–48 ended in stalemate, but fighting continued sporadically if unofficially after the end of the war, particularly in the Ohio valley to which both France and Britain laid claim. In 1758, during the French and Indian War, the British took Louisbourg,

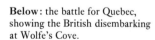

Below: the battle for Quebec, showing the British disembarking at Wolfe's Cove.

the key to the St. Lawrence. The following year they captured Quebec and in 1760 British troops entered Montreal. The treaty of Paris of 1763, which ended the war, also ended France's ambitions in the Americas. All French territory east of the Mississippi was ceded to Britain, and those west of the river to Spain.

The disappearance of France from North America removed a hostile presence from the frontier of the British colonies, but it also removed one of the principal links that tied the colonies to Britain – that of the need for security against a common enemy. Without the French threat, the British colonies became progressively more alienated from their motherland. In the 1760s and 1770s, their grievances focussed on British attempts to regulate their trade and to raise revenue by new tariffs – tariffs imposed by a government overseas in which the American colonies had no voice. In 1775 the first shots of the American Revolution were fired. The following year, the Second Continental Congress, meeting in Philadelphia, adopted the Declaration of Independence, and war continued. In 1783, defeated in battle, Britain recognized the independence of its 13 American colonies, which became the first 13 states of the new nation.

The treaty ending the American Revolution gave the United States all the territory south of the Great Lakes and west to the Mississippi

Below: an engraving of British troops landing at Boston's Long Wharf in 1768. Two years later an encounter between such troops and colonists, in which three Bostonians were killed, came to be known as the "Boston Massacre."

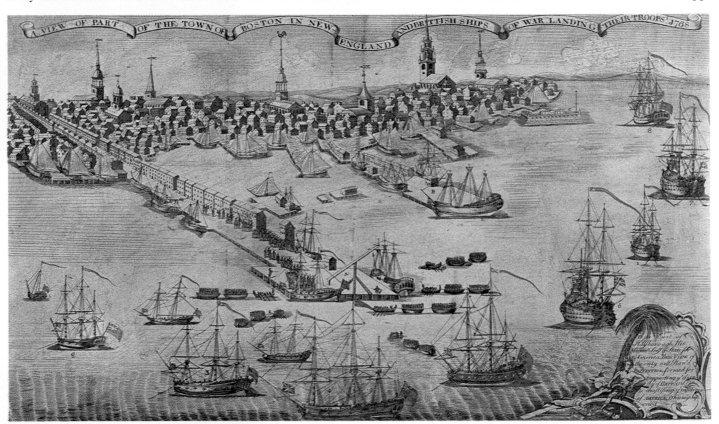

Left: the adoption of the Declaration of Independence by the Second Continental Congress of the American colonies on July 4, 1776. After this, war with Britain for self-government was almost inevitable.

River, but North America north of the Great Lakes remained in British hands. In 1803 President Thomas Jefferson bought Louisiana from Napoleon Bonaparte, who had acquired the region from Spain three years earlier, and in 1818 the 49th parallel was established as the Louisiana territory's frontier with the British lands to the north. In 1846 the 49th parallel was also fixed as the frontier between the United States and Canada as it related to Oregon, which had been in dispute until then.

In 1836 the part of Mexico called Texas became independent, a move made in order to enable annexation by the United States, which came in 1845. That same year, California also became independent of Mexico and three years later joined the United States. Only 65 years after independence, the United States of America stretched from the Atlantic to the Pacific coast.

David Thompson 1770-1857

David Thompson did not set out to be an explorer. His career – and his life work – were not originally of his choosing, and throughout his life exploration and surveying were seldom more than adjuncts to his main occupation, the fur trade. Yet this man has been called the greatest of all the explorers of North America. He was responsible for opening up the north-western part of the continent and he accurately surveyed and charted every mile of the country he explored.

Thompson was born in 1770 in the Westminster district of London, and from the age of seven to 14 attended the Grey Coat Charity school. In 1783 the Hudson's Bay Company requested the Grey Coat School to send four boys to work in the company's North American settlements and, because Thompson had learned navigation at the school, he was chosen. For a fee of £5, which was paid by the Grey Coat School, Thompson was apprenticed to the Hudson's Bay Company for seven years in May 1784. In September he arrived in Churchill, the company's post on the west coast of Hudson Bay.

Thompson spent his first winter in Canada in Churchill working for Samuel Hearne, who had already carried out some exploration in the interior and who, more than 10 years earlier, had reached the Arctic Ocean overland. In the autumn of the following year, Thompson was sent south to York Factory near the mouth of the

Right: Samuel Hearne, who explored much of present-day Manitoba and Saskatchewan for the Hudson's Bay Company. He and David Thompson, who later outdid him in feats of exploration, worked together in Churchill during Thompson's first winter in Canada.

Nelson River. York Factory was 150 miles from Churchill and winter was already approaching, but Thompson made the journey on foot accompanied only by two local guides. It was his first experience of travel in northwestern Canada and it must have left a deep impression on him. He made his first venture into the interior in July 1786 when he joined an expedition that had been formed to establish trading posts on the North Saskatchewan River, and he helped to establish the post of Manchester House.

The Hudson's Bay Company did not have a monopoly of trade with northwestern Canada. In fact, there was always fierce competition between its employees and those of the Northwest Company, which traded out of Montreal.

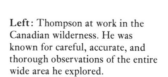

Left: Thompson at work in the Canadian wilderness. He was known for careful, accurate, and thorough observations of the entire wide area he explored.

Right: a medicine man of the Blackfoot Indians. Thompson traded with these Amerindians of southern Canada and northern United States and learned to appreciate their culture and society.

The rivalry between the groups of traders was as old as that between Britain and France in Canada. The Hudson's Bay Company represented the British interest, while the Northwest Company had been formed from various independent traders who came after Champlain and his successors. They operated from the French city of Montreal. In 1786 the Northwest Company already had a trading post on the North Saskatchewan, 40 miles north of Manchester House, but as far as is known, this post was then the limit of European exploration.

It was probably in 1787 that Thompson, with six other men, was instructed to travel southwest from Manchester House to find a new source of furs. Blackfoot and Piegan Indians from the plains had been bringing wolfskins to the traders, and the Hudson's Bay Company officials hoped that they might be persuaded to catch beaver and other more valuable fur animals instead. Thompson's party reached a Piegan camp on the Great Plains, probably in the region of present-day

Above: an outer trading station in the lowlands of Ontario. It is a typical inland station of the Hudson's Bay Company, fortified to protect the people living away from the bigger company forts.

Calgary, and while most of the men returned to Manchester House, Thompson spent the winter with the Indians. His visit gave him an appreciation of their way of life and culture, which enabled him to win the friendship of other tribes over the years.

The years 1788 and 1789 found Thompson trading on the Saskatchewan River, and in the winter of 1789-90 he was at Cumberland House on Pine Island Lake northwest of Lake Winnipeg. He had always had an interest in surveying, and during that winter he made a series of astronomical observations that enabled him to plot the position of Cumberland House with great accuracy. He also began keeping a meteorological journal, noting various aspects of the climate and weather. His studies marked the beginning of the constant, painstaking, and meticulous observation that characterized his entire career. When in 1790 he was ordered to return to York Factory, he took the opportunity to survey the route of some 750 miles.

From York Factory, Thompson was ordred in 1792 to the region he himself called Muskrat Country, roughly west of the Nelson River between the Churchill River in the north and the Saskatchewan in the south. Although Muskrat Country was rich in fur animals and compara-

Left: a surveying instrument of the kind available in the early 19th century. It measures the horizontal angle between two far objects or angles of elevation or depression.

Below: a drawing by Samuel Hearne of Lake Athabasca, made to illustrate the account of his journey around the Hudson Bay.

tively accessible from York Factory, trade there had been allowed to fall into the hands of the Northwest Company.

In 1793 Thompson tried to explore a new route from Muskrat Country via Reindeer Lake to Athabasca Country and, although he was forced to turn back because he could find no local canoe men, he surveyed and described in detail each part of his route. It appears that the opening of a route to Lake Athabasca was a priority of the Hudson's Bay Company directors in London, but the company's representatives at York Factory did little to promote the search. Despite their failure to assist him, however, Thompson himself remained determined to reach Lake Athabasca. In 1796 – with two untried Indian canoe men and a canoe he had built himself – he finally reached the lake. On his return journey to York, he wintered at Reindeer Lake, but while he was there a letter reached him from the Hudson's Bay Company representative at York Factory ordering him to cease his surveys. Thompson was wounded by this lack of appre-

Above: Mandan Indians crossing the frozen Missouri River. Their methods had to be adopted by non-Indian explorers of the region.

ciation, and felt that the order must be against the wishes of the company's directors in London. Since he had served out his time with the company, he decided to seek employment elsewhere. From Reindeer Lake he walked the 75-odd miles south to the nearest Northwest Company outpost. When Thompson left there, he was a Northwest Company man.

Thompson's new employers were more far-sighted and progressive than the leaders of the older Hudson's Bay Company, and they appreciated the importance of accurate knowledge of the country in which they were carrying out their trade. Thompson's first assignment for the Northwest Company was purely as a surveyor, with no responsibility for trading. He was instructed to plot the course of the 49th parallel of latitude – the boundary line between the United States and British territory – to visit the Mandan Indians on the Missouri River, and to establish the positions of Northwest Company trading posts. His journey led him from Grand Portage on Lake Superior via the Lake of the Woods to Lake Winnipeg, then to Lake Winnipegosis and cross country to the Assiniboine River. The winter of 1797 was setting in, and he had still not reached the Missouri River. Despite the difficulties and dangers of winter travel on the plains, Thompson resolved to push on. He was unable to find a guide for part of the journey and had to lead his party himself, but on December 29 he reached the Missouri only six miles above the uppermost Mandan village.

Thompson spent nearly two weeks with the Mandan Indians in an attempt to persuade them to come north to trade, but his attempt was unsuccessful because of the Mandans' fear of the

Sioux. He employed his time profitably, however, in writing down a vocabulary of the Mandan language, which ran to some 375 words. On January 10, 1798 he and his party left the Mandans and began gradually to make their way east. As the months passed and the thaws began, the journey became more and more difficult. Lakes and rivers remained at least partially frozen while thawing snow turned the open country into a muddy lake and made cross-country travel impossible. At last, by building a sled to carry his canoe and baggage and harnessing himself and his men to it, Thompson arrived at the headwaters of the Mississippi River.

On April 27 Thompson reached Turtle Lake, which he believed to be the source of the Mississippi. The true source of the river is in fact Lake Itasca, a few miles farther south, but the two lakes are so close together that the confusion was understandable. From the Mississippi, Thompson made his way back to Lake Superior, which he reached at the place where the city of Duluth now stands. He continued his survey around the shores of the lake before reaching the northwest shore of Grand Portage in June.

Delighted as the Northwest Company was with the results of Thompson's journey, as a commercial concern it could not afford to sponsor other such unprofitable ventures. It was therefore decided that in future Thompson should return to fur trading, but with the privilege of making surveys wherever he went. He spent the years 1798 and 1799 in the country north of the North Saskatchewan River and on the Athabasca River. In June 1799 at Isle à la Crosse Lake, he married Charlotte Small, the 14-year-old daughter of a Scottish trader and a

Chippewa Indian woman. Thompson and his wife had 13 children, seven sons and six daughters, although not all of them survived childhood. This increasing family accompanied him on many of his journeys in the northwest.

After their marriage, Thompson and his bride journeyed east to Lake Superior, but in 1800 Thompson was again on the North Saskatchewan where he remained until 1802. He explored west to the Rocky Mountains and made an unsuccessful attempt to cross the mountains in 1801. In 1802, after a visit to Lake Superior, he was back in the northwest, this time on the Peace River; there he remained until 1804. In 1804 he was sent back to Muskrat Country where the Hudson's Bay Company had taken over the position formerly enjoyed by the Northwest Company. This time, Thompson found himself in competition not only with the Hudson's Bay Company traders but also with those of the XY Company of Montreal. In November 1804, however, the Northwest Company and the XY Company agreed to join forces

and this gave them the added strength they needed to push west over the Rockies to the Pacific coast.

In 1806 Thompson was sent up the Saskatchewan River to prepare for the crossing of the Rocky Mountains, which was planned for 1807. Unlike the previous unsuccessful crossing of 1801, this time Thompson himself was in charge. In 1807 he and his family crossed the Rockies through Howse Pass and reached the Columbia River, and the next three years were spent traveling back and forth over the mountains, setting up trading posts on the Columbia, trading with the Kutenai Indians, and making careful surveys of this previously unknown country.

The Hudson's Bay Company, alarmed by reports of Thompson's work west of the Rockies on behalf of the Northwest Company, sent Joseph Howse to investigate Thompson's activities. In 1809 Howse made a short foray across the Rockies, actually meeting Thompson on his return journey, and the following year he

Below: a waterfall on the Columbia River painted in 1847. Thompson reached the Columbia in 1807 and spent three years surveying the region of the Columbia valley.

headed west again, this time to set up a trading post. The country he chose for his post was, however, near the battlegrounds of the Piegan and Flathead Indians, and in the spring of 1811 Howse and the other Hudson's Bay Company employees abandoned their post. Hudson's Bay Company traders did not venture into the Columbia valley again until after the Hudson's Bay Company and the Northwest Company were merged in 1821. Ironically, however, the pass first used by Thompson to cross the Rockies bears the name of Joseph Howse.

Howse Pass did not long remain Thompson's route for crossing the Rockies. His path up the Saskatchewan lay in the territory of the Piegan Indians who were enemies of the Kutenai west of the Rockies. They objected to Thompson's trade with the Kutenai on the grounds that he provided them with weapons and ammunition that made them more formidable in battle than before. In 1810 the Piegans forced Thompson's men to turn back from the mountains, and Thompson decided that he must open a new

Above: the Rockies, in which the Columbia River, among others, has its source. Thompson crossed these formidable mountains by way of Howse Pass.

pass farther north, out of the Piegan lands. It was already late in the season, but Thompson continued on his journey of exploration north through the mountains and on January 10, 1811 discovered the Athabasca Pass. For many years, this pass was the usual route of Hudson's Bay Company traders traveling from the Great Plains to the Columbia valley.

The year of 1811 saw Thompson's last great exploratory exploit, when he descended the Columbia River to the Pacific Ocean. He found, however, that the United States' Pacific Fur Company was already established at Fort Astoria near the river mouth. The following year, Thompson made his way east to Montreal, and never visited the northwest territories of Canada again.

Thompson's first task on his retirement was to complete his map of western Canada, made from the information he had collected over the previous years. Between 1816 and 1826 he was the British representative on a commission surveying and defining the boundary line between Canada and the United States, and in the following years he made a number of other surveys. He was comfortably off when he retired, but he was poverty stricken in his last years. He had so little money that he was forced to sell his surveying instruments and even to pawn his coat to buy food. He died on February 10, 1857, nearly 87 years old.

The Lewis and Clark Expedition

Below: Napoleon offering to sell the territory of Louisiana to the United States. It was a huge area that needed charting and surveying.

territory because the Mississippi River was vital to the trade of the westernmost states. The transfer of Spanish Louisiana to France, news of which reached the United States in May 1801, created a dangerous situation for the young nation. The weak Spanish government, which controlled the west bank of the Mississippi, was suddenly replaced by the dynamic and expanding French empire of Napoleon Bonaparte. President Thomas Jefferson therefore opened

In 1803, for the sum of $15 million, the United States bought Louisiana from France. Within four months, an American expedition was on its way to explore this vast new territorial gain. The expedition, commanded by Meriwether Lewis and William Clark, marked the beginning of a new era in United States exploration, an era notable both for its emphasis on accurate topographical surveys and scientific observation and for the new spirit of expansion that was abroad. Lewis and Clark not only opened a new route across North America and gave the United States an accurate picture of the western part of the continent, but they also strengthened the United States' claim to Oregon Country on the Pacific and ushered in the age of American expansion west.

The United States' interest in Louisiana existed before the nation's purchase of the

Above: Thomas Jefferson, president of the United States who quickly grasped the opportunity to extend the country's borders west.

negotiations with France to try to buy the all-important port of New Orleans. When James Monroe, Jefferson's minister "extraordinary and plenipotentiary" in the negotiations, reached Paris, he found the American minister already bargaining for the entire territory of Louisiana rather than just for New Orleans. The disasters which had befallen the French army in Haiti had made Napoleon think again about his New World ventures, and he determined to sell all of Louisiana to the United States. On April 30, 1803 the deal was concluded – and the size of the American nation was doubled at a stroke.

Even before the purchase of Louisiana, Jefferson had been planning an expedition west. As early as 1802 he was suggesting the possibility of such a venture, and his message requesting funds from Congress was sent in January 1803. The ostensible aims of the expedition were geographical and scientific, but in reality Jefferson hoped to discover a new water route to the Pacific for use by American fur traders in competition with the British, who had well-established routes. When the purchase of Louisiana took place, other more urgent reasons emerged for a journey of exploration, foremost among them being the need for information about the United States' new western lands.

The man chosen as leader of the expedition was Jefferson's private secretary Meriwether Lewis, a regular soldier and captain in the First Infantry, who was 29 years old in 1803. Lewis was much better fitted to be a leader of an expedition of discovery than to be a private secretary, and it could be that Jefferson saw the position as his secretary as a way to prepare Lewis for the expedition. For his partner in the enterprise, Lewis chose William Clark under whom he had served for a time in the army and for whom he had a great respect. Clark, 33 years old in 1803, was the oldest member of the expedition that set out the following year.

The winter of 1803-04 was spent in quarters north of the proposed starting point, St. Louis, in training and preparation for the journey in the spring. The official transfer of Louisiana to the United States took place in St. Louis on March 10, 1804, and two months later the 45-strong party started out. The first stage of their journey was the 1600-odd miles to the Mandan villages on the Missouri, a trip that was not one of original discovery because the Mandan were visited regularly by both French and British traders. The Mandan villages were reached in October, and the weather turned so cold that it

Meriwether Lewis (**top**) and William Clark (**above**), leaders of the first United States overland expedition to the Pacific.

Below: St. Louis, Missouri, in the mid-19th century. This city was the starting point of the Lewis and Clark expedition.

was decided to build winter quarters in the neighborhood. Fort Mandan was completed on November 20, and there the men spent the winter of 1804-05. They were visited at Fort Mandan by traders from the Northwest Company and by French woodsmen, one of whom, Toussaint Charbonneau, was married to a woman of the Shoshoni or Snake tribe. Charbonneau was engaged as interpreter and he, his wife Sacagawea, and their eight-week-old son Jean-Baptiste accompanied Lewis and Clark when they set out on their second stage in April 1805.

On April 12, five days away from Fort Mandan, the expedition passed the Little Missouri River. Beyond that, the Missouri was entirely unexplored. On April 25, they reached the Yellowstone and one of the party traveled a few miles up that river. A month later the snow-capped Rocky Mountains came into sight. At first the journey was straightforward, but early in June the party reached the junction of two rivers and was unsure which was the Missouri. Eventually, they decided against taking the northern stream, the present-day Marias, which they named Maria's River after Lewis' cousin, and Lewis pushed ahead along the southern fork. The Mandans had told them of a series of waterfalls on the Missouri, and when Lewis reached these on June 13 he was sure that their choice had been right. Seating himself on a rock under the middle of the falls he "enjoyed the sublime spectacle of this stupendous object, which since the creation had been lavishing its magnificence upon the desert, unknown to civilization."

It took a long hard portage to pass the 10 miles of rapids that Lewis had greeted with such verbal

enthusiasm, but thereafter the expedition was in the homeland of the Shoshoni Indians, Sacagawea's people, from whom they could expect help. They reached the Three Forks of the Missouri toward the end of July and took the southwest fork, which they named after Jefferson. At the beginning of August, they found the river was no longer navigable and abandoned their canoes. Following the Jefferson upstream, they crossed the Bitterroot Mountains by way of Lemhi Pass.

Soon afterward, Lewis and Clark discovered the first stream they had seen flowing westward, but the Shoshoni Indians told them that the Salmon River, into which the stream flowed, could not be navigated all the way to the sea. Clark traveled some way down the river, proving the accuracy of the Shoshoni description. The expedition then altered course north, then west, crossing and recrossing the Bitterroots in gradually worsening weather until, on September 20, they reached "a beautiful open plain." On October 10 they arrived at the Snake River, and on October 16 saw the waters of the Columbia for the first time. Later in the month, they met tribes that had previously met Europeans.

On November 2, after portaging around Cascade Falls, Lewis and Clark found the waters of the Columbia to be tidal. The country they

Above: a Shoshoni woman catching a horse. The Shoshonis proved very helpful to the Lewis and Clark expedition when the Shoshoni wife of the French interpreter joined the party. The Amerindians gave the Americans needed advice about crossing the Rocky mountains.

Below: Captain Clark and his men building huts for shelter.

were then passing through was forested, unlike that they had left, and the weather was also different. It rained constantly, and on several days they were held up by fog. On November 7 the Pacific Ocean at last came into view. A site on the south bank of the Columbia was chosen for winter quarters, and Fort Clatsop was completed on the first day of the new year of 1806. During the time the expedition stayed there, it rained almost continuously, but Lewis and Clark took the opportunity to compile their accounts of the country, of the Indian tribes they had encountered, and of the different species of plants and animals they had seen. Clark also completed a map of the region through which they had passed.

The long journey back to St. Louis began on March 23, 1806, partly because the elk that the men had been shooting for food had begun migrating from the coast to the hills. The early start meant, however, that the expedition was held up for nearly three weeks while the snows melted enough for them to attempt the crossing of the Bitterroots. That July in the mountains, the expedition divided. Lewis and a party of nine crossed directly to the Missouri and explored

Right: a sketch map by Clark of the mouth of the Columbia River. The Lewis and Clark survey of the huge territory of the Louisiana Purchase took over two years.

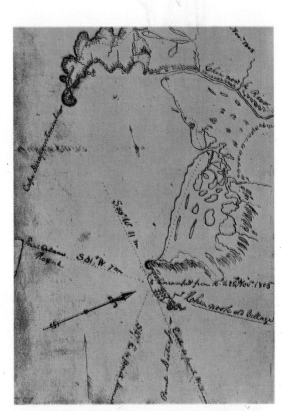

Left: the expedition in general maintained friendly relations with most of the Amerindians encountered. Clark in particular had a gift for dealing with the native inhabitants of North America.

Maria's River, while Clark and the remainder of the expedition followed a route closer to that of their outward journey as far as Three Forks. From there, 10 men went by canoe on the Missouri River while Clark and 10 others traveled overland to the Yellowstone and then down the Yellowstone to the Missouri. The parties were reunited on August 12, having explored much new country. On September 23, 1806, they reached St. Louis – their starting point more than two years before.

The Lewis and Clark expedition was almost entirely successful. Only one man had died – probably from a ruptured appendix – and in

Above: the annual gathering of fur trappers, this one near the border of Wyoming and Utah. Fur hunters and traders were among the first to move into and learn about the regions charted by Lewis and Clark. By the early 1820s they had organised the trade enough to hold annual meetings that became a social as well as a business event.

itself this is high tribute to the precision and care with which the journey had been organized and to the quality of its leadership. The mysterious west had been transformed into reality and, though the expedition revealed that there was no water route across the continent, it discovered a wealth of fur animals which opened new fur trading regions of its own for the United States. The fact that the Columbia River had been reached overland by a United States expedition bolstered the United States claim to Oregon Country around the mouth of the river. In the wake of Lewis and Clark, the American nation began pushing west.

John Charles Frémont 1813-1890

Rash, energetic, and ambitious, John Charles Frémont became an American national hero through his exploits as an explorer and adventurer, earning himself the nickname of "Pathfinder." His career was not one of original discovery, because the routes he followed had often been traveled by intrepid traders or mountaineers. However, it was he who surveyed and mapped these new areas to make them generally known. His sense of the dramatic led to ventures that caught the popular imagination, and when he took up the political banner on his journeys in California he became the personification of the spirit of "manifest destiny" in the United States.

Frémont was born in 1813 in Savannah, Georgia, the son of a French immigrant who had died when Frémont was six. His mother moved to Charleston, South Carolina and there Frémont spent his youth. In 1829 he entered the College of Charleston, where he showed a pronounced flair for mathematics, but his failure to attend classes regularly led to the withholding of his degree. Even without an official degree, Frémont in 1833 was appointed teacher of mathematics on the United States Navy's sloop of war *Natchez*, and held the post for two-and-a-half years. After leaving the navy, he served as assistant engineer on a team making a survey for a railway between Charleston and Cincinnati, Ohio, and it was in the field of surveying that he found his niche for a career. In

Above: John Charles Frémont, explorer, soldier, and politician. As an army topographer, he surveyed much of the country between the Rockies and the Pacific coast.

Below left: a 50-foot linen measuring tape in a leather case that also holds a notepad and pencil, as used by 19th-century surveyors.

Below right: a prismatic compass made in the late 19th century for taking accurate bearings.

1836 he received his college degree belatedly, and in 1838 was commissioned a second lieutenant in the Topographical Corps of the United States Army. This corps had been founded to assist in the surveying and mapping of the lesser known regions of the United States.

In 1838 the Topographical Corps appointed Frémont assistant to J N Nicollet in mapping the region between the upper Mississippi and Missouri Rivers. He later described this assignment as his "Yale College and his Harvard," and it gave him the taste for life in the American wilderness that remained with him throughout his career. On his return, he was supposed to help Nicollet in the assessment and classification of the expedition, but in 1841 he was suddenly sent to survey the Des Moines River, a tributary of the Mississippi, even though another member of the Topographical Corps had already done so less than a year before. It was said that so many settlers were making for the area that an accurate map had become a necessity, but Frémont always believed that the survey was just a pretext to end his romance with Jessie Benton, daughter of Thomas Hart Benton, a powerful member of the Senate. If so, it was unsuccessful, because Frémont and Jessie Benton were married upon his return.

Senator Benton was one of the foremost champions of American expansion westward. As the phrase coined in a newspaper article just a few years later expressed it, he believed that it was the "manifest destiny" of the United States to rule North America from coast to coast. In such a father-in-law, Frémont acquired an influential supporter whose interest in the American West matched his own. Backed by Benton, Frémont was able to survey and map the region from the Mississippi to the Pacific, probably working more freely than was usually possible

case it proved that, contrary to prevailing opinion, the country west of the Mississippi was suitable for agricultural settlement. After the publication of Frémont's report, the flow of settlers to the west increased.

Although Frémont's next expedition in 1843–44 was officially made under the aegis of the Topographical Corps, the project was originally Benton's. The purpose of the expedition was to connect Frémont's previous explorations around South Pass with the work of other American explorers on the Pacific Coast. Carson was his guide again, and the party again crossed the mountains by South Pass. Then, while a group followed the Oregon Trail westward, Frémont struck out for the Great Salt Lake and made a partial survey of its northern shores. Four years later, inspired by his descriptions, Brigham Young led the Mormons west to make their home on the Great Salt Lake.

From the Great Salt Lake, Frémont made his way north to the Snake River, then crossed to the Columbia which he followed to Fort Vancouver near the mouth. His official work was complete, but instead of retracing his route to Kansas City,

for an army officer. Under Benton's influence he also became an enthusiastic if sometimes unwise supporter of "manifest destiny."

Since 1818 Benton had been particularly interested in Oregon Country, whose ownership was disputed with Britain. By the 1840s a steady stream of American settlers was making for Oregon. Frémont's next expedition, in 1842, was therefore made to survey the route from the Mississippi to South Pass, Wyoming, which was used by pioneers going to Oregon to settle. Frémont was lucky to obtain as guide Kit Carson, an adventurous frontiersman who had built up a sound knowledge of the country west of the Mississippi and the Rocky Mountains. Under Carson's guidance the expedition made its way on the Missouri and Platte Rivers to South Pass, then detoured north into the Wind River Mountains where Frémont climbed the peak now named for him.

The value of Frémont's survey is today disputed by some authorities, even though Frémont's own commander in the Topographical Corps was in no doubt of its importance. In any

Above: a photograph of the 2000-mile-long Oregon Trail, which looked like this for miles of its length. Settlers taking this route west faced a feat of endurance. It took six months for the trip on which people braved rutted trails, water and food shortages, flooded rivers, and attacks from Amerindians protecting their lands.

Right: a map of 1830 still showing the mythical Buenaventura River. The myth persisted although numerous travelers knew that such a river did not exist.

he turned south with the intention of solving some long-standing mysteries of western geography. His plan was to search for a "lake called Mary's" in the Great Basin, then to strike southwest for the Buenaventura River. Not surprisingly, he could find neither of these mythical topographical features. In mid-January 1844 the expedition reached a point east of the Sierra Nevada, and Frémont resolved to cross the mountains into California on the pretext of replenishing his supplies. California was then still part of Mexico, so in crossing the Sierra Nevada, Frémont was trespassing on Mexican territory.

The pass across the Sierra Nevada lay nearly 9500 feet above sea level, a great height for a winter crossing, and Frémont's men suffered terribly before they reached California. The success of such a rash venture, however, added greatly to Frémont's fame. Sutter's Fort on the Sacramento River was reached early in March, and from there, on March 24, Frémont set out on his journey eastward. Rather than recrossing the Sierra, he led his men along the San Joaquin valley, rounded the southern end of the Sierra

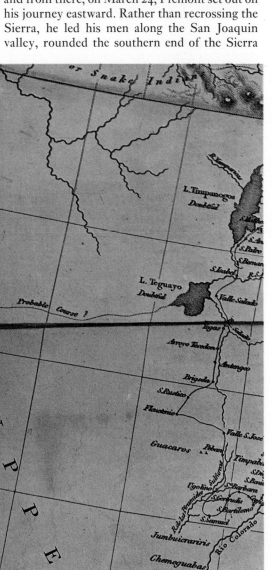

Top: the Great Salt Lake, Utah. Frémont thought that Lake Utah was a projection of this large shallow lake, but he was badly mistaken.

Above: Brigham Young, who led his persecuted Mormon followers to the Salt Lake valley about three years after Frémont reported on it.

Nevada, and skirted the Great Basin toward the Great Salt Lake. At the end of May, they reached Lake Utah. In describing this freshwater lake as a southern projection of the Great Salt Lake, Frémont made the biggest geographical blunder of his career. At the beginning of August 1844 Frémont and his men were back in St. Louis, having completed the most important journey to the American West since that of Lewis and Clark 40 years before. The story of Frémont's expedition, and in particular its heroic crossing of the Sierra Nevada, stimulated the public imagination and further encouraged people to go west.

In March 1845, the year after Frémont's return from California, a joint resolution of the United States Congress approved the annexation of Texas, the state that had won its independence from Mexico nine years before. The sensitivity of the issue made war between Mexico and the United States likely, and when Frémont again went west in June 1845, he was at the head of a well-armed 62-man party. He also carried secret instructions for action in case of war. At first his journey was one of exploration and observation. He surveyed the southern end of the Great Salt Lake, and then divided his party into two for the crossing of the Great Basin in order to cover as much ground as possible. The two groups were reunited at Walker Lake, having proved that the crossing of the desert was manageable and could possibly be a new route for overland communication. Frémont then crossed the Sierra Nevada to Sutter's Fort, reaching California in December. Others of his party detoured around the southern end of the mountains and rejoined him near San José.

So tense was the situation between the United States and Mexico that the appearance of

Left: the Sierra Nevada, the range that forms the eastern boundary of California. Frémont made a hazardous winter crossing of the Sierras in 1843.

Right: the San Juan mountains in Colorado. Because the slopes are so gradually inclined, explorers were surprised by the heights they attained after easy climbs.

Below: James Polk, 11th president of the United States. It was during his term of office that moves were made to take Texas and California from Mexico.

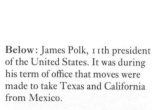

Frémont's party in California excited the suspicions of the Mexican authorities, and Frémont was ordered out of the province. At first he refused to leave and withdrew to the Gabilon Mountains where he fortified his position and raised the Stars and Stripes, but thinking better of his premature action, he abandoned the post and led his party north toward Oregon. He was in the region of Upper Klamath Lake, south of the Cascade Mountains, when he was overtaken by a confidential messenger from Washington. It is still not known exactly what orders the messenger brought but after meeting him Frémont turned south and led his force back into the Mexican territory of California.

A small group of American settlers in California had revolted against their Mexican rulers, proclaiming the "California Republic" and raising a new flag picturing a bear. Frémont supported the fight, which came to be known as the Bear Flag Revolt. Later, when news of the official outbreak of war with Mexico reached California, he and the naval officer Commodore Robert F Stockton led American volunteers from among the settlers and the United States armed forces in California to victory over Mexico. Frémont himself received the surrender at Cahuenga pass near Los Angeles, and Stockton appointed him governor of the newly conquered province.

Meanwhile, General Stephen W Kearny had entered California from the southeast. Kearny's orders were to conquer the province and to establish a government, but Frémont refused to recognize his authority and continued to act as governor for two more months. Then Kearny received confirmation of his authority, and Frémont was placed under arrest. In January 1848 in Washington, he was found guilty by court martial of mutiny, disobedience, and conduct prejudicial to military discipline. The sentence was dismissal from the army, but President James Polk intervened to get the conviction for mutiny quashed and the penalty withdrawn. In disgust with the way he had been treated, Frémont resigned his army commission.

After leaving the army, Frémont planned to make his home on a large estate he had purchased in the foothills of the Sierra Nevada. He combined his journey to his new home with another project dear to his heart – the survey of a route for a railway to the West, a survey to be funded by himself and Senator Benton. To see conditions at their worst, Frémont resolved to undertake the journey in mid-winter. Against all advice he made his way west from the Arkansas River across the mighty San Juan Mountains, which he reached in December. "On our first attempt to cross," he wrote to his wife, "we encountered a *pouderié* [dry snow driven thick

Above: a drawing of the Bear Flag adopted by American settlers who revolted against the Mexican government of California in 1846.

Above: surveyors setting up a baseline station in the Utah desert in 1850. Many army teams followed after Frémont in the search for good routes to the west.

through the air by violent wind] . . . and were driven back, having some 10 or 12 men variously frozen, face, hands, or feet. The guide became nigh frozen to death here, and dead mules were already lying about the fires. Meantime, it snowed steadily. The next day we . . . crossed the crest in defiance of the *pouderié*. . . . The trail showed as if a defeated party had passed by; pack saddles and packs, scattered articles of clothing, and dead mules strewed along. A continuance of stormy weather paralyzed all movement. . . . It was impossible to advance and to turn back was equally impracticable." At last, after 11 men had died, Frémont was able to retire to the headwaters of the Rio Grande and eventually made his way to California by way of a vast sweep to the south along the Gila River.

When Frémont arrived in California in 1849, he was greeted with the news that gold had been found in the province. The rich deposits on his own estate made him a multimillionaire. In 1853 the United States government undertook a series of surveys for a railway across the continent – Frémont's pet project – but despite Frémont's knowledge of the West, he was not invited to participate. That same year, therefore, he undertook a "railway survey" on his own initiative, to complete the one he had been forced to abandon in 1848. His 1853 journey, which took him from the Arkansas to the upper Colorado and across the southern part of the Great Basin, was the last one he made as an explorer. The rest of his life was much concerned with politics, except for a period during the Civil War when he returned to the army. That return was not altogether happy and he resigned his commission for the second time in 1862.

In 1856 Frémont was the new Republican party's presidential candidate, riding on the publicity of his 1853 expedition and his popularity following the conquest of California, but he was defeated in the election by James Buchanan. Although he was again considered as the candidate in 1864, he withdrew from the contest and then from public life. For some years he devoted himself to projects for railways in the West but in 1878, after losing his fortune, he was appointed governor of Arizona territory for a five-year term. He died in New York City on July 13, 1890 at the age of 77.

Chapter 6

South America Unveiled

The continent that stretches south from the isthmus of Panama presented a very different aspect to explorers from that of its northern neighbor. The most obvious difference was that of climate. Because the equator runs through northern South America, the explorer there was faced with the particular difficulties and dangers of travel in the tropics. Then, too, explorers were lured by the great wealth of the thriving civilizations in the region, and consequently it became a goal of the Spanish conquistadors. After conquest some of the earliest Spanish colonies in the New World were established. The colonizers of these areas ascertained the principal geographical features, at least of the coastlands, but the Spanish were so secretive about their colonies that knowledge of these discoveries was confined to Spain. It took scientists many years to get around the Spanish desire for secrecy and to open South America to the outside world.

Left: this contemporary print depicts the Fort of St. Gabriel on the Negro River in Brazil in the mid-19th century. Small settlements like St. Gabriel were few and far between, but they meant haven for the intrepid scientists who exposed themselves to the hardships of exploration in South America to collect scientific information. Three naturalists – Henry Wallace Bates, Richard Spruce, and Alfred Russel Wallace – spent a great deal of time on and around the Negro.

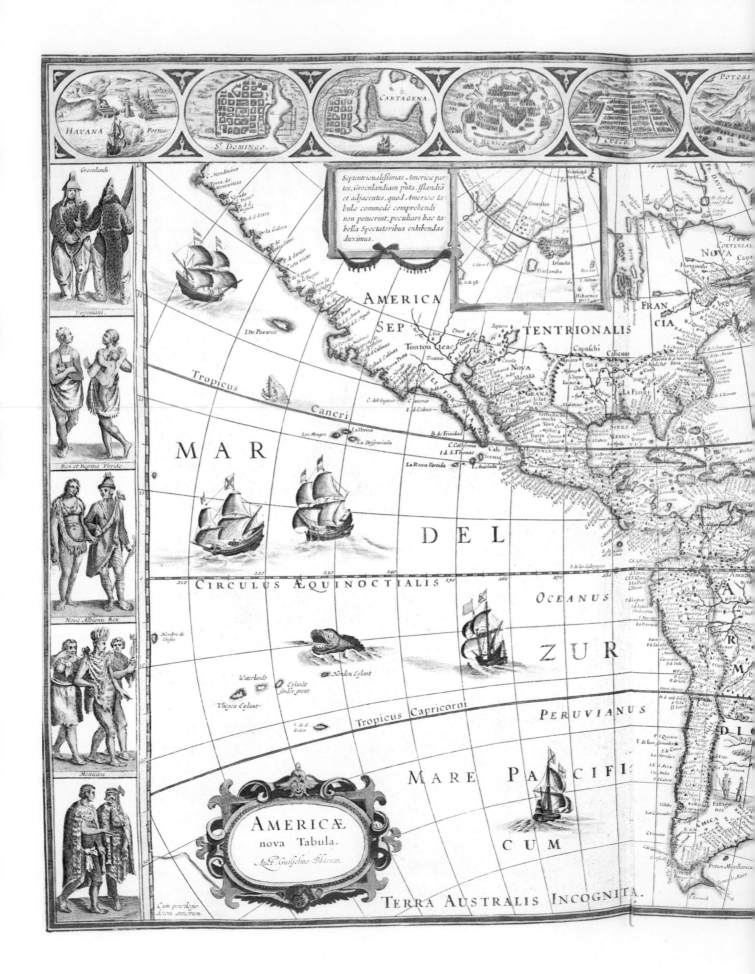

The Blaeu Map–1630?

When the Dutch cartographer Willem Blaeu mapped the Americas around 1630, he had at his disposal the accumulated knowledge of nearly 150 years of discovery. This knowledge enabled him to chart the continental coastlines and to mark numerous rivers and towns, but the area of which he had accurate information was small compared with the vast size of the American continents. In South America, generally speaking, the explored regions either hugged the coastline or pushed inland along river valleys. Of the vast mass of the interior, virtually nothing was known.

Naturally, this lack of information gave rise to supposition and invention. Mythical geographical features appeared, and it took many years to displace them. For example, straddling the equator in the region Blaeu calls Guiana, he places a vast inland sea named Lake Parime. Word of this body of water had first reached Europe from Sir Walter Raleigh's unsuccessful gold-seeking expeditions to the Orinoco River at the start of the 16th century. Lake Parime, also known as the Lake of Manoa or the Lake of Guiana, had no foundation whatever in reality, yet it persisted on maps until late in the 18th century. The English map maker Aaron Arrowsmith even theorized that the Orinoco River had its source in Lake Parime.

On Blaeu's map, Tierra del Fuego is at last correctly depicted as an island and not as part of some great southern continent. In fact, unlike earlier map makers, Blaeu does not even include the outline of Terra Australis on his map. He is careful, however, not to discount the existence of such a land mass because the legend "Pacific Ocean" includes the words "with the unknown southern land."

The margins of Blaeu's map are decorated with vignettes of the peoples and towns of the Americas; the inhabitants of North America appear in the left-hand margin, while those of South America are pictured to the right. It is an interesting fact that not one of all the towns featured in the top border is in North America. The only cities depicted by Blaeu are in the Caribbean and Central and South America, which shows how much more advanced colonization by the Spanish was.

Charles-Marie de la Condamine 1701-1774

The controversy raged in European scientific circles. Did the earth bulge at the equator and become flattened at the poles, as asserted by the English mathematician Isaac Newton, or was it lengthened at the poles and nipped in at the equator, as the followers of French astronomer Jacques Cassini held? Without the answer to this question, it was impossible to calculate the length of a degree of latitude correctly, and without knowing the correct length of a degree of latitude, it was impossible to construct an accurate map. In 1734, therefore, the French Academy of Sciences decided to send out two

expeditions to take the measurements that would solve this problem. The first, led by Pierre de Maupertuis, carried out its task in Lapland in the region of the Arctic Circle. The second, under Charles-Marie de la Condamine, worked in South America on the equator. Though La Condamine and his companions traveled in regions where the principal geographical features had already been discovered, theirs was the first scientific exploration of those regions, and their exploits brought South America to the attention of the outside world.

La Condamine was 33 years old in the year the French Academy of Sciences proposed to measure the earth, and at that time he had been a member of the Academy for four years. His early training, however, had been as a soldier and he had served in the French army, distinguishing himself by his courage and daring. He was nearly 20 years old when his interests turned to science and in particular to geodesy, the branch of mathematics concerned with establishing the

Left: Charles Marie de la Condamine, the French scientist assigned to calculate the exact length of a degree of longitude at the equator. He made his measurements in the Andes mountains.

Above: Isaac Newton, the influential English scientist whose theory of the shape of the earth was challenged by Jacques Cassini. The argument led to La Condamine's trip of verification.

shape and size of the earth. This interest made him a natural choice for the French Academy's expedition. His companions in the venture included Pierre Bouguer, a mathematician; Louis Godin, an astronomer; Godin's cousin Jean Godin des Odonais, a naturalist; Joseph de Jussieu, a botanist, and Jean Senièrgues, a doctor. In May 1735 the party sailed from La Rochelle.

The expedition's first South American landfall was at Cartagena in present-day Colombia, at that time the gateway to the Spanish possessions in the New World. At Cartagena they were joined by two Spanish naval officers, Don Jorge Juan y Santacilla and Don Antonio de Ulloa, who had been charged by the King of Spain with assisting the Frenchmen in their work. The Spanish court had an ulterior motive in attaching Spanish officials to the French party, however. La Condamine's expedition was the first official body to be allowed to enter Spain's South American colonies and the Spanish government, jealous of its colonial secrets, had determined that the visiting Frenchmen would not see more than the Spanish desired. Everything they saw was new and interesting to the French travelers, however.

The expedition's ultimate goal was the city of Quito, Ecuador, at that time the only spot on the whole equator sufficiently accessible for them

to carry out their work. Rather than traveling inland by way of the Magdalena River, they took a ship from Cartagena to Puerto Bello, Panama, then crossed the isthmus and sailed from Panama City for Manta, Ecuador. There La Condamine and Bouguer landed to begin their measurements, while the rest of the party continued by ship to Guayaquil.

After La Condamine and Bouguer had completed their measurements near Manta, Bouguer wanted to join the other scientists in Guayaquil but La Condamine was determined to push north to take his first measurements on the actual equator. One day Pedro Vicente Maldonado, the governor of Esmeraldas in northwest Ecuador, road into their camp. Maldonado, who had been born in Ecuador and knew the country intimately, was a mathematician, a cartographer, and an explorer. He wanted to persuade La Condamine to make the journey with him to Quito, which lay on the way back to Esmeraldas, by a little-known route along the Esmeraldas River instead of by the more usual route via Guayaquil. La Condamine, anxious to learn as much as he could about the country, was delighted to accept Maldonado's offer and so, while Bouguer took the heavier instruments south to Guayaquil, Maldonado and La Condamine made for the Esmeraldas jungles. They spent the entire month of May exploring the

Above: street vendors in Cartagena, Colombia. The French scientists were charmed with the townspeople, who proved hospitable and helpful.

Right: *Chiasognathus Granti*, one of the beetles that scientists like those with La Condamine's party would find of interest.

river and the surrounding region. La Condamine studied the forest birds and animals and discovered a strange stretchy substance that the natives called *caoutchouc* (rubber), which La Condamine was the first to bring to Europe. He also discovered the precious metal platinum.

From the Esmeraldas River the route followed by Maldonado and La Condamine lay over the high passes of the Andes. When they reached Quito, La Condamine found that in the rarefied air 12,000 feet above sea level he had difficulty in keeping up with Maldonado, who had been accustomed to such altitudes from his earliest years. The two men reached Quito on June 4, some time after the main body of the party. Six days later, Bouguer arrived.

Once in Quito the French scientists wanted to take the measurements that were the object of their expedition, but innumerable problems faced them. To begin with, it was difficult to find a strentch of level ground where they could take the first measurement on which they based all the others. In addition, the climate was bad. Although it was hot by day, the temperature dropped to freezing point at night. Besides the natural problems of working in a remote region, the scientists were exposed to the suspicions and interference of the settlers, who could not believe in a disinterested desire for knowledge and thought that the Frenchmen were searching for hidden Inca gold. When the Spanish governor began to interfere, La Condamine decided it was time to appeal to a higher authority. He undertook a 1000-mile journey south to Lima to protest to the Spanish viceroy, and although his journey added to the time necessary to complete the work of the expedition, it enabled him to see much more of South America than he would otherwise have done.

By June 1739, nearly four years after leaving Paris, La Condamine's party had completed the

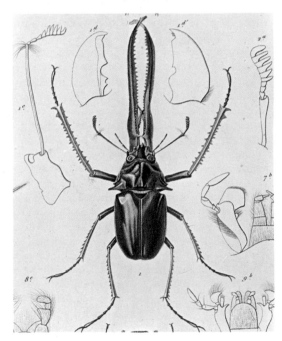

series of measurements from which they would be able to calculate the shape of the earth. At that moment a letter reached them from the Academy of Sciences telling them that the other scientific expedition had already solved the problem. Maupertuis, working in Lapland, had in only 18 months taken the measurements necessary to prove that the earth bulged at the equator and was flattened at the poles. Newton had been proved right, but to La Condamine and his companions after their years of hard work, the disappointment was necessarily great. The four remaining years of La Condamine's stay in Ecuador were marred by the suspicions and hostility of the Spanish and also by personal tragedies of his expedition companions. Senièrgues became involved in a family feud and was killed in a brawl; Morainville, the draftsman, died when a church he had helped design collapsed on him. Jussieu went out of his mind

Below: the city of Quito, looking much as it did when La Condamine and his companions were there.

when the plant collection it had taken him five years to build up was lost. By March 1743, when La Condamine took his last measurement near Cuenca, he was more than ready to leave.

The hardships and difficulties of La Condamine's scientific work had, however, in no way dulled his desire for adventure and, rather than retracing his outward journey, he decided to travel the Amazon River to its mouth. He was accompanied by the intrepid Maldonado, and during their two-month-long journey down the river, the two men were constantly making the first scientific observations of the world's second longest river. They were not the first Europeans to travel down the river, but they were the first trained scientists to do so, and their work was of immense value to the study of the geography and peoples of the Amazon valley. La Condamine's map of the Amazon remained generally unchanged until the 20th century. On his voyage down this river, La Condamine also heard of a water connection between the Negro River, a

tributary of the Amazon, and the Orinoco river system to the north. He could not take the journey to prove it, however.

In September, four months after leaving Ecuador, La Condamine and Maldonado reached Pará (present-day Belém) at the southern mouth of the Amazon, and from there they took ship for Europe. La Condamine reached Paris in the spring of 1745 after an absence of 10 years. His voyage down the Amazon was duplicated more than 10 years later by Isabela Godin des Odonais, the wife of La Condamine's expedition member. In 1769 she traveled down the Amazon to rejoin her husband in French Guiana, but she sailed into tragedy. Her vessels were lost, her companions died, and she herself was found by Amerinds wandering alone in the hostile unexplored Amazon jungles. With their help, however, she managed to get out of the jungle and at last completed her journey to the river's mouth.

Right: a map showing the meridian at Quito drawn by La Condamine. The maps made by La Condamine and Pedro Vincente Maldonado as they sailed down the Amazon were so accurate that they are still applicable today.

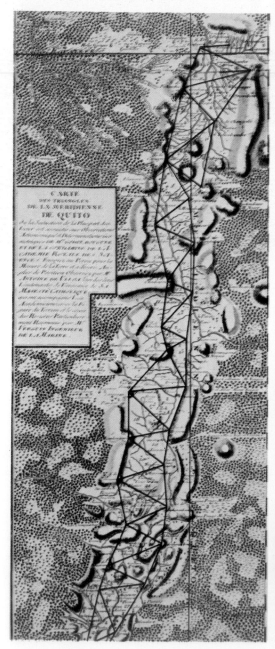

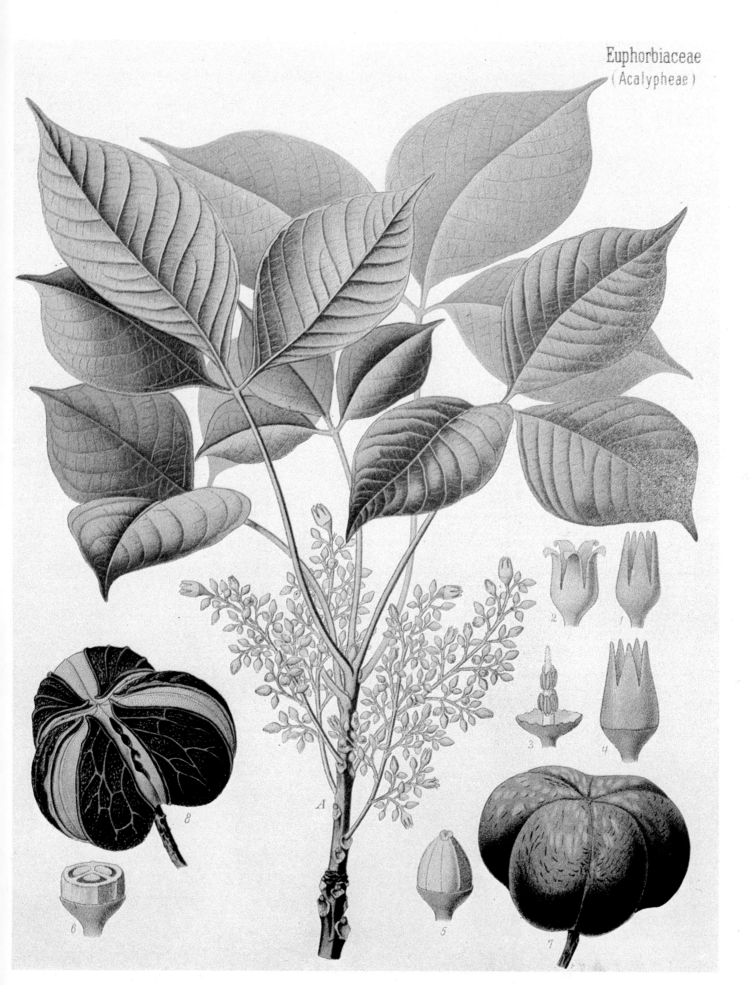

Alexander von Humboldt 1769-1859

According to Charles Darwin, the naturalist famous for his theory of evolution and himself no mean explorer, Alexander von Humboldt was "the greatest scientific traveler who ever lived." Yet apart from a short visit to Russia and Siberia, Humboldt made only one expedition – a five-year long exploration of the Americas. To this journey that lasted from 1799 to 1804, he brought immense scientific knowledge and a rare ability to analyze and classify his observations. The sciences of physical geography and meteorology are based on Humboldt's work in South America, and his travels stimulated exploration of the continent, calling attention to its geographical riches and to the many unknown regions it contained.

Von Humboldt was born in 1769 – the same year as Napoleon Bonaparte and the Duke of Wellington – in Berlin, then capital of Prussia. He was the scion of a noble family. His father was an officer in Frederick the Great's army, and his mother the offspring of a French Huguenot family that had fled to Prussia from France following Louis XIV's withdrawal of religious liberty for French Protestants in 1685. Humboldt's father died in 1779, and although their mother saw to it that Alexander and his elder brother received an education destined to fit them for high public office, it was in science that both made their career.

After a short stay at the university of Frankfurt an der Oder, Humboldt spent a year at the University of Berlin where he studied engineering. During his stay in Berlin, he acquired a passionate interest in botany, collected specimens in the woods and fields around the city, and learned to classify them correctly. It was at the University of Göttingen that his interest turned toward mineralogy and geology. To obtain a thorough training in these subjects, he entered the School of Mines in Freiburg in 1790. He spent two years there, but left without taking a degree. This did not prevent him from getting an appointment in the Mining Department of the Prussian Government, for whom he worked for five years.

During that time, Humboldt became increasingly sure that the main purpose of his life was scientific exploration. His chance came in 1796 with the death of his mother, which not only gave him possession of a modest fortune, but also cut the most important of the ties binding him to Prussia. In 1797 he resigned

Above: the *Melastoma coccinea*, one of the thousands of plants that the botanist Aimé Bonpland identified for the first time on his South American journey.

Below: Alexander von Humboldt in 1796 when he was 26 years old. A man of great intellectual curiosity, Von Humboldt fulfilled his childhood dream of following La Condamine's footsteps across South America.

Below right: Bonpland, lifelong friend and working companion of Von Humboldt. He was a physician as well as a botanist.

from his post in the Mining Department to study astronomy and the various systems of scientific measurement that he would need on his travels. Then he left for Paris, the center of the European scientific world. In the autumn of 1798, accompanied by the botanist Aimé Bonpland, Humboldt left Paris for the Mediterranean seaport of Marseille.

Humboldt's meeting with Bonpland had been totally accidental and proved to be remarkably lucky. The Frenchman was a physician by training but a botanist by inclination. The two formed a partnership that was ideal. Humboldt himself wrote on describing his South American travels, "I was aided by a courageous and enlightened friend, and, what is singularly propitious to the success of participated labor, whose zeal and equanimity never failed, amid the

Above: an illustration from Von Humboldt's book of him and Bonpland in a striking vista of valley and mountains. The two men made an immeasurable contribution to the knowledge of South America – and in a form that remains usable today.

fatigues and dangers to which we were sometimes exposed."

When Humboldt and Bonpland started for Marseille, they were bound for North Africa. They chose that destination because the upheavals of the Napoleonic Wars were making travel outside Europe difficult, and North Africa seemed to be possible to reach. Once in Marseille, however, the boat they were hoping to ship out on failed to appear, so they journeyed westward across the Pyrenees into Spain. Suddenly a whole new world opened to them. Humboldt's noble connections gave him access to the Spanish court, and he was able to obtain permission to visit the Spanish colonies in Central and South America. The Spanish overseas empire was still generally closed to foreigners and, despite La Condamine's expedition there, a vast amount of work remained for the scientific explorer.

In July 1799 Humboldt and Bonpland landed at Cumaná east of Caracas on the coast of what is now Venezuela. Their first project was the exploration of the Orinoco River and the investigation of the water link between the Orinoco and the Negro, which had been reported by La Condamine. In Cumaná they were told that such an expedition was impossible at that season because of the rains. The two men spent several months collecting specimens of flora and fauna around Cumaná and then, in November, set off for Caracas where they prepared for their expedition. To reach the Orinoco it was necessary to cross the llanos, the dry tropical grasslands stretching 150 miles south of Caracas, which in the dry season virtually became a desert. The annual mean temperatute on the llanos is 90°F. "Not a breath

Right: one of the dry and dusty plains that Von Humboldt and Bonpland trudged across on their way from Venezuela to the Orinoco.

Below left: a drawing by Bonpland of *Rhexia sarmentosa*. The botanist cataloged 3500 new species of plants, nearly doubling the known plants in the world.

Below: a boat on the Guayaquil River, from Von Humboldt's book. This may not have been his own because his description mentions an open boat requiring the travelers to stop to camp on shore at night.

of air was felt at the height at which we were on our mules;" wrote Humboldt, "yet, in the midst of this apparent calm, whirls of dust incessantly arose.... These *sand winds* augment the suffocating heat of the air. Every grain of quartz, hotter than the surrounding air, radiates heat in every direction.... All around us, the plains seemed to ascend toward the sky, and that vast and profound solitude appeared to our eyes like an ocean covered with seaweeds."

Above: a bat of the species *Stenoderma chilensis*. Von Humboldt reported that his pet dog was bitten by a vampire bat while they were camping along the Apure River.

Despite the heat and the discomforts of their journey, Humboldt and Bonpland tirelessly gathered information about the country through which they were traveling. They learned that because of the leaf-cutting ants, the only crops that could be grown on the llanos were cotton and indigo, and they made a detailed study of the ants and their lifestyle. They learned of a "cow-tree" the sap of which was like milk, they drank the sap to confirm this, and made drawings of the tree to identify it – and it turned out to be Arto-carpus, actually introduced to South America by Spanish explorers. When the scientists marveled at the cow tree, their guide told them of an even stranger phenomenon – the *tembladores* or electric eels whose shock could kill a horse. Electricity was then a new field of science and greatly interested Humboldt who managed with difficulty to obtain specimens to examine. Imprudently standing on one of the fish after it had been taken from the water, he received a terrible shock which for the rest of the day produced "a violent pain in the knees, and in almost every joint."

In March 1800 the travelers reached the Apure River, a tributary of the Orinoco, and on March 30 they set sail down the Apure in a large dugout canoe. By the middle of April they were on the waters of the Orinoco and sailing up river. They suffered acutely from the hordes of insects that tormented them – mosquitoes, flies, gnats, chigões, and ants were accompanied by minute piumes, which stung as hard as a wasp. Early in May they reached the mission of San Antonio de Yavita, which was separated by only a narrow neck of land from a stream in the Negro river drainage. Indian porters dragged the canoe across the land bridge, and the trek down the Negro began. Below the explorers' portage point there is another link between the Negro and the Orinoco, the Canal Casiquiare, and Humboldt and Bonpland used the Casiquiare to return to the Orinoco. Before beginning their homeward journey, they measured the precise point at which the two river systems were joined.

Humboldt's journey on the Orinoco opened a barely known part of South America. He later pointed out, for example, that on the upper Orinoco there existed an area three times as large as Spain in which not one single point had had its position established astronomically. In proving the link between the Orinoco and the Amazon river systems, he had disproved the existence of the mythical Lake Parime, placed by map makers in that region, and on their journey he and Bonpland had discovered great numbers of previously unknown plants. When in November 1800 the two men set sail for Cuba, Humboldt had no intention of returning to South America. Nonetheless by April 1801 he was once more on the mainland of the continent, and the second part of his South American odyssey began.

The Magdalena River, which Jiménez de Quesada had traversed to Bogotá to conquer the

Chibcha in the 1530s, was still the principal means of trade and communication in Colombia in 1801, and it was up this river that Humboldt and Bonpland set sail. As they journeyed, Humboldt studied the river, surveying its course to enable him to make a map. When they reached the limit of navigation, they took to mules and horses for their climb up the Andes to Bogotá. By September they were on their way to Quito, which they reached the following January and where they spent some months. One of Humboldt's dearest plans was to climb to the top of Chimborazo, a volcanic mountain south of Quito that had never been scaled.

Chimborazo, towering 20,577 feet above sea level, was a formidable project for any climber, but particularly for an inexperienced party in the days when oxygen equipment did not exist. Humboldt prepared for his ascent by climbing Pichincha, the smallest volcano in the valley of Añaquito. Then, on June 9 he left for Chimborazo itself. The first 6000 feet of the climb were relatively easy but thereafter the path became ever steeper and more dangerous. At the snow-line, 7000 feet from the summit, the American Indian porters deserted and Humboldt, Bonpland, the son of their host in Quito, and a half-caste were left to complete the ascent alone. Snow, ice, and the mist that clung to the mountain made their project increasingly dangerous. In addition the climbers began to suffer from sickness and dizziness, and to bleed from eyes, lips, and gums – signs of the onset of altitude sickness. In spite of this they persevered until, little more than 1000 feet from the summit, they found themselves on the brink of a vast abyss which it was impossible to cross. Though they had failed in their project to scale the mountain, they had climbed 19,286 feet – which remained a world record for nearly 30 years.

From Quito, Humboldt and Bonpland set out on horseback on a 1000-mile journey down the Andes to Lima, capital of Peru, where they intended to observe a passage of the planet Mercury across the sun. Humboldt studied and described the remains of Inca buildings, so becoming the first archaeologist of South America for, although Inca architecture had been mentioned before, it had never been described in an accurate scientific way. Near Loja, Bonpland collected specimens of the bark of the cinchona – the source of the medicine quinine – and the travelers also descended into the Amazon valley because Humboldt wanted to improve La Condamine's map. The final 600 miles of their journey led them from Trujillo south through the near deserts of the Peruvian coastlands, and Humboldt immediately began a series of studies to establish why the coast was so dry. In doing so he identified the cool current that flows north along the shores of Peru, which was named the Humboldt Current in his honor. Now it is as frequently known by the name of the Peru Current, however.

Above: a view of the Negro River in Brazil. During their journey on this river the scientists saw the Amerindians making the deadly poison curare, of which they took away some samples.

Right: Mount Chimborazo from the Plain of Tapia. The two scientists tried to climb to the top of this formidable peak, but failed.

Early in January 1803, after spending some time in Lima, Humboldt and Bonpland boarded a ship bound for Mexico. Besides Mexico, they visited Cuba and the United States before sailing for France in July 1804. There they received a tumultuous welcome, having caught the popular imagination through the descriptions of South America that Humboldt had written in letters to friends in Europe. He and Bonpland had traveled 40,000 miles in South America, made

had previously been known.

After his return from the Americas, Humboldt lived in Paris until 1827, at which time he had completed the work on his American material. The cost of his South American expedition and of publishing his works had eaten into his fortune, and in 1827 he returned to Berlin to take up a court appointment. Two years later he made an expedition to Russia and Siberia, but Berlin was his home for the rest of his life. He devoted much of his time and energy to furthering the cause of science, organizing one of the first international scientific conferences in 1828, and was always ready to assist young scientists at the start of their career. In 1845, at the age of 76, he began the publication of *Kosmos*, a vast account of the structure of the universe written at a generally popular level. Four volumes of *Kosmos* had already been published when Humboldt died in May 1859. The last was published after his death.

1500 measurements, and collected 30 chests of specimens and 60,000 plants, thousands of which were previously unknown. It took Humboldt 23 years to prepare the information collected on his expedition for publication. His complete work on the Americas filled 29 volumes and included nearly 1500 maps and plates. The abundance of data he brought back from South America completely changed European thinking about the New World continent of which so little

Right: Von Humboldt in old age, seen in his study in Germany. He spent most of his later years compiling his voluminous notes.

Naturalists as Explorers

The work of Henry Bates, Richard Spruce, and Alfred Russel Wallace gave Europe a minutely detailed picture of the natural history of the Amazon region, and in so doing revealed the true nature of the valley to the world. The three men had much in common. All were naturalists. All were English and came from remarkably similar backgrounds – respectable but by no means wealthy. All three owed their education more to their own efforts than to any formal schooling. Yet these men's dreams of more exotic fields for study than those existing in their homeland led them to South America and to the Amazon river valley.

Bates and Wallace first met in Leicester, England, in the 1840s. Bates was a clerk, but far more interested in his hobby of studying insects than in his job. Wallace taught English at the Collegiate School, Leicester, and used his spare time for botanical study. Under Bates' influence, Wallace turned from botany to entomology, and like Bates, concentrated on beetles. After Wallace left Leicester for South Wales, the two men corresponded. In the autumn of 1847 Wallace wrote to Bates suggesting that they travel together to the Amazon River on a collecting expedition. He proposed that they finance their expedition by making and selling duplicate collections of specimens, and this is what they did.

Early in 1848 Wallace and Bates met in London to study the collections of South American animals and plants that were already in Britain, and then visited the Duke of Devonshire's seat in Chatsworth, Derbyshire to study his orchids. On April 26 they embarked at Liverpool for Pará, the principal seaport of the Amazon region. A month later they had their first view of South America, and on May 28 their ship made port at Pará. "When the sun rose in a cloudless sky," wrote Wallace in his account of their journey, "the city of Pará, surrounded by the dense forest, and overtopped by palms and plantains, greeted our sight, appearing doubly beautiful from the presence of those luxuriant tropical productions in a state of nature, which we had so often admired in the conservatories of ... Chatsworth."

Pará was built on ground cleared from the Amazon forest, and the country around the town was a paradise for a naturalist. According to Wallace, he and Bates captured 150 distinct species of butterfly in about three weeks – more

Top: Henry Walter Bates. Although he was an amateur, his knowledge of beetles in particular and entomology in general was extensive.

Above: Alfred Russel Wallace. Like Bates, Wallace went from botany and entomology as a hobby to natural history as a career.

Above right: the coast of Brazil in the 1820s. Bates and Wallace remained in and around the port of Pará for a year.

Opposite: a page from Bates' notebook with his sketches of butterflies from the jungle.

than twice as many as the entire number known to exist in Britain. The two men made their base in Pará for 18 months, collecting specimens in the surrounding forests and undertaking a number of longer expeditions. In the year of their arrival, they traveled by canoe up the Tocantins, the first great southern tributary of the Amazon. Later that year Wallace visited the island of Mexiana, which is situated on the equator north of the island of Marajó.

Early in July 1849 Wallace was joined in Pará by his younger brother, Herbert, who had traveled to South America to help him in his work. The botanist Richard Spruce was on the same ship as Herbert Wallace. Spruce, a teacher and the son of a teacher, had abandoned teaching for botany in 1844, spent two years studying and collecting specimens of the plants of Spain, and paid for his journey by the sale of specimens. In 1848 he had reached agreement with another British botanist, George Bentham, to market any specimens he collected in South America in order to finance an expedition there.

Soon after Herbert Wallace's arrival in Pará, the two brothers started up the Amazon for Santarém at the mouth of the Tapajós River. A few weeks later they were joined by Bates, and in October Spruce arrived. No botanist had collected on the Amazon. Even Aimé Bonpland, Humboldt's companion, had only visited its uppermost headwaters. Spruce spent a year in and around Santarém. Methodically he divided the country into ecological zones and systematically collected all the plants of one zone before moving on to another. Almost all his specimens were new to science, but he also included those already known in order to give a representative picture.

Meanwhile, in November 1849 Bates and the two Wallaces had left Santarém for Manaus at the mouth of the Negro River. In March of the following year they parted company, "finding it more convenient to explore separate districts and collect independently." Wallace's goal was the Negro River and he spent his first months in Manaus making preparations for his journey. He left Manaus in August, but his brother stayed behind to go back to Pará and return to England from there. Pushing up the Negro, Wallace reached the waters of the Orinoco river system. Among his adventures on this journey was an encounter, at a distance of only 20 yards, with a black jaguar, "the most powerful and dangerous animal inhabiting the American continent . . . "In the middle of the road," wrote Wallace, "he turned his head, and for an instant paused and gazed at me, but having, I suppose, other business of his own to attend to, walked steadily on, and disappeared in the thicket. As he advanced, I heard the scampering of small animals, and the whizzing flight of ground birds, clearing the path for their dreaded enemy."

From the Orinoco, Wallace continued to the Uaupés, the tributary of the Negro that enters the river north of the present-day town of Uaupés. Because the wildlife on the river was so plentiful, Wallace abandoned his intention of making a journey to the Andes in favor of another voyage up the Uaupés to make a collection of live birds and animals to take back to England. Knowing he would have to take his

Right: Richard Spruce. He had long been planning a collecting trip to South America when he got the opportunity to join forces with Bates and Wallace.

Below: Manaus in 1880. The small port had become a booming town between Spruce's visits to it because of the European demand for rubber.

Bottom: a drawing by Wallace of the fish *Osteoglossium bicirrhasirm* from the Negro River.

live specimens to England himself, he decided to return home a year earlier, and in the midst of the tropical forests of the Amazon, he began to long for the simple pleasures of home. But before he could even embark on his second Uaupés voyage, he had to undertake the 1500-mile journey to Manaus and back to send off his existing collection of specimens and to buy the supplies he would need.

Wallace arrived in Manaus in September 1851 to find that Spruce had been there since the previous December, continuing his systematic col-

retrace his steps and explore the Amazon valley in detail. He left Pará in October 1851 and arrived in Santarém in November. There he made his headquarters for three-and-a-half years.

Bates had already left Santarém for an expedition to the Tapajós River when Wallace arrived in the town on his way from the Uaupés to Pará in June 1852. Wallace had also been very sick with malaria during his journey, and he found it so difficult to make a collection of live birds and animals that he often said he wished he "had had nothing whatever to do with them." On land, "it was a constant trouble to get food for them in sufficient variety, and to prevent them from escaping," and in a small canoe "52 live animals (monkeys, parrots, etc.) . . . were no little trouble and annoyance." Nevertheless, Wallace had succeeded in going into regions never before seen by a European. Despite his weakness after his fever, he even regretted his lack of the necessary instruments to measure latitude, longitude, and height above the sea. He finally reached Pará on July 2, 1852, and 10 days later he embarked for home on the brig *Helen*. On August 6, the *Helen* caught fire and all the specimens

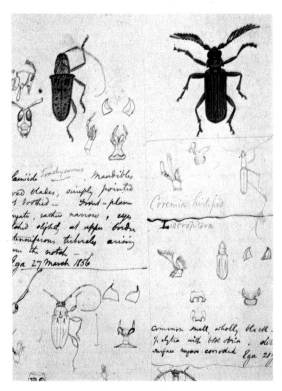

lection of botanical specimens in the rich hunting grounds around the town. Bad news awaited Wallace. A letter more than three months old informed him that his brother Herbert was sick with yellow fever in Pará, and that there was little hope of his recovery. Wallace had to leave Manaus for the Uaupés without learning of his brother's fate.

It was Bates who gave Herbert Wallace companionship during his illness. Bates had been in Ega, 750 miles from Manaus, for more than a year and had built up a collection of 7553 insect specimens. He had become ill and depressed, however, partly through loneliness and lack of contact with the outside world. In addition, he ended up penniless, having been robbed by his servant. In March 1851 he had left for Pará, arriving in April and meeting Herbert Wallace just before he went down with yellow fever. Bates nursed Herbert before himself succumbing to the same disease, and he recovered. But Herbert died. Despite the hardships of his previous stay in Ega, Bates then decided to

Above: a curl-crested toucan, one of the brilliant birds of the jungle observed by Bates while he was on his own in the Negro River region. He sighted dozens of birds that he recorded for the first time.

Right: a page from Bates' notebook. It demonstrates what care Bates took to make a complete and accurate catalog of the animal and plant life he found.

that Wallace had so painfully collected were lost. He spent nine days in a lifeboat before being picked up, and did not arrive in England until October 1.

Bates remained in South America for seven years after Wallace's departure. In 1855 he left Santarém for another stay in Ega, which became his base for four more years. During that time he found over 7000 insect species, of which 550 were distinct butterfly species. From Ega, Bates made many expeditions into the surrounding countryside and on the Amazon or Solimões, as

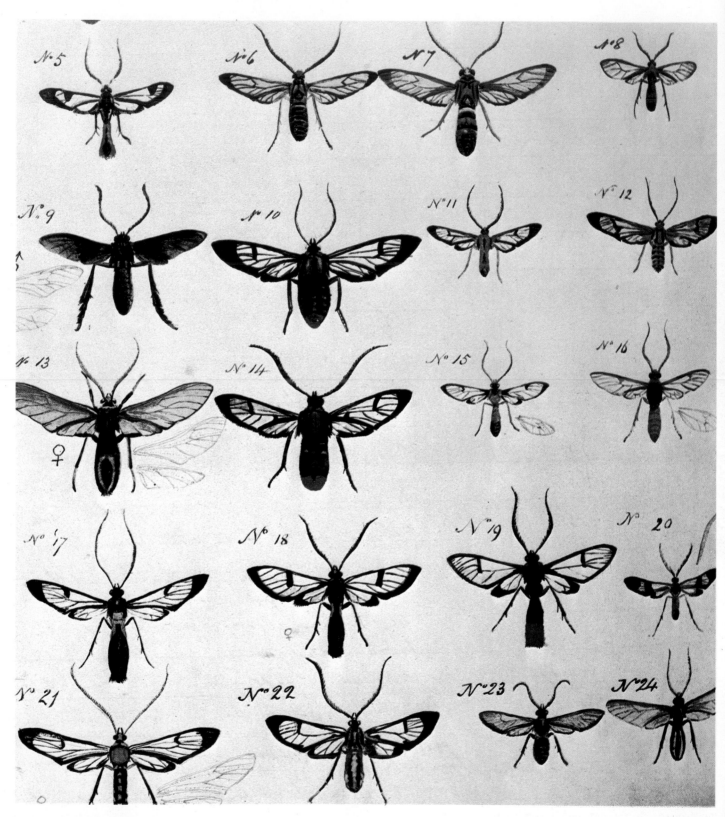

it is known in its upper reaches. In 1853 steamers were introduced on the river, and it was in the comparative comfort of a steamer that Bates sailed to Fonteboa – the "headquarters of mosquitoes" – in 1856 and to St. Paulo de Olivença, 400 miles by water from Ega, the following year. While in St. Paulo, Bates had a serious attack of an ague common to the region and had to give up his plan to explore the

Above: another page of drawings by Bates. He painted each insect meticulously in color and numbered them carefully in sequence.

Amazon to the foot of the Andes. He returned to Ega but, too weak to continue working, in February 1859 left to make the long journey home. In the 11 years he had spent in South America he had collected 14,000 species of insect of which 8000 were new to science.

Spruce, meanwhile, had remained in and around Manaus, finding the surrounding forests a fascinating botanical textbook. "Nearly every natural order of plants," he wrote to a friend, "has here *trees* among its representatives. Here are grasses (bamboos) of 40, 60, or more feet in height, sometimes growing erect, sometimes tangled in thorny thickets, through which an elephant could not penetrate. . . . Instead of your Periwinkles we have here handsome trees exuding a milk which is sometimes salutiferous, at others a most deadly poison, and bearing fruits of corresponding qualities. Violets of the size of apple trees. Daisies (or what might seem daisies) borne on trees like Alders."

Below: prickly palms, entangling undergrowth, biting insects, and constant damp – these were the ordeals involved in jungle travel.

Through such forests lay Spruce's route when in November 1851 he left Manaus for the Negro River. In the autumn of 1852 he was on the Uaupés River. Along the way he observed the effects on local revellers of *caapi* – the "drink-that-makes-one-brave". He investigated the plant from which caapi was made and discovered that it had narcotic properties. From the Uaupés he continued to the Casiquiare and the Orinoco, where the mosquitoes were particularly ferocious. "If I passed my hand across my face," he wrote to a friend, "I brought it away covered with blood and with the crushed bodies of gorged mosquitoes . . . they are an indescribable annoyance." Not surprisingly, on the Orinoco Spruce was striken with the scourge of the tropics that is carried by mosquitoes – malaria. By November 1854 he was on his way back to Manaus. In four years he had collected more than 20,000 plants, mapped unknown rivers, and made vocabularies of 21 Amerind languages.

In 1855 Spruce embarked by steamer on the Amazon bound for the Andes. The 1500 miles to the Peruvian border were covered in 18 days whereas before the introduction of steamers on

the river it had taken Spruce 63 days to travel 450 miles. For two years Spruce made his home in Tarapoto, Peru, "the most agreeably placed . . . in my South American wanderings." In the Amazon valley, he had already made the studies of rubber trees that 20 years later resulted in the "snatch" of rubber seedlings from which rubber plantations were established in the Malay peninsula. He was then asked by the British government to study the tree from which quinine – the preventative against and treatment for malaria – was produced. This necessitated a journey to Ecuador on a trip Spruce considered the worst he had ever undertaken in South America. Despite the fact that he arrived in Ecuador to find the country in a state of revolution, he managed to make the desired studies and to acquire seeds and cuttings which the British government attempted without success to establish in India. It was 1864 before Spruce sailed for England, 30,000 botanical specimens to the good.

What of the naturalists after their return from America? Wallace went to Malaysia to gather evidence on evolution, and while there formulated his theory of evolution by natural selection simultaneously with Darwin. He received an Order of Merit honor for his work as a scientist and writer three years before his death. Bates became Assistant Secretary to the Royal Geographical Society, a post which freed him from financial worry and which he retained until his death. He was also made a fellow of the Society. In contrast, Spruce spent the rest of his life in his native Yorkshire, living on a meager annual pension granted to him by the government for all his valuable work.

Right: a drawing by Spruce of the bark, leaves, and flowers of the cinchona tree, source of quinine.

143

Percy Fawcett 1867-1925?

On April 20, 1925 Percy Fawcett, veteran of nearly 20 years of exploration in South America, set out from Cuyaba into the Mato Grosso in search of a fabled lost city. On May 29 he wrote a letter to his wife from a place he called Dead Horse Camp between the upper Tapajós and Xingu rivers. Thereafter no word was received from him. From time to time during the following years, rumors of what had happened to Fawcett and his companions came out of the jungle, but none could be proved. Fawcett, his son Jack, and Jack's friend Raleigh Rimell had

Left: Percy Harrison Fawcett, the explorer who disappeared without trace in South America while searching for a mysterious lost city and civilization.

simply disappeared as though swallowed.

Fawcett hoped to find the lost city – which he called Z "for the sake of convenience" – as a way to prove some of the theories about the continent that he had formed on other journeys there. Tales of abandoned and forgotten cities hidden deep in the jungle were common. Travelers also related rumors of a race of white-skinned people living in the interior. Fawcett believed that both might be the relics of a former civilization. "Between the outer world and the secrets of ancient South America a veil has descended," wrote Fawcett, and it was his ambition to lift that veil and discover what it hid.

Fawcett was born in Torquay, England, in 1867, and about his childhood he later wrote that

Below: Fawcett (second from the left) on one of his earlier survey trips in the jungle.

Fawcett spent five years exploring and surveying on behalf of the Bolivian government, in 1910 resigning his commission because the British army was no longer willing to release him for the work. His first expedition in 1906–7 took him to the headwaters of the Madeira and Purus rivers, and in particular to the Abuna and Acre rivers which mark Bolivia's northern boundary. He soon discovered the difficulties of working in

Right: a drawing by Fawcett's younger son Brian of an attack by piranhas. These deadly fish were one of the many river hazards.

Left: Fawcett (center front) and his party at the source of the Verde in the Mato Grosso.

the interior – lack of communications, primitive settlements with few comforts or aids for the explorer returning from the wilderness, hostile locals, and the ever-present animal pests. Crocodiles and man-eating fish lurked in the rivers, deadly snakes infested the forests, and the swarms of insects drove the explorers nearly crazy. "There was no respite from them," wrote Fawcett, "for the night shift of biting insects was nearly as bad as the day shift," and soon the explorers' hands and faces were "a mass of tiny, itching blood-blisters." In addition, the surveying instruments, which were to have been provided by the Bolivian government, failed to arrive. Nevertheless, when Fawcett presented his report he was invited to undertake further work in the uncharted country to the east of Bolivia on the Paraguay River. Before embarking on this next expedition, he returned to England to see his family.

The boundary line Fawcett was to survey ran along the little known and unmapped Verde River, but the country was so wild and difficult that he was lucky to return alive. In fact, five of the bearers who accompanied him died soon after the expedition's return. In 1909 he returned to the Verde River with the boundary commissions from both Brazil and Bolivia to confirm the frontier he had just investigated. Then from Montevideo he sailed for Bolivia via the Strait of Magellan. At La Paz, the Bolivian capital, the president of Bolivia invited Fawcett to continue his work on the boundary between Peru and Bolivia, which involved the exploration of the Heath River whose course was unknown. During this journey Fawcett succeeded in making friends with a group of the warlike Guarayos Indians, who were especially hostile to travelers – proof of the success of his policy of not using arms against the local inhabitants. He returned to the

he had known no parental affection. His general unhappiness continued in the army, in which he was commissioned as an officer of the Royal Artillery in 1886. His army training did, however, prepare him well for a life of exploration. By 1906 he had risen to the rank of major, and at that time received the offer which was to change his life. The government of Bolivia had requested the Royal Geographical Society of Great Britain to arbitrate in a boundary dispute between Bolivia, Peru, and Brazil, and an army officer was to be appointed to survey the frontiers on Bolivia's behalf. In fact, the officer really needed to be an explorer rather than a surveyor because much of the disputed territory was unknown. Fawcett, who had completed a Royal Geographi-

Above: Jack Fawcett, the explorer's eldest son, and Raleigh Rimmell at Dead Horse Camp. It was from there that Fawcett wrote his last letter to his wife.

Left: remains of a past civilization lying deep in the Mato Grosso jungle. These traces lured Fawcett to search for more evidence of great lost cities.

Heath River in 1911. When he got back to La Paz in December 1911, he found that the boundary survey had created such tension between Peru and Bolivia that the two countries were on the brink of war. Fawcett therefore resigned his post. He then had time to pursue his personal quest for the secret of South America's past.

In 1913 and 1914 Fawcett made expeditions that linked up his work in northeastern Bolivia with his explorations in 1908 and 1909 on the Verde River and the Paraguay River, but in September 1914 he heard that Britain and Germany were at war and he made a difficult journey home to participate in the fight. When the war ended in 1918, Fawcett was eager to return to his work in South America, but he had great problems in trying to obtain backing for his proposed expedition in search of lost civilizations. Backing by the Brazilian government was forthcoming in 1920, but his attempt to unveil the lost city in the Mato Grosso failed because of the lack of stamina of his companions. On a journey south of Salvador the following year, Fawcett found evidence which convinced him that he must venture into the interior again. This time he was determined not to be hampered by the possible weakness of any companions. He was to be accompanied by his eldest son Jack, 21 years old in 1925, and by Raleigh Rimell, a school friend of Jack's. Their route was to lead from Dead Horse Camp, west of the upper Xingu, roughly east across the Araguaia and anxiety was felt, because Fawcett had been prepared to spend about two years in the forests and it was known that he would have no means of sending out a message. But as the months passed it was felt that all might not be well. In 1928 the North American Newspaper Alliance financed a rescue expedition led by Commander George Dyott, an experienced South American explorer, who followed Fawcett's trail beyond Dead Horse Camp and met Amerinds who remembered seeing Fawcett's party. Dyott returned convinced that Fawcett and his companions had been murdered by the inhabitants, but he had no definite evidence to support his belief.

In 1932 a Swiss trapper asserted that the previous year he had met a European held prisoner by Amerinds, and identified the captive as Fawcett. Two years later the compass belonging to one of Fawcett's surveying instruments was delivered to his wife by the Royal Geographical Society, having been found in the Mato Grosso. That same year, an expedition to the Kuluene River reported meeting a local woman who described three European men living with a tribe of Indians, but rumors that reached the outside world were of the murder of Fawcett, his son, and Rimell. In 1950 the mystery of Fawcett's disappearance appeared to have been solved when the chief of one of the

Tocantins rivers, then southeast across the São Francisco to Salvador on the coast. Somewhere in that unknown region of unfriendly inhabitants, Fawcett surmised, he would discover the forgotten city Z.

Fawcett's party set out from Cuyaba on the western fringe of the Mato Grosso on April 20, 1925, and by May 20, the day after Jack Fawcett's twenty-second birthday, they had reached Dead Horse Camp. All three men were pestered by the insects, but Rimell appeared to be particularly allergic to them and was soon lame and unable to walk. On May 20 Fawcett sent a report from Dead Horse Camp to the North American Newspaper Alliance, to whom he had sold the newspaper rights of his story, and nine days later he penned his last letter to his wife. "You need have no fear of any failure. . . ." he wrote.

A year passed without news of Fawcett's party, and then another. At first, no particular

Above: the splendid Gateway to the Sun in Tiahuanaco, Bolivia. It is a reminder of the magnificence of past cultures of South America.

Right: an exhibition of bones claimed to be those of Colonel Fawcett. They were found in 1951 in a shallow jungle grave and are on display in a Rio de Janeiro museum of anthropology.

tribes met by Dyott confessed on his deathbed to Fawcett's murder. The bones found in the grave identified by his successor were not those of Fawcett, however, and may not even have been a European's. The puzzle of Fawcett's disappearance, therefore, still remains as much a mystery today as ever.

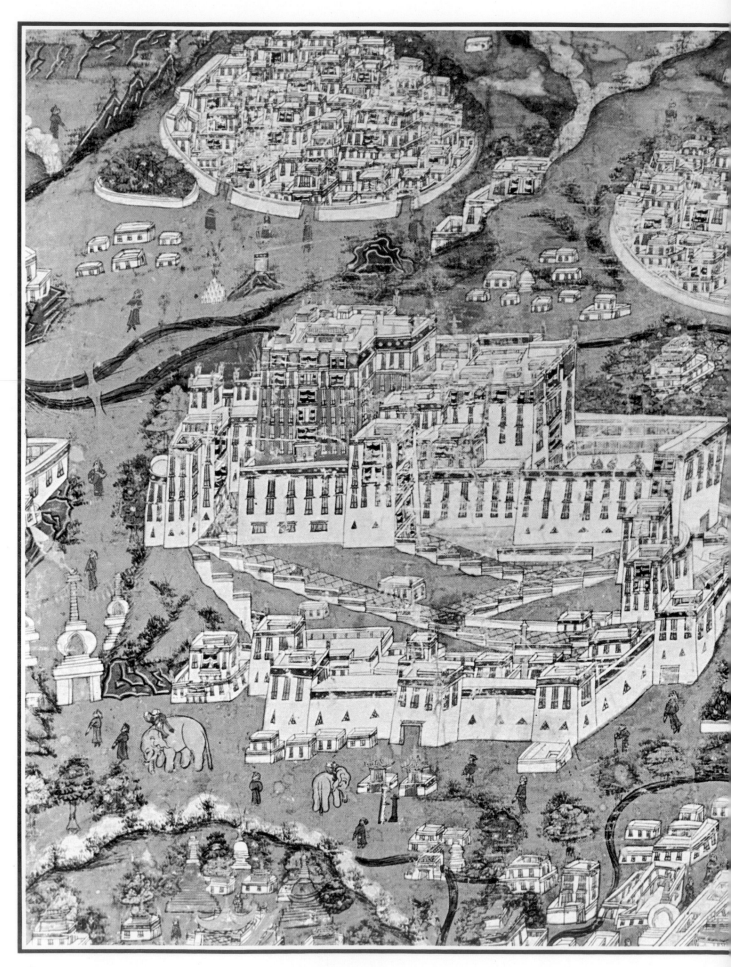

Chapter 7

Asia Explored

Asia, unlike the Americas, was not a total unknown to Europeans because from the earliest times the histories of the continents were entwined. The desire for conquest took Alexander the Great east to India; trade existed between Europe and Asia in the days of the Roman Empire; and the Mongols reached the Dnieper River in their invasion of East Europe. The European voyages of the Great Age of Discovery had as their goal the treasures of Asia, and they succeeded in opening the sea route to the continent's fabled lands. Asia – more than 17 million square miles in area – is so vast, however, that the exploration of its interior was a slow and laborious process, made still more difficult by the inhospitable nature of the terrain. Certain countries were themselves inhospitable – hostile or even entirely closed to foreigners – and particular hardship and danger attended the traveler there. Not until the 20th century was Asia fully explored.

Left: the country of Tibet held its mysteries through the centuries. Although a few hardy Jesuit missionaries managed to reach its capital of Lhasa in the 17th century, the land remained closed to Europeans even after travel to and from China had become almost commonplace. Hidden in the fastness of the mountain lay the Potala, former grand palace of the Dalai Lamas, shown in this 13th-century painting. Not till about 200 years after the Jesuits did such explorers as Nikolay Przhevalsky and Sven Hedin gain access to the remote country.

ASIA
noviter delineata
Auctore
Guil. Gansſonio

EVRO
PÆ
PARS

CALECVTH   GOA   DAMASCO   IERVSALE

Syri

Arabes

Armenius Persa

Balaquato

Insulani Sumatrae

MARIS MEDITERRANEI PARS

MARE RVBRVM

AFRI:
CÆ PARS

ABISSINÆ
PARS

AYAMAN
olim
ARABIA
FELIX

Aden

MARE
ARABICVM
et INDICVM

OCEANVS
Æquator

ORI   E N T A L I S

ARABIA
DESERTA
Calde

PERSI
FARSIA

INDIA INTRA GANGEM

INDIA
EXTRA
GANGEM

GOLFO DI
BENGALA
Gangeticus
Sinus

Zeylan

NOVA
ZEMBLA

Circulus

TARTARIA

Mare de
Sala vel Bachu
seu Chualenſko
more

150

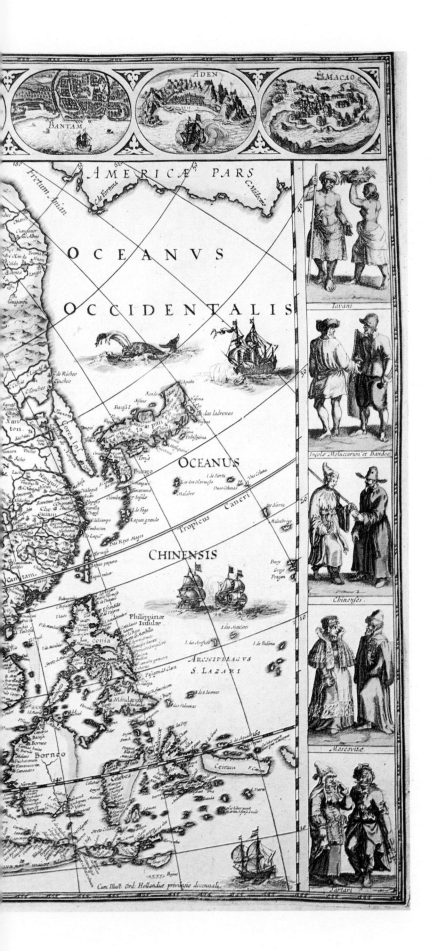

A New Map of Asia – 1617?

The Dutch cartographer William Blaeu made this map of Asia around 1617. As was his custom until 1619, he signed it with his middle name Janszoon. In 1623 it was included in that year's edition of the Mercator-Hondius atlas – begun in 1585 by Gerardus Mercator and bought in 1604 by Jodocus Hondius – to replace an earlier and less accurate map. Even Blaeu's map provides little real information about the interior of Asia, relying chiefly on hearsay and legend as did most maps of the time.

By the time Blaeu drew his map, the coastlines of southern and southeastern Asia were already familiar to European mariners, and their knowledge is reflected in Blaeu's picture of these coasts. He possessed no such first-hand information about the north and northeastern coasts of the continent, however. Northeastern Siberia is foreshortened and the Kamchatka Peninsula and Sea of Okhotsk are missing, while Sakhalin and the northern Japanese island of Hokkaido also fail to appear. It is interesting to speculate about how Blaeu knew to divide Siberia from north-western America by a strait which he calls the Strait of Anian. For, although Siberia and Alaska are in fact separated by the Bering Strait, this was not discovered until the 1640s and its existence was not generally recognized for more than another century.

Blaeu was indebted to Marco Polo's account of his journey to the court of Kublai Khan for information about the interior of Asia. He marks the desert that Polo called Lop and illustrates it with a drawing of a traveler with a camel. Polo's book was also indirectly responsible for a conspicuous error in Blaeu's map in the geography of eastern Asia. The great Venetian traveler had called the land he visited "Cathay." When European seamen reached eastern Asia in the 16th century, they found themselves in a country called China, and discovered no trace of Cathay. Geographers, unwilling to abandon Polo's fabulous country, failed to identify Cathay with China and Blaeu, in common with other map makers, simply pushed Cathay to the north. On this map, therefore, Cathay and its capital Cambaluc, which is present-day Peking, appear in the easternmost part of what is now Siberia.

Jesuit Missionaries in Asia

The center of the Asian continent is a bleak region of deserts and lofty plateaus, broken and enclosed by some of the most formidable mountain ranges in the world. Mountain and desert cut off central Asia from the more accessible lands of India and China, forming an intimidating barrier to the would-be traveler there. In the 17th century, these awe-inspiring natural obstacles were faced and overcome by a handful of intrepid Jesuit missionaries. These men sought souls rather than new lands, but they succeeded in opening mountain-fast Tibet and in crossing the barren wastes of central Asia. They were the pioneers of Asian exploration, although their journeys remained virtually unknown for centuries.

Early in the 17th century, the land that Marco

Right: Matteo Ricci, head of the Jesuit mission in Peking. He was one of the first Europeans to believe that the mysterious land of Cathay was the same as China.

Below: a bandit attack on the caravan of Bento de Goes. The perils of travel were so great that a small army had to go along with every caravan for protection.

Polo called Cathay was still not generally identified with the land the Portuguese knew as China. Jesuit missionaries in Peking, led by Father Matteo Ricci, had become convinced that the two countries were the same, but the fact remained that 250 years had passed since a European had made the overland journey to China.

well as some of the horses died. At last the caravan reached Yarkand, capital of Kashgar, where it disbanded. De Goes could not continue alone because his way lay across the great deserts of central Asia. So he was faced with another protracted delay while a China-bound caravan was formed.

During the year he spent in Yarkand awaiting the formation of a caravan to China, De Goes visited the mines of Khotan to the southeast. There a form of jade valued in the East, and especially in China, was found. It was November 1604 when his caravan left Yarkand and made its way around the northern fringes of the Taklamakan Desert toward the Chinese frontier. In Korla, between Aksu and Turfan, his patience was so sorely tried by another three-month holdup that he finally obtained permission to continue his journey alone. He was on the point of leaving Korla when he met a party of merchants traveling west from Cathay. They had stayed with Matteo Ricci in a city they called Cambaluc. This demonstrated that Cambaluc and Peking were the same, and therefore that Cathay and China were as well.

Anxious to complete his journey, De Goes pressed on to Turfan and then to Hami, accom-

It was to remedy this omission, and to prove Ricci's contention, that the first Jesuit journey across central Asia was made. It was undertaken by Bento de Goes, a lay member of the holy order, who set out from Agra, India in October 1602. De Goes made his journey disguised as a Persian trader because he had to pass through Muslim countries in which a Christian would be unwelcome.

From Agra De Goes traveled first to Lahore, where he intended to join a caravan for the journey to Kashgar beyond the Pamirs; but because the Kashgar caravan left Lahore only once a year, he was forced to spend several months in Lahore before continuing on his way. There he hired an Armenian named Isaac to be his traveling companion, and Isaac accompanied him when he finally left with the Kashgar caravan on February 24, 1603. The caravan consisted of about 500 travelers accompanied by a long baggage train, but the strength of the party did nothing to deter robbers. After leaving Peshawar, the caravan hired an escort of 400 soldiers to protect it. The journey from Lahore to Kabul took more than six months. Many of the travelers were wounded or killed by bandits, and many more became afraid of continuing, so that a lengthy delay occurred at Kabul while the depleted ranks of the caravan were filled.

When at last De Goes and his companions quit Kabul, the great Hindu Kush lay before them. Crossing the mountains, they continued into Badakhshān, then up into the Pamirs – the "roof of the world." The cold was intense. All suffered badly from altitude sickness induced by the great height, and some of the travelers as

Above: cliffs studded with figures cut from stone and caves in the Bamian valley of Afghanistan. Behind rises the Hindu Kush, one of Asia's highest ranges. De Goes crossed this formidable mountain in the early 17th century.

Right: an engraving of the 18th century showing De Goes being poisoned by his fellow travelers. The priest was already dying when help reached him, but there is no proof that he was murdered.

panied only by Isaac and a small party. Toward the end of 1605 he and his companions reached Suchow. From there De Goes wrote to Ricci requesting his help to get to Peking. It was the middle of November 1606 when his letter reached Ricci and the following March when Ricci's messenger came to Suchow. De Goes had been ill for a month, and Ricci's communication came too late. Weak from lack of medical attention and the hardships of the journey, De Goes died on April 11, 1607. He had the satisfaction of knowing that he had succeeded in the object of

his journey and proved that Cathay was China. Even so, the legend of a fabulous and undiscovered Cathay continued to linger on.

De Goes had had to travel by a roundabout way to China because no caravan route crossed the Himalaya, the vast mountains guarding India's northern frontier. Beyond the Himalaya and cut off by them from the Indian subcontinent lies the high and windswept plateau of Tibet, the next land the Jesuits attempted to reach. Rumors had arisen in the Jesuit missions in India that there were Christian communities in Tibet and Antonio de Andrade, superior of the Jesuit missions in the Mogul Empire, determined to discover the truth.

Andrade's opportunity came in the spring of 1624 when he joined the Mogul emperor on a journey to Kashmir. In Delhi he learned that a large party of Hindus was planning a pilgrimage to a temple in the Himalaya more than two months' journey away. Realizing that their company would provide him with disguise and protection on the first part of his journey, Andrade and Brother Manuel Marques donned Hindu apparel and joined them. With their Hindu companions, the two Jesuits slowly made their way into the Himalaya along paths so narrow that they could advance only in single file, clinging to the rock face to avoid slipping down into the mountain torrents far below. Fifteen days after leaving Srinagar, capital of Garhwal, they found themselves amid the snows. No longer did they cross rivers by frail rope bridges, but by "bridges formed by frozen masses of snow, which fill up the whole width of the river and underneath which the river-water breaks itself in a foaming passage."

Toward the end of May or early June 1624, the travelers reached the shrine of Badrinath which was sacred to the Hindus. Then at Mana, from which they were to cross the high Mana Pass into

Above: Jahangir, the Mogul emperor with whom Andrade traveled to Kashmir.

Tibet, orders were given that they could not go on. Nevertheless, Andrade was determined to continue his mission and, hiring a guide from Mana, started up the Mana Pass. A party sent after them succeeded in forcing the guide to return, but not Andrade. After struggling through deep snows to the summit of the pass, however, he and his companions were so badly affected by frostbite and snowblindness that they had to turn back. They waited until the snows had melted before attempting the crossing again.

It was early August 1624 when Andrade reached Tsaparang. He had resolved to return to India before the autumn snows began, but the king was so delighted with him that he could only obtain leave to depart on condition that he return the following year. Impressed by the religious fervor that had led Andrade to undertake such a journey, the king promised him help in establishing a Christian mission in Tsaparang.

Andrade reached Tsaparang for the second

Above: a river gorge in the foothills of the eastern Himalaya. Andrade went through this region on his way to Tibet.

Below: Leh, the capital of what is now the district of Ladakh in Kashmir. Francisco de Azevado went to Leh to see if he could help the Christians who had been forced to go there from Tsapapang.

time at the end of August 1625. A church was built in Tsaparang, and three other Jesuits joined Andrade to help in the mission work. Andrade left to become the Jesuit superior in Goa in 1630, and shortly after a revolution deposed the friendly king. The church was sacked, but none of the missionaries was hurt although they were made to leave. It was not until the following year that Andrade received news of the revolution, and he then sent Francisco de Azevado to Tsaparang to find out what had occurred.

At Srinagar Azevado met Brother Marques on his way from Mana to get supplies and to send Andrade a report on the Tsaparang situation, and together the two men began the journey to Tsaparang. However, Marques remained in Mana to wait for pack animals to carry his provisions, while Azevado continued alone to Tsaparang. He found the mission in great difficulties. Tsaparang was then ruled by the king of Ladakh, represented in Tsaparang by a governor greatly hostile to the Jesuits. To Azevado the only solution seemed to be to continue his journey to Leh, the Ladakhi capital, to appeal to the king in person. Various holdups prevented Azevado from setting out immediately but early in October 1631, in a caravan of horse dealers, Azevado was on his way to Leh.

The journey from Tsaparang to Leh took 21 days with the caravan traveling from sunrise to sunset. The route was little used and led through mountains covered with snow. The day after Azevado's arrival in Leh, the king of Ladakh sent for him, and a week after receiving the Jesuit's proposals, gave his permission for the mission work to continue. Once he had achieved the object of his journey, Azevado was anxious to return to India to make his report. It was the beginning of November when he left Leh and the cold was already intense. Rather than retracing his steps to Tsaparang, he turned southwest toward Lahore, which he hoped would be an easier route. In November, however, winter was already setting in – it was bitterly cold and there was much snow and ice. Azevado's boots wore out, and although he managed to obtain

locally made shoes of twisted straw, his feet were so badly hurt that for the final stages of his journey he had to be carried in a litter. Four days from Lahore, Azevado turned south for Agra, reaching the city on January 3, 1632. Not only had he obtained permission for the Tsaparang mission to continue, but also he had linked the area of Andrade's travels with the beginning of the route followed by De Goes.

In 1625, during Andrade's second visit to Tsaparang, merchants from China had told him of Utsang, a country to the east. Thinking that Utsang might be a fruitful field for a mission, he wrote to the Jesuits in India to suggest that an attempt be made to reach Utsang from Bengal. The mission was entrusted to Fathers Estêvão Cacella and João Cabral, who left Hugli on the Ganges delta in August 1626. Making their way northeast across the Brahmaputra, they turned west for Cooch Behar, then began their ascent of

the Himalaya. They seem to have been the first Europeans to visit the mountain country of Bhutan, where they were warmly received and spent some time at the court of the Dharma Rajah. It was evident, however, that mission work would have little chance of success, so they decided to continue to Utsang. Cacella left first and within three weeks he had reached Shigatse, seat of the king of Utsang. Being kindly received, he sent for Cabral to join him there. In January 1628 the two priests were reunited at Shigatse, given a house, food, and permission to preach.

The route by which the Jesuits had reached Shigatse was very long and difficult. Cabral therefore attempted to return to India via Nepal, hoping to find an easier way by which the Shigatse mission could be supplied. He made the crossing of Nepal successfully – probably the first European to do so – but missed the season for the return journey via Nepal. He therefore

Left: the chief lama of Bhutan. He was in conflict with a reform sect when Estêvão Cacella and João Cabral reached his capital.

Below: a letter of patent of the kind that served as a passport for the missionaries of the Far East.

set out for Cooch Behar from which he wrote to Cacella requesting a royal escort to continue his journey. Cacella, meanwhile, had also left for Bengal, having first made an unsuccessful attempt to reach Tsaparang. Hearing that Cabral was at Cooch Behar, he rejoined him there.

In September 1629 Cacella again left for Shigatse, leaving Cabral at Cooch Behar. When he

Left: the Great Wall of China, which Johann Grueber and Albert d'Orville passed while traveling overland back to the West.

appears to have been recalled to India because he was back in Hugli in 1632. By 1635 the Shigatse mission had been abandoned for good. That year the decision was also made to give up the Tsaparang mission.

The years passed and with them the heyday of the Portuguese eastern empire. By the third quarter of the 17th century, Portuguese control of the sea route to China had been lost to the Dutch. So it was that when the superior of the Jesuit Mission in Peking wanted to contact Rome, it was decided to send his representatives overland. In April 1661 Johann Grueber and Albert d'Orville set out on their trek to the west. Two months after leaving Peking they reached the Chinese frontier at Hsining, where they spent two weeks, and then they entered territory that was almost unknown. They sighted Koko Nor

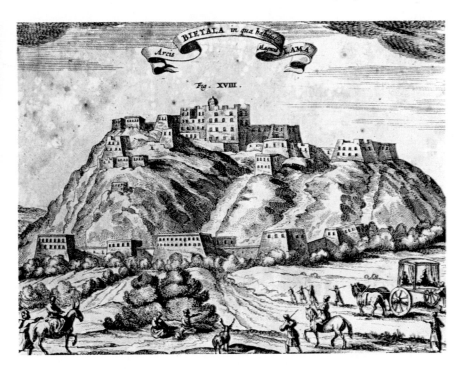

arrived at the end of the following April he was seriously ill, and within a week he was dead. The king of Utsang immediately sent word to Cabral to come to Shigatse, and the missionary reached the town accompanied by a royal escort in 1631. Despite the promise of the mission, which Cabral had believed might become "one of the most glorious of the Society of Jesus," Cabral

Above: an engraving of 1667 of the Potala, former grand palace of the Dalai Lamas in Lhasa. It was made from sketches by Grueber.

Left: a prayer wheel, which is used by spinning a small cylinder that contains a prayer on it. Tibetans believe that this action transmits the prayer without need of words or thoughts. Grueber was fascinated by this device.

and crossed the salty marshes of the Tsaidam basin, then crossed the Burchan Buddha mountains, the eastern wing of the Kun Lun, and the Shuga mountains to reach the plateau of Tibet. Making their way across this lofty, cold, and windswept region, they reached Lhasa, the Tibetan capital and Tibet's most sacred city, in October 1661. They were the first Europeans to enter Lhasa for more than 300 years.

The necessity of finding a caravan with which to continue their journey meant that Grueber and d'Orville had to spend some time in Lhasa, and it was probably toward the end of November that they left the city for the south. The journey from Lhasa to Nepal over the Himalaya took a month. Then from Katmandu the two priests continued to Agra, which they reached toward the end of March 1662. By that time d'Orville's health had broken down under the hardships and privations of the journey, and he died in Agra. Grueber continued his mission westward,

158

reaching Rome in February 1664. Nearly 200 years later, his remarkable journey from Peking to Lhasa was repeated by two other missionaries, Evariste Huc and Joseph Gabet, but they found that religious teaching was forbidden in the Tibetan capital and were forced to travel back across central Asia to rejoin their mission in Peking.

Meanwhile, in the early years of the 18th century, a new attempt was made to reestablish the Tsaparang mission. It was carried out by Father Ippolito Desideri accompanied by Father Emmanuel Freyre. Desideri, who had but recently arrived in India, met Freyre in Delhi, and on September 24, 1714, the two men started for Lahore. In November they reached the Kashmiri capital called Srinagar like the capital of Garhwal. Winter was setting in, the mountain passes were closed, and Desideri was weak and ill from repeated lung hemorrhages. The missionaries therefore spent the winter in Srinagar, resuming their journey northward in May the following year.

Forty days after leaving Srinagar, Desideri and Freyre arrived at Leh. The King of Ladakh welcomed them, hoping that they would settle in Leh, but the hardships of the journey outward had so exhausted Freyre that he was determined to return home. At first he hoped to find an alternative route south from Leh, and then he decided to continue to Lhasa. On August 17 Desideri and Freyre were on the move again. Although from Srinagar to Leh they had traveled on foot, they now had horses. They also had guides to help them on their journey, but joined a caravan bound for Lhasa in Gartok as protection against the terrible dangers. It was led by a charming Tartar princess.

Opposite: an Indian miniature of the holy family of Siva and Parvati on Mount Kailas. Desideri's journey took him past this mountain that is sacred to Buddhists and Hindus.

Left: an engraving of the Tree of Ten Thousand Images from the English edition of Father Evariste Huc's book. He traveled the same overland route that Grueber had 200 years before him.

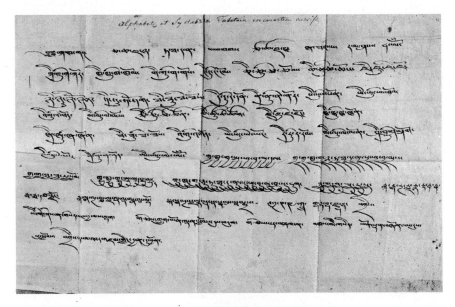

Above: a page of the alphabet and syllables in Tibetan characters from Desideri's collection. He was the first European to learn how to read and write Tibetan.

The road followed by Desideri and Freyre after leaving Gartok was unknown to Europeans – and after their journey no other European traveled it for nearly 200 years. It skirted Mount Kailas, which Desideri called the Mountain of Urghien, one of the most sacred places in Buddhist Tibet. Tibetan legend recounted how Urghien, founder of the Tibetan religion, had lived in seclusion on the mountain. By 1715 it was the site of a temple and a monastery, the goal of countless pilgrims. Early in December the travelers passed Lake Mansarowar and in March, after a delay of nearly a month because of the illness of the princess, the travelers reached Lhasa. Freyre remained there for a few days only before returning to India by way of Nepal.

Desideri was the only European in Lhasa after Freyre's departure, and he was granted permission to preach Christianity. He became so proficient in the Tibetan language that in January 1717 he was able to present the king with an exposition on Christianity in Tibetan. For four months that year, Desideri stayed in a monastery studying the sacred works of Lamaism. In August he withdrew to the University of Sera outside Lhasa to continue his studies. He was in Sera when the Mongols invaded Tibet and took and sacked Lhasa. Unharmed, Desideri moved to the province of Takpó-Khier, eight days' journey from the capital. Apart from a few months at Lhasa, he remained in Takpó-Khier until April 1721 when he received orders to leave Tibet.

Ippolito Desideri left a lengthy account of his journey to Lhasa including a geographical description of Tibet. It was unrivaled for about 200 years. However, his manuscript was unknown for a long period, not being rediscovered until the mid-1870s and remaining unedited until the early years of the 20th century. By that time, other European travelers had reached the country, and the modern exploration of Tibet had begun.

Vitus Bering
1680-1741

In December 1741 the Danish navigator Vitus Bering died of scurvy on a remote island off the east coast of the Kamchatka Peninsula. He was returning from a voyage across the north Pacific to Alaska, and was less than 300 miles from Petropavlovsk, his home port. Already he had achieved the aim of this expedition, which was the exploration of the unknown seas between Asia and Alaska, and on an earlier voyage from Kamchatka he had confirmed that Asia was divided from America by sea. Together these voyages entitle Bering to a place among the great navigators of the world.

Although Bering was by birth a Dane, his voyages were made in the service of Russia as an officer in the navy of that country. The impetus for his explorations sprang from a profound change that had taken place in Russia in the early years of the 18th century. It came through Czar Peter I who had found himself monarch of a country turned inward on itself and still in many respects unchanged since the Middle Ages. Peter resolved to make Russia a modern nation and he used all the powers of an absolute ruler to carry out his aims. He was also

Below left: Vitus Bering, the Danish navigator who was one of the first to explore the waters of the far north.

Below: Peter the Great, the Russian monarch who hired Bering to work for Russia.

been carried out in the 17th century by Cossack explorers who, gradually pushing eastward, had reached the Sea of Okhotsk. It is even claimed that one of the Cossacks, Semen Ivanov Deshnef, had in the middle of the century sailed through the Bering Strait. Although these explorers opened Siberia, however, the knowledge acquired by them was fairly haphazard. Organized scientific exploration and accurate map making were required. The Kamchatka Peninsula, reached in the closing years of the 17th century, was the obvious starting point for any attempt to determine the eastern boundary of Asia, but Peter's first concern was to open a southern route to the peninsula across the Sea of Okhotsk to replace the difficult overland route in the north. A successful voyage to Kamchatka was made in 1716-17, but two years later an

eager to learn more about Siberia, the vast and little known eastern part of his empire, in particular to obtain accurate information about Siberia's eastern extent.

The preliminary exploration of Siberia had

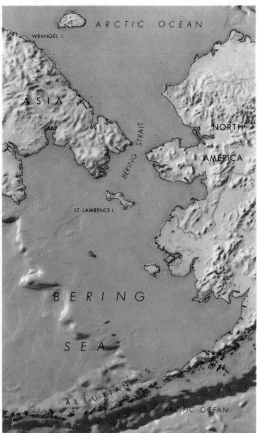

Above: Mount Augustin in the Aleutian Islands. Bering sailed to the south of them in seeking the mythical Gamaland.

Left: a map of the Bering Strait, named after the man who found it.

Below: a Canadian Indian carving of a trader, probably a Russian. After Bering's trip, many Russians went to Alaska and south.

attempt to reach the area where Asia was nearest to North America failed. It was not until 1725, the year of his death, that Peter renewed this scheme and commissioned Vitus Bering to undertake a voyage to discover whether Asia and North America were joined.

Eighteenth-century ships were not strong enough for Bering to sail to Kamchatka and then begin an arduous voyage of exploration, so it was necessary for the expedition to travel overland to Siberia with all the supplies they would need to build the ship for their voyage there. Bering left St. Petersburg, present-day Leningrad, in February 1725 accompanied by Lieutenants Martin Spangberg and Aleksey Chirikov, his seconds-in-command. It was July 1727 before the party left for Kamchatka on their newly built ship. During the winter, they sledged across the Kamchatka Peninsula, and on the east coast built another ship named the *Gabriel*. In July 1728, more than three years after leaving St. Petersburg, Bering's voyage of discovery began.

Setting their course northward up the east coast of Kamchatka and carefully charting the coastline, the explorers sighted a large island at the beginning of August. They named it St. Lawrence. A few days later they reached a point where the coast tended decidedly to the west. In Bering's view, this proved that the *Gabriel* had rounded the eastern extremity of Asia, and confirmed that a strait divided Asia from Alaska. Afraid of being caught in the ice fields of the Arctic Ocean, he therefore turned back. The expedition again spent the winter of 1728–29 on the Kamchatka Peninsula, and in June 1729 set out for Okhotsk on the first stage of their long journey back to St. Petersburg. When adverse winds prevented the ship from making headway, Bering turned back and rounded southern Kamchatka, fixing the position of the southern end of the peninsula for the first time. Toward the end of July he and his companions arrived back in Okhotsk.

It was largely on Bering's instigation that an extensive series of expeditions was planned at the beginning of the 1730s. The aims were to complete the survey of the north coasts of Siberia, to explore the unknown seas between Asia and the Americas, and to chart the Siberian interior. A number of members of the Academy of Sciences agreed to take part as researchers. In February 1733 Martin Spangberg was sent ahead to Okhotsk with the bulk of heavy materials to superintend the building of ships for the expedition. Later the same year Bering went in the company of three scholars, Johann Gmelin, a naturalist, De la Croyère, an astronomer, and G F Müller, an historian. There was considerable delay before the start of the voyage toward North America – the main aim of the expedition – but the scientists used the time to explore the interior; some of the party made several voyages along the north coast of Siberia, and Spangberg sailed south to Japan. It was September 1740 when Bering and Chirikov left Okhotsk with their two new ships, the *St. Paul* and the *St. Peter*. They made first for Kamchatka where

Above: the Uzon volcano on Kamchatka Peninsula. Bering traveled across the peninsula by sledge to reach the coast where ships for his voyage were to be built.

they wintered at a spot they called Petropavlovsk, the Russian names of their two ships. Before June 1741 they were joined by De la Croyère, who sailed with Chirikov, and the naturalist Georg Steller, who had traveled to Siberia to join the expedition in 1738.

Soon after the beginning of the voyage a severe storm separated Bering and Chirikov, and although the two ships appear to have been in the same region around the middle of August, they did not meet again. Chirikov reached the coast of the North American mainland and sent his ship's boats ashore, one after the other, for supplies or information. Neither was ever seen again. Unable to land without his boats, Chirikov could not replenish his water supplies when they began to run out. Then he was delayed by fog and contrary winds, and finally scurvy broke out among the crew. Many men died, including De La Croyère, and the battered survivors were thankful to reach Petropavlovsk in October after a voyage of four months.

Bering, meanwhile, had followed his instructions to search for a mythical country called Gamaland, which was believed to have been discovered by the Spanish south of the nearer Aleutian Islands early in the 17th century. Not surprisingly, Bering found no trace of it. At the end of July he sighted Mount St. Elias on the coast of Alaska, a landfall a little to the north and west of Chirikov's. Then he tried to follow the coast northwest, but was hampered by the fog which had delayed Chirikov. Passing outside the Kodiak Islands, he then set his course south of the Aleutians, discovering a number of the volcanoes that distinguish this island chain. However, his crew, like Chirikov's, was attacked by scurvy. Bering himself fell sick and so many of his men caught the disease that it was impossible to continue. In November they discovered Bering Island, which at first was believed to be part of the mainland, and because the crew was so weak, it was decided to winter there. The un-

Left: the spectacled cormorant (*Phalacrocorax Perspicillatus*). It was discovered by Georg Steller, the naturalist who sailed with Bering on his second voyage.

Left: a recent reconstruction of Bering's ship the *St. Peter*. It was made by the Danish marine artist Per Bøgh, based on the descriptions in Bering's own diaries.

Below: an oil painting depicting the death of Vitus Bering, made about 100 years later. He died on the island named in his honor.

inhabited island was treeless and the only way they could shelter was to dig shallow pits in the sandhills, protecting them with the ships' sails. Bering died little more than a month after the expedition's arrival on the island, and before the end of the winter many of the crew members were also dead. The only man to remain well throughout was Steller. He made himself responsible for the survivors, but still found time to compile an invaluable description of the regions' natural characteristics and animal life.

The winter of 1741–42 saw not only the loss of the expedition's leader, but also that of its vessel. In the spring the 45 survivors had to build a new ship with material saved from the wreck. It was launched toward the end of August, and early in September arrived safely in Petropavlovsk.

Bering was dead, but his voyage had been successful. It greatly improved knowledge of the relation between Asia and North America and of the formerly unknown seas between. Despite the importance of Bering's achievement, however, little was done to follow up his explorations, and for many years his work was scarcely known.

Nikolay Przhevalsky 1839-1888

Nikolay Przhevalsky did more than any single explorer before him to reveal the secrets of central Asia. Between 1871, when he set out on his first major expedition, and his death 17 years later, he helped wrought an immense change in the map of Asia. Through him, many of the major geographical features had been accurately located for the first time, and vast areas of formerly unknown country had been surveyed. For the Russians, the knowledge Przhevalsky gained was of political as well as geographical importance because the country was then preoccupied with expansion into central Asia. However, Przhevalsky's expeditions were also of immense botanical and zoological value because Przhevalsky was a collector as well as a traveler. In the unknown country he passed through, he amassed a huge number of specimens of often unknown animals and plants.

Przhevalsky was born in April 1839 near Smolensk, southwest of Moscow. When he was 10 years old he and his younger brother entered school in Smolensk where they remained until the May of 1855. By the time he left school, Przhevalsky had resolved to enter the army like his father before him and in September 1855 he joined the infantry. The Crimean War was raging and young Przhevalsky was sent straight to the front, but he saw little active service because peace was declared the following year. He soon discovered that he loathed the peacetime army and began to dream of making his career as an explorer of unknown places. In 1860 he asked for a transfer to the Amur military district of Siberia, which had been ceded to Russia by China only that year and which was still virtually unexplored. Far from granting his request, the military authorities confined him to barracks for three days under arrest.

Disgusted by his treatment, Przhevalsky evolved another plan. It was to enter the Academy of the General Staff in St. Petersburg, where he would receive training vital to the work he longed to do. He studied hard and passed the difficult entrance examination among the first of the 180 candidates competing for the 90 available places. The academy's curriculum included geography, surveying, navigation, and astronomy, all important for a career of exploration. While still a student, Przhevalsky wrote a dissertation on the military and statistical importance of the Amur region, compiled from all the existing information. On the strength of this

work he was later elected a member of the St. Petersburg Imperial Geographical Society.

Przhevalsky never finished his course at the military academy. He was already becoming bored by his studies when the authorities offered the officers of his year the benefits of graduation, including a commission, in return for a period of active service helping to crush a rebellion in Poland. The following year, 1864, with the Polish revolt over, Przhevalsky became a teacher at a newly established college for officer cadets in Warsaw. His subjects were history and geography, and he also acted as the college librarian. He took advantage of his relative freedom to study botany and zoology in preparation for his later work, but he found his Warsaw life fairly

Above: St. Petersburg in 1803 during the centenary celebration of its founding. Nikolay Przhevalsky studied there about 60 years later.

Below: Przhevalsky in his army uniform. The giant of exploration in central Asia up to his day, he was the first to delineate the Astin Tagh mountains as well as the first to make a systematic survey of the sources of the Hwang Ho.

humdrum. He was longing for "wildness, breadth, and freedom" when, toward the end of 1866, the realization of his dream began. He was posted to the East Siberian military district, the region he had written about in his student dissertation and which was still relatively unknown.

In June 1867 Przhevalsky began his first journey of exploration. He was commissioned to make a military and general survey of the newly acquired Ussuri River region. Besides fulfilling the strict letter of his orders, he gathered enough information for an account of the population and of the area's geography, animals, and plants. "My material will be the best enhancement of the Siberian section of the Geographical Society's coming *Notes*," he wrote proudly in a letter to his brothers. He was also anxious to write a full account of his journey, but having insufficient funds to pay for publication, he started to gamble at cards to raise money. During the winter of 1868 he won enough not only to publish his book but also to help finance his first major expedition into central Asia.

In 1869 Przhevalsky was promoted to staff captain by the army and awarded a lesser silver medal by the Geographical Society for his expedition in the Ussuri region. By the New Year he had returned on leave to St. Petersburg with the prime aim of raising funds for a lengthy journey to central Asia. Permission was eventually given for such an expedition, and financial

Right: Przhevalsky in the kind of clothes he would have worn for travel and exploration.

backing came from the Geographical Society, the War Ministry, and the Botanical Gardens in addition to that provided by Przhevalsky himself. "On this expedition, of course," wrote Przhevalsky to his mother, "my entire future depends." In August 1870 *Travels in the Ussuri Region* was published, and Przhevalsky returned to his home near Smolensk on the first stage of his journey east.

The starting point of Przhevalsky's first central Asian expedition was Kyakhta, situated south of Lake Baikal on Russia's border with Mongolia. From there he set out for Kalgan, northwest of Peking, in a Chinese two-wheeled cart. At Urga (now Ulan Bator), he was able to join a Mongol caravan for the trek across the Gobi Desert to Kalgan. Because the camel's pace

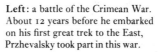

Left: a battle of the Crimean War. About 12 years before he embarked on his first great trek to the East, Przhevalsky took part in this war.

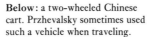

Below: a two-wheeled Chinese cart. Przhevalsky sometimes used such a vehicle when traveling.

death, Przhevalsky had to send two of his men 50 miles for help. The round journey took them 17 days, and the half-lame camels they acquired took the last of Przhevalsky's money. However, they enabled him and his men to struggle back to Kalgan for the New Year of 1872.

In March 1872 Przhevalsky started out again and, following much the same route as that taken by the Jesuit missionaries Evariste Huc and Joseph Gabet nearly 30 years earlier, made his way southwest to Koko Nor, the Blue Lake. "In all my life," he exclaimed, "I have never beheld such a beautiful lake as this. . . ." While he was at Koko Nor, he visited a Mongol encampment where he was surprised to meet the Tibetan ambassador to Peking on his way home to Lhasa. The ambassador assured Przhevalsky that the Dalai Lama, Tibet's supreme ruler, would be glad to welcome him to his capital. It was the only invitation to Tibet that Przhevalsky received during his career.

The way to Tibet from Koko Nor lay through the Tsaidam depression, a salty marsh stretching some 500 miles from east to west. In Przhevalsky's opinion, it had recently been covered by a saline lake. As he traveled south he was able to correct some of the inaccuracies about the region that had been perpetrated by Huc's account. From Tsaidam the party made its way up into the Burchan Buddha Mountains and so into northern Tibet. The route they followed was one that had been forged by Buddhist pilgrims on their way to Lhasa, but Przhevalsky was following it in winter when conditions were extremely hard. By the time his party reached the Mur Usu, a headstream of the Yangtze River, three of his camels were dead, others were dying, and he had little money left with which to buy more pack animals. He was only some 500 miles from

was slow, Przhevalsky walked ahead of the caravan to hunt – always a favorite occupation of his.

Kalgan gave the explorer his first experience of the Chinese, whom he did not take to. He felt that Chinese authority thwarted him and he responded by formulating plans for a rebellion among China's Buddhist and Muslim subjects in central Asia – a rebellion that would bring them under Russian rule. With this end in mind, his dream of reaching Lhasa, the Tibetan capital, took on political coloration.

From Kalgan, Przhevalsky made a 200-mile journey northeast to explore Dalai Nor, the Great Lake, and its vicinity. Then in May 1871 he headed west from Kalgan into the Ordos Desert south of the great northern loop of the Hwang-Ho. This was in his eyes the start of the expedition proper. By October he found that it had become necessary for him to return to Kalgan for more money and supplies. The journey was difficult, and the season already late. At one stage the camels wandered off, leaving the expedition only one sick camel and two horses. When the sick animal died and one of the horses froze to

Lhasa, but he had no alternative except to turn back. Nonetheless he was the first Russian to penetrate so far into central Asia. He had determined the geography of a vast, formerly unknown area, had surveyed some 3000 miles of route, and had collected numerous specimens of the regions animal and plant life. In recognition of Przhevalsky's achievement, he was promoted to lieutenant-colonel and awarded an annual pension. In addition, the Academy of Sciences bought his zoological collection and the Imperial Geographical Society paid for the publication of his three-volume account of his journey, *Mongolia and the Country of the Tanguts*.

Przhevalsky's next journey had a definite political objective – he was to lead an embassy to Kashgaria whose ruler, Yakub Beg, had broken with the Chinese and wanted closer links with Russia. On the investigative side, Przhevalsky planned to try to discover Lake Lop Nor on his way to Lhasa. In the autumn of 1876 Przhevalsky left Kuldja southeast of Lake Balkhash in the upper Ili valley, which was then occupied by Russia. He crossed the Tien Shan into the domains of Yakub Beg. Less friendly than had been anticipated, Yakub Beg seems to have suspected Przhevalsky's party of being the vanguard of a Russian invasion, and he sent a party of his men to escort the Russians along the Tarim River and across the desert to Lop Nor. The lake was reached by the end of December, and south of it Przhevalsky made the most important discovery of this expedition, the Astin Tagh range of mountains. His attempt to cross them was unsuccessful, however. He had no guides, and had lost a number of his camels. Unable to continue his journey, he had to make the 600-mile trek back to Kuldja to form another caravan. There he learned that his mission had been

Above: the wild horse named after Przhevalsky as the first European to sight it.

Opposite: Lake Baikal. It was from south of the lake that Przhevalsky started his first journey.

Below: a Mongol camp of the 19th century – probably a common sight to Przhevalsky.

fruitless – Yakub Beg was dead, and his empire had fallen to the Chinese.

In Kuldja Przhevalsky fell victim to an unpleasant skin disease which, aggravated by the primitive treatments which were all that was available to him, helped to bring his second expedition to a premature end. Despite his illness while in Kuldja, he wrote *From Kuldja across the Tien Shan and to Lop Nor*. He also

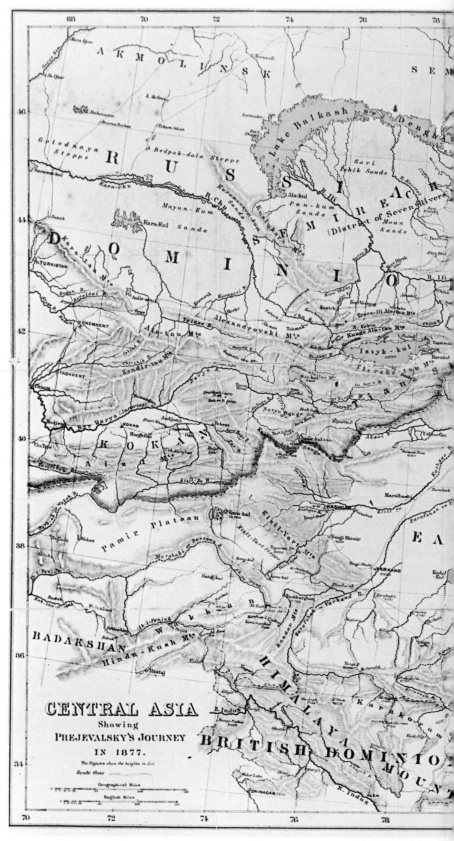

received news of his promotion to full colonel. Leaving on his next trip, he traveled south down the Ili valley, crossed the Tien Shan mountains and turned northeast parallel to the Russian border, and crossed the desert of Dzungaria which lies northeast of the Tien Shan. By then he was suffering so badly that he turned north again, reaching the Russian border at Zaysan east of Lake Balkhash. There he learned that the political situation between Russia and China had deteriorated so much that his journey into Chinese territory was inadvisable. He abandoned his expedition with some relief, hoping to recover and recuperate before setting out for Lhasa again.

The expedition on which Przhevalsky embarked in 1879 was perhaps his greatest journey and certainly his most successful attempt to penetrate the Tibetan plateau. He was spurred on in his attempt to establish the Russians in Lhasa in the face of the political interest of the British, who were well established in India. As usual, he started from the town at which he had ended his previous expedition, in this case Zaysan. Less than a mile away from the town he was brought the skin of an animal that he immediately recognized as the primitive Mongolian wild horse, often reported but never seen by a European. Later the explorer came upon herds of this animal, now named after him, but despite his skill with a rifle, he never managed to shoot one.

From Zaysan Przhevalsky and his party made their way east and south, crossing the desert of Dzungaria. There Przhevalsky studied and described in detail the climate, soil, flora, and fauna. Besides Przhevalsky's horse, the animal life included a wild camel from which the domesticated

Above left: an idol from the caves of the Thousand Buddhas, which Przhevalsky visited.

Bactrian two-humped species had been bred. After crossing the Tien Shan and reaching the oasis of Hami, Przhevalsky again plunged into the desert, making for Sa-chou (present-day Tunhwang) at the foot of the Nan Shan mountains.

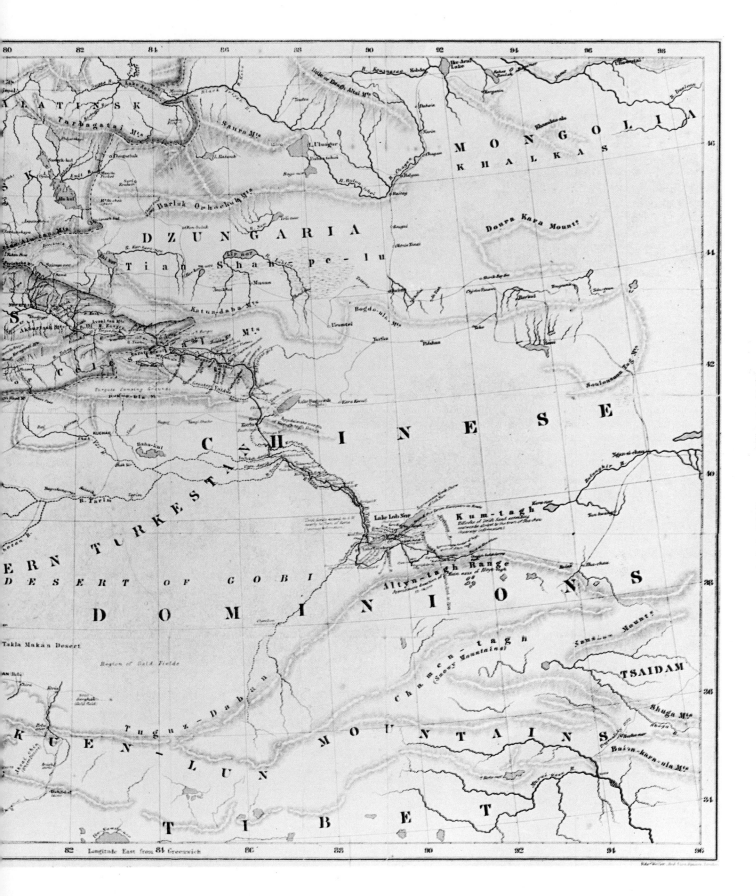

Near Sa-chou there is an 8th-century Buddhist shrine – the caves of the Thousand Buddhas – and Przhevalsky visited these caves before continuing up into the Nan Shan. He and his men spent some time in the mountains, exploring,

hunting, and adding to their zoological collections. One member of the party nearly died of hunger and exposure when he got lost pursuing a wounded yak.

Descending from the Nan Shan, the party

found itself in the salt marshes of Tsaidam. The inhabitants were friendly, but would not show Przhevalsky the direct route to Tibet for fear of the Chinese. He therefore had to make a detour around the north of Tsaidam before breaking out for the south. At last it seemed that Przhevalsky was on the verge of achieving his ambition as he climbed up into the mountains "that guard the inaccessible world of the plateaus beyond the clouds . . . still utterly unknown to science." As he advanced into Tibet, he heard rumors that troops had been assembled to prevent him from reaching the Tibetan capital, but this did not deter him. Neither did the climate which, although it was only October, was very cold and snowy. On one occasion the sun was so bright after two days of bad weather that the men's eyes became inflamed and one of the sheep went blind. Crossing the Tanglha range, Przhevalsky found the way barred by the local Yograi tribesmen and had to fight his way out.

It was on the way south from the Tanglha mountains that Przhevalsky again heard that he would not be allowed to enter Lhasa. His impending arrival had apparently generated great excitement in the Tibetan capital, and a rumor was circulating that he intended to kidnap the Dalai Lama and destroy the Buddhist faith. All at once Przhevalsky and his men found themselves surrounded by Tibetan soldiers who demanded that they wait until they had received permission to go on to Lhasa. It took more than two weeks for an answer to reach them, but then it was final. Przhevalsky was less than 200 miles from the Tibetan capital, but he would not be allowed to proceed. He made his way slowly back to Russia, turning east rather than following his outward route. He skirted the Hwang-Ho and Koko Nor before crossing the Gobi to

Kyakhta, where his first expedition had begun.

Once Przhevalsky had completed his account of his third expedition, *From Zaysan via Hami to Tibet and the Upper Reaches of the Yellow River*, his only thought was his next journey to central Asia. His object was a more detailed examination of those regions in northern Tibet and

Below left: a lama in ceremonial dress, from Przhevalsky's book about Mongolia.

Right: the Cossack guard that traveled with Przhevalsky at the czar's behest for protection.

Far right: Lake Issyk-Kul, the first point in Russia reached by Przhevalsky on his last trip.

Below: an engraving showing how Tibetan guards made the Russian expedition turn back before reaching Lhasa.

eastern Turkestan through which his route had led before. He left St. Petersburg in August 1883 and went to Kyakhta where he carried out his final preparations before setting out to cross the Gobi. His first goal was the source of the Hwang-Ho, and his next objective the Do-chu or Blue River. The latter was reached at a point

where its deep rapidly flowing stream was hemmed in by mountains. Przhevalsky's camels were unable to cross it, so he returned to the Hwang-Ho to survey the two lakes through which the Hwang-Ho's headwaters flow. From there he headed west, traveling through a wide valley running roughly east to west and so swept by the prevailing westerlies that Przhevalsky named it the "Valley of the Winds." To the east of the Kun Lun he discovered a series of mountain ranges that he named Marco Polo, Columbus, Moscow, and Mysterious. The last mountain was renamed Przhevalsky's Range by the Imperial Geographical Society.

Crossing the Astin Tagh, Przhevalsky returned to Lop Nor where he spent nearly two months surveying and hunting before turning west along the southern fringes of the Taklamakan Desert via the oases of Cherchen and Khotan. From Khotan he turned north along the Khotan River and crossed the Taklamakan. Then, making his way over the Tien Shan by the Bedel Pass, he reached Russia again at Lake Issyk-Kul. His return to St. Petersburg in January 1886 was marked by his promotion to major-general as well as by the award of gold medals from many of the leading geographical societies of Europe; but he was not yet content to abandon exploration. He planned a new expedition to make another assault on Lhasa. By the autumn of 1888 preparations were almost complete and Przhevalsky was already in Karakol on Issyk-kul – which was to be his starting point – when he was suddenly taken ill and died shortly after. He was buried overlooking the waters of the lake dominated by the Tien Shan mountains that he had crossed so often. In his honor, the town in which he died is today called Przhevalsky.

Sven Hedin 1865-1952

"We were like sleepwalkers; but still we fought for our lives. Suddenly Kasim grabbed my arm and pointed downward at the sand. There were distinct tracks of human beings! In a twinkling we were wide awake. . . . Kasim bent down, examined the prints, and gasped: 'It is our own trail!' In our listless, somnolent state, we had described a circle without knowing it. That was enough for a while; we could not endure any more."

Sven Hedin, on his first major expedition to the deserts of central Asia, faced death because his caravan had run out of water, but he survived to become one of the most important explorers that the Asian continent has seen. He expanded European knowledge of the deserts of central Asia, the Tibetan plateau, and the region north of the Himalaya, and he gave Europe its first knowledge of areas that had never been explored.

Hedin was born in Stockholm on February 19, 1865, the son of an architect. He was fascinated by exploration from the time he was a child. Shortly before he left school at the age of 20, he was offered a post tutoring a Swedish child whose family was stationed in the Russian town of Baku on the Caspian. Such was his interest in travel that he accepted eagerly. The assignment lasted seven months, and after its completion Hedin made his first journey in Asia. He traveled overland to the Persian Gulf, then by steamer up

Above left: Sven Hedin, the Swedish explorer who covered thousands of miles in little-known areas of central Asia in a period of about 40 years.

Right: a watercolor by Hedin of one of his mountain camps, dated 1908. The explorer made hundreds of drawings and sketches of a remarkably high quality.

the Tigris to Baghdad, and from there across the desert to Teheran. On his return to Sweden he studied geography and geology at a school in Stockholm and at the Universities of Uppsala and Berlin. He also published his first book, the story of his experiences in Persia, and the publisher's interest made Hedin "ready to leap for joy."

Hedin had learned Persian during his visit to the country, and in 1889 was appointed interpreter to an embassy sent to the Persian shah by the king of Norway and Sweden, which were at that time united under a single crown. The mission left in April 1890 and its work was completed by July, but instead of returning to Sweden with

Above: a caravan in a valley of the Pamir mountains, northeast Afghanistan. Most travelers in this region joined such a caravan at one time or another.

Above right: a sketch by Hedin showing a market village near the town and oasis of Khotan.

Right: Hedin's drawing of a Mongolian beggar.

European had ever set foot."

Hedin's first major expedition began in October 1893 and centered on the region between the Tien Shan and Astin Tagh mountains occupied by the Tarim Basin and the Taklamakan Desert. He also explored in the Pamirs, the lofty "roof of the world." There, where the mighty Hindu Kush, Tien Shan, Kun Lun, and Karakoram mountain ranges come together, he attempted unsuccessfully to scale the summit of Muztagh Ata, 24,386 feet high. When he continued into the Taklamakan Desert with its great sand dunes and vast waterless reaches, his career of exploration nearly reached an untimely end. The caravan was about 200 miles east of Kashgar when water began to run short, and although the remainder was strictly rationed, Hedin's supplies were soon completely gone. The sand

the other members of the embassy, Hedin remained in Teheran. He had determined to travel into central Asia. Visiting Merv, Bukhara, and Samarkand, he made his way east to Kashgar and then, with three Cossack companions, crossed the Tien Shan mountains to Lake Issyk-Kul. From Issyk-Kul Hedin made a 126-mile pilgrimage to the grave of Nikolay Przhevalsky, who had died on the eve of embarking on his fifth journey to central Asia barely two years before. Hedin returned to Europe eager to solve the immense geographical problems still presented by Asia, "burning with desire once more to take the road of wild adventure . . . content with nothing less than to tread paths where no

dunes of the Taklamakan stretched to every horizon with no sign of waterhole or stream.

The camels began to die first. To keep themselves alive the men drank rancid camel oil. Hedin even sampled some Chinese brandy intended as fuel for a lamp stove, which made him very ill. A sheep was slaughtered for its blood, but no one could stomach it and fell by the wayside one by one. Finally only Hedin and his servant Kasim were left trudging "like sleepwalkers" across the dunes. When they discovered that they had been going around in circles, they gave way to despair, stopped where they stood, and fell asleep. The following morning, however, "from the top of a dune, where nothing obstructed the view toward the east, we noticed that the horizon, which for two weeks had revealed a row of yellow saw-teeth, now disclosed an absolutely even, dark green line." It was the forest which lined the Khotan River, and the discovery gave them strength to struggle on. They were but a few hundred yards from the forest when Kasim collapsed, unable to go farther, but Hedin continued alone to the river. Although he used the handle of a spade as a staff, he was so weak that he had to travel long distances on all fours. At last he reached the river bed, only to discover that it was dry.

The perseverance that throughout his career aided Hedin came to his rescue. Determined not to die of thirst in the very bed of a river, he pushed himself to search for a pool. He was rewarded when a bird rose into the air ahead of him and he heard the splash of water. In the deepest part of the river bed lay a large pool 70 feet by 15. "In the silent night I thanked God for my miraculous deliverance," Hedin wrote later. "I drank, and drank again." He had no water bottle with him, but filled his boots with the precious liquid and returned to save Kasim. The two lived.

The traveler in the Taklamakan Desert faced other dangers besides that of running out of water because the climate of the region fluctuates wildly. On a later visit Hedin was confronted by snowstorms and heavy frosts and once his caravan was caught in a dust storm, the *Kara-buran*. The wind blew so fiercely that the tent poles snapped in two, and the "drift sand

Scenes and events caught by the pen and brush of Hedin: the onset of a storm in northern Tibet (**above**); self-portrait of his agonizing search for water in the desert (**opposite**); and a caravan at sunset in the desert (**below**).

beat against the tent cloth, and the particles filtered through and covered everything within." On that particular occasion the storm lasted for more than 24 hours and Hedin later recalled that when at last it had passed "we all felt queerly dazed as after a long illness".

During his first expedition, Hedin made some valuable archaeological discoveries, although he was not essentially an archaeologist. Guides from Khotan took the explorer to one buried township that they called Takla-makan or Dandan-uilik, the "Ivory Houses," and later a shepherd directed Hedin to another ruined city known as Kara-dung, the "Black Hill." The most important of Hedin's archaeological discoveries however, was the town of Loulan near the lake of Lop Nor. This turned out to have

been a frontier town on the Silk Route, that great ancient trade route by which Chinese silk had reached the West in the days of the Roman Empire. From the documents found in Loulan it was possible to piece together a picture of life in this remote Asian city in the 3rd century AD. Hedin felt to the full the fascination of these long forgotten cities. "Here I stand," he wrote after his first discovery, "like the prince in the enchanted wood, having wakened to new life the

Below: map of Hedin's route through north China and Mongolia, from his book *Through Asia*. He made a point of visiting the burial place of Nikolay Przhevalsky, the Russian traveler who preceded him in the area by two years.

city which has slumbered for a thousand years."

Hedin's travels in the Taklamakan Desert on his first great expedition were succeeded by explorations in the Lake Lop Nor region. The surveys he made there showed that the lake's position had changed since Przhevalsky had located it some 20 years before. Gradually making his way east, he visited Koko Nor and then trekked across the Ordos Desert to Kalgan northwest of Peking. Kalgan was Hedin's starting point for a crossing of the dreaded Gobi Desert to Siberia, where he ended that expedition. Only two years later in 1899 he was in central Asia again exploring in the area of Lop Nor. From there he made his first visit to the shuttered and mysterious land of Tibet.

Lhasa, which had been visited by Jesuit missionaries in the 17th and 18th centuries, was by that time closed to foreigners, and Hedin's only chance of reaching the city was by stealth. Disguising himself as a Mongol and hiring a Tibetan monk as his interpreter, he led a large and well-equipped caravan south across the plateau of Tibet. It would obviously be impossible for him to enter the Tibetan capital at the head of such a large company, so in July 1901 he left the caravan and, accompanied only by his interpreter and another man, pushed swiftly toward the south. His map, notebook, and a few scientific instruments were well concealed in hidden pockets in his mongol cloak. As visible proof of his assumed identity, he wore a 108-beaded rosary and carried

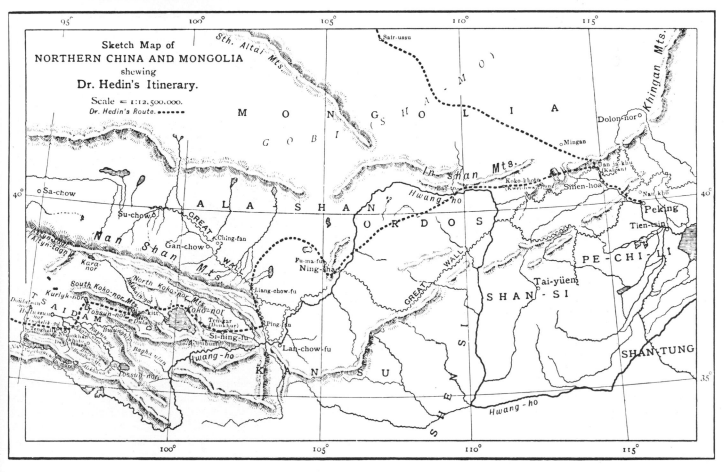

an image of Buddha. The journey was hazardous in spite of careful preparations. On the second night out two of the horses were stolen. Later the remaining horses lost their footing and were nearly swept away while crossing a ford. Hedin and his companions succeeded in reaching the main road to Lhasa, but soon found their way barred by a party of Tibetan warriors who informed them that the road south was closed.

Escorted by the soldiers, Hedin made his way back to his caravan. Then he made another attempt to cross Tibet, aiming for India to the south. Once more he was stopped, this time by orders sent direct from the Dalai Lama, Tibet's supreme ruler. "It is quite beyond any need," wrote the Dalai Lama to the governors of the provinces through which Hedin was going to travel, "for Europeans to enter the Land of the Holy Books to look about them. . . . If . . . they should proceed, your heads will be forfeit. Oblige them to turn and to retreat on the path over which they came." The route by which Hedin and his caravan were escorted from Tibet led west to Leh across the plateau of Tibet, so that Hedin was able to explore and map many formerly unknown areas before the Tibetan frontier was reached.

Right: lamas of Tashilhumpo, a photograph by Hedin. He managed to reach his important shrine although impediments were placed in his way.

Despite the problems he had encountered in trying to reach Lhasa, Hedin went back to Tibet in 1906, aiming for a region that the latest British map simply designated "unexplored." It covered a mountainous area north of the Tsangpo or upper Brahmaputra River and, as far as was known, no European had entered it before. This time Hedin reached Tibet from the south, as the Jesuits had long before. He traveled from Srinagar in Kashmir to Leh, then over the Karakoram

Below left: Hedin's drawing of a Tibetan soldier. The explorer met armed guards barring his way more than once in his travels.

Below right: Hedin dressed for travel in harsh conditions.

mountains to the plateau of Tibet. He intended to cross the plateau to Tashilhumpo on the Tsangpo River, which was Tibet's second most important shrine. Tibet seemed even more unwelcoming on Hedin's second visit than on his previous one. It was intensely cold. One night the temperature fell to 50° below freezing point. Horses and sheep froze to death and Hedin had to provide his dogs with felt sleeping jackets to keep them alive. For months the expedition saw no other human beings, which at least reduced

Above: the Tsangpo River as photographed by Hedin. He explored the beautiful valley of this river.

Left: another of Hedin's own sketches, this one of a Tibetan woman in traditional garments.

their chances of discovery by the Tibetan authorities. At last they stood on the very fringes of the region they had come to explore.

It was at this crucial moment that Hedin received a visit from the governor of Naktsang province, one of the rulers who had turned him back on his previous journey. He again told Hedin that he could not pass through Naktsang and would have to retrace his steps. "I started out on this journey with 130 beasts of burden," retorted Hedin. "I have eight horses and one mule left. How can you ask me to go back . . . ?" Adamant at first in his refusal to allow Hedin into his province, the governor relented the following day for no apparent reason. Hedin was able to go on his way. Passing through regions in which every step was a new discovery, he at last reached the valley of the Tsangpo. The land abounded in villages and gardens, in contrast with the desolate regions through which Hedin had passed.

The season of the New Year celebrations was approaching as Hedin made his way toward Tashilhumpo, and he found himself in company with many Buddhist pilgrims on the journey toward the shrine. Some of the pilgrims embarked on the river in boats made of yak hides fastened to rectangular frames, and for the last day of his journey Hedin joined them, thinking that he had more chance of being allowed to continue in this way. He reached Shigatse safely, and while there received a welcome from the Tashi Lama, head of the Tashilhumpo monastery and second in importance only to the Dalai Lama. The Tashi Lama told Hedin to attend the celebrations for the New Year and Hedin therefore continued to

177

Tashilhumpo. Surprisingly, in view of the Tibetans' persistant hostility to foreigners, Hedin was interviewed by the Tashi Lama who gave him permission to visit and photograph any part of the town he wanted to. The explorer witnessed the *Losar*, or New Year festival, with its traditional devil dance, visited the huge kitchens where tea for 3800 monks was "brewed in six enormous cauldrons," and observed the customs, rituals, and inhabitants of this centuries-old monastic town. After more than six weeks, messages came from Lhasa making it clear that his stay had been too long.

Leaving Tashilhumpo, Hedin attempted to reach the holy lake of Dangra-yum-tso, but was turned back. He was more successful in reaching the source of the Tsangpo River and in exploring Lake Manasarowar in a region that was hardly known to Europeans. To investigate the shores of the lake, Hedin sailed across it – to the horror

Above: Hedin's watercolor of Mount Kailas on a summer evening after sunset.

Left: a huge buddha enshrined in a temple in Inner Mongolia.

Right: a picture of the source of the Indus from Hedin's camera.

of the Tibetans who believed that he was inviting divine retribution by defiling a sacred place. At Mount Kailas, Hedin joined the Buddhist pilgrims coming from all over Tibet to make a circuit of the holy mountain, a custom the Jesuit missionary Ippolito Desideri had described nearly 200 years earlier. At last, in September 1907 he reached the source of the Indus River.

A large part of the region Hedin had planned to explore still remained unknown, largely because of the hostility of Tibetans to foreign travelers. Undeterred, Hedin disguised himself and formed a fresh caravan, heading eastward. It was December and the explorers were faced with bitter cold and frequent snowstorms. This forced them to travel very slowly over a route that Hedin described as the highest and possibly the most difficult on earth. Sixty-four days passed and many of the caravan animals had died before the first nomad encampment was reached. From then on, Hedin pretended to be a shepherd, and at the first sign of human life would take charge

of the caravan's sheep. This time, however, he was found out and forced to turn west again under escort to Lake Manasarowar. From there he followed the Sutlej River to the Indian frontier.

Hedin's explorations resulted in the first maps of the formerly unknown areas through which

he had traveled – maps which included, among other discoveries, the Kailas mountain range lying parallel with the Himalaya and to the north. He had cleared up so many problems of Tibetan geography that no major discoveries remained to be made; the work of future explorers would be simply to fill in the details on Hedin's map.

After nearly 20 years of adventure and discovery in Asia, Hedin had a long break before his next journey of exploration. His life was less than half over, but his major work was already complete. His journey brought him fame and many honors. In 1902 he was created a Swedish noble and in 1909 Great Britain named him an honorary Knight Commander of the Indian Empire. In addition he received awards from the leading European geographical societies for his work.

It was late in the 1920s when Hedin next visited central Asia. More than 60 years old, he returned to the continent that had witnessed his greatest daredevil triumphs as the respected leader of a large scientific expedition sponsored jointly by Sweden and China. The Sino-Swedish expedition lasted for six years during which its members covered a vast amount of ground and filled in other blanks on the map. No sooner had the expedition ended than Hedin, then in his 69th year, set out on his last journey into Asia. Its purpose was to survey the eastern part of the Silk Route. It was Hedin's last expedition although he did not die until the age of 87.

Below: Hedin in Mongolia, taken on his way to Peking. He learned the rudiments of the Mongolian language from a yak hunter, and was altogether adaptable, open-minded, and conscientious.

The Lure of Arabia

Since Europe became civilized, there has probably never been a time when the Arabian peninsula was utterly unknown. The first European account of the country appears in the *Histories* written by the Greek historian Herodotus in the 5th century BC. By the time of the Roman Empire, Arabia was described as *Felix* – "happy" or "fortunate" – because the country was the source of many of the luxuries that were craved in Imperial Rome. Even before the Christian era, Arabia supplied Rome with precious stones and metals, incense, and costly spices. Not all of these were produced in Arabia, but came through Arabia after being imported from farther afield. It was in an attempt to break the Arab monopoly of the luxury trade that the first Roman emperor, Augustus, promoted the unsuccessful military expedition to Arabia under the leadership of Aelius Gallus in 25 BC.

Gallus' expedition was the only attempt made in ancient times to explore Arabia, and the hardships his men suffered on their journey should have been enough to dispel the image of Arabia as a land where "milk and honey" flowed. However, when Ptolemy wrote his *Geography* some 200 years later, he still referred to the peninsula as *Arabia Felix*. The original maps accompany-

Below: a map of Arabia made around 1460 but based on Ptolemy's map of 1300 years before.

Above: Marib, Yemen, in a view from the surrounding desert. Sent to conquer it in 25 BC, Aelius Gallus failed in the mission, defeated as much by the hardships of the journey as by his opponents.

ing the *Geography* have not survived but many reconstructions exist, made from the text of the *Geography* after it was first translated into Latin in the 15th century. This reconstructed Ptolemy map of Arabia Felix was made around 1460, some 1300 years after the original *Geography* appeared.

Ptolemy was aware that Arabia was a peninsula and he also had a rough idea of its coastline, but he misrepresented the proportions owing to one of the more serious errors in his work. This fault – an overestimate of the breadth of the Eurasian land mass – meant that Ptolemy had to increase the east–west measurements of various sections. He solved the problem on Arabia by enlarging the little known Persian Gulf in the north into an inland sea. In the south he had to increase the width of Arabia, since it was already known that only narrow straits separated the peninsula from Africa on the west and Persia on the east.

For his knowledge of the Arabian interior, Ptolemy was chiefly indebted to information supplied by the men who followed the traditional caravan routes across the peninsula. Because distances were measured in camel marches and directions by the sun, it is hardly surprising that the geographical positions of the places he includes are not perfectly correct. However, in many respects Ptolemy's information was remarkably accurate. He depicts a number of mountain ranges – which appear on this map as distinct darker areas – and places them where mountains actually exist. Similarly, although Arabia does not have and probably never has had a true river, the five rivers whose sources are recorded by Ptolemy are all *wadis* (dried-up river valleys) where water does flow in the wet season. Ptolemy also listed 114 cities and villages in Arabia, many of which can be identified with settlements known in the 20th century. Ptolemy's picture of Arabia provided the world's image of the peninsula for many centuries.

Travelers soon found, like Aelius Gallus, that the country was one of the most inhospitable in

it was only around oases that permanent villages and towns could grow. Most of the peninsula's inhabitants were therefore nomads, living in tents, herding camels, sheep, or goats, and moving from place to place in search of water or pasture for their flocks. The harsh life of the nomad Arabs bred insularity and suspicion of strangers who might steal the vital secrets of water or pasture. The Arabs became proud of their liberty, and jealous of it, preserving their rights by violence if necessary.

In the 7th century AD Arabia and Europe came into a new relationship. Early in that century in Arabia the religion of Islam was born. It was founded by Muhammad, who taught that there was only one god – Allah – and that he was

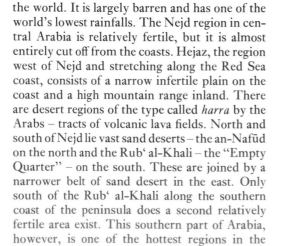

the world. It is largely barren and has one of the world's lowest rainfalls. The Nejd region in central Arabia is relatively fertile, but it is almost entirely cut off from the coasts. Hejaz, the region west of Nejd and stretching along the Red Sea coast, consists of a narrow infertile plain on the coast and a high mountain range inland. There are desert regions of the type called *harra* by the Arabs – tracts of volcanic lava fields. North and south of Nejd lie vast sand deserts – the an-Nafūd on the north and the Rub' al-Khali – the "Empty Quarter" – on the south. These are joined by a narrower belt of sand desert in the east. Only south of the Rub' al-Khali along the southern coast of the peninsula does a second relatively fertile area exist. This southern part of Arabia, however, is one of the hottest regions in the world.

The geography and climate of Arabia did not encourage a settled life among its people because

Above: a Turkish miniature of the 16th century of a desert scene with nomads.

Right: a herder tending her herd of camels. Nomadic women do all the heavy work, including taking down and putting up the tents.

degree of tolerance was extended to other faiths.

In the country of Islam's birthplace, however, the characteristics of the new religion – perhaps like all new sects – were fanaticism, intolerance, and distrust of anyone who did not follow the Islamic creed. The two holy cities of Mecca, birthplace of Muhammad, and nearby Medina were closed to all except Muslims, and travel in Arabia for non-Muslims became even more dangerous than it had previously been. However, Muslims from all parts of the world flocked to the country to fulfill the Islamic obligation of making the *hajj* or pilgrimage to Mecca at least once during their life. Not surprisingly therefore, the first explorer of Arabia was a Muslim. His name was Ibn-Battūtah and he made his pilgrimage in the second quarter of the 14th century, leaving one of the first accounts of the holy places. As the centuries passed, Ibn-Battūtah was followed by Christian explorers, who suffered great hardship to penetrate unknown Arabia and risked their lives to enter Mecca and Medina. The difficulties of travel in Arabia were in fact so great that only in the present century have parts of the peninsula been explored.

Allah's prophet, and its teachings were aimed at a reformation of Arab society and the establishment of a purer way of life. Islamic law forbade the use of violence except in self-defense or in the Islamic cause.

Muhammad's successors waged a long series of wars, in which they felt justified because they were launched in the Islamic cause. These holy wars carried Islam east to India and west along the Mediterranean coast of Africa, across the Strait of Gibraltar, and as far north as the Pyrenees. Only the defeat of the forces of Islam by Charles Martel at Poitiers in 732 prevented more of Europe from falling under Islamic rule. In most of the countries conquered by the Arabs, Islam became the principal religion, although a

Charles Montagu Doughty 1843-1926

Charles Montagu Doughty spent less than two years in Arabia and his wanderings were confined to a relatively small area of the Arabian peninsula, but he has been called the greatest of all the travelers in that land. He started out by wanting to live the life of the Arabs, and he remained sympathetic to them despite frequent hostility and even ill-treatment. In fact, he understood the Arab mentality better than any of his European contemporaries. He observed in detail the physical characteristics of the country and the life of its people, building up a more detailed picture of the peninsula than any traveler before. On his return to England, he amplified and refined his rough sketches into the monumental *Travels in Arabia Deserta*, one of the greatest of all travel epics. To this day it is vital reading for anyone interested in Arabia.

Doughty was born in the county of Suffolk, England on August 19, 1843, the son of a clergy-

man. He was educated at Cambridge University and acquired a taste for scholarly pursuits which he indulged by traveling widely in Europe and the Middle East after graduation. In the early summer of 1875 he was in Palestine and anxious to penetrate Arabia, still a difficult and dangerous country for a Christian European to enter. Doughty had heard of ancient monuments at Medā'in Sālih, which lay on the borders of Hejaz province and on the traditional pilgrim

Left: pilgrims dressed in the traditional clothing of the pilgrimage. The entire journey is bound by strict rules of ritual.

Above: Charles Doughty as an old man. After his great Arabian travels, he settled down to a sedentary life of writing.

route to Mecca, but it was impossible for him to journey there alone. He therefore made his way north to Damascus and joined the annual caravan of Muslims making the obligatory *hajj* or pilgrimage to the holy city of Mecca. By the November of 1876, Doughty and the caravan were in Arabia. They reached Medā'in Sālih by traveling south from Damascus via Tabuk.

The monuments of Medā'in Sālih, which inspired Doughty to explore Arabia, were known more than 500 years before Doughty's visit. In the 1320s, the Muslim traveler Ibn-Battūtah, Arabia's first explorer, passed through al-Hajar—

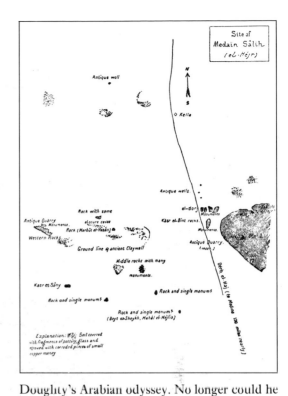

as Medā'in Sālih was then known – and described dwellings with carved thresholds cut in hills of red rock. Ibn-Battūtah called them the "dwellings of Thamūd," and the story of the destruction of the Thamūd tribe for disobedience is told in the Koran. It says: "Whereupon a great earthquake overtook them with a noise of thunder, and in the morning they lay dead in their houses, flat upon their breasts." The "dwellings" are in fact tombs hewn from the rock and bearing inscriptions in Nabathean and Himyaritic. Doughty visited the tombs as far south as Al 'Ulā, an oasis a little beyond Medā'in Sālih. He spent four months in and around Medā'in Sālih, and then left the *hajj* caravan for the desert. "I commit him [Doughty] to thee," said the caravan leader to the Bedouin with whom Doughty was to travel, "have thou a care of him as of mine own eye."

Medā'in Sālih was the true beginning of

Doughty's Arabian odyssey. No longer could he rely on the protective color imparted by the pilgrim caravan. He was alone, an Englishman and a Christian, among the Muslim Bedouin tribes. He made no attempt to hide his nationality or religion, though he did assume the guise of a

doctor with the group of Bedouin tribesmen he joined in their wanderings. Throughout his Arabian wanderings, Doughty was known by the Arabs as "Khalil," a title of honor.

With his Bedouin companions, Doughty went back and forth through the southern fringes of the an-Nafūd desert, closely observing and studying his companions and their customs as well as the country through which they passed. He visited Taymā', a "tall island of palms, enclosed by long clay orchard-walls, fortified with high towers ... [and] overlaid with blossoming boughs of plum trees; of how much amorous contentment to our parched eyes." He made his way to Hā'il, where he was received by the ruler Ibn Rashīd whom he regarded, apparently with justification, as "a murderous man." Doughty was expelled from Hā'il with such intense hostility that he feared for his life, but luckily his *rafiq* –

Above: the an-Nafūd, an enormous and desolate expanse of desert to the north of the Nejd. Doughty traveled widely in and around its southern fringe.

Right: the house inhabited by Doughty in Khaibar in 1877. The photograph was taken by Harry St. John Philby when he visited the village in the 1950s.

the traditional camel pillion rider, both servant and companion – was a trustworthy man and Doughty was able to make his way southwest toward the oasis of Khaibar. As he approached Khaibar he crossed a 6000-foot-high range of volcanic origin, "the greatest height which I had passed hitherto in Arabia . . . a stony flood which has stiffened," he wrote; "long rolling heads, like horse-manes, of those slaggy waves ride and over-ride the rest: and as they are risen they stand petrified, many being sharply split lengthwise, and the hollow laps are partly fallen down in vast shells and in ruinous heaps as of massy masonry."

More trouble awaited Doughty at Khaibar, a village which was under Turkish control. He was arrested by the village governor, accused of

being a "Muscovite spy," and had all his books and papers sent to the Governor of Medina so that he could decide what action should be taken. At last, orders for Doughty's release and good treatment reached Khaibar and the explorer was able to resume his wanderings. When he returned to Hā'il, however, he faced even greater hostility than on his previous visit. He was thrown out of the town, and the men who were to guide him onward tried first to murder him, then to abandon him – which was tantamount to murder. Having succeeded in reaching Buraydah, he was set upon and robbed, although he later retrieved his belongings. Then, on his way from Buraydah to 'Unayzah, his *rafiq* deserted him. Remarkably, he managed to get to 'Unayzah where he stayed for several months awaiting the arrival of the annual "butter caravan" for Mecca. Although he was befriended by the governor of 'Unayzah, Doughty's months there were not free from danger; once he was even driven from the town.

Doughty's intention was to accompany the butter caravan to Mecca and then to make his way to the Red Sea port of Juddah from which he would leave Arabia by sea. Even this final section of his journey was far from uneventful. At the last halt before Mecca, Doughty fell into the hands of a fanatical *sharif* – the title given to descendants of Muhammad – who robbed and beat the helpless Doughty until he feared for his life. It was only through the help of the prince of at-Tā'if that Doughty was able to reach Juddah. The prince clothed and fed the explorer, and

conveyed him on his way. At last, "'Rejoice, Khalil!' quoth my *rafiqs*, 'for from the next brow we will show thee Juddah.' – I beheld the white sea gleaming far under the sun, and tall ships riding, and minarets of the town!" It was August 1878 and nearly two years had passed since Doughty had first set foot on Arabian soil.

Doughty returned to England exhausted by the hardships and privations of his Arabian journey. He spent the next 10 years of his life transforming the notes he had made in Arabia into a 1100-page epic, *Travels in Arabia Deserta*. The book was published in 1888, but at the time received remarkably little notice. Certainly, Doughty himself regarded *Arabia Deserta* as less important than the epic poetry with which he occupied the rest of his life. He had published *The Dawn in Britain*, *Adam Cast Forth*, *The Clouds*, and *The Titans* among other poetic works before his death on January 20, 1926 at the age of 82.

History disagrees with Doughty about the relative importance of his literary output. His poetic works are almost forgotten today, but *Arabia Deserta* is recognized as one of the masterpieces of travel literature, a classic of its kind. Doughty used the work not only to record the story of his own travels, adventures, and misadventures in Arabia, but also to convey his feelings for Arabia and the Arabs, bringing both country and people to vivid exuberant life. "To read his *Arabia Deserta*," wrote Sir Percy Sykes, "is to travel with him," and this is in spite of the difficulties of the prose style in which Doughty wrote. He attempted to write what he considered to be pure English, expressed in a direct Elizabethan style which, when he was writing, was about 300 years out of date. The complications of language and expression cannot, however, obscure Doughty's achievement. Later explorers may have done more to clarify the geographical problems of Arabia, but none has given a truer picture of the country to outsiders.

Harry St.John Philby 1885-1960

In the first part of 1932 Harry St. John Philby made a crossing of the scarcely known Rub' al-Khali, the dreaded "Empty Quarter" of Arabia, a desert so fearsome that even the hardy Bedouin hardly dared to enter it. By 1932 Philby had already spent more than 10 years in Arabia as explorer and political adviser, acquiring an immense sympathy for the Arabs which culminated in his conversion to the Islamic faith. His feeling for Arabia greatly eased his journeys

Left: Harry St. John Philby in Arab dress. The British explorer so identified with Arabia that he converted to Islam.

Right: windblown sand dunes in the vast Rub' al-Khali or Empty Quarter of Arabia. To survive in its desolation calls for great endurance in a constant battle.

Below: Abdul Aziz Ibn Sa'ūd in 1911 when he was leading the uprising against the Turks. The photograph was taken by a British officer at Ibn Sa'ūd's camp.

tribes against their Turkish rulers and, in the case of the independent Arab states, to secure Arab cooperation against the Turks.

Political events within Arabia seemed to favor British tactics. A new spirit of Arab nationalism had arisen, promoted by Abdul Aziz Ibn Sa'ūd, ruler of the southern Nejd province. Ibn Sa'ūd's

in the open country, and his explorations helped to open one of the last areas in the world to remain unknown.

Philby's first opportunity to travel in Arabia came about as a direct result of World War I. At that time Arabia was broken up into a number of kingdoms, often at odds with each other. Part of the peninsula even fell within the empire of the Ottoman Turks. Turkey had entered the war on the side of Germany and the weak underbelly of her empire, running down through the Middle East and into Arabia, was obviously of strategic importance. Britain hoped to stir up the Arab

plan was to unite the nomad tribes of Arabia and to drive the Turks from the peninsula. The means he chose was a revival of Muslim fanaticism – a holy war. More than a century earlier, much of Arabia had been briefly united by the fanatical Wahhābiyah movement, which preached a reformation of Islam and a return to the teachings of Muhammad. In the 20th century, Ibn Sa'ūd aimed at nothing less than a revival of the Wahhābiyah sect. Realizing that the Turks would take the first opportunity to destroy his authority – which threatened their Arabian possessions – Ibn Sa'ūd looked to Great Britain for protection. He struck his first blow at the Turks in the first year of the war. In 1916 Britain signed a formal treaty with Ibn Sa'ūd and the following year, to promote further active operations against the Turks, it was decided to send a British mission to Riyadh, Ibn Sa'ūd's capital. At that time St. John Philby was on the staff of the Chief Political Officer to the British Expeditionary Force in Mesopotamia, and when the mission left Baghdad in the autumn of 1917, Philby was in charge.

Philby had taken advantage of his two years of service in Mesopotamia to learn as much as he could about Arabia and Arab life and customs, and to perfect his Arabic. Setting out from Bahrain, he and his companions donned Arab dress. They made the journey to Riyadh safely, surveying the route as they went. In Riyadh,

Below: the oasis near Riyadh. Philby went to Riyadh when it was Ibn Sa'ūd's capital on a mission to help the Arab nationalist leader against the ruling Turks.

Philby had expected to meet an officer representing the British High Commissioner in Egypt, who was to travel to Riyadh via the province of Hejaz. Relations were bad between King Husayn of Hejaz and Ibn Sa'ūd, and Philby heard that Husayn had detained the Englishman on the pretext of the danger of the journey into Nejd. This was not a good sign for getting Husayn and Ibn Sa'ūd to take joint action against the Turks, but Philby decided to cross Arabia to bring back the British representative, and to try to get the two Arab leaders together.

On December 9, 1917 Philby started for the Red Sea port of Juddah. He was accompanied by a picked party of Ibn Sa'ūd's men, and all were mounted on camels. The route they followed was one used by Muslims making the pilgrimage to Mecca, and it enabled Philby to study the topography of the Arabian peninsula. From the poli-

tical viewpoint, however, his mission was totally fruitless because King Husayn refused to cooperate with Ibn Sa'ūd.

In 1918 Philby embarked on a journey of exploration into the unknown southern Nejd. On this journey he traveled deeper into Nejd than any Christian before him. His most southerly landfall was as-Sulayyil in the beautiful Wadi Dawasir where he was told that only seven days' travel would take him to Yemen. He was on the northeastern fringes of the Rub' al-Khali, the great Empty Quarter of southern Arabia where no European had ever penetrated. When Philby was starting across this stretch of desert, the Arabs wept to see their friends going into the "abode of death."

After the war, Philby was given a political appointment putting him in charge of British affairs in Trans-Jordan. This gave him the opportunity for travel and from 1920 to 1922 he made a journey from Amman, Jordan to the

Euphrates. He wanted to investigate the political situation in al-Jawf, an oasis on which Ibn Sa'ūd, who had already annexed Hā'il, had set his sights for conquest. Philby was accompanied on this journey by Major A L Holt, who was examining the possibility of constructing a railway across the desert. Their first attempt to reach al-Jawf ended in failure, but they made a second try in May 1922 and, in spite of the unsettled and often dangerous situation, reached the oasis safely on the 20th of the month. From al-Jawf they decided to cross the desert to Karbalā', where they arrived safely after an adventurous journey. In July, Ibn Sa'ūd took possession of al-Jawf.

After his term in Trans-Jordan, Philby left the British civil service and took a post as adviser to Ibn Sa'ūd. At that period in his life, he also became a convert to the Islamic faith.

For years Philby had dreamed of and prepared for a crossing of the Rub' al-Khali, but the honor of being the first to traverse the hazardous desert was destined not to be his. His plans to make the crossing during the winter of 1930–31 had to be cancelled and Bertram Thomas, an Englishman who was vizier to the Sultan of Muscat, accomplished the first crossing of the desert from south to north that very winter.

Philby's journey into the Rub' al-Khali began on January 7, 1932 at al-Hufūf on the Arabian mainland west of Bahrain. There he joined his party of 19 men, six of them members of the Murra tribe through whose territory the route across the desert lay. For transport the party had 32 camels, carefully chosen and in excellent condition. They crossed the al-Jāfūrah desert to the oasis of Jabrin in weather so cold that every morning before breakfast the waterskins had to be unfrozen. They left Jabrin on January 31, entering the unknown country to the south. Philby hoped that somewhere in the desert he would discover the ruins of the legendary city of

Wabar which, according to the Arabs, had been destroyed by fire from heaven as punishment for its wickedness. Suddenly one day he found himself looking down from a hilltop "not on the ruins of a city, but into the open mouth of what I took to be a volcano with twin craters side by side." Later he wrote, "I scarcely knew whether to laugh or weep." In fact, there were five craters in all at the location, three of them filled with sand. It was later proved that they had been caused by a shower of meteorites, which must have given the impression of heavenly fire in antiquity.

The southernmost point reached by Philby in the Rub' al-Khali was Shanna, from which Bertram Thomas had started his crossing. From there, Philby decided to make the 360-mile trek across the waterless desert to as-Sulayyil in the west. His first attempt ended in failure when the

Above: camels watering at the well of Naifa, photographed by Philby before starting across the waterless desert.

Left: Philby's coffee mill and roaster used in the desert. Coffee was roasted over the campfire.

camels could go no farther, but once the party had rested and revived, Philby decided to make another attempt. Accompanied only by 11 picked men and 15 camels, he headed into the desert on March 5, 1932. They traveled light, carrying only 24 waterskins, some dried camel meat, and a large can of peppermints for Philby to "suck on thirsty days." After six successive days of lengthy marches, the camels were exhausted but the back of the desert had been broken. The party returned to as-Sulayyil on March 15. They had made the journey safely, crossing the Rub' al-Khali from east to west for the first time. It was an adventure, Philby wrote later, "not to be lightly undertaken by the uninitiated." He and his party had accomplished a journey of 1800 miles through almost waterless desert in only 90 days.

Below: Philby's photograph of the wells near as-Sulayyil in 1932. They must have been most welcome to the travelers who had just crossed the waterless Rub' al-Khali.

Philby's last extensive journey in Arabia took place in 1936 when he traveled in the southwest of the peninsula between Mecca and al-Mukallā on the Gulf of Aden.

Chapter 8

The African Challenge

While the adventurous were successfully charting the oceans and exploring new lands elsewhere in the world, the great land mass of Africa obstinately withheld its secrets. The Mediterranean coastline had been known since Roman times. Portuguese mariners and their successors had traced the outline of the continent's southern coasts with reasonable accuracy. A small number of forts and trading posts had been built on the Atlantic and Indian Ocean shores. But the way inland was barred by dense jungle, dangerous rivers, hostile tribes, and vast deserts of burning sand. In the 19th century these barriers began to be breached at last. Exploration centered on three main areas: the Nile and the lake region of eastern Africa, the southern and central parts, and the Niger River and the Sahara Desert. Gradually the geographical problems of each region were unraveled, and the true face of the Dark Continent slowly became clear.

Left: the name of David Livingstone is almost magical in connection with exploration in Africa – though he was preceded and followed by others more adventure-minded and just as motivated. This painting shows Livingstone sailing up the Shire River in his boat the *Ma-Robert*, which is what the Africans called his wife Mary. The artist used the elephant symbolically to stand for the strange sights and potential dangers likely to face all the explorers of the great continent.

The Continent Outlined

The fragmentary knowledge of Africa was reflected in the geographers' maps. These provided detailed and for the most part accurate information concerning the coastlines but the interior, though often impressively crowded with cities and mountains, was almost entirely guesswork. This double standard of accuracy can be seen in the map published by Abraham Ortelius in his atlas *Theatrum Orbis Terrarum*. Ortelius, a Fleming who latinized his name from Ortels, was not himself an explorer but a scholarly craftsman and businessman. He used a great deal from the work of his predecessors, whose names he scrupulously acknowledged; in the first edition of his atlas he listed 87 other cartographers. His map of Africa is both an imaginative interpretation of their achievements and a record of contemporary rumor.

Ortelius' version of the Nile owes much to the Greek geographer Ptolemy and his work of

Above: Ortelius' map of Africa.

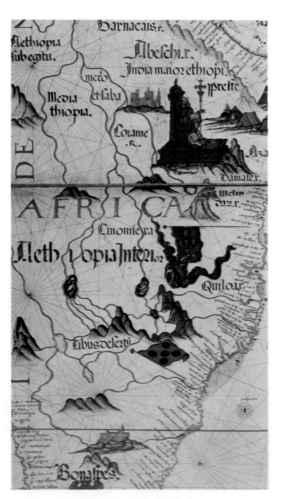

Left: detail from a map showing how well charted the east coast of Africa was after the voyages of Vasco Da Gama and his immediate successors.

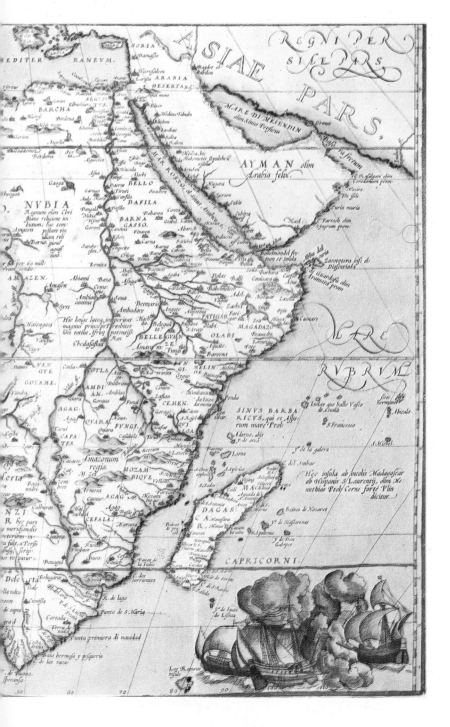

the 2nd century AD. Ptolemy showed the river rising in two lakes far to the south, fed by melting snow from a high range he called the Mountains of the Moon. In Ortelius' map, the Nile also rises in two lakes deep in the interior. The rivers flowing from these lakes join together just north of the equator, and near that he marked the land he believed to be ruled by the legendary Christian king and priest Prester John. Surprisingly, Ortelius omits from his map the great eastward bend of the Nile south of Aswan that had been recorded by Ptolemy.

The lake represented as the source of the westernmost branch of the Upper Nile is shown as the source of two other rivers as well. To the west flows the Zaire, through a region named as the Congo, and to the south flows the Zuama, soon branching into two separate rivers. Here Ortelius seems to have incorporated definite knowledge because the two rivers presumably represent the Zambezi and the Limpopo.

Ortelius gives a totally false impression of the Niger River, showing it flowing from east to west instead of the other way around. After rising close to the equator in a lake also designated as Niger, it flows north and then west past

Above right: a Benin bronze of a warrior. The sculpture of black African civilizations such as the Benin has influenced modern art and sculpture.

Left: a view of the Upper Nile. The source of this great river was not verified until Morton Stanley's African travels of 1876, although John Hanning Speke had made the correct deductions 14 years before.

some imagined towns and others that actually existed – Kano and Tombouctou (Timbuktu). It then enters the Atlantic Ocean through a delta greater than the Nile delta. The true mouth of the Niger, south of Benin, is drawn as a minor river with a different name. Unreliable though it was, the information given in the Ortelius map remained substantially uncorrected for over 250 years. Even in the 1730s the English satirist Jonathan Swift was writing that:

"... geographers, in Afric-maps,
With savage-pictures fill their gaps;
And o'er unhabitable downs
Place elephants for want of towns."

The Arrival
of the Dutch

Below: Jan van Riebeeck, first explorer of southern Africa, meets the Hottentots near Table Bay in 1652. He planted the Dutch flag to claim the territory.

The Portuguese were the first Europeans to reach the southern point of Africa with the landing of Bartholomew Dias at the Cape of Good Hope, which he called the Cape of Storms, in 1488. Disputes with the native Hottentots led to a massacre of Portuguese sailors in Table Bay in 1510, and thereafter the Portuguese took care to sail past the coast without setting foot on it except when driven ashore by bad weather. Even then, they never ventured beyond the low belt of land bordering the coast.

The first explorers of mainland southern Africa were the Dutch. On April 7, 1652 a party of about 90 of them, led by the energetic Jan van Riebeeck, ran up the flag of the Dutch East India Company beside Table Bay. They planned to establish a station for the supply of food, fresh water, vegetables, and firewood to the company's ships sailing between The Netherlands and the East Indies. The crops they planted flourished, but it was not so easy to provide meat. Therefore expeditions were sent inland and along the coast to hunt game and to barter for cattle with the Hottentots. Other than this, the early Dutch settlers were reluctant to go far from their small settlement next to the fortified castle in Table Bay, and knowledge of the interior remained fragmentary.

In 1681 a party of Namaquas, a branch of the Hottentots who lived on the Atlantic seaboard north of the Cape, arrived at the Dutch settlement. They brought with them lumps of very rich copper ore dug out of a mountain near a great river. They also said that beyond the river lived a tall black people unlike themselves. The Dutch governor, Simon van der Stel, saw potential wealth in the copper and wondered whether the place described was Mwanamutapa. For it was believed that beyond a river marked on old maps as Vigiti Magna lay the mysterious land of Mwanamutapa, a region of great wealth ruled over by a black emperor. In the next few years three parties were sent to investigate but had to turn back, unable to cross an inhospitable region turned to desert by years of drought. In August 1685 Van der Stel himself set out with a retinue of 56 Europeans and a number of Hottentot servants equipped with horses, mules, oxen, seven wagons, eight carts, and a coach. There was also a boat to cross the river into the empire of Mwanamutapa – if they found the legendary land.

Their guides led them into steep mountains and swamps where travel was exceedingly difficult. Their wagons overturned in the ravines

Above: copper ore, such as is mined in the mountains of Namaqualand in the African southwest.

Below: the Namaqualand mountains that produce copper. Part of the region is also rich in diamonds.

filled with boulders, or sank to the hubs in the mire. Nevertheless, three months after leaving Table Bay they reached Copper Mountain near the site of modern Springbok, and spent two weeks gathering ore and exploring the surrounding countryside. They spent another month exploring the country between Copper Mountain and the sea, but the coast was barren and fresh water virtually unobtainable, and there was great relief when Van der Stel gave the order to turn homeward. The expedition had accumulated much geographical information even though the "great river," 10 days march beyond the mountain, remained undiscovered, and it had been decided that Copper Mountain was too remote to mine the ore profitably.

As the colony on the Cape grew, the Dutch pushed eastward toward the Indian Ocean. In 1736 a party of Dutch elephant hunters led by Hermanus Hubner crossed the Great Fish and Kei rivers and reached the *Transkei* (beyond the Kei) where the more warlike Xhosa and Bantu nations lived. An official expedition of 1752 made accurate maps and surveys of the eastern Cape, but was prevented from exploring beyond the Kei when Bantu warriors attacked them.

Interest had never died in the great river beyond the Copper Mountain which, though still unvisited, had come to be known as the *Groote* (Big) River. The first European known to have crossed it was the elephant hunter Jacob Coestsee on the search for ivory in 1760. In August 1779 Colonel Robert Jacob Gordon finally reached the long-undiscovered mouth of the Groote River on the South Atlantic and renamed it the Orange in honor of the ruling house of The Netherlands. Gordon later mapped the course of the river from the sea to its confluence with the Vaal 500 miles to the east. It was he who sent the first skin and skeleton of a giraffe back to The Netherlands. By then, other European nations were also becoming increasingly interested in Africa. The dawn of the great age of African exploration was at hand.

Mungo Park
1771-1806

Above: Mungo Park, the man who explored the Niger River at the cost of his life.

The first of the great African rivers to be systematically explored was the Niger, about which almost nothing was known in the late 18th century – neither its source nor its mouth nor even the direction in which it flowed. Ibn-Battūtah, the great Medieval Arab traveler, was one of the few to see the river, having crossed the Sahara from Tangier and reached Timbuktu in 1352. He assumed it to be the Nile or one of its major tributaries. In 1788 the Association for Promoting the Discovery of the Interior Parts of Africa was founded in London by Sir Joseph Banks, the most eminent British scientist of the day and an experienced traveler who had explored the Pacific with Captain Cook. The Association decided to make the mysterious Niger the first object of their research.

The first explorer recruited by Banks was John Ledyard, an American who had also sailed with Captain Cook. He made first for Egypt to find a caravan that would take him across the desert to Timbuktu, but in Cairo he fell ill with dysentery and died. The Association's next recruit was Major Daniel Houghton, a British Army officer who, instead of attempting the Sahara crossing, landed at the mouth of the

Right: a pocket sextant dating from about 1800 and probably similar to that carried by Park.

Below: Park surrounded by African Muslim women of Benown, where he was held captive. They were particularly curious about his white color.

Gambia River and started east. He thought the journey to Timbuktu would take him about a month. After sending two letters back to England, he disappeared without trace. The Association believed that the large amount of merchandise carried by Houghton had prompted robbery and murder, and it decided that Houghton's successor would have to be "a traveler of good temper and conciliatory manner, who has nothing with him to tempt rapacity." It was not until 1794 that a suitable candidate offered his services. It was Mungo Park.

Park was a 23-year-old Scottish surgeon who had just returned from a journey to Sumatra on a ship of the East India Company. There he had discovered eight new species of fish, and on his

return to London he published a description of them in a scientific journal. This article brought him to the attention of Banks who suggested to the African Association that he was their man for the Niger exploration. Park accepted the offer at once and sailed from England in May 1795, arriving at the small trading village of Pisania on the Gambia River in July. A severe attack of fever confined him to his house for several months, but by the end of the year he had learned the Mandingo language, the common tongue in that part of Africa, and had collected extensive information about the regions he was to visit.

In December 1795 Park set out for the interior of Africa. With him went a former black slave named Johnson and a slave boy who was promised his freedom if he behaved well. Park rode a horse while the other two rode donkeys. They carried few provisions – food for two days, beads, amber, and tobacco for bartering, a compass and pocket sextant, a thermometer, some firearms, and an umbrella.

After three days he entered the country of a local king who urged him to go no further. The tribesmen farther east had never seen a white man, he said, and would certainly kill him. Park thanked the king for his warning but expressed his determination to proceed. Within a few days he was surrounded by the horsemen of another king and robbed of half his goods. Elsewhere he was more fortunate. In fact, the whiteness of his skin and the size of his nose excited much interest among the women who insisted that he must have been dipped in milk as an infant and had his nose pinched daily to lengthen it. Wherever he went the people found it hard to believe that he was traveling not as a spy nor for reasons of trade but out of curiosity.

When Park and his companions approached Muslim country, their situation became increasingly perilous. Near the village of Simbing he was shown the spot where a party of Muslims had robbed Daniel Houghton of all his possessions and left him to die. (In his journal Park used Moors to describe all non-black Muslims.) Shortly after, Park himself was captured and taken to a chief in Benown on the edge of the desert. There he was treated with great harshness and, much to his distress, the slave boy whose loyalty had earned him his freedom was taken from him and resold into slavery. After

three very unpleasant months, Park resolved to escape from his captors. Shortly before dawn one morning he stepped over his sleeping guards and slipped away unseen. In his journal he recorded: "I had not one single bead, nor any other article of value in my possession, to purchase victuals for myself, or corn for my horse."

He nearly perished from starvation and thirst before making his way to the relative safety of non-Muslim country, where he had the good fortune to meet a party of refugees who were making their way to the flourishing market town of Ségou on the Niger. For two weeks he traveled in their company. On July 20, 1796, nearly eight months after leaving the Gambia, he approached the outskirts of the town and was able to write: "I saw with infinite pleasure the great object of my mission – the long sought for majestic Niger, glittering to the morning sun, as broad as the Thames at Westminster, and flowing slowly *to the eastward.*"

Park waited several days at Ségou, hoping in vain to visit the ruler of the area, King Mansong of Bambarra. Finally the king sent him the generous present of 5000 cowries, a sum of money that could purchase 50 days provisions

Below: Park catches his first sight of the Niger River, an illustration from his book *Travels in the Interior of Africa.*

for Park and corn for his horse. Park interpreted this as a wish to speed him on his way out of Mansong's kingdom. After leaving Ségou, Park followed the north bank of the Niger downstream for six days until he reached the town of Silla. There he realized he could travel no further. The tropical rains were causing widespread flooding, he was feverish and in constant torment from the swarms of mosquitoes, and more serious still, he was approaching land ruled by the Muslims. After his experience in Benown,

Right: a view of the Niger at sunset. Park first saw it in the light of the morning sun.

Left: at one point in his journey Park was robbed and left alone to his fate. Fortunately, he retained his hat in which he had secreted his irreplaceable notes, and he made his way to safety.

Below: an engraving of a West African village made from a sketch of Park's. The bearded figure was added by the engraver, probably to represent Park himself.

Park dreaded falling into their hands again. So at the end of July he began his return journey.

After a month of uneventful travel he was attacked by robbers who stripped him of everything he possessed except for his shirt, his trousers, and his hat, in the crown of which he had concealed his notes. In September he fell seriously ill with fever at the small town of

started to suffer from the inevitable dysentery and malaria. Still Park pressed forward. Those who became too ill to keep up with the rest were left behind to die. Only 10 were still alive when the Niger was reached at Bamako in August 1805.

From there the much reduced party traveled downstream to Sansanding where Park managed to build a large boat by breaking up two big canoes of local style. The HMS *Joliba*, the local name for the Niger, was 40 feet long and six feet wide, and was equipped with an awning of bullock hides to protect those on board from the spears of tribesmen on the banks. On this boat Park proposed to sail down the Niger to the sea and in a last letter to his wife, dated November 19, 1805, he wrote that "the sails are hoisting for our departure to the coast." His party of Europeans by then consisted only of himself, the lieutenant, and three soldiers, one of whom was crazy.

For more than five years nothing more was heard of Park's party. In 1810 the Mandingo guide who had brought Park's letters back to the Gambia was sent out to discover what had happened to him. He succeeded in finding the interpreter who had accompanied Park from Sansanding and traveled with him beyond Timbuktu down the Niger as far as the Falls of Bussa in modern Nigeria. According to the interpreter's account, the rapids were impassable because it was the season of low water (March or April 1806) and the boat jammed in the rocks. The party was then attacked by the tribesmen of

Kamalia and was only saved through the kindness of a slave dealer. He remained there for seven months before starting for Pisania with a slave caravan. He reached it 18 months later.

Back in London, Park wrote an account of his travels and became famous on its publication in 1799. He returned to Scotland and married but longed to go back to Africa to complete his exploration of the Niger. In 1804 the British government, anxious to establish a commercial foothold in western Africa, invited him to lead an expedition and gave him the rank and pay of an army captain. His departure was postponed again and again, so Park did not reach the Gambia until May 1805 at the height of the hot season and with the rains imminent. His party of 44 Europeans included his brother-in-law, an army lieutenant, and 30 soldiers unsuitably clad in the red coats then worn by the British Army on active duty. Park would have been wiser to delay departure until the rainy season was over, but he was anxious to begin. Three weeks out from Pisania the rains began and the soldiers

Above: the falls near the town of Bussa where Park and his expedition met their end.

a local king who had not received the present sent to him by Park. Greatly outnumbered, the entire remaining party jumped from the boat and all were drowned.

With a little more luck the *Joliba* might have sailed on to reach the sea. Although this final success eluded Park, his two journeys into the African interior and his description of the physical features and customs of the regions hold a firm place in the history of exploration.

René Caillié 1799-1838

Timbuktu, legendary city of fabulous wealth, drew explorers like a magnet. The first to reach the city was a young Scotsman, Alexander Laing, who had spent a year on a gruelling crossing of the Sahara before entering Timbuktu in August 1826. By the time he got there, however, the grandeur of the city was a thing of the past. Furthermore, Laing may hold the honor of being the first explorer to set foot in Timbuktu, but his letters are the only record of his achievement. Three nights after leaving the city for the hazardous return journey he was murdered by the sheik in charge of the caravan in which he was traveling.

The first European to make the journey to

Above: Alexander Laing, the first to reach Timbuktu, died by violence on his return journey.

Left: René Caillié not only visited Timbuktu, but also returned alive. He had difficulty proving that he had completed the hazardous adventure.

Timbuktu and return alive was the 27-year-old Frenchman René-Auguste Caillié. The son of a drunken baker who had died in prison, Caillié had been fascinated by stories of travel almost as soon as he had been able to read. When he was 16 he got a job as a servant on a French ship sailing to Senegal, where he joined several small expeditions and read Mungo Park's account of his first journey to the Niger River. This strengthened his desire to explore the interior of Africa himself, and when the French Geo-

Above: Caillié in Arab dress. His disguise did not always work, but he was generally lucky enough to meet with kindness.

Right: Koran boards of the kind studied by Caillié in preparation for passing himself off as a Muslim. He spent nine months learning the Koran, the Arabic language, and Arab and African customs.

graphical Society announced a monetary prize to the first European to reach Timbuktu and return, Caillié wrote, "Dead or alive, the prize shall be mine."

The many tales of Muslim hostility toward European travelers made him decide to travel as a Muslim, and in preparation he lived among the Braknas, a primitive tribe of Muslim nomads on the banks of the Senegal river, for nine months. He studied the Koran and learned to speak Arabic. Unlike almost all other explorers, Caillié received no assistance from his country, financing his expedition from his own meager savings. In March 1827 he arrived at the estuary of the Rio Nuñez between Senegal and Sierra Leone. Dressed as an Arab, he told his guides and companions that he had been born in Egypt, that he had there been captured by the French, and that he was on his way to make the pilgrimage to Mecca and seek his family. Accompanied by a slave to carry his small bundle of luggage, he joined a salt caravan and started on his 3000 mile walk across Africa.

In June the caravan reached the Niger at Kouroussa and Caillié joined another that would take him on to Djenné. Though he scrupulously played the part of a devout Muslim, his paler complexion sometimes aroused the suspicions of his fellow travelers. But his courage and resourcefulness always succeeded in convincing doubters. In general he was treated with great kindness. When he collapsed with malaria and then scurvy in the town of Tieme, his life was saved by an old black woman who nursed him for five months.

In March 1828 he at last reached Djenné, which was situated on a tributary of the Niger, and boarded a boat for Timbuktu. The heat was appalling and Caillié was forced to travel with the slaves in cramped conditions below decks. After a 500-mile voyage of great discomfort, he caught sight of Kabara, the port of Timbuktu. His first glimpse of the city of Timbuktu that evening proved to be an anticlimax. There were

no palaces, no golden domes. He wrote: " ... the city presented, at first view, nothing but a mass of ill-looking houses, built of earth. Nothing was to be seen in all directions but immense plains of quicksand of a yellowish-white color. The sky was a pale red as far as the horizon; all nature wore a dreary aspect, and the most profound silence prevailed; not even the warbling of a

Above: a waterhole in Timbuktu. Far from being the fabulous city of legend, the town Laing and Caillié saw was small and insignificant.

Below: the dig for Laing's remains. In 1910, 84 years after the Scotsman had been killed, an official inquiry was made. As a result, Laing's grave was found.

bird was to be heard."

Caillié was staying opposite the house where the unfortunate Laing had stayed, and he made what inquiries he could about Laing's death without arousing suspicion. After remaining in Timbuktu for two weeks, he left on May 4 for Morocco with a caravan of 1200 animals. Four days out from Timbuktu the scene of Laing's murder was pointed out to him.

In his journey across the Sahara, Caillié endured all the horrors of desert heat. Temperatures reached 160°F (70°C), and he experienced such thirst that he could think of nothing but water. His disguise seemed to be slipping, perhaps because of his stress, and he was terrified when the others said that he looked like a Christian because it made him recall Laing's death. When the the caravan finally reached the Atlas Mountains, Caillié was six weeks more making his way across them through Fez and Rabat to reach Tangier where he could ask for help from the French Consul.

He did not find it easy to prove to the French authorities that a young man without any financial or scientific backing had really been to Timbuktu, and a special commission was set up to consider his claim. It found in his favor and he was awarded the prize back in France.

Heinrich Barth
1821-1865

In the 50 years that followed René-Auguste Caillié's pioneering journey to Timbuktu and back, a succession of other travelers tried to cross the Sahara to the cities on the southern fringe of the desert. Most of those who went never returned. Of about 200 who attempted the journey, 165 died from starvation or disease or were killed by the Tuareg. The Tuareg were fanatical Muslims who attacked many explorers simply because they were Christians. In other cases travelers' deaths were instigated by powerful Arab merchants, who were worried that their monopoly of the caravan routes across the desert would be broken if Europeans were allowed to interfere.

European merchants were certainly interested in the possibilities for trade in that part of Africa, but there was also a desire in Europe to find out more about the slave trade across the Sahara. It was to investigate slave trading that the Englishman James Richardson was assigned by a British Bible Society when he left Tripoli in August 1845. Traveling openly as a Christian, he journeyed southwest to the oasis of Ghudāmis, and then 400 miles due south to the small town of Ghāt. He was warmly welcomed by the local sultan who presented him with gifts to take back to Queen Victoria, and after recording details of the slave traffic, Richardson set out on the return journey to the Mediterranean. His

Right: Tuareg tribesmen, drawn in 1821. The fierce Tuareg roamed the Sahara, a danger to travelers crossing the desert on their way to reach Timbuktu.

Below: an engraving of black slaves and their Arab captors. As repelled as Caillié and other travelers often were by the bestial treatment of the blacks, they just as often were compelled to take help from the slave traders.

exploration had been a limited one in that he had penetrated only 700 miles into the Sahara, but the published account of his travels aroused great interest in London. In particular, his description of the cruelty of the slave traders stirred up strong feelings in Britain.

A few years later the British government appointed Richardson to lead an expedition to explore the great caravan routes extending south from Tripoli across the Sahara to the inhabited regions in the far south. Richardson wanted his team to contain men with a more scientific approach to exploration than some of the romantic adventurers of the past. The Prussian ambassador in London suggested to him the name of Heinrich Barth, a young German who had already had experience of exploration in North Africa, having traveled from Rabat, Morocco the length of the Mediterranean coastline as far as Alexandria. Barth had studied archaeology, geography, history, and law at the University of Berlin, and had also spent some time in London learning Arabic. He seemed an ideal companion and Richardson asked him to join his expedition. Barth eagerly accepted. During his travels in North Africa he had often cast a wistful look at the unknown or little-known regions in the interior. Once in Tunis he had spoken to a Hausa slave from the great city of Kano, now in modern Nigeria, who on seeing the interest Barth took in his native country said, "Please God, you shall go and visit Kano." The words had rung in Barth's ears ever since,

Above: a drawing of Ghāt by Heinrich Barth. He devoted five years to travel and study of the southern fringe of the Sahara between Lake Chad and Timbuktu.

and Richardson's expedition offered the opportunity he had long desired. The third member of the party was another young German, a geologist named Adolf Overweg, who had had no previous experience of desert travel.

The expedition that left Tripoli in March 1850 appears to have been the best organized and equipped ever to have ventured across the Sahara. In addition to the usual retinue of guides and servants, the three Europeans took with them great quantities of stores, equipment, scientific instruments, and a large wooden boat in which they planned to explore Lake Chad. The boat was in four sections to make it easier to carry, although Barth recorded in his journal that the camel found the long oars and poles most awkward to carry. Barth meticulously recorded and made frequent sketches of everything that attracted his attention.

Unfortunately for the harmony of the expedition, Richardson and Barth soon developed an intense personal dislike for each other. From the day the party left Tripoli it was split into distinct national groups. The two Germans rode ahead, followed at a considerable distance by Richardson and a British sailor who had been sent along to manage the boat. At night the two groups and their servants ate and slept in separate camps.

Barth comments briefly that the choice of the sailor was "unfortunate" and Richardson must have agreed because he decided to send him back from Marzūq. In this desert settlement they had to wait five weeks while negotiating safe

conducts to Ghāt, the next town on their route and the farthest point reached by Richardson on his previous journey. Similar negotiations and the inevitable distribution of presents later delayed them at all stages of their travels. A few days out from Ghāt, Barth decided to climb the mysterious Mount Idinen, believed by the Tuareg to be inhabited by demons. He reached the bare summit of the mountain but was so exhausted and thirsty that, by the time he made his descent, he had drunk all the water he had with him. He then lost his way and eventually fell to the ground in a state of semiconsciousness. On regaining his senses, he managed to prevent himself from panic, and cut open one of his

Right: an ancient rock painting of cows grazing in the Tassili region of Algeria shows that the Sahara was not always a desert.

veins to quench his thirst by drinking his own blood. A Tuareg found him and helped him to get back to the expedition. He was able to proceed the next morning and had a quick recovery, even though he could eat scarcely anything for three days.

From Ghāt the travelers made their way through the Tassili-n-Ajjer where, nearly a century later, thousands of Neolithic rock paintings were discovered. Barth himself saw rock carvings of bulls and buffaloes which led him to conjecture that at one time they were common

205

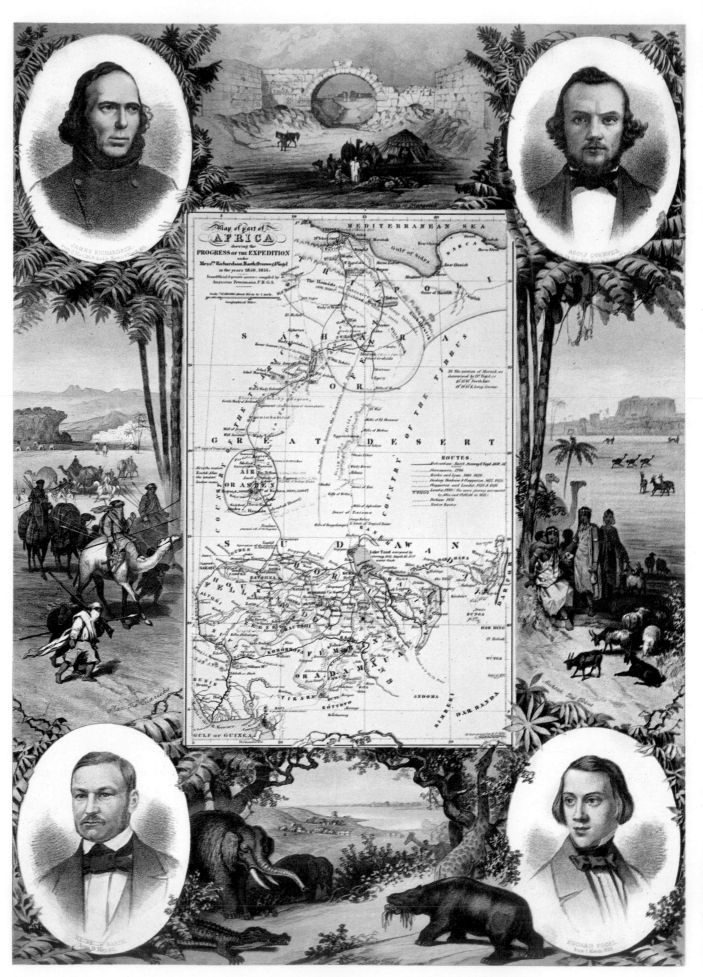

animals in a region where only the camel then survived. After passing through the Air Mountains, Barth took himself off from his companions to visit the ancient city of Agadez, in decline after once having been one of the great commercial centers of the Sahara. Barth stayed there a month, recording the history of the region and the customs of the people. He was fortunate enough to watch the installation of the new sultan from the seclusion of an upper terrace. Perhaps because of his happy experience in Agadez, Barth and his companions agreed to go their separate ways. Richardson headed directly for Lake Chad, and the Germans explored two more westerly routes to the lake. On February 2, 1851 Barth at last entered Kano and found it a rich and flourishing city of about 30,000 people. He made copious notes on the kind of European goods that would be welcomed in this part of Africa, urging speed because American slave dealers, in their drive to obtain large supplies of slaves, were inundating the whole of Central Africa with American merchandise.

The three explorers had arranged to meet at Kukawa on the western shores of Lake Chad in April, but Richardson never kept the rendezvous. Three weeks before Barth arrived at Kukawa, Richardson died of malaria. When Overweg arrived, he was also suffering from malaria but he recovered sufficiently to explore Lake Chad in the boat they had brought. Barth explored the territory to the south and east of the lake. When the British government heard of the death of Richardson, they appointed Barth as the new leader of the expedition. Before the two men could start on their next objective of visiting Timbuktu, Overweg collapsed with malaria

Above: another drawing by Barth, this one of the town of Kano. When he arrived there in 1851, it was an important city open to trade.

Opposite: a map of Africa made in 1854 with the routes and portraits of four well-known African travelers. Barth is in the lower left, James Richardson in the upper left, Adolf Overweg in the upper right, and Edward Vogel in the lower right.

Below: a drawing of the Chad area based on the reports of Vogel. His description of the vegetation was highly imaginative.

again. With his last remnant of energy he crawled from his bed to lie beside the boat on which he had traveled the lake, and there he died. He was only 29.

Barth had also suffered many attacks of dysentery and malaria but he was determined to go on. His journey westward to Timbuktu, which he had expected to take him about two years, was accomplished in 10 months. He was fortunate in his dealings with the local tribesmen and he attributed his luck to the incident in which, surrounded by a particularly hostile group of townspeople, he had fired off six rounds from his revolver into the air. In his journal he says that this show of force led to his future safety because the Africans were afraid of his power. They believed he had guns hidden in all his pockets and could fire them whenever he wished.

In September 1853 Barth became the first European to enter Timbuktu since Caillié had 25 years before. The city's prosperity had slightly recovered but still did not equal that of Kano or even Agadez. In March 1854 he started down the Niger River to return to Lake Chad, and on the way he learned that a party of Europeans had already arrived there to look for him. This expedition was led by Edward Vogel, who explained to Barth that people in London had given him up for dead.

Vogel decided to stay in Africa, and was murdered two years later on his way to the Nile. Barth decided that after five years of ceaseless exploration, he must return to Europe with his invaluable store of information. In May 1855 he began the crossing of the desert along a caravan route to the east of his southern journey. In spite of the fact that it was the hottest time of the year, he managed to get to Tripoli and from there to London, which he reached in September.

The expedition of 1850–1855 was a triumphant success. Despite the discomfort and dangers, Barth's single-minded determination carried him through. He was the first man to make reliable maps of huge areas of Africa, and the first to study the customs of the blacks he met in detail. No one before him had accomplished so much.

Richard Burton
1821-1890

Africa was a land of many mysteries, but its greatest mystery for many years was the source of the Nile River. For over 2000 years people had wondered at the miracle that each September brought the life-giving floods to the land of Egypt. The floods had never been known to fail – but where did such quantities of water come from?

In the 1st century AD a Greek merchant named Diogenes had claimed to have landed on the east coast of Africa in present-day Tanzania, and after a 25-day journey inland had arrived "in the vicinity of two great lakes, and the snowy range

Tana in the northern highlands of Ethiopia and were told that it was the source of the Blue Nile. The Scottish explorer James Bruce confirmed their findings in 1770, but his belief that he had seen the long dreamed-of source of the Nile was mistaken. The source of the Nile is considered to be the point at which the White Nile, the longer of the two branches, rises.

The first real information concerning the possible source of the White Nile came from two German missionaries working in East Africa in the area where Diogenes may have landed 1800 years before. In 1848 Johann Rebmann caught sight of the snow-covered peak of Mount Kilimanjaro, Africa's highest mountain, and the following year his colleague Johann Krapf became the first European to see Mount Kenya. Believing these might be Ptolemy's "Mountains of the Moon," they questioned ivory traders about any lakes in the vicinity. They learned that there were two lakes, really great inland seas, and beyond them a range of mountains. The two missionaries sent a report to the Royal Geographical Society in London, which raised money for an expedition to explore the region in 1856. Its leader was instructed to "penetrate inland from some place on the east coast and make the best of your way to the reputed great lake of the interior."

The man selected to lead the expedition was Richard Francis Burton, at 35 already a celebrated Oriental scholar and linguist. Burton had mastered half a dozen languages before he was 18 and later became fluent in 29. Flamboyant, hottempered, fearless, and proud, he was a natural rebel. After being expelled from Oxford University, he joined the army and spent seven years in India. While in the service of army intelligence, he started to wear Indian dress and stained

Left: Richard Burton, whose sense of the dramatic and air of flamboyance is caught in this portrait of 1876.

Below: the fez that Burton wore. He particularly liked to dress up in local costume and pass himself off as a native.

of mountains whence the Nile draws its twin sources." This fact, if fact it was, was included by Ptolemy in his great map of the world, and for hundreds of years represented all that was known concerning the source of the Nile.

In its upper reaches the Nile is really two rivers that join at Khartoum to flow together to the sea. These two branches are known as the White Nile and the Blue Nile from the color of the waters, although the White Nile is more a muddy gray and the Blue Nile, laden with sediment from the mountains of Ethiopia, is more a brownish-green. In the 1600s some Portuguese missionaries at the Ethiopian court visited Lake

his face with walnut juice in order to pass as an Indian. In 1853, disguised as a Muslim holy man, he visited Mecca, which was still forbidden to non-Muslims. Two years later he reached the Ethiopian city of Harar, another "forbidden holy city." His companion on this daring journey was the army lieutenant, John Hanning Speke, whom he also invited to join the Nile expedition. Speke immediately agreed and in 1856 the two men sailed to East Africa to put their expedition together. Almost immediately both were struck down with malaria, the curse of all the African explorers, but on June 16, 1857 they left Zanzibar and crossed over to the main-

land. They were accompanied by about 130 porters, 30 donkeys, and trade goods to last for two years.

The expedition struck westward from the coast along the slavers' route to what the Arabs called the Sea of Ujiji. Covering about 10 miles a day, they were beset by the usual troubles of flooded rivers, dying animals, deserting porters, and shortage of food. Burton and Speke were both constantly ill. By August they were almost

deaf from ear infections and, too weak to walk, could barely sit on their donkeys. Not until November did they reach Kazé (modern Tabora) some 500 miles inland, an Arab oasis of civilization for all its dependence on the slave trade.

A week later the two explorers left Kazé for the desolate wilderness further west. Soon after Burton was struck by a paralysis that crippled him for over a year and Speke went almost totally blind. They kept on in spite of all their infirmities and on February 13, 1858 climbed a hill so steep that it killed Speke's donkey. Burton, who was more than half blind himself by then, asked of his guide, "What is that sheet of light that lies below?" "That is *the* water," his guide replied, "the Sea of Ujiji". The first Europeans to reach its shore, Burton and Speke could scarcely see it.

The discovery of the vast Sea of Ujiji – now called Lake Tanganyika – was a major triumph, but Burton's next endeavor ended in disappointment. He hoped that the Ruzizi River, described by the Arabs as flowing out of the lake on the north, might prove to be a part of the Nile river system and so make the lake the source of the great stream. However, when he and Speke arrived at the northernmost trading post on the lake, they learned from Arabs living in the area that the Ruzizi River flows into rather than out of the lake. "I felt sick at heart," wrote Burton of his dashed hopes.

The two explorers were unable to verify this for themselves because the crew, terrified of cannibals, refused to go any farther and they were too ill to insist. In June 1858 they were back at Kazé, Burton still semiparalyzed and Speke nearly deaf from painful abscesses in his ears. Then occurred the incident that led to bitter disputes between the two men – and ultimately to Speke's death. While Burton rested with his Arab friends in Kazé, Speke set off to investigate reports of another great lake to the north, the Nyanza.

After a surprisingly easy journey of 16 days, Speke reached the shore of the lake on August 3,

Below: an engraving of Ujiji made from a photograph by Morton Stanley. It appeared more than 12 years after Burton and Speke saw it.

Bottom: sunset on Lake Victoria, named for the queen of Britain.

1858 and saw the immense stretch of water that a local tribesman said "probably extended to the end of the world." In a flash of inspiration Speke decided that he had found "the fountainhead of that mighty stream . . . the Nile." He named the lake Victoria after the British queen and returned to Kazé with the news. Burton greeted his claim coldly, refusing to believe it. He later wrote, "the fortunate discoverer's conviction was

strong, his reasons weak." On the return journey the relationship of the two men was strained and they avoided any mention of the lake. When Speke arrived in London 12 days ahead of Burton, however, he lost no time in acquainting the president of the Royal Geographical Society with his discovery of the source of the Nile. By the time Burton arrived, Speke had already lectured to the Society and become a popular

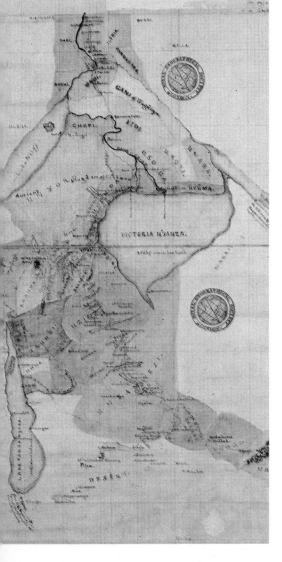

hero. The two men's joint discovery of Lake Tanganyika was almost ignored.

In the spring of 1860 Speke went to Africa again, this time with Captain James Augustus Grant, an amiable young brother officer who proved to be an admirable traveling companion. From Zanzibar they proceeded once more to Kazé and then up the western side of Lake Victoria to find the spot where, Speke was convinced, the Nile issued from the lake. The inevitable attacks of sickness laid both men low, Grant suffering for four months in a remote village while Speke tried without success to round up some porters. The two had to leave in separate parties and Grant's group was attacked and robbed. Together again in Karagwe, they

Below: James Augustus Grant, the army officer who accompanied Speke on his second trip to Africa. Grant made many watercolors of the places they visited.

Left: Grant's map of his and Speke's journey. There was one gap in it which fed the controversy between supporters of Burton and those of Speke.

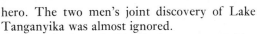

Below: Mutesa's palace, today preserved as a national monument.

spent a month at some ease with the king, though Grant was painfully ill again. Before they could reach the lake, the expedition had to go through Buganda whose ruler, Mutesa, was a young tyrant. His capital, located on the present-day site of Kampala, astonished the Europeans. "The whole brow and sides of the hill were covered with gigantic grass huts, thatched as neatly as so many heads dressed by a London barber, and fenced all round with tall yellow reeds," Speke wrote.

At first Speke had difficulty with Mutesa, partly because he would not grovel before the young king, and he was detained for five months in negotiations for guides and porters to take his party to Gondokoro. He was finally able to leave on July 7, 1862.

On July 28, 1862 Speke at last stood beside a great waterfall about 40 miles east of Mutesa's capital. He gazed entranced as the waters of the lake flowed like a broad tidal wave northward into a river. He knew that his flash of inspiration on the southern shore of the lake had been proved right. Unfortunately, warring tribesmen prevented him from following the river's course downstream. For two months Speke and Grant had to march overland before reaching Gondokoro, unmistakably on the Upper Nile. This gap on the map gave Burton his chance for revenge. Speke had not proved that the river flowing out of Lake Victoria became the Nile. Geographers were divided into rival camps, some believing Speke had found the source, others supporting Burton's counterclaim that the Nile originated in another river flowing out of Lake Tanganyika. Finally, it was arranged for the two rivals to confront one another at a public meeting in the resort city of Bath, England. But on September 16, 1864, the morning of the meeting, Speke went out to shoot partridges and, in climbing over a low wall, shot himself fatally in the chest.

In spite of the official verdict that the death was accidental, many people wondered whether it had been suicide. Was Speke afraid to debate with the more experienced, fluent, and brilliant Burton? If so, there was a terrible irony in his death – for he was right and Burton was wrong.

David Livingstone 1813-1873

The 19th-century explorer needed to possess an iron constitution and immense strength of character to survive, especially in Africa. Travel required the capacity to endure fearful extremes of heat and drought, physical danger from warring tribes, repeated disappointments, betrayals, and the ravages of tropical disease. The wish to free the African people from the terrible scourge of the slave trade was a professed desire of many of the explorers, yet this noble aim was linked to an intense longing for personal fame and, often, a harsh insensitivity to the weaknesses of others.

No explorer exhibited these contrasts more sharply than David Livingstone, the poor Scottish boy who succeeded in becoming a doctor and, as a medical missionary, spent most of the last 30 years of his life in solitary wandering

through the heart of Africa. Revered by the late-Victorian English as a saintly hero who sacrificed himself for love of the African, his reputation has been somewhat dented in recent years by disclosures that at crucial periods of his life he behaved in a mean-spirited way that was only all too human. But to his contemporaries, the force of his personality and the scale of his achievements obscured the inconsistencies of his character. To them he seemed the perfect embodiment of an African explorer.

Livingstone was born near Glasgow on March 19, 1813, the son of a traveling tea merchant. The family was poor, and at the age of 10 David started to work in a local cotton mill.

Below: the Kalahari Desert showing a dried-up salt pan. When Livingstone saw one, he thought he had found the water he so badly needed because the sun made the white incrustations so shimmery.

Below left: David Livingstone in 1864. A man of tremendous determination and piety, he became one of the most famous African travelers of all time.

After a 12-hour day he studied for two hours at night school, and when the school was forced to close, he continued his studies at work by "placing the book on a portion of the spinning jenny, so that I could catch sentence after sentence as I went by." In this way he taught himself Latin, Greek, and mathematics, and later gained university admittance to study medicine and theology in Glasgow.

A deep and undoubting religious faith formed the basis of Livingstone's character. It was expressed by a practical aim: he wanted to become a missionary as well as a doctor. After gaining his medical degree he approached the London Missionary Society and was ordained.

On March 15, 1841, four days short of his 28th birthday, David Livingstone stepped onto African soil at Cape Town for the first time. A 700-mile journey from the coast by ox wagon took him to Kuruman, a mission among the Batswana people. It was headed by Dr Robert Moffat, a missionary who had worked in South Africa for 25 years. From there he moved farther north to find a place for a new mission station, and while traveling along the fringe of the Kalahari Desert, he preached his first sermon to the Bakaa, a tribe that had recently murdered four Europeans. They caused Livingstone no

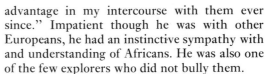

advantage in my intercourse with them ever since." Impatient though he was with other Europeans, he had an instinctive sympathy with and understanding of Africans. He was also one of the few explorers who did not bully them.

In 1843 Livingstone established his mission station in Mabotsa 220 miles north of Kuruman, and it was there that he was attacked and almost killed by a lion. He owed his life to a companion who distracted the lion's attention, and also to the fact that he was wearing a tartan jacket that wiped off all the virus from the lion's teeth before they pierced his flesh. He never fully regained the use of his left arm, which he was unable to lift above his shoulder.

Livingstone returned to Kuruman to recover and fell in love with Mary Moffat, daughter of the mission head. They were married in 1845. Converts at the mission were few and Livingstone proposed a scheme for training African evangelists. This sensible idea was turned down by his colleagues and by the London directors of the mission who at that time considered him too impulsive and secretive. In 1847 he moved his wife and young family to Kolobeng on the eastern edge of the Kalahari Desert, but after two years there he felt the need to go even farther afield. The Boers were encroaching upon

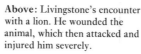

trouble, which convinced him that he would succeed in Africa where others had failed. "In order to obtain an accurate knowledge of the language, I cut myself off from all European society for about six months, and gained by this ordeal an insight into the habits, ways of thinking, laws, and language of the Botswana [Batswana] people which proved of incalculable

Above: Livingstone's encounter with a lion. He wounded the animal, which then attacked and injured him severely.

Above: a jungle village in which Livingstone was received with great friendliness and welcome.

them from the south; north lay the arid waste of the Kalahari which no European had ever crossed. But to the north of the desert was Lake Ngami, known by reputation to Europeans but never seen by them. Beyond the lake lived the Makololo, a Batswana tribe ruled over by Sebituane, a respected chief. Livingstone hoped that he could find a healthy site, build a church, a house, and a school, and bring his family to live there. They would then be safe from the Boers whose cattle could not cross the waterless Kalahari. In this way, Livingstone's ambitions as a missionary led him to become an explorer.

Livingstone was still a poor man but the problem of how to equip a desert expedition was solved by the arrival of Captain Cotton Oswell, a well-to-do young hunter who had already explored one of the tributaries of the Limpopo

River. He presented Livingstone with a wagon and paid for all the supplies. On June 1, 1849 Livingstone, Oswell, another Englishman named Mungo Murray, and a guide started across the Kalahari for Lake Ngami. The expedition of 80 oxen, 20 horses, and 30 or 40 men faced a journey of about 600 miles. Before long they found themselves struggling through a sea of soft white sand. The wagons sank to the wheel hubs and at the end of the day there was nothing for the animals to eat but "grass so dry as to crumble into powder in the hands." The guide advised them to dig deep in the sand for water. By nightfall they had dug far enough to give all the horses a sip. The oxen had to wait two more days before four pits had been opened to a depth of nine feet, enough to give all the animals a good drink. Soon after this their guide lost his way, and everyone would have perished had Oswell not caught sight of a Bushman woman running away. He caught her and, persuading her to help, she led him to a large pool eight miles away. It saved their lives. At last they reached a hitherto unknown river, the Zouga (now Botletle) and followed it for 280 miles to the lake. "None save those who have suffered from the want, know the beauty of water," wrote Oswell. "A magnificent sheet without bound that we could see, gladdened our eyes."

The Makololo lived another 200 miles to the north. The three explorers felt they could not make this journey and returned to Kolobeng. Livingstone lost no time in sending an account of the exploration back to London where it was read at a meeting of the Royal Geographical Society. He barely mentioned Oswell and Murray.

In 1850 Livingstone crossed the desert again, this time taking with him his pregnant wife and three small children. They followed the Zouga "with great labour, having to cut down trees to allow the wagons to pass." They lost some oxen that fell into pits dug by local tribesmen to catch game. They were attacked by tsetse flies,

carrier of the parasites that cause sleeping sickness, and two of the children caught malaria from the porters. Oswell, who was exploring Lake Ngami independently, came to their aid and escorted them back to Kolobeng where Mary Livingstone gave birth to a daughter. Almost immediately the baby caught a fever from her elder brother or sister and died in agony at six weeks of age. Her screams are said to have haunted Livingstone for a long time.

However, soon after this he wrote, "I mean to follow a useful motto and *try again*." Against the protests of the Moffats he once more took his wife, who was pregnant again, and his surviving children across the wilderness of the Kalahari. This was to be the most important of his early explorations, and once again he was accompanied by the loyal Oswell, a man who seems to have had no desire for personal fame and was happy to take a back seat.

This time they took a different route, only to find the hardships more severe than before. Oswell was an expert shot and provided them with meat whenever there was anything to shoot, but Livingstone's journal reports that in many places there was nothing but "low scrub in deep sand: not a bird or insect enlivens that

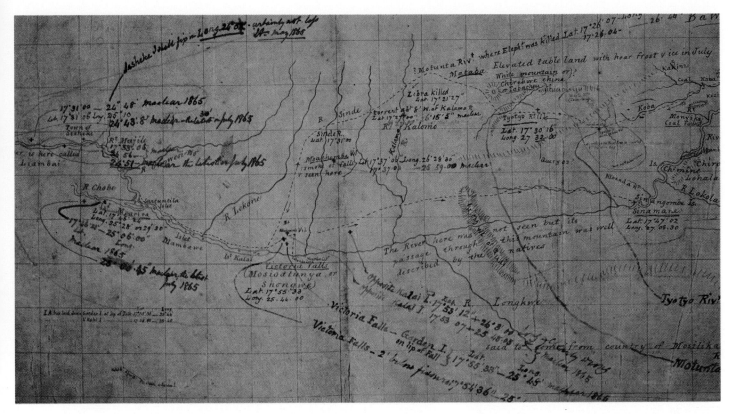

Above: Livingstone's map of the Zambezi River, showing Victoria Falls. He said that he recorded many places only as a point of reference for future investigation.

Left: the Zambezi River at Tete. To express its huge size, the Barotses described it to Livingstone as, "when you look up the river the sun rises on one chief and sets on the other."

landscape; it was without exception the most uninviting prospect I ever beheld." Their guide deserted and a few days later they ran out of water. In his *Missionary Travels* he reveals a strange sense of humor when he writes of his children, "The less there was of water, the more thirsty the little rogues became." There was, however, the real prospect of seeing the three children "perishing before our eyes." Water was found in the nick of time and four days later the party reached the Chobe (or Linyanti) River, a tributary of the Zambezi. Livingstone and Oswell went on alone by canoe to meet the chief of the Makololo at last. He was standing "upon an island with all his principal men around him, and engaged in singing when we arrived."

Sebituane, "a gentleman in thought and manner," welcomed them but thoughout the first day remained ill at ease in their presence, as though he sensed that the Europeans' friendship brought risks as well as advantage. He wanted Livingstone to set up a Christian mission in the hope that it would stop the unceasing tribal warfare and put an end to the slave trade. Greatly to Livingstone's sorrow, Sebituane died within a month of their meeting. After the burial Livingstone and Oswell rode 130 miles to the northeast over country cut by numerous small rivers, and in August 1851 they were rewarded by the sight of a great river. "All that we could say to each other was . . . How glorious! How magnificent! How beautiful!" The river was flowing eastward and could only be the Zambezi. "This was an important point," Livingstone wrote later, "for this river was not previously known to exist there at all."

On the banks of the Zambezi, Livingstone discovered something even more important to him than a great river – his true vocation of exploration. In Oswell's words, "He suddenly announced his intention of going down to the west coast. We were about 1800 miles off it. To my reiterated objections that it would be impossible – 'I'm going down. I mean to go down,' was the only answer." In his own journal the explorer put it more soberly. "I at once resolved to save my family from exposure to this unhealthy region by sending them home to England, and to return alone, with a view to

exploring the country in search of a healthy district that might prove a centre of civilization, and to open up by the interior a path to either the east or west coast."

Livingstone and Oswell rejoined Mary and the children on the Chobe river and embarked on the long journey back to Kolobeng. In April 1852 they were in Cape Town where Mary and her four children, of which the last had been born in the desert, left for England. They did not see Livingstone again for four years.

Once again he crossed the Kalahari where he found the new chief of the Makololo as amenable as Sebituane had been. He provided Livingstone with canoes for the journey up the Zambezi and, more important, with 27 men whose loyalty and endurance proved outstanding.

Livingstone's aim was to follow the river to its source, continue to the west coast, turn around, rejoin the Zambezi, and follow it down to its mouth on the east coast near the Portuguese city of Quelimane in Mozambique. The journey across the continent would be over 3000 miles and the total distance covered almost 5000.

Unlike most of the other explorers, Livingstone traveled light. Three muskets and a shotgun were to support the party with game. The Makololo carried 20 pounds of beads. Livingstone provided himself with a small tent and a spare set of clothes. His most precious possessions were his scientific instruments, a journal for recording his many detailed observations, and a medicine chest. The party set off in January 1854 and within days Livingstone was

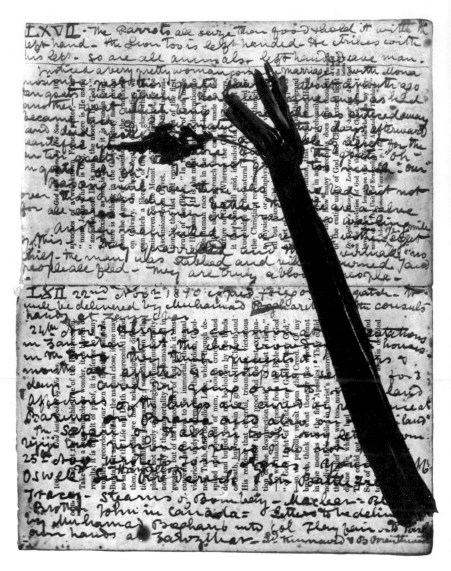

Above left: the Livingstones in 1857. Robert, the first-born, is on the right and the others, going left in order of age, are Agnes, Thomas, and Oswell. The family suffered great privation and danger on journeys to and from new missions.

Above: a set of Livingstone's notes written on the pages of a book. He used any paper at hand to make notes at any given moment, later transcribing them neatly into a locked diary.

prostrated with malaria. Drenching rain reduced his tent to shreds so that he was obliged to sleep on the sodden ground. In the uninhabited regions there was no game and they went hungry; in inhabited regions the local chiefs extorted everything they had from them, even Livingstone's tattered shirts.

Nonetheless the expedition traced the Zambezi, crossed the divide where the streams began to drain toward the Atlantic, and in May – sick and exhausted – reached the coast at Luanda. In four months they had covered over 1500 miles of unmapped country. The return journey along a different route proved more difficult, and it took a year of slogging through forest and wilderness before the Makololo saw their homeland again. Livingstone was provided with a larger retinue of volunteers for further exploration. In November 1855 they reached the great falls called by the Africans "smoke that thunders" but named by Livingstone the Victoria Falls. "It had never before been seen by European eyes; but scenes so lovely must have been gazed upon by angels in their flight."

Continuing eastward, the expedition circled the Quebrabasa Rapids without realizing they

were there. Six months later they were still struggling downstream, once more without food, and were saved from death by a party of men sent out from the Portuguese outpost of Tete to find them. The expedition reached Quelimane on May 20, 1856. Livingstone had become the first European known to travel across the continent.

A ship of the Royal Navy was sent to bring him back to England where he found himself famous. Honors and prizes were loaded upon him but all the time he longed to return to Africa. Finally he persuaded the British government that the only way to defeat the slave trade was to open up the interior to commerce and Christianity. He was clear that one would not succeed without the other. The way to do this,

Above: Victoria Falls in a painting of 1863. Livingstone was the first European to see them, sighting them in 1855.

Right: black slaves were yoked in pairs for the cruel forced march to the ports of export. Such treatment sickened Livingstone.

Below: Livingstone's boat the *Ma-Robert* on the Zambezi River. The explorer traced this river from its mouth to its source.

he argued, was by way of the Zambezi River, and in 1858 he was back there with £5000 from the British government, a steamer named *Ma-Robert* – the Africans' name for Mary Livingstone – and a scientific party. The *Ma-Robert* steamed up the Zambezi past Tete and suddenly came upon the Quebrabasa Rapids that Livingstone had by-passed in his journey across Africa. They extended for 40 miles and some of the waterfalls were 30 feet high, making the river clearly impassable.

Livingstone next tried one of the Zambezi tributaries, the Shire River, but once again impassable rapids blocked the route inland. A small party that went ahead discovered Lake Nyasa (now also known as Lake Malawi). They also discovered one of the busiest slave routes from the interior to the coast, with Arab dhows speeding captives across the lake. Livingstone reckoned that only one in 10 would survive to reach the slave markets in Zanzibar, and he became convinced that the traffic could only be stopped by having an armed vessel patrol the

lake. Although two boats were provided for the purpose, one at Livingstone's own expense, the program was never carried out because too much else happened. A mission that was established at his recommendation among the Makololo was destroyed in horrible circumstances and another mission that he sent up the Zambezi also ended in total disaster with the deaths of many of the party, including the first missionary bishop. The London Missionary Society withdrew support from Livingstone, and the British government

Left: Mary Livingstone's grave in Shupanga. After years of living away in Britain, Livingstone's wife returned to Africa only to die within months. Livingstone was desolated by her death.

Below: the chronometer was one of the few instruments available to 19th-century explorers of unknown territory, and one of the most important. In 1872 Livingstone borrowed one from a navy captain, putting a note on the receipt that "... it will be of very signal benefit in my exploration."

They passed through "village after village all deserted and strewn with corpses and skulls." There was little food to be found in the ravaged land, and by the time Livingstone's party reached the Shire River south of Lake Nyasa it had shrunk to 11 half-starved men. Worse was to happen on the slow journey to Lake Tanganyika. A porter dropped the precious chronometer, damaging it so that Livingstone could no longer make accurate observations of his position. Another porter deserted with Livingstone's medicine chest. Ill and weak, Livingstone wrote in his journal, "I feel as if I had now received sentence of death."

ordered the recall of the expedition. As a final blow, he found his wife much changed when she came to Africa to visit him. She had become a heavy drinker as well as developing a hearty dislike of missionaries. However, within a few weeks she was dead of fever and Livingstone apparently felt her death keenly, saying: "I feel as if I had lost all heart now." When Livingstone returned to London in 1864 the general public ignored him.

The problem of the origin of the Nile was still unsettled because a smaller lake, Lake Albert, had been found to the west of Lake Victoria and the river Speke had seen flowing north out of Lake Victoria was discovered to flow into Lake Albert. It flowed almost immediately out again, northward, to become the Nile, but did another river flow into Lake Albert from the south? If so, did it come from Lake Tanganyika as Burton then believed? Livingstone believed that it must, and was further convinced that the real source of the Nile was to be found south of Lake Tanganyika in a river and a lake the local peoples called Bangweulu. He could not know that Lake Bangweulu, which did exist, was surrounded by great swamps, and that its water flowed westward to the Congo River.

So it was with every confidence that in 1865 Livingstone left England for what proved to be the last time. Because East and Central Africa had been despoiled by the slavers, he could find only 60 porters willing to risk the journey inland.

Below: the point at which the Nile enters Lake Albert. Livingstone was on the search for the final answers to the source of the Nile when he returned to Africa for the last time.

He was found by a party of Arab slavers, the very people he opposed so strongly, and they nursed and fed him. In their company he discovered the small Lake Mweru, and then parted from them to search for Bangweulu. Only four men would accompany him on this terrible journey, wandering through swamps waist-deep in leech-infested water. In June 1868 they penetrated to the lake, but the men could not be persuaded to go any further. There was nothing for it but to turn around and rejoin the Arabs. "I am nearly toothless and in my second childhood," Livingstone wrote. Yet despite constant sickness and hunger he went on, searching for the river he hoped would lead to the Nile. In a district called Bamberre he was marooned for eight months, sick with malaria and dysentery. During this time he read the whole Bible four times.

In March 1871 Livingstone and three faithful attendants, Susi, Chuma, and Gardner, reached the Lualaba River which, unknown to Livingstone, was a tributary of the Upper Congo. The Arabs had established a trading post at Nyangwe on the banks of the Lualaba, and there Livingstone witnessed an atrocious massacre by some of the armed Arabs who fired into the crowd at the market where many women and children

Left: Chuma and Susi, two of the faithful men who served Livingstone for many years. With him at his death, they lovingly and with great sacrifice carried his body back to the settlement of Zanzibar.

Below: a massacre of Africans by Arab slave traders. Livingstone once witnessed such a cruel scene of carnage that he determined to make a fight against the traffic in human beings.

were peacefully going about their business. Terrified Africans jumped into the river where more bullets were sprayed at them until over 400 had been shot or drowned.

Sickened by this senseless cruelty, Livingstone determined to tell the outside world of the true horrors of the brutal traffic in human beings. Unable to bear the company of Arabs any longer, he turned back with his three faithful companions for a 350-mile walk to Ujiji, "almost every step in pain." He was certain he would find a good supply of stores waiting for him, but when he arrived he found they had all been plundered by the headman of the caravan on the way up from Zanzibar. Livingstone was destitute and close to despair. At this low point in his fortunes, he later recounted: "Susi came running at the top of his speed and gasped out: 'An Englishman! I see him!' and off he darted to meet him. The American flag at the head of the caravan told me the nationality of the stranger." Henry Morton Stanley had arrived. The most famous meeting in the history of African exploration was about to occur.

Henry Morton Stanley 1841-1904

The name of Henry Morton Stanley is so entwined with that of David Livingstone that his story must begin with the background leading up to their famous meeting.

In 1866 David Livingstone entered the African bush to search for the source of the Nile. The months passed and no word was heard from him. By 1868 it was feared he might be dead and the Royal Geographical Society prepared an expedition to search for him. Then letters written by Livingstone from the shores of Lake Nyasa arrived at Zanzibar and the search was called off.

Fears for Livingstone arose again when several months passed and no further news emerged. Livingstone had always been an assiduous letter writer who as often as possible reported on his progress. When he ran out of paper, he even used scraps or the blank margins of books. When he came to an end of his ink, he concocted a substitute from the juice of berries. The long silence after 1868 was therefore ominous. James Gordon Bennett, owner of the *New York Herald*, decided that news of the whereabouts of Livingstone would give a boost to the circulation of his newspaper, and he instructed one of the journalists on his staff to try to find him. "If he is dead bring back every possible proof of his death," Bennett said.

The journalist assigned to the job was Henry Morton Stanley who, like Livingstone had risen from the humblest level of society. His real name was John Rowlands and he was born in Wales in 1841. He was illegitimate and spent most of his childhood in a workhouse run by a sadistic schoolmaster from whose tyranny he finally ran away. After going to sea as a cabin boy, he was adopted by a New Orleans cotton merchant named Henry Morton Stanley in 1859, and he took his protector's name and nationality. He fought in the American Civil War – first on one side and then on the other – drifted into journalism, and supplied the *New York Herald* with such vivid reports on a war in Ethiopia that Bennett gave him a succession of other foreign assignments including the search for Livingstone.

Stanley arrived in Zanzibar at the beginning of 1871, five years after Livingstone had vanished into the still uncharted interior of the Dark Continent. Stanley's newspaper had provided him with unlimited funds of which he spent a small fortune to equip one of the most elaborate

Above: Henry Morton Stanley. After his meeting with David Livingstone when he saved the elder man's life, he decided to carry on the work of exploration.

expeditions ever seen. He bought the best supplies and hired 192 of the best porters at the highest rates. Even with this advantage, his eight-month march from the coast to Ujiji was a considerable achievement because he had to face fighting in the area between Arab slave dealers and African tribes, an attack of malaria, and the death of his two non-African assistants. Stanley had joined in the war on the Arab side, and thereafter had to travel cautiously to avoid African raiders.

On November 10 his caravan climbed the last hill and saw the broad expanse of Lake Tanganyika ahead. Below them lay the port of Ujiji among its palm trees where, unknown to Stanley, Livingstone had just arrived. Stanley ordered the American flag unfurled at the front of the caravan and the Zanzibar flag at the rear, 50 guns were fired simultaneously, and the caravan marched down into Ujiji. In his book *How I Found Livingstone*, Stanley described how he had to make his way through dense crowds.

"Suddenly I hear a voice on my right say, 'Good morning, sir!'

"Startled at hearing this greeting in the midst of such a crowd of black people, I turn sharply around in search of the man, and see him at my

side, with the blackest of faces, but animated and joyous – a man dressed in a long white shirt, with a turban of American sheeting around his wooly head, and I ask:

"'Who the mischief are you!'

"'I am Susi, the servant of Dr Livingstone,' said he, smiling, and showing a gleaming row of teeth.

"'What! Is Dr Livingstone here?'

"'Yes, sir.'

"'In this village?'

"'Yes, sir.'

"'Are you sure?'

"'Sure, sure, sir. Why, I leave him just now.'"

Susi raced off to inform the doctor of Stanley's arrival, and after a moment of disbelief Livingstone came onto his veranda to greet him.

"As I advanced slowly toward him," Stanley recalled, "I noticed he was pale, look wearied, had a gray beard, wore a bluish cap with a faded gold braid round it, had on a red-sleeved waistcoat, and a pair of gray tweed trousers. I would have run to him, only I was a coward in the presence of such a mob – would have embraced him, only, he being an Englishman, I did not know how he would receive me. So I did what cowardice and false pride suggested was the best

thing – walked deliberately to him, took off my hat, and said:

"'Dr Livingstone, I presume?'

"'Yes,' said he, with a kind smile, lifting his cap slightly.

"I replace my hat on my head, and he puts on his cap, and we both grasp hands, and then I say aloud:

"'I thank God, Doctor, I have been permitted to see you.'

"He answered, 'I feel thankful that I am here to welcome you.'"

Right: Livingstone's battered blue cap, which he was wearing when Stanley found him in Ujiji.

Below right: the hat that Stanley wore at his first meeting with Livingstone.

Left: a newspaper illustration of the Stanley-Livingstone meeting published around the time of the much publicized event.

The contrast between these two men could hardly have been greater. The aging missionary still had his humility and unshaken faith, his humor and love of nature. Stanley was brash, self-confident, and thrusting; he had his own career to make and his paper to serve. Yet in the five months they spent together a close warm relationship – almost like father and son – developed between them. For Stanley the meeting was the supreme experience and turning point of his life.

Medicine, good food, and rest brought about a recovery in Livingstone's health, and the two men set off together to explore the north end of

Lake Tanganyika. When their canoes were attacked by a local tribe maddened by the persecutions of the slavers, they were saved by the calm and unprovocative behavior of Livingstone. This astonished his companion and deeply impressed him – though he himself was seldom prepared to do the same on his own subsequent explorations. The two men went farther up the lake than Burton and Speke had been able to in 1858, and were able to settle one important

wished to uncover more evidence concerning the slave trade; others that he may simply have been reluctant to return to England with so little new information concerning the river he had been sent out to explore.

Five months after Stanley wished Livingstone an emotional farewell at Tabora, the stores promised to Livingstone arrived from the coast. On August 25, 1872 Livingstone began his last journey around the south shore of Lake Tangan-

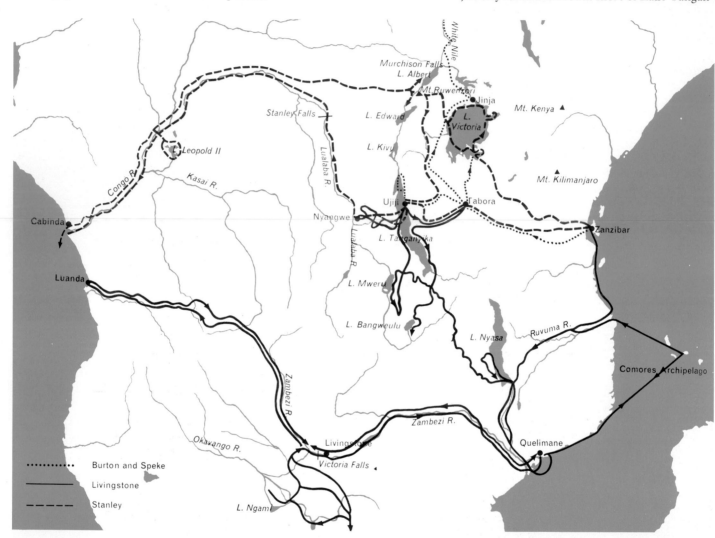

Above: the main routes charted by Stanley, Livingstone, Speke, and Burton. Most of Stanley's exploration was in the Congo region.

question about the source of the Nile by discovering that the Ruzizi River, despite Burton's belief to the contrary, flowed into and not out of the lake. Unfortunately, this only confirmed Livingstone's belief in his error that the Lualaba River, 200 miles to the west of the lake, would turn out to be the Nile. He determined to explore the Lualaba to make sure but this meant hiring new porters, which could not be done in Ujiji. The two men walked to Tambora 300 miles away and there they parted, Stanley going on to Zanzibar to obtain the porters and the necessary supplies.

Historian's have wondered at Livingstone's refusal to return to civilization with Stanley, his determination to go again on a fruitless journey after the Nile. Some speculate that he may have

yika, where the weather was intensely hot in the period before the rains, and down toward Lake Bangweulu. The land had been ravaged by famine and, with the rains, became a vast swamp. Relying on his own inaccurate instruments rather than the new ones Stanley had given him, Livingstone was soon hopelessly lost. Progress was slowed to one or one-and-a-half miles a day, the water was bitterly cold, and Livingstone was once again desperately ill. Yet one month before his death he could write in his journal: "Nothing earthly will make me give up my work in despair. I encourage myself in the Lord my God, and go forward."

Two weeks later, though bleeding copiously, his powers of observation were still acute. "A species of soft moss grows on most plants, and

Left: Livingstone's home in Ilala. With the help of his loyal black companions, he managed to reach it a couple of days before he died in April 1873.

Below: the plaque over Livingstone's grave in Westminster Abbey, London. His body lies there, but his heart is buried in the Africa he knew and loved so well.

seems good fodder for fishes, fitted by hooked or turned-up noses to guide it into their mouths.'' His men refused to leave him although he was plainly dying. When he could no longer walk, they carried him in a litter. Toward the end he noted, ''It is not all pleasure, this exploration.'' At a village called Chitambo's in the district of Ulala, he made his last entry in his diary on April 27, 1873. Too weak to turn the key himself, he signalled to Susi to wind up his chronometer. On April 30 he died, kneeling across his bed in an attitude of prayer.

The sequel is unique in African exploration. Livingstone's companions, directed by Susi and Chuma, cut out his heart and buried it under a tree. They embalmed his body with raw salt, dried it in the sun, and lashed it to a pole, wrapped in cloth and bark. For eight months they carried it through swamp and forest, over lake and mountain, to deliver it to the Zanzibar authorities. With his body they carried all his precious journals, notes, and scientific observations. David Livingstone was buried in Westminster Abbey, London, among many of the

BROUGHT BY FAITHFUL HANDS
OVER LAND AND SEA
HERE RESTS
DAVID LIVINGSTONE,
MISSIONARY,
TRAVELLER,
PHILANTHROPIST,
BORN MARCH 19.1813,
AT BLANTYRE, LANARKSHIRE,
DIED MAY 1.1873,
AT CHITAMBO'S VILLAGE, ULALA.

FOR 30 YEARS HIS LIFE WAS SPENT
IN AN UNWEARIED EFFORT
TO EVANGELIZE THE NATIVE RACES,
TO EXPLORE THE UNDISCOVERED SECRETS,
TO ABOLISH THE DESOLATING SLAVE TRADE,
OF CENTRAL AFRICA,
WHERE WITH HIS LAST WORDS HE WROTE,
"ALL I CAN ADD IN MY SOLITUDE, IS,
MAY HEAVEN'S RICH BLESSING COME DOWN
ON EVERY ONE, AMERICAN, ENGLISH, OR TURK
WHO WILL HELP TO HEAL
THIS OPEN SORE OF THE WORLD."

"OTHER SHEEP I HAVE, WHICH ARE NOT OF THIS FOLD: THEM ALSO I MUST BRING, AND THEY SHALL HEAR MY VOICE."

"TANTUS AMOR VERI, NIHIL EST QUOD NOSCERE MALIM, QUAM FLUVII CAUSAS PER SÆCULA TANTA LATENTES."

national heroes of Britain. But his heart remained in Africa.

Stanley was one of the pall bearers at Livingstone's funeral. On hearing of the death of his hero he wrote, "May I be selected to succeed him in the opening up of Africa to the shining light of Christianity!" He added significantly, "but not after his method." Stanley may have regarded Livingstone almost as a saint, but in his opinion, "this selfish, wooden-headed world requires promptings other than the Gospel."

When Stanley returned to England with news of his meeting with Livingstone, his reception was decidedly mixed. Many people, including the president of the Royal Geographical Society, believed his account to be a journalistic hoax. Eventually his account was accepted – though bitterness at this initial mistrust never left him. Seven months after Livingstone's funeral he was back in Zanzibar, determined to complete the task his hero had left unfinished. His great

Edward (**left**) and Frank Pocock, the two young brothers chosen by Stanley to accompany him on his first trip to Africa to continue in the footsteps of Livingstone.

Below: the *Lady Alice*, designed by Stanley so that it could be dismantled into the five sections shown for easier portage around impassable rivers.

Left: the Congo forest. After reaching Yambuya, Stanley had to penetrate hundreds of miles of such jungle on foot.

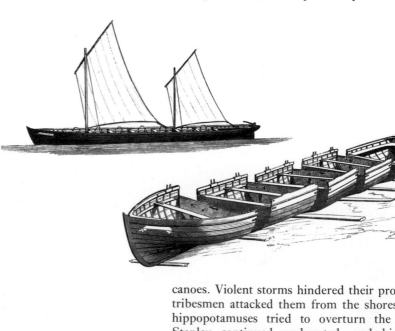

Congo Expedition, numbering 356 assorted porters, gun bearers, and camp followers, was being paid for by his New York patron, Bennett, and the London newspaper *The Daily Telegraph*. For his companions he chose almost at random the two young Pocock brothers, Frank and Edward, sons of an English fisherman, and, Frederick Barker, a London hotel clerk. None had ever been to Africa before and all would be dead before the expedition was over.

Stanley set himself three objectives. The first was to sail all around Lake Victoria, map it accurately, and establish whether it was one great lake or, as some critics of Speke suggested, a number of smaller ones. After this he proposed to do the same on Lake Tanganyika, find out which rivers flowed into it, and where if at all a river flowed out. The third and most dangerous of his objectives was to sail down the Lualaba River from where Livingstone had abandoned it and follow wherever it led. These voyages he would make in the *Lady Alice*, a cedarwood boat that could be taken apart in five sections when portage was required.

Stanley marshalled his column of porters with military efficiency: the tallest carried the heavy bales of cloth, the shorter carried sacks of beads, and the older more reliable carried the precious instruments. Edward Pocock taught the men to obey the call of his bugle – but by the time the expedition reached Mwanza on the south shore of Lake Victoria, Edward Pocock was dead of typhus and 100 other men had deserted, died of disease, or been killed in skirmishes with tribesmen. Stanley launched the *Lady Alice* and set sail up the lake, accompanied by a flotilla of

canoes. Violent storms hindered their progress, tribesmen attacked them from the shores, and hippopotamuses tried to overturn the boat. Stanley continued undaunted, and his trip around the lake proved Speke's belief in a single great lake with a single outlet at the north to be right. He also visited King Mutesa of Buganda, as Speke had 13 years before when he taught the ruler how to handle a gun. A salute of between

200 and 300 muskets greeted Stanley's approach. Africa was becoming "civilized."

On his way back to Mwanza, Stanley was angered by the behavior of tribesmen on Bumbire Island and ordered his men to fire into the crowd. Many were killed. This incident and others similar to it aroused a storm of criticism in Europe, and Stanley's position was not improved by such written comments as, "The savage only respects force, power, boldness, and decision." Stanley was undeniably brutal to the Africans, but in his defense it might be argued that conditions had considerably deteriorated since Burton and Speke had first made their way there. The

persecutions of the slave trade had provoked fierce tribal wars. Without Stanley's ruthlessness his expedition would have achieved nothing – whereas with him in command it achieved a great deal.

After Lake Victoria he had the *Lady Alice* carried over to Lake Tanganyika where again he sailed all the way around the lake and established that the only outflow was through the reed-choked Lukuga River on the west shore. He also established that this was a tributary of the Lualaba. In October 1876 the 154 surviving members of the expedition reached Nyangwe on the edge of the unknown. Ahead lay vast tropical rain forests. Many of the inhabitants were known to be cannibals, so Stanley enlisted the aid of Tippu Tib, a slave trader of mixed Arab-African parentage, who had made himself the richest and most powerful individual in Central Africa. For a substantial payment, Tippu Tib agreed to accompany Stanley with a force of 700 men, and in November the combined party set off. Stanley called the jungle a Turkish bath. Moving through it was like struggling continually in a "feeble solemn twilight" with hardly a glimpse of the sun. Everything was drenched in moisture and deep in mold and

Below left: Tippu Tib, a slave trader of mixed Arab and African blood. He was always friendly and helpful to Europeans.

Below: a view of the Congo River near Yangambi in what is now the Congo (Kinshasa). Stanley was the first to navigate the full length of the mighty river.

decaying vegetation. In one village they walked along a road 500 yards long flanked on each side by skulls that numbered 186. The village chief informed them that they were the skulls of chimpanzees, but Stanley bought two which he took back to England and had identified. They were human.

At this point Stanley had the *Lady Alice* assembled again and paddled down the river in her with 36 men, everyone else following on foot. Starvation, smallpox, dysentery, and ulcers attacked the land party and every day two or three bodies had to be tossed into the water. In December Tippu Tib and his party had had

enough and turned back, but Stanley urged his own men on. They came to a chain of seven cataracts and had to unload all the supplies, dismantle the boat, and carry everything through jungle and over rocks and cliffs. Nearly all the way they were under attack from cannibals whose "fierce yells came pealing to our ears, even above the roar and tremendous crack of the cataract." When they could take to the water again, the river narrowed to four miles wide and the *Lady Alice* was frequently in danger of shipwreck through storms. Food was always scarce and sometimes nonexistent. "It is a bad world, master, and you have lost your way in it," said the dying wife of one of his men. At last they reached a stretch of the river where the inhabitants were friendly. Stanley asked their chief the river's name. "Ikuta ya Kongo," was the reply. The Lualaba and the Congo were one and the same river. The question Livingstone had died trying to answer was solved.

After they had paddled and hauled for 1000 miles, they came upon another series of cataracts that turned the river into the wildest stretch of water Stanley had ever seen. Nine of the 17 canoes were lost and Frank Pocock, his last surviving London companion, was drowned while trying to shoot the rapids. "I am weary, oh so weary, of this constant tale of woes and death,"

wrote the grieving Stanley. Toward the end of July they reached a point from which Boma, a European trading post, was only five days journey overland. With his men starving and mutinous, Stanley decided to make for it.

The expedition was reduced to 115 people including three mothers with newborn children. Stanley wrote a letter appealing for aid from "any gentleman who speaks English at Embomma," and persuaded a local chief to send it on ahead. Three days later the bearers returned with a message signed by the agent of an English company. Supplies followed close behind, and Stanley's surviving men and women fell upon the provisions with a "glorious loud-swelling chant of triumph and success." On August 9, 1877, exactly 999 days after the departure from Zanzibar, Stanley led the expedition into Boma, to be greeted by a group of men whose "pale color, after so long on gazing on rich black and richer brown, had something of an unaccountable ghastliness." Stanley had achieved all three of his objectives. The last of Africa's four great rivers had been mastered.

Ten years later Stanley embarked on his final African exploration, a long trek through the Ituri forests of the central Congo to reach Lake Albert. The purpose of the expedition was to rescue Eduard Schnitzer, a remarkable German

reveal peaks rising to nearly 17,000 feet and white with snow. This was the Ruwenzori range, the legendary Mountains of the Moon that Ptolemy had drawn on his map 1900 years before. The early Greeks and Romans who believed them to be the source of the Nile were partly right. Water from snows melting on the Ruwenzori range flows into Lake Edward and Lake Victoria and so to the White Nile.

With this discovery the heroic age of African exploration was virtually at an end. The European governments soon imposed a network of frontiers on the maps that a handful of courageous men had laboriously drawn. Names of colonies, protectorates, and dependencies took the place of what had been, only a few years before, a great blank space dotted with the quaint names of legendary cities. The Dark Continent was dark no longer.

Below: the meeting of Stanley and Emin Pasha, who turned out not to need or want help from the outside. He had to be persuaded to return with Stanley.

explorer and surgeon who had become a Muslim, changed his name to Emin Pasha, and since 1878 had established himself in the southern part of present-day Sudan. When the fanatical Mahdist Revolution engulfed the whole of the Sudan, Emin retreated up the Nile to Lake Albert and, with war raging all around Lake Victoria, became cut off from all contact with the outside world.

Stanley's rescue expedition had to hack a path through one of the densest, darkest, most impenetrable forests on earth. Pygmies discharged poison arrows at them and planted poisoned skewers in their path. The death toll was appalling. When finally the expedition forced its way through, Stanley was dismayed to discover that Emin did not particularly wish to be rescued. He had planted crops around his settlement, built comfortable quarters and a small dockyard, and amassed a fortune in ivory. Finally he reluctantly agreed to accompany Stanley to Zanzibar, and on their way they explored the land south of Lake Albert. They discovered another lake which Stanley named Albert Edward Nyanza after Britain's Prince of Wales. It is now called Lake Edward. A great range of mountains could be seen on the farther side of the lake. The clouds that hung about the upper slopes drew aside just long enough to

227

Chapter 9

Terra Australis

In the far southern regions of the world, according to the ancients, there lay a great continent. This land mass was necessary, they argued, to offset the weight of the continents in the Northern Hemisphere. Without it the earth would overbalance and "topple to destruction amidst the stars." The Greek geographer Ptolemy called this continent Terra Australis Incognita, the Unknown Southern Land. Belief in Terra Australis persisted throughout the Middle Ages and into the Great Age of Discovery. It was thought to be a land of gentle climate and fabulous wealth, and many explorers sailed the southern seas in search of it. Their voyages revealed the Pacific Ocean and led to the discovery of its islands and of Australia and New Zealand – but of the southern continent of legend not a trace was found. When the sightings of Antarctica pushed the bounds of Terra Australis farther and farther south, the myth dissolved.

Left: the vastness and danger of the Pacific Ocean is caught in this picture of Captain James Cook's boat fighting its way through a waterspout, a tornado at sea that takes the form of a huge whirling column of wind and water. Weathering such storms and other adversities, Cook left little of the great ocean uncharted at the end of his explorations. This led to the opening and mapping of Australia, New Zealand, and many of the Pacific islands.

The Mysterious Southern Continent

In the days before the European explorers established the true geography of the world, map makers were obliged to speculate about the unknown regions. One of the most enduring theories was that a great continent stretched across the southern hemisphere – not the icebound land mass we call Antarctica but a temperate region that was inhabited. The Greek historian Theopompus, writing in about 350 BC, placed this continent beyond the Ocean Sea he described as encircling the islands of Europe, Asia, and Africa. In the infinite green meadows of this continent, he said, could be found "big and mighty beasts" and "gigantic men who, in the same climate, exceed the stature of us twice."

Five hundred years later, Ptolemy of Alexandria drew his famous map of the world and, like many geographers before and after, invented what he did not know. Reaching the limit of his knowledge of Africa about halfway down the east coast, and knowing nothing of Asia beyond the Malay Peninsula, he joined the two together with an imaginary southern continent. This turned the Indian Ocean into a vast inland sea. The made-up land mass he called Terra Australis Incognita.

For over a thousand years Ptolemy's theories represented the sum of human knowledge about the southern lands except, of course, for those who were already living there – the Aborigines of Australia, the Maoris of New Zealand, and the inhabitants of the East Indies and the innumerable Pacific islands. They should be considered the first explorers of these parts of the world, but because they left no written testimony and only fragmentary accounts in the form of myths, the story of their arrival is impossible to establish with certainty. It is believed that the Aborigines originated in Java and made their way southeast to Australia more than 16,000 years ago when the level of the sea was at least 270 feet lower than it is today. People did not reach the smaller Pacific islands until much later, some migrating east from Asia while others sailed west from South America. The process must have been a slow one, with voyagers gradually finding their way from one island group to another. The Maoris, guided by a legendary navigator named Kupe, did not reach New Zealand until about 1000, probably from Tahiti.

European knowledge of these journeys is relatively recent, and has been pieced together from myth and archaeological remains. The first

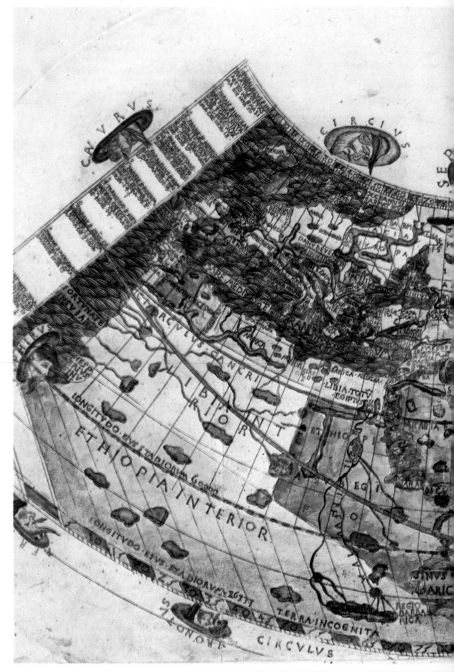

Above: an early map, based on a description by the Greek geographer Ptolemy, showing Terra Australis Incognita, the Unknown Southern Continent. The belief that such a land mass existed in the South Pacific endured for many hundreds of years before being disproved in the 18th century.

Right: an early drawing of the Aborigines. These original inhabitants of Australia lived in the open, able to bear extremes of heat, cold, and humidity.

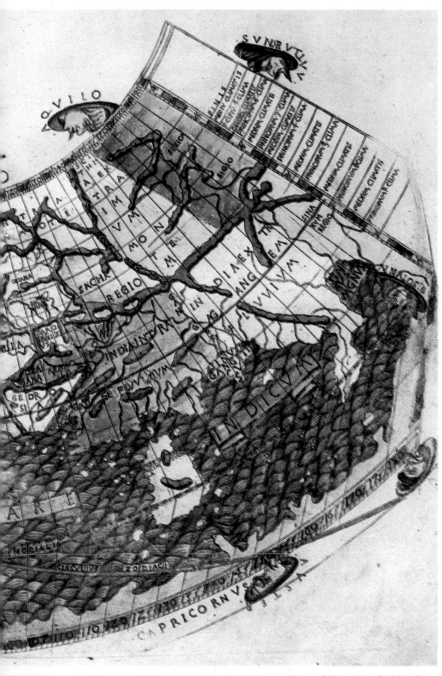

European sailors to search for Terra Australis went as travelers into the unknown – although they did not think of it in that way. They were confident that such a place existed because Ptolemy and his successors all showed it on the maps. All they had to do was discover exactly where it was.

The voyages of the early Portuguese explorers forced the map makers to make their first alterations. The rounding of the Cape of Good Hope at the southernmost point of Africa showed that no connection with a southern continent existed there. Within a few years of this achievement, the Portuguese were venturing among the islands of present-day Indonesia and in 1513 conquered the Moluccas, the famed Spice Islands with their plantations of cinnamon, clove, and nutmeg. It is possible that they reached Australia as well but the documentation is scanty, principally because, in an effort to keep details of the spice routes secret, the king of Portugal

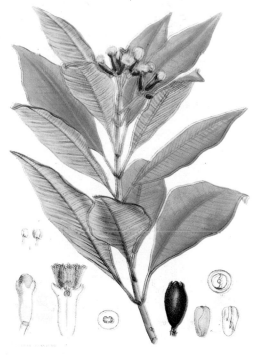

Above right: a botanical drawing of the clove, whose dried unopened flower is a much-used spice. The desire of Europeans for cloves and other spices of the East inspired a great deal of the exploration that took place in the 15th and 16th centuries.

threatened death on the export of any marine chart. The evidence for the Portuguese discovery of Australia rests essentially on the Dieppe Maps, a series of maps produced in France. The earliest of these is dated 1541. At that time the French had undertaken no long voyages, yet this map actually showed a recognizable part of Australia instead of the great southern continent depicted on earlier maps. The information had undoubtedly come from the observation of people who had been to the lands shown, and the major clue to the Portuguese as the pioneer explorers lies in the considerable number of Portuguese place names to be found on the map. For example, Terre Ennegade plainly comes from Tierra Anegada, meaning "land under water," and Baie Bassa is from Bahia Bassa, meaning "low bay."

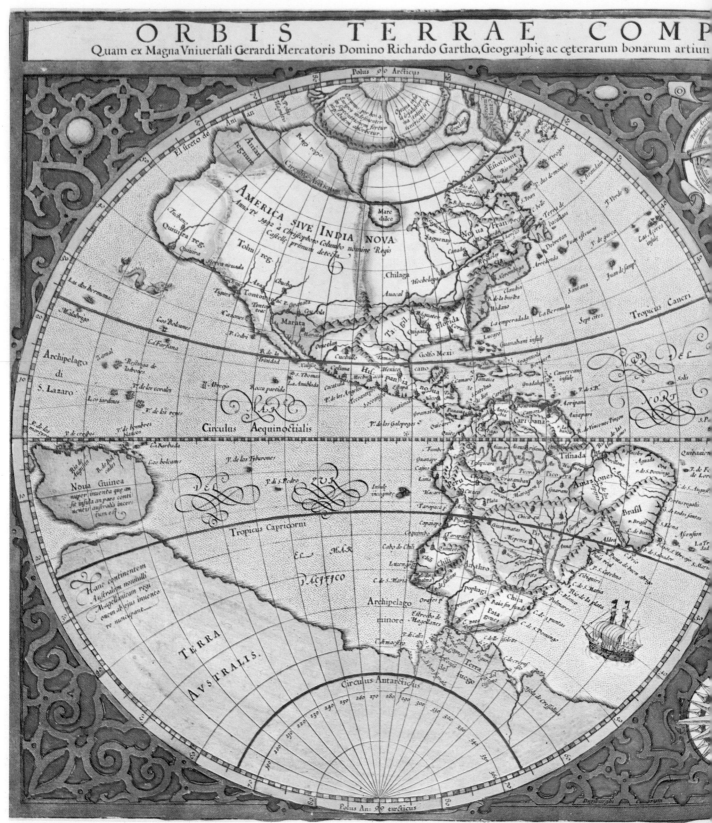

Because of Portugal's unwillingness to reveal its knowledge of the real lands along their spice routes, the search for Terra Australis continued. There was an increase in the demand for maps and charts, and cartographers rivaled one another to produce maps incorporating the latest information. One of the greatest of these map makers was Gerhard Kramer, born in East Flanders in 1512 of German descent, and known by his latinized name of Gerardus Mercator. He was a man of many skills – a land surveyor, a scientific instrument maker, and above all an engraver. He was patronized by Emperor Charles V, who had a room entirely hung with maps, and this patronage brought him in touch with Portuguese and Spanish navigators. On the

NDIOSA DESCRIPTIO

ac fautori summo, in veteris amicitię ac familiaritatis memoriã Rumoldus Mercator fieri curabat Aᵒ. M.D.Lxxxvii.

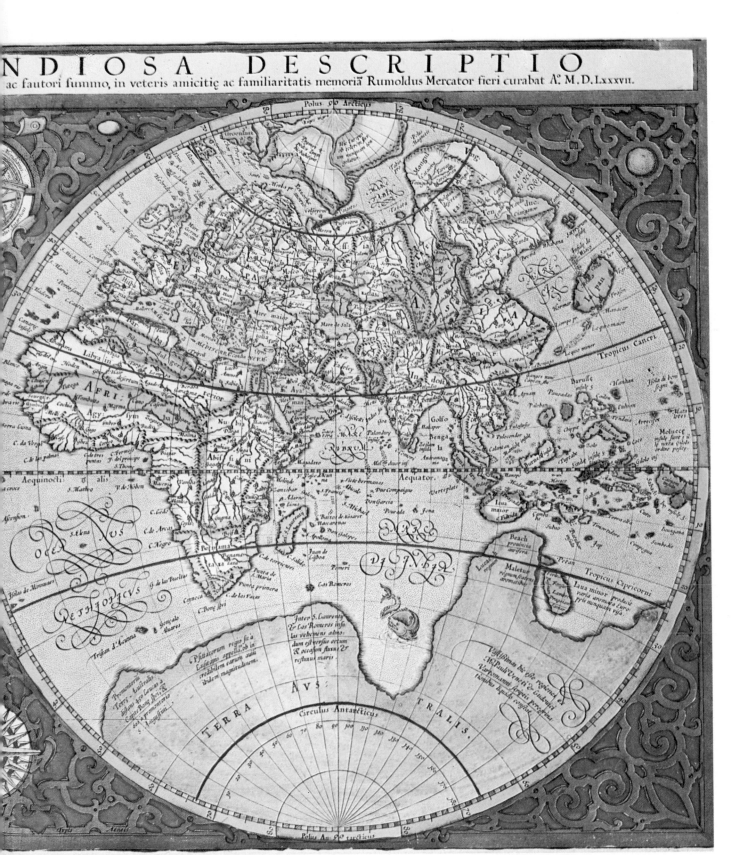

Above: Rumold Mercator's map of the world.

world map he drew in 1569, however, the coastline south of the Spice Islands is given no Portuguese place names.

In 1587 Mercator's son Rumold drew a world map for the collection of over 100 maps bound and published together after his father's death. On the title page of this edition the word "atlas" was used for the first time, tied in with an en-

graving of the Greek mythological hero Atlas holding the world on his back.

Rumold Mercator's map was broadly similar to his father's earlier one. A huge continent occupies much of the space south of the Tropic of Capricorn. Tierra del Fuego, seen by Magellan to the south of the strait named after him, is shown as a promontory of this southern conti-

233

nent, after which the coastline climbs steadily toward the equator. The map gives the impression that something was known of Australia, for a peninsula is shown with its western coastline roughly parallel to Australia's west coast. Terra Australis is also separated from New Guinea, even though no one is known to have sailed through the Torres Strait at that date.

One of the reasons for the survival of Terra Australis is that place had to be found for all the legendary lands once shown in Asia or Africa and known not to exist there by the time of Mercator's map. He therefore designated the kingdom of Lucach and the Land of Parrots as part of the unknown southern continent.

Spain was determined to share in the profitable East Indies trade and from the time of Magellan onward made many attempts to get back and forth from Mexico. However, the prevailing trade winds kept the ships away from the main island groups of Polynesia, and the same winds prevented an easy return voyage. Not until 1565 did Alonso de Arellano, separated from an expedition fleet, sail his 40-ton *San Lucas* north from the Philippine Islands into the east-flowing Japan current. Whether he did so by accident or design, the current and the prevailing westerlies took him back to Mexico. The first west–east crossing of the Pacific had been achieved.

Pedro Sarmiento de Gamboa, historian, mathe-

Above: a contemporary painting of Hernando de Grijalva embarking from Mexico in 1537 on his way to win some of the spice trade in the name of Spain.

Right: an ornament for the prow of a canoe from the Solomon Islands. It is made of blackened wood inlaid with mother-of-pearl and represents the spirit that protects the canoe.

matician, astronomer, and sea captain, persuaded the Spanish government to mount an expedition in 1567 with the express purpose of searching for Terra Australis. Sarmiento had studied Inca legends of the Pacific and was convinced that a gigantic southern continent lay within easy sailing distance of Peru. His argu-

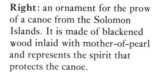

through Polynesia, missing every island except one small atoll in the Ellice group. A navigational error prevented them from landing on that one island sighted, and they did not see land again until they reached the palm-fringed bays of what is now the Solomon Islands. Mendaña believed he had reached the shores of the elusive southern continent, but found the land to be an island in a few days. When he discovered his error, he spent three months exploring other islands in the group and then sailed for home.

Right: Francis Drake, the first Englishman to sail around the world. Drake was more pirate than explorer, but documents indicate that he had instructions from Queen Elizabeth I to promote trade and claim new territories.

ments were so impressive that the viceroy of Peru decided to keep the command in his own family; though Sarmiento was a member of the expedition, the leadership was given to the viceroy's relatively inexperienced nephew, 25-year-old Álvaro de Mendaña de Neyra.

For three weeks the ships sailed westward and then, contrary to Sarmiento's advice, changed course to the northwest. By doing this Mendaña performed the remarkable feat of sailing right

Below: the fleet led by Cornelius Houtman rounding the Cape of Good Hope. Houtman commanded the first Dutch expedition to India and the East Indies.

The islands remained unvisited for another 200 years.

After Spain it was the turn of England. Queen Elizabeth I instructed the buccaneer Francis Drake to sail for the Pacific by way of the Strait of Magellan and to take possession of whatever parts of the coast of Terra Australis he could find. Having passed through the strait in 1578, he was blown to the south and saw enough of Tierra del Fuego to guess that it must be an island. He could see no sign of any land farther south.

The Dutch displaced the Portuguese in the Spice Islands, and from there it was they who made the first recorded landfalls on the Australian coast. In 1642 Abel Tasman separated Australia, still called New Holland at that time, from Terra Australis but it was not until James Cook sailed along the antarctic coast in the following century that Terra Australis was finally removed from the maps.

Pedro Fernández de Quirós 1565-1615
Luis Vaez de Torres ?-1613?

On February 11, 1596 a rotting galleon limped into Manila Bay. Its Spanish crew members were little more than ragged, fever-ridden skeletons, their teeth dropping from their ulcerated gums. High on the poop stood an astonishingly different figure, well-fed and dressed in a brilliant silk gown. It was Doña Ysabel, widow of the commander of the ship, Álvaro de Mendaña de Neyra. It mattered nothing to her that the crew was starving while at her feet scampered two pet pigs.

The man who had miraculously brought this death ship to harbor was Mendaña's pilot, Pedro Fernández de Quirós. He was a Portuguese navigator and visionary who, his enemies said, had been born in the slums of Lisbon. The story of the death ship had started when four ships sailed from Callao, Peru in April 1595 with 378 people on board, 100 of them women. They were going to live in the Solomon Islands, which Mendaña had discovered 25 years before and which he had

been trying for all that time to get colonized. Doña Ysabel Barrato, a high-strung and dominating woman, accompanied her husband with three of her brothers and a sister. From the start the voyage was marred by family disputes and Mendaña proved incapable of withstanding his wife.

On July 21 the ships reached a group of beautiful islands to which Mendaña gave the name they are still known by today, Las Islas Marquesas de Mondoza, after his sponsor the Viceroy of Peru. Mendaña and Quirós were charmed by the islanders and impressed by their skill in building canoes, but several of the Spanish soldiers shot them needlessly and heedlessly. Two hundred were killed, to the great distress of Quirós who hoped to bring Christianity to the inhabitants of the islands.

The ship continued to the west after leaving the Marquesas but as the weeks passed the crews became restless and many began to question the existence of Mendaña's Solomon Islands. On September 7 the ships ran into dense fog. When it cleared one of the ships had vanished – possibly taking advantage of the opportunity to return to Peru. Whatever the explanation, the ship was never seen again. That same evening a tree-covered island was sighted near a smoking volcano. The islanders who approached the ships in outrigger canoes were much darker than those who inhabited the Marquesas, with frizzy hair and red-dyed teeth, and Mendaña again

Below: a view of the Marquesas, a series of volcanic islands which were named by Álvara de Mendaña de Neyra. The Spanish explorer was the first European to sight them.

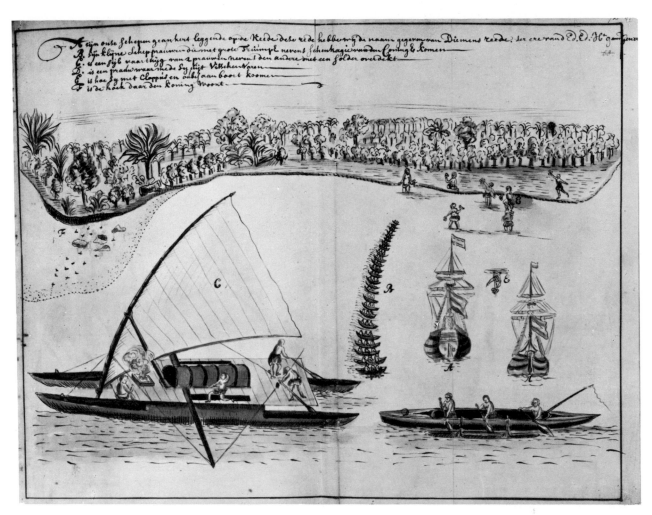

thought he had reached the Solomon Islands. In fact he had reached a different island group 300 miles to the east.

Mendaña named the largest island Santa Cruz and the large bay on the northern side Graciosa Bay. Relationships with the islanders quickly deteriorated into warfare when the Spanish tried

Above: a study of the two kinds of canoes used by Pacific islanders when they came to meet European ships off their shores.

Below: a sailing ship similar to the one used by Mendaña.

to build a settlement. Then the Spanish began to fight among themselves, many of them wanting to leave. This Doña Ysabel, who had money invested in the endeavor, was not prepared to do, and she had some of the rebels executed. Soon after this malaria began to kill off the Spaniards and the islanders attacked the survivors with poisoned arrows, choosing moments after showers when they knew the Spanish guns were useless. Mendaña himself died of malaria on October 18, but though Quirós took charge, it was a full month before Doña Ysabel consented to abandon the disastrous colony and make for the Philippines.

The wooden ships had been attacked by worms while at Santa Cruz and were so rotten that the sea ran in and out of the warped planks of their sides. Two ships sank and the sails of the surviving flagship disintegrated. The daily ration for the crew was reduced to a handful of flour mixed with seawater. Doña Ysabel had her own provisions, and though the men, women, and children on board were dying of scurvy, she refused to part with any. She did not even allow the little fresh water that remained to be distributed to the crew, but used it to wash her clothes. The sailors implored Quirós to run the ship onto the next reef in order to end their agony. Ninety-six days out from Santa Cruz, they at last sighted Manila and were rescued. Quirós returned to

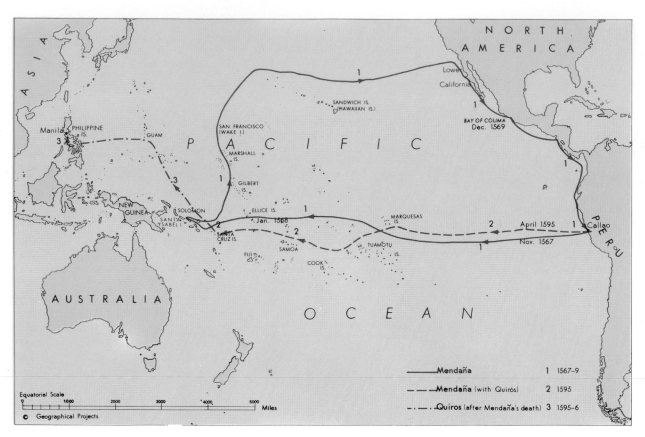

Mendaña   1   1567-9
Mendaña (with Quirós)   2   1595
Quiros (after Mendaña's death)   3   1595-6

Mexico, docking at Acapulco on December 11, 1596.

The frightful experiences of this voyage did not deter Quirós from wanting to convert the inhabitants of the elusive southern continent to Christianity. When he could not persuade the viceroy of Peru or the king of Spain to finance him, he journeyed to Rome in 1601 as a simple pilgrim and pleaded his case before the pope. The audience was successful and Quirós returned to the Spanish court bearing a papal letter. He was fired with missionary zeal. Intrigue

Above: a route map of the voyages made by Mendaña and Pedro Fernández de Quirós.

Left: Quirós' appeal to Pope Clement VIII for support of a voyage to the Pacific for the purpose of conversion. His approval imbued Quirós with a missionary zeal that was at variance with the motivations of his crews.

and obstructions delayed his departure, and there were further delays in Peru before he was given command of three ships – the *San Pedro y Paulo*, the *San Pedrico*, and the *Los Tres Reyes*, a small pinnace about the size of a modern launch. In command of the *San Pedrico* was a proud Spanish aristocrat, Don Diego de Prado y Tovar. The captain of the pinnace was another Spaniard, a navigator named Luis Vaez de Torres.

Quirós displayed a passion for the moral well-being of his men. Six Franciscans and four friars of the Order of St. John accompanied the crew and on the day of departure, December 21, 1605, Quirós insisted that all his officers put on friars' habit at the quayside. He forbade all card playing or gambling in any form and ordered the backgammon boards to be thrown into the sea. This did not endear him either to his officers or to the men, who were interested in treasure rather than missionary work.

Food was ample and good because Quirós was determined to prevent scurvy. He was the first expedition leader to carry distilling apparatus to make fresh water from the sea. His care for his men's diet was so successful that during the nine months the *San Pedro y Paulo* was at sea only one man died, and he was over 80.

Urged on by a group of troublemakers that included the chief pilot, the crews protested at going into the unfamiliar cold and squalls beyond 30° S. Quirós was obliged to turn northwest but even then many of the men, unused to long Pacific voyages, became alarmed at the vast size of the ocean. Intrigues and mutiny were avoided by the fortunate discovery of the island of

Taumako in what is now the Duff group. There the islanders' chief told of many islands to the south, one of which Quirós understood to be a large continent. He of course assumed that this was the longed-for Terra Australis and set sail for it.

On may 1, 1606 the ships entered a wide bay, described by Torres as "big enough for all the fleets in the world." Quirós named it the Bay of St. Philip and St. James. Landing parties confirmed that it was a most beautiful place, with a broad river flowing into the bay, rolling plains, a forest, and an abundance of plants and domestic animals. In a strange ceremony Quirós made his men members of a new Holy Order of his own invention, the Knights of the Holy Ghost, who were to be dedicated to the ideals of chivalry. Amid the fluttering of banners, Quirós knelt and kissed the warm sand of the beach. "O Land," he cried, "sought for so long, intended for so many and so desired by me!" He took possession of the territory in the name of the king of Spain, and because the king was also an Archduke of Austria, he named it Austrialia del Espiritu Santo. The colony was to be called New Jerusalem and the nearby river the Jordan. It was the climax of Quirós' life.

Disillusion soon set in. There was no sign of the expected riches and none but Quirós was interested in saving souls. Though not actually hostile, the inhabitants were far from friendly. After barely five weeks in New Jerusalem, the Spaniards abruptly abandoned it – and the circumstances of the departure were never satisfactorily explained. Quirós sailed alone, first going to Mexico and then to Spain to raise royal support for another voyage. He died on his way back to Peru in 1614, unappreciated and sick.

There is an important epilogue to this otherwise unrewarding tale. On the morning of June 12, 1606 Don Diego and Torres had awakened to find Quirós and his ship gone. On searching for the possible wreckage of the ship along the coast, they were convinced that Espiritu Santo was an island rather than the sought for Terra Australis. Don Diego was officially in command but he wisely let Torres, a more resolute and decisive man than Quirós, take charge. Torres had sailed southwest into the Coral Sea, and if he had continued on this course he would have come to the coast of the real Australia. However, he had turned north, planning to sail along the north coast of New Guinea which was a land already claimed for Spain. That plan had to be altered when headwinds prevented them rounding the eastern tip of New Guinea. Torres observed, "I could not weather the east point, so I coasted along to the westward on the south side." This simple statement concealed a sensational discovery. For as they battled through seas infested by sharks and littered with dangerous reefs, Torres unwittingly came upon the southern coast of New Guinea and proved it to be an enormous island also instead of part of a greater

Above: the Philippine Islands, to which Luis Vaez de Torres returned after the Spanish attempt at colonizing Austrialia del Espiritu Santo had failed and Quirós had sailed away alone.

continent. For the next two and a half months, Torres charted a coast no other European had ever seen. He then touched two islands of the Moluccas and sailed back to Manila, arriving on May 22, 1607.

Torres' wrote his report on his discovery in the Philippines, and it was buried in the archives for about a century and a half. Only after the British occupied the city of Manila briefly from 1762 to 1764 did Torres' discovery become generally known, and the name of Torres Strait was given to the passage through which the *San Pedrico* had sailed. Of Torres himself, nothing further is known, and after the death of Quirós there were no more Spanish attempts to discover Terra Australis. The great era of Spanish exploration was at an end.

Right: Manila, capital of the Philippines today. It was founded by Miguel Lopez de Legaspi in 1571 on a Spanish colonizing mission that left from Mexico.

Jan Pieterszoon Coen 1587-1629

Spices came second to gold dust for the merchant traders in the East, and Portugal was the first European country to exploit the Spice Islands. In the second half of the 16th century Portugal became a province of Spain, however, and the Dutch sailed in to seize the rich prize of the spice trade. They were urged to do so by Jan Huyghen van Linschoten who at the age of 20 had obtained the post of junior clerk to the Portuguese Archbishop of Goa, and six years later had returned to the Netherlands with a store of useful information. He urged Dutch merchants to send their ships around the Cape of Good Hope, "especially to Java, an island not yet frequented by the Portuguese, but abounding in diamonds, frankincense, and spices."

The first merchant ships sailed from the Netherlands in 1595 and soon 10 different companies were competing with one another. They saw the advantages of amalgamation and formed the United East Indies Company in 1602 with

Above: Jan Pieterszoon Coen. He was largely responsible for the ascendency of the Dutch in the Spice Islands.

Left: Jan Huyghen van Linschoten. His suggestions and information on the Spice Islands helped prompt organized Dutch activity in the East Indian spice trade.

the monopoly of all Dutch trade east of the Cape of Good Hope.

It was necessary to discover something of the eastern approaches to Java and the Moluccas so as not to be taken by surprise by the merchant ships and raiding vessels of other nations. Steven van der Hagen sailed from the Netherlands in 1603 in command of an expedition of 13 ships to do

this, and after making treaties of friendship with the rulers of Ternate and the Banda group of islands of the Moluccas, brought the Netherlands its first territorial conquest by ousting the Portuguese garrison from the island of Amboine. When Van der Hagen turned for home he left a small sailing ship behind to continue exploration east of the Moluccas. It was the *Duyfken* commanded by Willem Jansz. Jansz sailed eastward along the southern coast of New Guinea – in the very same year that Torres sailed along it in the opposite direction – and was attacked by the inhabitants who murdered some of the crew. He missed the Torres Strait and coasted south for 150 miles along the western shore of Cape York, Australia's northernmost peninsula. Jansz thought he was still following the coast of New Guinea, but his voyage was the first recorded discovery of Australia.

During most of the 17th century the Dutch were aiming for complete monopoly of trade in the East Indies, and the man chiefly responsible for this policy was Jan Pieterszoon Coen. Born in 1587 in Hoorn, North Holland, he was 20 when he sailed to the Spice Islands for the first time as an assistant merchant of the company. He was promoted swiftly, becoming head of the company's principal trading post in Bantam, Java in 1613. At first he showed patience and restraint in his dealings with local rulers, securing a clove monopoly in the Moluccas followed by a nutmeg monopoly in the Banda Islands. The

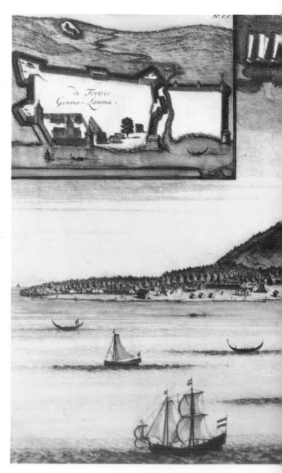

pepper trade proved more difficult to control because pepper vines grew in many parts of the East Indies islands. The sultan of Bantam resisted his attempts to introduce controls and in 1619 Coen, governor-general at the age of 31, transferred his headquarters to the nearby port of what is now Djakarta.

In May 1619 the sultan besieged the newly built Dutch fort but Coen, temporarily absent from the town, returned with a force large enough to defeat the Bantams. On the site of his

Above: Dutch nutmeg traders in the Moluccas. The wooden weight measure shown in the foreground is still in use today.

Above right: an early woodcut showing the leaves and fruit of the nutmeg tree.

victory he founded the Dutch city of Batavia. This soon became the political and commercial center of the Dutch East Indies, and today as Djakarta is the capital of Indonesia.

In pursuit of his plan to control the supply and price of spices, Coen decided to restrict the clove crop to the island of Amboine. He headed a military expedition which attacked and laid waste the Banda islands, exterminating the population of 15,000. He drew up plans for attracting Dutch colonists to the East Indies and went back to the Netherlands to put the plan in action. While he was gone, 10 English merchants suspected of plotting to take over the settlement were tortured and executed by Dutch officials. This provoked public outrage in London and, since England and the Netherlands were on

Above: the Dutch East Indies Company headquarters in Batavia, now the capital of Indonesia and known as Djakarta.

Left: Ternate, one of the Molucca Islands, in about 1720. This drawing shows the fort built by the Portuguese, but the ships sailing in are Dutch.

friendly terms at the time, the Dutch considered it diplomatic to hold Coen responsible and forbid him to return to the Moluccas.

Coen again became governor-general in 1527 but his former energy seemed to have flagged. Two years later a Javanese army besieged Batavia and Coen died, probably from dysentery. Ruthless in his pursuit of the mercantile interest, he is representative of those who follow in the wake of discoverers and explorers.

Jakob Le Maire 1585-1616 Willem Schouten 1527?-1625

Few of the early explorers gained lasting profit from their discoveries. Some returned to honors and reward but later fell from favor. Some met death during their exploration. Several died on their very way home. The Dutchman Jakob le Maire, commander of one of the most daring and enterprising voyages of exploration in those adventurous years, was one of these last unfortunates.

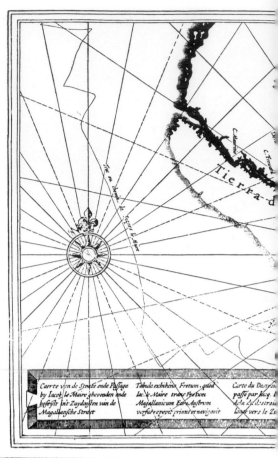

Left: Jakob le Maire who, with Willem Schouten as his sailing master, charted a new route to the Spice Islands by way of the unexplored tip of South America.

Below: an illustration of Porto Desire, Patagonia, in a book about Le Maire and Schouten's journey. It depicts the rheas (M) and llamas (L) they saw for the first time.

His story is tied to that of his father Isaac. A merchant himself, Isaac disapproved of the monopoly of the United East Indies Company and wished to break it. A letter written to the king of Spain by Pedro Fernández Quirós had come into Le Maire's possession and fired him with the ambition to travel to the South Seas and trade with the inhabitants of Terra Australis. The terms of the monopoly granted to the East Indies Company by the Dutch government gave it the exclusive right to send ships by way of the Cape of Good Hope and the Strait of Magellan. This effectively blocked both known routes to the Indies but Le Maire reasoned that if another route could be found, the company would have no legal power to prevent him from trading there. The more he studied the records of voyages in the vicinity of the Strait of Magellan, the more he came to believe that a route might exist around the unexplored tip of South America.

Isaac le Maire had no practical experience of the sea, so he consulted Willem Schouten because he was "a man well experienced and very

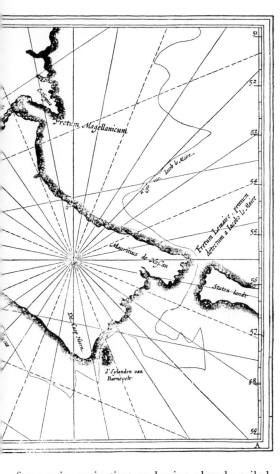

Left: a map showing the route taken by Le Maire and the strait later named after him. Le Maire's father fought the Dutch East India Company in the courts for two years to get his son's achievement properly recognized.

an island "almost entirely covered with eggs. A man standing still, with his feet together, could touch with his hands 54 nests, each containing three or four eggs." They were the eggs of the black-backed gull and the crew brought them on board by the thousands to eat. While at Porto Desire the *Hoorn* caught fire and burned to the waterline; nothing but the guns and anchors could be recovered for later reuse.

On January 20 Le Maire calculated that the *Eendracht* was passing the entrance to the Strait of Magellan and still sailing south. The high land of Tierra del Fuego to the west was white with snow, and soon more snow-capped hills came into view to the south. The coast appeared threatening, but on January 24 they came to an eight-mile-wide channel separating Tierra del Fuego from the land farther south. Because this land extended as far as they could see, they believed it to be a part of the great southern continent. It is in fact a fairly small island now called Staten Island. Along the southern coast of Tierra del Fuego they saw sandy beaches, penguins and other sea birds, and "whales by thousands," but they found no anchorage.

Leaving the channel that was later named after Le Maire, they sailed to the southwest, finding themselves in deep blue water. They battled against heavy rollers from the west – the Antarctic Drift. Then on the evening of January 29 they

famous in navigation, as having already sailed three times to nearly all places in the East Indies as skipper, pilot, and merchant, and still very eager after strange voyages and the visiting of new and unknown lands." At the town of Hoorn they equipped the 220-ton ship *Eendracht* and the 110-ton vessel the *Hoorn*. With Willem on the *Eendracht* was Jakob le Maire as commander of the expedition. Schouten's brother Jan was captain of the smaller ship. The crew was not told of the intended destination, and there were many rumors as to where it might be. The directors of the expedition called their venture the "Australian Company," but they were known on the waterfront as the Goldseekers.

The two ships sailed on June 14, 1615. By mid-August, with some members of the crew showing symptoms of scurvy, the ships stopped at Sierra Leone on the west coast of Africa. There Le Maire led a party ashore and traded "a few beads and some poor Nuremberg knives" for 25,000 lemons. This stock undoubtedly contributed to the remarkable good health of the crew; in the course of a voyage that lasted 15 months only three men died out of the total of 87.

When they reached the equator the men were told that they were sailing to Terra Australis by a new passage into the South Sea, and received the news with "great joy." For the next two months they coasted down the east side of South America and on December 8 anchored at Porto Desire in Patagonia. The men saw rheas, llamas, and the bones of an 11-foot "giant." Nearby they found

Below: Cocos and Traitors Islands in the South Pacific. These are two of the several islands visited by Le Maire on his way to the East Indies.

Hoornse Jnsel.
Insula Horn.

were astonished to lose sight of land ahead, seeing only high and sinister cliffs looming above and stretching back to the north. It was the southernmost tip of the American continent, which they named Cape Hoorn after their native town. They had rounded the tip in 10 days, showing that this route was quicker as well as safer than the narrow, reef-scattered Strait of Magellan which, six months earlier, had taken the Dutch admiral Joris van Spilbergen a month to navigate.

Steering a northerly course, the *Eendracht* reached the Juan Fernández Islands but, unable to land for fresh water, resumed their voyage to the northwest. They made good progress across the Pacific and on April 15 caught sight of the first of a succession of Polynesian islands that studded their route westward from then on. It was no more than a fringe of land encircling a lagoon, and because the sea was too deep for anchoring they named it *Sonder Grondt* (bottomless land). The islanders were "quite naked and red of color, with very black and long hair." Some approached the ship in canoes and one managed to make his way aboard and into Le Maire's cabin. There he pulled out the nails in the portholes hiding them away in his hair. In all the islands they visited they found the islanders most eager for metal objects. An atoll on which they succeeded in finding fresh water they called

Above: the Horn Islands, sighted by Le Maire in 1616. The Dutch established friendly relations with the islanders, who invited their exploration. They found no signs of cultivation in a land where food simply grew on trees.

Opposite top: the New Guinea coastline, looking much like it did when Le Maire sailed past it in the 17th century.

Waterlandt, and another on which they were attacked by vast swarms of flies they named *Vliegen* (Flies) Island. All these have been identified as part of the Tuamotu group.

A few days later they sighted a double canoe carrying "red folk who smeared themselves with oil." Their island, on which the *Eendracht* at last found an anchorage, was so thickly covered with coconut trees that they named it Cocos – which is now Tafahi in the northern Tonga group. At a neighboring island the inhabitants began by trading pigs and bananas for nails, but then tried to attack the ship. The discoverers called this *Verraders* (Traitors) Island.

The most pleasant period of their long voyage across the South Seas began on May 1, 1616 when they dropped anchor in the pleasant bay of a mountainous island which, with its neighbor, they named the Hoorn Islands. They are now Futuna and Alofi in the Horn Islands, midway between Samoa and Fiji. The islanders were a tall strongly built and intelligent people with yellowish-brown skin. Some wore their hair curled, "others beautifully crimped, others again had it tied up in four, five, or six plaits, whilst a few (a strange thing to behold) had their hair standing straight on end more than a quarter of an ell [about 10 inches] long, as if it had been pigs' bristles." The Dutch entertained the inhabitants with songs and dances to the

birds in the forest," as they expressed it.

Le Maire felt sure that the island was one of the Solomons and proposed continuing westward in an effort to find Quirós' continent, but Schouten favored a safer course to the northwest that would bring them to the Moluccas. Schouten's plan was adopted, which probably lost the explorers the chance of rediscovering the real Solomon Islands. In July and August they passed the long north coast of New Guinea, arriving at Ternate in the Moluccas in September and at Djakarta on October 18.

It had been a courageous and eventful voyage, but the East Indies Company was not prepared to allow any threat to its monopoly. Jan Pieterszoon Coen, the future governor-general, refused to believe that Le Maire and Schouten had found a new route to reach the Pacific. He declared their log to be a forgery and confiscated the ship and its contents. Both men, together with 16 members of the crew, were sent back to the Netherlands with Admiral van Spilbergen but after only eight days at sea Jakob le Maire died, a disillusioned man.

His father refused to let matters rest and sued the East Indies Company. After two years of legal argument he succeeded in recovering the ship, the cargo, and the court costs as well as establishing the existence of the strait that bears his and his son's name.

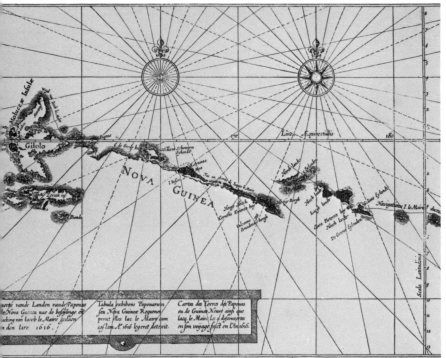

accompaniment of trumpets and drums, and the islanders returned the compliment in their way. Living on a fertile island that provided them with all their needs, the islanders seemed to the Dutchmen to enjoy "a life free of care, like the

Above: a map giving the route of the *Eendracht* as far as Ternate.

245

The Dutch Explore Australia

Below: a map of the west coast of Australia marked with the landfalls made by explorers in the 17th century and showing where the first Europeans were put ashore in 1629.

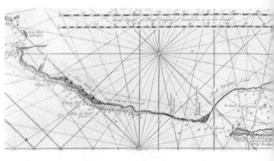

Below left: the pewter plate left by Dirk Hartog on the island named after him. It was found in a battered state 81 years later.

The most popular route to the East Indies lay around Africa's Cape of Good Hope. For many years all ships sailed northeast after rounding the Cape, but in 1611 Captain Hendrik Brouwer took advantage of the prevailing westerlies and sailed due east for 4000 miles before turning north toward the East Indies. This route proved so much easier that the Dutch East Indies Company ordered all its navigators to follow it. It was inevitable that a ship would one day overshoot the eastward leg of the journey and reach the west coast of Australia.

The first to do so was Dirk Hartog, captain of a merchant ship. On October 25, 1616 he made a landfall on Dirk Hartog Island off the west coast of Australia. He left a record of his visit in the form of a pewter plate that was hammered flat and nailed to a post. On the plate were scratched the details of his visit and the names of his companions. Eighty-one years later in 1697 the captain of another Dutch ship found the plate, battered but still decipherable, and brought it back to Amsterdam.

Several Dutch seafarers visited the west coast during the 10 years following Hartog's landfall. In 1618 Captain Jacobszoon discovered the Northwest Cape and Captain Claeszoon touched on the coast farther north near Port Hedland. In the following year Captain Edel sailed south of Dirk Hartog Island to a part of the coast that was named Edel's Land. In 1622 the *Leeuwin* reached the southwest corner of Australia and the cape was named after the ship. The East Indies Company became sufficiently interested in this new land to dispatch a small

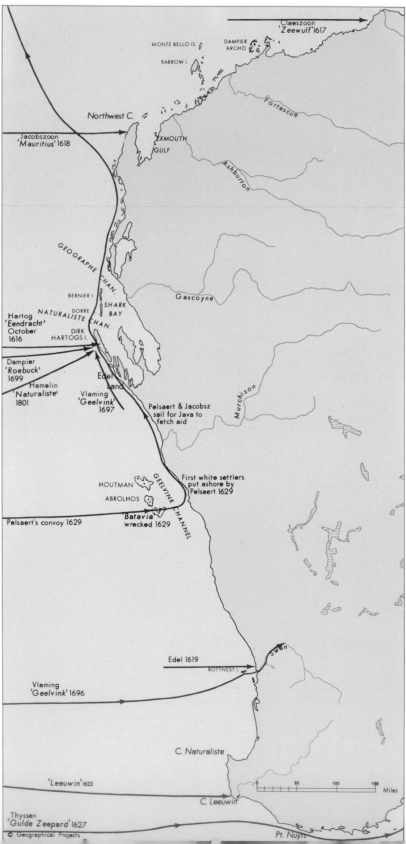

expedition under the command of Jan Carstensz to search for gold and spices. The ships, the *Pera* and the *Arnhem*, were blown westward across the Gulf of Carpentaria to a region they called Arnhem Land, but they brought back such discouraging reports of barren land and savage inhabitants that several years passed before the company decided to send out any more expeditions.

The south coast of Australia was discovered in 1627 when Captain Thyssen in the *Gulde Zeepaert* passed Cape Leeuwin and sailed for 1000 miles along the Great Australian Bight. The land to the north became known as Nuyts Land after Peter Nuyts, an important passenger who later became the Dutch ambassador to Japan. The existence of a great southern continent had finally been shown to be a fact. Though it was not the Terra Australis of legend, it was evidently a land mass of considerable size. Within a few years of its discovery, it was known as New Holland.

In 1629 the *Batavia* was wrecked on the reefs of the islets of Houtman Abrolhos off the coast of Edel's Land. All but 70 of the 290 men, women, and children abroad managed to reach two of the small islands, bringing with them food rescued from the *Batavia* before it sank; but no water could be found on the islands. François Pelsaert, the commander, put out in a small boat in the hope of finding water on the mainland 25 miles away, but the shore was rocky and barren and bad weather prevented a landing. After sailing 500 miles from the wreck, he decided that the best course was to make for Java to obtain help.

Meanwhile the shipwreck victims had discovered that the water lying on the rocks was fit to drink. With that problem solved, the ship's under-merchant Jerome Cornelis seized control and proclaimed himself captain general. About 30 people who questioned his authority were immediately executed and 45 others fled to a small island where they rallied under another leader. Cornelis attempted an invasion but was repulsed by the defenders armed with spiked clubs. Next Cornelis tried to bribe the others into joining him while proposing a peace treaty to the leader, but was captured instead.

At that moment Pelsaert returned from Java, and was overjoyed to find some of his party alive. The mutineers were rounded up, tried, and all but two executed. The fate of these two was to be marooned on the shore of the Australian continent, so becoming the first Europeans to land on the mainland. They were never seen again.

Abel Janszoon Tasman 1603-1659

The newly discovered land of New Holland, though its coastline seemed barren and its people hostile, could not safely be ignored by the Dutch East Indies Company. In 1642 the enterprising governor-general Antony van Diemen commissioned Abel Janszoon Tasman to make a full investigation of the seas to the south of it. Van Diemen's instructions were: "All continents and islands which you shall discover, touch, and set foot on, you will take possession of on behalf of their High Mightinesses the States General of the United Provinces."

The voyage had several important aims. The Dutch were eager to find the reputedly rich Solomon Islands, which had been lost since their original discovery by the Spanish in 1568. They were anxious to find a southern sea passage from the Spice Islands to Chile where they had established a valuable trade with the Spanish colonists, and they hoped Tasman might find a route to take the place of sailing around the north coast of New Guinea before proceeding southeast across the Pacific. They also wanted a more detailed exploration of the New Guinea coastline. Finally, they wanted to discover more about the mysterious New Holland.

Tasman's orders were to sail from Batavia westward to Mauritius and into the zone of prevailing westerly winds. Taking advantage of these he was to sail eastward, farther east than any other ship had ventured before. He was then to turn north and search for the Solomons and for Austrialia del Espiritu Santo, examine the east coast of New Guinea, and make his way back to Batavia. This voyage was excellently planned, both in terms of the new regions it would penetrate and the use it would make of the pre-

Above: Abel Tasman and his family. Tasman established his home in Indonesia after he made his historic voyages of discovery around the Australia continent.

Above: Anthony Van Dieman, the governor-general of New Holland for whom Tasman named the island that is now Tasmania.

Left: a plan of a Dutch fort in Batavia. The Dutch constructed their forts to give them a full field of fire against any attack.

vailing winds. If successful, it would also lead to the circumnavigation of Australia – although neither Van Diemen nor anyone else at that time suspected that Australia was not a peninsula of the great southern continent but an island-continent. As it happened, Tasman sailed right around Australia without seeing it.

On August 14, 1642 Tasman sailed from Batavia with the two ships *Heemskerck* and *Zeehaen*. He arrived at Mauritius on October 8, and after taking on fresh water supplies, set sail into the west wind zone of the Roaring Forties. The ships reached 47° S, which was too cold for a crew accustomed to the warm weather of tropic seas. When they complained, Tasman altered the course northward to 44° S. On the afternoon of November 24 they sighted the mountains and rocky shore of what is now Tasmania. He was just north of the Elliot Bay area, and he followed the coast to the south and east but at too great a distance to make an adequate survey. It is hard to understand why he did not try to anchor there because the new land was no barren stretch of desert such as had been discovered by Dutch sailors on the northwest coast of Australia. It was a fertile and thickly wooded island which had on the south coast three of the best harbors in the southern hemisphere. Tasman sailed past all of this, and when he anchored off Cape Frederick Hendrick on the southeast corner he chose a place where the seas were too rough and the surf too high for boats to reach the shore. The ship's carpenter had to swim ashore on his own with the flagpole and claim the land for the Netherlands.

Tasman called the island Van Diemen's Land in honor of the governor-general. The discovery of Australia may always be in dispute but there is no controversy over this island lying on its southeastern tip. In 1856, in recognition of its Dutch discoverer, the island's name was changed by the British colonists to Tasmania.

The *Heemskerck* and the *Zeehaen* sailed eastward and after nine days sighted land again. Seeing a long coastline to starboard, Tasman was convinced he had found the southern continent. He was in fact looking at the western coast of New Zealand's South Island. Unable to land, the ships sailed north for three days until,

ing four of the Dutch, the Maoris rowed rapidly back to shore. Tasman ordered the ship's guns to be fired but the Maoris escaped. The speed of their canoes and the skill with which they handled them surprised and impressed the Europeans. To avoid more deaths, Tasman ordered the ships to leave. He named the place Murderers' Bay.

The ships continued north. Had they sailed east they would have found the strait that separ-

rounding the northernmost cape of the South Island, they swung east into what is now called Golden Bay. That evening they dropped anchor in the sheltered harbor.

Though anxious to replenish his supply of fresh water, Tasman was uncertain of the temper of the island's inhabitants. He called the *Zeehaen*'s officers for a counsel aboard the *Heemskerck*, and it was decided to wait for the islanders to make the first move. No unnecessary risk was to be taken. Even while the Dutch were discussing what to do, however, the islanders were preparing their assault. As the officers of the *Zeehaen* were returning, a boatload of Maori warriors swiftly rowed out and attacked them. After kill-

Above: ships like these were used by the Dutch East India Company. They were superior to those of the rest of Europe.

ates the two islands and beyond it the wide Pacific stretching more than 4000 miles to Cape Hoorn. Taking the northern course meant that the legend of the great southern continent survived a few years longer.

The Maoris of New Zealand's North Island proved as hostile as those of South Island, and Tasman gave up the attempt to land. Within two weeks of sailing away, the ships were among the islands of the Tonga group, later to be known also as the Friendly Islands. The inhabitants certainly proved more hospitable than the Maoris, readily exchanging fresh water, fruit, coconuts, pigs, and chickens for old nails, beads, and cheap looking glasses. The chief, says Tasman, "behaved to us with great friendship, and inquired of us whence we came and where we intended to go. We told him that we had been more than one hundred days at sea, at which he and the natives were much astonished . . . We saw no arms among them; so that here was altogether peace and friendship."

Sailing northwest the Dutch soon came to the

Right: a proa of the kind that greeted Tasman at many of the South Sea islands he approached.

Below: a drawing of Tasman's ships while anchored off an island.

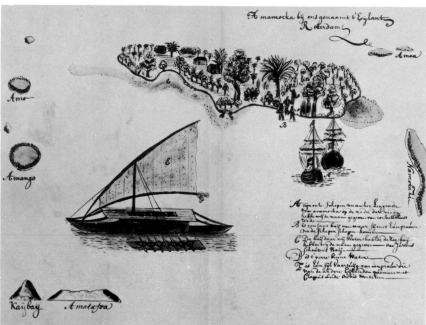

dangerous outer reefs of the Fiji Islands. Here both ships came close to being wrecked when they found themselves within a bay of reefs shaped like an arrowhead, with the wind driving them fast toward the point. Tasman in the *Heemskerck* chose the only possible course for escape. He looked for the place in the reefs where there was the least sea breaking and therefore offered the most chance of sailing over, and he boldly drove the ship toward it. The *Heemskerck* was just able to scrape across. The smaller *Zeehaen* managed even a little better, and they both survived.

Tasman's chief navigator on this voyage was Francis Jakobszoon Visscher, a brilliant and imaginative seaman who deserves as much credit as Tasman for the voyage's achievements. Visscher wanted to sail the ships due west from Fiji toward the southern coast of New Guinea. If they had done so, they would have filled a gap in the maps and would also have rediscovered the Torres Strait. Tasman had had enough of reefs, however, and took the known and safer course along New Guinea's northern coast.

When the ship returned to Batavia after barely 10 months away, Van Diemen did not conceal his disappointment. In a letter to the company in Amsterdam he criticized Tasman for being "somewhat remiss in investigating the situation, conformation, and nature of the lands and peoples discovered." Nonetheless, when another expedition set sail in January 1644, Tasman

Below: a view of the Tasman Sea, named in honor of the Dutch explorer who first charted it. The British settlers of Australia also named the island of Tasmania after him in recognition of his work.

was again placed in charge of it.

This time he had three ships, one a fishing boat. He first explored the southern coast of New Guinea so that "we may be certain whether this land is divided from the great South Land or not." Once again Tasman had the benefit of Visscher's experience but, although at one time he was actually in the entrance of one of the three channels of the Torres Strait, he was deterred by the reefs south of New Guinea. He sailed south into the Gulf of Carpentaria and then followed the north Australian coast back toward the west, this time more closely than on his previous

voyage. He made several observations on the land and its people. At Anson Bay south of Darwin he wrote, "The coast is barren. The people are bad and wicked, shooting at the Dutch with arrows without provocation when they were coming on shore."

When Tasman returned to Batavia, Van Diemen was even angrier than before. He wrote, "We intend to have everything more closely investigated by more vigilant and courageous persons than have hitherto been employed in this service," but he died in 1645. The company decided that it was making enough profit from the lands it already possessed, and Tasman remained in its employ without making more voyages. He became a wealthy and respected landowner in Batavia, dying there in 1659. Tasman had encircled New Holland without being aware of it, and had shown that it did not stretch indefinitely eastward. What he discovered – and curiously, what he failed to discover – proved of much importance to those who followed him into the South Pacific, not least Captain James Cook of Britain. The Dutch had no other grand designs for exploration.

Below: a map of 1680 which takes account of the most up-to-date information, including Tasman's establishment of the continuity of the coastline from Cape York to the Northwest Cape.

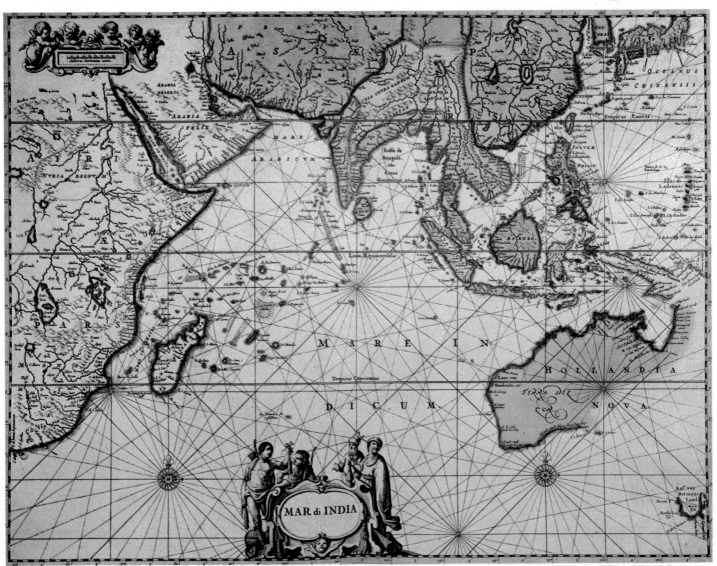

James Cook
1728-1779

Until the latter half of the 18th century, doubts and disputes clouded human knowledge of the South Seas and the many large and small islands that lay scattered across it. The east coast of Australia was unknown. The two islands of New Zealand were still assumed to be one – and possibly the edge of a much larger southern continent. It was James Cook, not quite the last but undoubtedly the greatest of the Pacific explorers, who solved almost all the outstanding mysteries. He accurately charted the coasts of New Zealand and eastern Australia, and he sailed south into Antarctic waters. He proved conclusively that a southern continent extending to the Pole was a figment of the imagination. By discovering the Society and Sandwich Islands, now called Hawaii, he also filled in almost all the missing gaps on the map of the Pacific.

Cook was born in 1728 near Whitby in northern England, the son of a Scottish farm laborer. Not until the late age of 18, after having worked as a farmer's boy and grocer's assistant, did Cook

Right: James Cook, the son of a farm laborer who became one of the greatest navigators in history. After his voyages, little of the vast Pacific remained unknown.

Below: an example of the early cartography work done by Cook. It shows the traverse of the St. Lawrence River near Quebec, and it was used to good effect by British warships that sailed up the river to besiege that city.

go to sea. He was apprenticed to a Whitby ship-owner who lodged the boy in his own home when he was ashore and encouraged him to study. When Cook was only 25, he was offered the command of a collier. Surprisingly, he turned the offer of commanding the coal transport vessel down, choosing instead to join the navy as an ordinary seaman. His ability was quickly recognized and he was soon raised to the rank of master. During the Seven Years War with

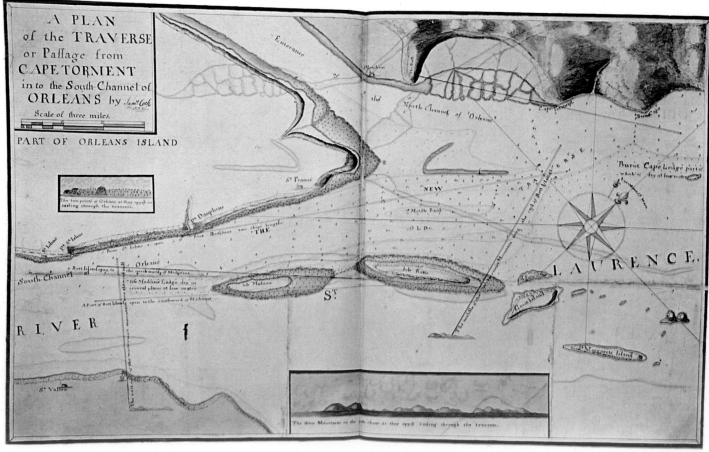

France, Cook saw active service in Canada and was present at the siege of Quebec. His meticulous charting of the St. Lawrence River was a major contribution to the British victory and testified to his patience and skill as a marine surveyor. The data he gathered was so accurate that his charts were not superseded for over a century. After the war he surveyed the coast of Newfoundland where his skill and industry gave him the deserved reputation as the best pilot in the navy. The governor of Newfoundland recommended him for his first command, which was of the schooner *Grenville*, and in the winter of 1767–68 he sailed the ship from Newfoundland to England.

In 1768 the British Royal Society requested that a ship be sent to the Pacific to study the transit of Venus across the sun. The observation of this phenomenon, due on June 3, 1769, was needed to determine the distance of the sun from the earth, and the Royal Society had calculated that the best vantage point for doing so was the newly discovered island of Tahiti. The British Admiralty at once seized the opportunity as a convenient cover for a thorough search for Terra Australis. The French were then active in the southern hemisphere, having already settled the Falkland Islands, and if there really were a rich southern continent, the British wanted to be there first. The Admiralty suggested that Cook

Above: Joseph Banks, the wealthy naturalist who accompanied Cook on his first journey in the Pacific to collect natural history data.

be given command of the ship and the Royal Society, which already knew of his work in Newfoundland, agreed. Cook, promoted to lieutenant, was able to select his own ship and chose a snub-nosed flat-bottomed collier from Whitby. The choice was an excellent one, though only a Whitby man would have made it. From his experience as an apprentice on the run between Yorkshire and London, Cook knew that a collier could maneuver well along tidal coasts. Its shallow draft was ideally suited for sailing channels of uncertain depth and if it did happen to go aground, the flat-bottomed hull would allow it to rest there without much risk of capsizing.

The ship was bought, completely refitted, and renamed the *Endeavour*. Provisioned for 18 months, it carried 94 men on board of whom 11 were civilians. Chief of these was the wealthy young Joseph Banks, later to become president of the Royal Society, and an ardent naturalist. He had contributed a large sum to the cost of the voyage and he brought with him two botanists, an astronomer, an artist, and four servants. Several members of the rest of the crew had sailed with the *Dolphin*, the ship that had discovered Tahiti the previous year under Samuel Wallis.

The *Endeavour* sailed from Plymouth on August 26, 1768. Tahiti was the official destina-

253

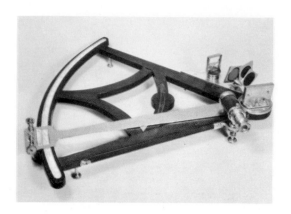

Left: a quadrant, a navigational instrument used by Cook. It is not nearly as accurate as modern scientific instruments, especially in bad weather.

coast of the island was charted, and on July 13 the *Endeavour* sailed from Tahiti. Cook took with him an islander named Tupia who proved invaluable as a pilot and interpreter. On his advice Cook visited other neighboring islands and then, following his instructions, sailed to the south. Cook followed a zigzag course but saw no sign of land until, on October 6, 1769, the ship touched on the east coast of New Zealand's North Island – the first European ship to sight the land since Tasman's voyage over a century before. Banks believed they had found the southern continent but Cook was unconvinced.

tion, but Cook carried secret instructions authorizing him to continue south after completing his astronomical observations in the hope of discovering "a continent or land of great extent." If he found no land he was to sail southwest between latitudes 40 and 50 until he reached the eastern coast of "the land discovered by Tasman now called New Zealand." He could then return by either the Horn or the Cape of Good Hope.

The outward voyage was by the Horn, which they passed in the southern hemisphere's midsummer, although the hills of Tierra del Fuego were thick with snow. Two of Banks' servants froze to death there when Banks took a party ashore to collect specimens and was unable to return to the ship before nightfall. After the Horn, Cook sailed the *Endeavour* farther south than anyone had ever done before, and the great roll of the sea from the west convinced him that there could be no great continent in that direction for many hundreds of miles. He knew he would have to sail there in order to make sure, but he did not do so at the time. First there were the observations to be made on Tahiti, and he turned north to sail there. Finding a small island in an ocean as vast as the Pacific was no easy task, and Cook had only the measurements of a previous navigator to go by. Estimates of longitude were often inaccurate in the days before the chronometer came into general use. Calculations of latitude were more reliable, so the only sure way of finding Tahiti was to get onto its latitude a few hundred miles to the east and to sail westward along that latitude until the land came into sight. That is what Cook did, and the peaks of the islands were sighted on April 11, 1769. As they approached the good anchorage of Matavai Bay, hundreds of Tahitians rowed out in their canoes to greet them, carrying the green bough of peace and crying, "Taio! Taio!" (Comrade!)

Tahiti proved a paradise for the naturalists, who occupied the three months they spent there collecting samples of the local plants and animals. The artist made sketches of the samples as well as of the landscape and the islanders. Cook had instructed everyone under his command to treat the population "with every imaginable humanity," and this injunction was followed to the letter – unlike many expeditions that followed.

The transit of Venus was duly observed, the

Above: *Arearea*, a painting by Paul Gauguin who lived and worked on Tahiti. This was one of his oils that helped create a romantic image of the South Seas island.

The truth could only be established by a careful survey of the coast, which had to wait until the *Endeavour* got fresh water. Cook dropped anchor in a protected bay and for two days watched the coast. On the third day he sent a boat ashore but the Maoris drove it away. A second attempt met with no more success and a third one led to a struggle in which Cook had to order his men to fire. The Maoris fought with great courage but four of their men were killed. Cook was distressed that his first attempts at friendship with them had ended so badly.

Farther north he found friendlier tribes of Maoris, and as the slow meticulous work of circumnavigating the two islands proceeded, he and they came to admire one another greatly. Cook pronounced the quality of their boats to be excellent and noted the expert construction of their fortified villages. He also respected their courage. "All their actions and behavior toward us," he wrote, "tended to prove that they are a brave, open, warlike people and void of treach-

ery." So great was his admiration that he returned to New Zealand on each subsequent voyage he made to the Pacific, using Queen Charlotte Sound on the north tip of South Island as his base and rendezvous. On their part, the Maoris were still handing down the story of Cook's humanity and gentle bearing toward them a hundred years later.

The *Endeavour* completed its 2500-mile close-in navigation in less than six months, a remarkable achievement on an unknown and often

Left: Cook's station at Venus Point, Tahiti. He built this fortified base for the scientific observations of the transit of Venus in June 1769.

Below: a clifftop fortification built by the Maoris of New Zealand. They also kept their war canoes at the ready to challenge any strangers approaching their homeland.

dangerous coast. Cook then turned for home, choosing the route around the Cape of Good Hope as being safer than the Horn for a ship that had already been at sea for 18 months. On April 19, 1770 the southeast corner of Australia was sighted. Sailing north for 10 days along the coast, surveying as he went, Cook at last found an anchorage in Botany Bay. Unlike the Maoris, the Aborigines avoided all contact with the European sailors. Tupia had been able to speak to the Maoris, whose ancestors had sailed from Tahiti, but he could not speak to the Aborigines. Wearing neither clothes nor ornaments, such things as beads, cloth, and nails meant nothing to them.

Cook continued northward and soon the *Endeavour* was within the treacherous area of the Great Barrier Reef – 1250 miles of coral ridges capable of ripping a ship to pieces. For weeks the *Endeavour* crawled forward a few yards at a time while boats ahead took soundings and men high in the rigging tried to spot the dark shadows of reefs in the water before the ship was on them. After navigating almost 1000 miles in this manner, the keel scraped across a pinnacle of coral and the sea gushed in. For a night and a day the ship was stuck on it, and only the flat-bottomed hull stopped it from turning over. Pumps were manned constantly but still there was water four feet deep in the ship's bottom when it was lifted on the tide. They had to fother the vessel – an intricate procedure by which a sail, filled with oakum, wool, rope ends, and dung, is passed

under the ship and pulled tight in the hope that the suction of the water will draw the refuse as a plug into the leak. The ship then slowly made its way to the mouth of a river a few miles to the north, where Cooktown now stands. When the *Endeavour* was finally beached, they discovered that it was not the fothering which had saved it but an immense piece of coral stuck like a plug in the largest of the holes. It took two months to get the ship seaworthy again.

Cook then decided to find a passage through the seemingly endless reef to the open sea, but once outside, the strong current and unpredictable winds threatened to carry them back onto the reef. A few days later the threat became greater when the wind died and the ship, unable to anchor in the deep water outside the reef and

Right: the *Endeavour* beached for repairs. Only once in the long voyage did the ship leak – and that after running aground on the Great Barrier Reef. It was made seaworthy within seven weeks.

Below: Captain Cook's route up the east coast of what is now the State of Queensland, Australia. It shows how he sailed in and out of the channel between the Great Barrier Reef and the mainland.

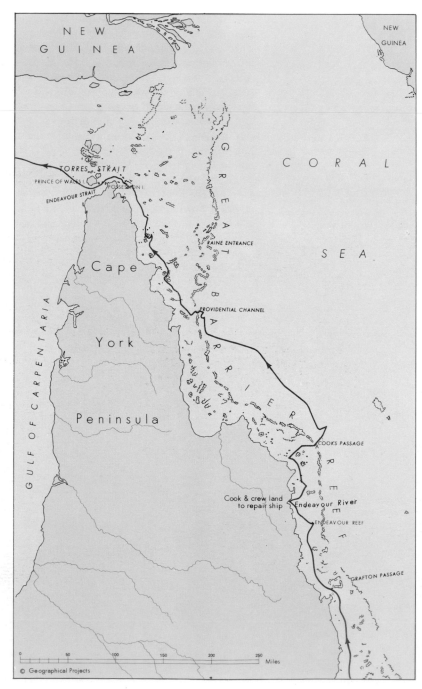

unable to move without wind against a strong tide, was only one yard from a wall of coral. A providential puff of wind carried it back out to sea for a moment. Cook saw an opening in the reef and managed to sail through the narrow gap into the comparative safety inside the reef. "It is but a few days ago that I rejoiced at having got without the reef; but that was nothing . . . to what I now felt at being safe at an anchor within it," he recorded.

The *Endeavour* continued on its painstaking way north to the Torres Strait and passed through it on August 21 and 22, 1770, the first to do so since Luis Vaez de Torres himself in 1606. After a long stay for repair at Batavia, it sailed for the Cape of Good Hope and home. Cook reached England in June 1771 almost two years and 11 months after embarking.

In spite of the doubt that the voyage cast on the existence of a southern continent, there were still scientists in England determined to believe in it. They felt that Cook had deliberately avoided the regions in which it must lie. Cook proposed that he lead another expedition, this time with two ships, in order to "put an end to all diversity of opinion about a matter so curious and important." The Admiralty promoted him to commander and provided for him the 462-ton *Resolution* and the 340-ton *Adventure*, two more converted Whitby colliers though handsomer ships than the *Endeavour*. The hulls were covered with an extra skin of planking as a protection against the borer worms of warm seas and the space between the two skins was packed with tar and oakum to deter the worms yet more. Banks had intended to go on this second voyage too, but withdrew angrily when Cook refused to accommodate his 15-member party of scientists, artists, secretaries, and servants.

The two ships sailed from Plymouth on July 13, 1772 and reached the Cape by October. From there they sailed south into the freezing storm belt that surrounds Antarctica. Soon the ships were having to make their way through a sea littered with floes and icebergs, some so enormous that sailors called them ice islands.

On January 17, 1773 Cook wrote: "At ¼ past 11 o'clock we crossed the Antarctic Circle, and are undoubtedly the first and only ship that ever crossed that line." On February 8 the two ships lost each other in a fog, and on March 16 Cook turned northeast in the face of impenetrable ice. One hundred and seventeen days after leaving the Cape and having sailed 11,000 miles – much of it where no other ship had been – Cook brought the *Resolution* into Dusky Sound on the coast of New Zealand's South Island. Some weeks later they found the *Adventure* safely moored in Queen Charlotte's Sound.

The ships passed the southern winter visiting

Below: the *Resolution*, shown near Antarctica where the crew collected and melted ice for drinking water. Cook was the first British captain to sail in the waters surrounding the frozen continent.

Pacific islands, including Tahiti, where they received the customary warm welcome. In September they sailed for New Zealand and on the way there the two ships were separated, this time for good. Cook left a message in a bottle for the captain of the *Adventure* and departed to explore the Pacific between New Zealand and Cape Horn. Battling through the ice, on January 30, 1774 they reached Latitude 71° 10', the farthest point south yet attained and only some 1250 miles from the Pole. By then Cook was certain that no continent existed in those latitudes. "I will not say it was impossible to get farther to the South," he wrote, "but the attempting of it would have been a dangerous and rash enterprise and what I believe no man in my situation would have thought of." The 16-year-old midshipman George Vancouver, later to win renown for his explorations on the west coast of Canada, clung to the bowsprit of the ship, determined to be the one to reach farthest south.

It would have been simple to head for the Horn and home from there but Cook, warmly supported by his officers and men, decided to head north and look for more islands. During the next six months they visited Easter Island, the Marquesas, Tahiti again, and Espiritu Santo. Farther south Cook charted the islands of the New Hebrides archipelago and the attractive island of New Caledonia. Returning to Queen Charlotte's Sound, he found that his message had been removed, but could not learn what had

happened to the *Adventure* from the local inhabitants. A month later he set off on a final attempt to find land between New Zealand and Cape Horn. None was sighted. The expedition spent Christmas in a cove off Tierra del Fuego, making merry with goose pie and Madeira wine and entertaining the local people. On December 28 they rounded the Horn into the South Atlantic, having shattered for ever the myth of a southern continent. Cook did not disguise his relief, writing: "I was sick of these high latitudes where nothing is to be found but ice and thick fogs."

Cook made one last voyage in the course of which he charted the coasts of west Canada and Alaska and discovered a group of islands that he named the Society Islands. They are now known as the Hawaiian Islands. On the morning of January 17, 1779 Cook stepped ashore at Kealakekua Bay on Hawaii itself. About 1500 canoes had surrounded the two ships and the

Below: Kauai, the first island that Cook landed on in Hawaii. He called this group of islands the Society Islands.

to return a week later because the *Resolution's* foremast had been damaged in a gale, and this time relationships with the islanders were not as good. When one of the seamen died and was buried ashore, the islanders were astonished to learn that Lono's followers were mortal after all. During the night of February 13 the cutter of Cook's second ship, the *Discovery*, was stolen. The next morning Cook strode ashore, escorted by 10 marines, to announce his intention of taking the local king on board his ship as hostage until the return of the cutter. A crowd began to throw stones and the boats lying offshore opened fire although Cook called out to them to stop. Turning his back to the islanders so that he could make his orders clearer, he stumbled. This was fatal. First he was stabbed in the neck, and then the mob descended to club and stab him wildly. His dismembered body was taken back to the village as the surviving marines made their way to the ship. A few days later the pitiful remains

islanders welcomed Cook with marks of adoration, taking him for the reincarnation of Lono, God of harvests and happiness. Cook, though unaware of this, treated the chiefs and priests with due solemnity and consideration, as was his natural way.

For a few weeks all went well, but even so, when Cook announced his departure there was undisguised relief on the part of the chiefs. Entertaining a god and his retinue had proved an exhausting and expensive business. Cook had

Below: the king of Hawaii being rowed out to greet Cook. The explorer was thought to be a god by the Hawaiians, and was entertained in the grand manner.

were brought to the ship by the villagers, who were penitent and grieving. It was Cook's fate to be killed in as tragic and unnecessary a way as his famous predecessor Ferdinand Magellan had been.

There was little left to discover in the Pacific after Cook had been there. He had disproved the southern land mass theory, established the true identity of New Zealand, and charted the east coast of Australia. He had also waged a successful battle against scurvy, the disease which had proved fatal on so many previous voyages of

Above: the death of Captain Cook. This romanticized version of the event fails to convey the horror and futility of the tragic killing of a man who had always treated local peoples with respect, dignity, and friendliness.

exploration by strictly regulating his crew's diet, issuing a daily supply of fresh vegetables and other foods containing the vital Vitamin C, and insisting on cleanliness and hygienic conditions. No man died of scurvy on any of his three voyages. He was admired and loved by his men, who knew he worked for their best interests both at sea and at home. He set an example of humanity and understanding in his relationship with the local peoples he encountered. With his death at the age of 51, the great age of seamen-explorers was near its end.

Matthew Flinders 1774-1814

"Cook had reaped the harvest of discovery, but the gleanings of the field remained to be gathered." This assessment of the state of Australian exploration at the end of the 18th century was made by Matthew Flinders, a young navigator and cartographer, as he set out to circumnavigate the continent.

British colonization of Australia was largely the result of the loss of the North American colonies through the Revolutionary War. When convicts could no longer be shipped to Virginia, they were sent to penal settlements in New South Wales. The first of these was established in Sydney Cove in 1788, and during the early years of the colony's struggle, little time could be spared for surveying territory farther afield. In

Above: Murray islanders rowing out to greet Matthew Flinders. The island inhabitants liked to get glass beads and other trinkets in exchange for food and information.

Below: Flinders and his companions on the tiny *Tom Thumb*, in which they weathered a terrible storm while exploring a river.

1795 Captain John Hunter arrived in Sydney to become the young colony's second governor. George Bass, the ship's surgeon, was a keen naturalist with ambitions as an explorer, and he convinced the governor of the benefits of charting the unexplored stretches of Australia's long coastline. Bass had brought a small sailing boat, the *Tom Thumb*, from England and within a few weeks of his arrival in Sydney he made his first expedition. With him in the *Tom Thumb* was his servant and Midshipman Matthew Flinders, whom Bass had come to know on the outward voyage.

Flinders was born in 1774 in Donington, England, the son and grandson of doctors. The surname had once been spelled Flanders be

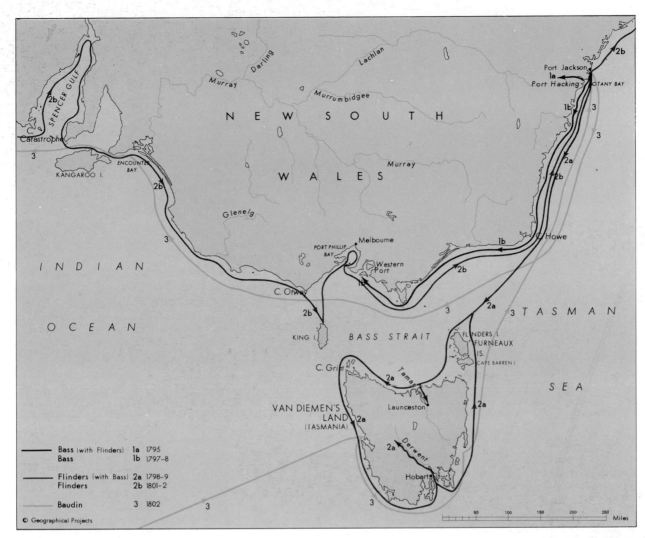

map legend

Bass (with Flinders) 1a 1795
Bass 1b 1797–8

Flinders (with Bass) 2a 1798–9
Flinders 2b 1801–2

Baudin 3 1802

© Geographical Projects

Above: the routes of Flinders, Bass, and Baudin around the coasts of southern Australia and Tasmania.

Below: George Bass. He teamed up with Flinders, and the two became Australia's first serious explorers.

cause the family was of Flemish origin. Young Matthew had been intended for a medical career in the family tradition, but at the age of 15 he decided to join the navy after reading a copy of Defoe's *Robinson Crusoe*. At the age of 17 he sailed through the Torres Strait with William Bligh, captain of the *Bounty*, and learned much from Bligh's skillful navigation.

In 1795 Flinders, Bass and the young servant took the 8-foot *Tom Thumb* south from Sydney Cove, through Botany Bay, and up the George's River. They were away for only eight days, but for the first time since the settlement of the colony, two men had shown themselves to be interested in exploration and Governor Hunter encouraged them. In March of the following year they again departed, this time to explore a large river said to flow into the sea to the south of Botany Bay. Their boat was nearly overwhelmed by a furious thunderstorm, and they were forced to go ashore where Flinders' quick thinking saved them from an attack by hostile Aborigines. The river proved to be no more than a large inlet, now Port Hacking, but they found a coal deposit – and again demonstrated that they were serious explorers.

Cook, Tasman, and the early Dutch explorers had charted the eastern, western, and northern coasts of Australia but little was known in detail of the southern coast. It was still uncertain whether Van Diemen's Land (Tasmania) was an island or a promontory jutting south from the Australian mainland. In September 1798 Flinders, then a lieutenant, was given his first command of the 28-ton sloop the *Norfolk*. With Bass and a crew of eight he set sail for Van Diemen's Land to establish positively whether or not it was an island. They stopped briefly at Twofold Bay to survey. Suddenly an Aborigine appeared. Flinders describes the encounter: ". . . We made much of him and gave him some biscuits; and he in return presented us with a piece of gristly fat, probably of whale. This I tasted; but watching an opportunity to spit it out when he should not be looking, I perceived him doing precisely the same thing with our biscuit, whose taste was probably no more agreeable to him, than his whale was to me."

The channel between Australia and Tasmania is 150 miles wide in places, but the relatively large islands at both the western and eastern entrances had long misled mariners into supposing that the land was continuous. The *Norfolk* sailed south by way of the Furneaux Islands and continued west along the north coast of Tasmania. Soon after passing the mouth of the

261

Above: the camp established by Flinders on the Great Barrier Reef while he went for help. This illustration appeared in his book.

beautiful Tamar River the coast turned north-west, and they began to fear that the channel was no more than a great gulf after all, and that they would arrive back on the Australian coast.

On December 9 the *Norfolk* turned south past Cape Grim and the two men saw a heavy ocean swell breaking on the shore ahead. "Mr Bass and myself hailed it with joy and mutual congratulation, as answering the long-wished-for discovery of a passage into the Indian Ocean," Flinders wrote.

That same day they observed a vast flock of sooty petrels, covering a space 1000 feet wide and 150 feet deep. The birds flew out to sea in an uninterrupted stream for a full hour and a half. Flinders calculated that this incredible flock must have numbered 151,500,000.

He and Bass sped down the west side of the island, spent Christmas exploring the Derwent River, and returned to Sydney having established that Tasmania was an island. The journey through Bass Strait, which was what Flinders named the channel, cut off a week of the voyage to Sydney.

This expedition was the last that the ailing Bass undertook, but Flinders sailed for England determined to persuade the Admiralty to entrust him with the circumnavigation, surveying, and charting of the whole of Australia. The Admiralty was sufficiently impressed by his achievements to give him command of the 334-ton *Investigator*, and in July 1801 he was ready to sail. At the last moment he was obliged to leave his new bride behind because of an Admiralty order, although it was not then uncommon for

Right: a view of Adventure Bay, Tasmania. The coasts of Australia and New Zealand have some of the finest natural harbors in the world.

wives to accompany their husbands on long voyages. Perhaps the officials thought Mrs Flinders would distract her husband from his duties, but if so, they misjudged their man. Flinders was passionately dedicated to the science of surveying and only crippling illness ever prevented him from working. He was the first man to study how a ship's ironwork affected its compass, and he proposed a compensating device that came to be known as the Flinders Bar.

The survey of Australia's southern coast began in December 1801 and for four months Flinders sailed the *Investigator* slowly eastward. It was believed that a great river must drain so vast a land mass, and one important object of the expedition was to discover the mouth of such a river. Flinders thought he had discovered it at

Left: a drawing of *Grevillea Banksii*, one of Australia's wild flowers. Many are hardy enough to grow in the harsh interior desert.

Above: Nicolas Baudin. He was sent by the French government to explore the south coast of Australia between Western Port and the Nuyts Archipelago.

Below: a letter promising not to take part in the war then on between Britain and France, signed by Flinders. It was a condition of his release from a French prison.

Spencer Gulf near present-day Adelaide, but the sides of the gulf narrowed and the inlet ended in mud flats. While they sailed across a broad sandy bay in April 1802, they sighted the French ship *Géographe* commanded by Nicolas Baudin. The two captains exchanged information before sailing on, and possibly because of the distraction of this unexpected meeting, they both missed the mouth of the Murray River which drains into the very bay where they met.

From Sydney the *Investigator* sailed up the east coast, surveying and occasionally exploring inland. Flinders sailed through the Torres Strait and into the Gulf of Carpentaria using the old charts of the Dutch mariners. Unfortunately the *Investigator* was not a good ship, and it began to leak badly. The carpenters found timber after timber rotten and reported that it would be unlikely to last more than six months. On November 26 Flinders wrote in his journal: "From this dreadful state of the ship, I find the complete examination of this extensive country, which is one of the nearest objects of my heart, to be greatly impeded, if not wholly frustrated."

He continued for as long as he could but was unable to take the ship beyond Arnhem Bay. In March 1803 he abandoned the hopeless task and set sail for Sydney, a weary and disappointed man. Ill-luck dogged him for the rest of his life. The ship on which he embarked for England was wrecked on the Great Barrier Reef and he sailed back to Sydney in an open boat to organize the rescue of the survivors on the reef. He then set sail in a 29-ton schooner, the *Cumberland*, to make the 13,000-mile journey back to England. The ship leaked so badly that he was forced to put into Mauritius where he was imprisoned by the French, then at war with England. He spent six and a half years in a Mauritius jail, suffering the added indignity of the French claiming his discoveries as their own. When he finally got back to England his health was broken. He never traveled again.

For four years Flinders worked on his book *A Voyage to Terra Australis*, and died on the very day that it was published in 1814.

I undersigned, captain in His Britannic Majesty's navy, having obtained leave of His Excellency the captain-general to return in my country by the way of Bengal, Promise on my word of honour not to act in any service which might be considered as directly or indirectly hostile to France or its Allies, during the course of the present war

Port Napoleon, Isle de France, 7th June 1810

(Signed) Matt.ew Flinders

Charles Sturt 1795-1869

Forty miles to the west of Sydney the precipitous ridges of the Blue Mountains rise steeply like an encircling wall. For a quarter of a century after the establishment of the first settlement, this barrier defied all attempts by the colonists to surmount it. Every expedition that laboriously made its way up one or other of the river valleys was forced to return, defeated by the rugged gorges and impassable waterfalls. Not until 1813 did Gregory Blaxland, a successful rancher, hit on the ingenious plan of conquering the mountains by climbing to the top of a ridge and track-

Above: Charles Sturt, who succeeded in charting Australia's main rivers but who was unable to conquer its hostile interior.

Below: the Murrumbidgee River.

ing it westward, rather than by following a valley. Having done so, he came upon mile after mile of rich well-watered country – "sufficient," he reported, "to support the stock of the colony for the next 30 years."

In the following decade a number of enterprising people discovered rivers that flowed westward from the Blue Mountains and the Great Dividing Range into the interior. In 1818 John Oxley, the surveyor-general, tried to explore the catchment area of the Macquarie River but unwittingly chose the wettest winter for years. At any other time he would have been walking over fine pastureland, but the wetness bogged him down in swamps. On his return to Sydney he crossed 12 rivers and guessed that they all drained into a great central lake. Neither he nor anyone else then suspected the existence of the great river system created by the Murray and the Darling.

The Murray was discovered in 1824 by Hamilton Hume, Australia's first native-born explorer. With William Hovell, he explored the land to the

south of the Murray as well, reaching the coast at Geelong a few miles west of what is now Melbourne.

In 1828 Captain Charles Sturt, a member of the governor's secretariat, was entrusted with the task of finding out where all the previously discovered rivers went to. For two years New South Wales had been suffering a severe drought, and Sturt reasoned that the swamps that had halted Oxley would be passable. With Hume, two soldiers, and eight convicts, he followed the Macquarie River far beyond the place at which Oxley had watched it disappear into the marshes. The journey was a nightmare. Twelve-foot high reeds often blocked their path. Leeches clung to their legs and mosquitoes and kangaroo flies bit their flesh. They squeezed river mud through their handkerchiefs to get drops of water to slake their thirst. Some of the Aborigine tribes they met proved to be hostile and set fire to the reeds ahead of them to hinder their passage. Sturt and his party were experiencing the ordeal that was to become a familiar pattern for all those who dared to seek out the secrets of this vast land.

In February 1829 Sturt wrote: "We suddenly found ourselves on the banks of a noble river . . . The channel of the river was from 70 to 80 yards broad and enclosed an unbroken sheet of water, evidently very deep, and literally covered with pelicans and other wildfowl." It was the Darling. To their dismay the water was salt, and though they followed it for 80 miles downstream, the water remained salt because of numerous brine springs along the river bed. It was clear from the height of the Darling's banks that "furious torrents must sometimes rage in it." But what happened to it when it was full? "Its course is involved in mystery," wrote Sturt. "Does it make its way to the south coast, or exhaust itself in feeding a succession of swamps in the centre

Above: an illustration of the Ana River, a tributary of the Darling, from Sturt's book entitled *Narrative of an Expedition into Central Australia.*

Below: the junction of the Murray and Darling rivers, which Sturt discovered.

of the island?" This was the puzzle he faced.

The question was solved by Sturt's expedition of 1829-30. This time he went down the Murrumbidgee River with George Macley, a young naturalist. They floated a 27-foot whale boat on the river and were carried westward through lakes of reeds and narrow channels all but choked with fallen trees. One afternoon their boat shot out into a broad swift-flowing river. They had reached the Murray, the same river that had been crossed by Hume and Hovell several hundred miles downstream.

The party made friends with many of the Aborigines and Sturt observed their customs. "The old men alone have the privilege of eating the emu. This evidently is a law of policy and necessity for if the emus were allowed to be indiscriminately slaughtered they would soon be-

come extinct. Civilized nations may learn a wholesome lesson even from savages, as in this instance of their forbearance. For somewhat similar reasons perhaps, married people alone are here permitted to eat ducks."

Not all the tribes let them sail by unimpeded. On one occasion 600 angry tribesmen gathered on a spit in the river ahead, "their spears quivering in their grasp ready to hurl." Sturt prepared to fight, but before he could fire into the cluster of Aborigines, Macley stopped him. Four men from a group they had befriended the previous day were hurrying toward the warriors. One went ahead and, when he reached the sandbank, succeeded in persuading the Aborigines to lay down their arms. After this providential rescue, Sturt noticed that they were at the junction of another river and they rowed up it for several miles. Sturt was convinced that this was where the Darling, the river he had discovered the previous year, flowed into the Murray.

Sturt then turned and continued down the Murray for about 400 miles. The party finally reached the shallows of Lake Alexandrina, which earlier coastal explorers had not recognized as the mouth of a great river. The men could hear

the thunder of the sea from Encounter Bay but mud flats and quicksands made it impossible to take the boat to the sea. There was nothing to do but turn back and row the 1000 miles upsteam for home. The return journey was harrowing, but the severe trial opened the way inland for the new settlers. Within two years, nine ranches had spread 50 miles down the Murrumbidgee, and the colonization of southern Australia followed soon after. The city of Adelaide was founded on the other side of the mountains from Alexandrina Bay, and it was from there that several important expeditions set out. They went westward along the Great Australian Bight and northward into the region of the central lakes, ultimately crossing the continent to the north coast.

The challenge of the center drew Sturt who declared, "I should like to put the finishing strokes to the career I began in New South Wales by unfolding the secrets of the interior and planting the ensign of my country in the center of this mysterious region. Truly it is an object worthy to perish one's life for."

In June 1844 Sturt and a party of 15 men started up the Murray and the Darling Rivers from Adelaide to the settlement of Menindee, there turning northwest for the center. In November he camped at Broken Hill, unaware that the mountain range contained vast wealth in silver ore. Unluckily it was one of the hottest of summers, and the suffering of men and animals was intense as they toiled over desert plains in the blistering heat. They walked the last 150 miles to Milparinka, watching the waterholes dry up before them or having to pull out dead frogs before they could get at the last drops. Milparinka offered them a good supply of water, but with temperatures ranging from 130° to 160° F, the party was forced to camp there for the next six months.

Above: Sturt on the edge of one
of Australia's stony interior deserts.
Because of his courageous efforts to
open the Australian interior, Sturt
is often called the "father of
Australian discovery."

Even in the underground room they dug for themselves the heat was so intense that ink evaporated from their pens and their hair stopped growing. In August 1845 Sturt and four men made a dash for the center. They found a few waterholes and some fish in the creeks, but then they came to a plain, burned and cracked by the heat of the sun. After 400 miles Sturt turned back. Although he was only 150 miles from the very center of the continent, his decision had come not a moment too soon. They were on the edge of the fearful Simpson Desert and he could not have gone farther and lived.

The return journey was another terrible ordeal. The stores ran out and they had to unearth scraps the dogs had buried. When they reached Malparinka Sturt collapsed, scurvy-ridden and on the verge of total blindness. From there the expedition returned to Adelaide in easy stages with Sturt carried on a litter.

That was Sturt's last expedition, although he considered another venture into the interior when he had recovered his health. Because of his courageous attempts to open up the country, he is often called the "father of Australian discovery," and unlike so many other explorers, his path was never stained with bloodshed. He

Right: Sturt's Desert Pea, a wild
flower of the desert named after
the explorer.

lived until 1869, long enough to see the continent crossed by a younger member of his Central Australian expedition, John McDouall Stuart.

267

Penetrating the Vast Interior

In 1859 the South Australian government offered a monetary prize to the first person to cross the continent from south to north. There were two contenders – John McDouall Stuart, who had almost reached the center of the continent with Charles Sturt in 1845, and Robert O'Hara Burke, a Melbourne police officer.

Stuart, the first to start out, was an experienced explorer. Born in Scotland, he had emigrated to Australia as a young man and had tried his hand at sheep farming before joining Sturt as a draftsman on his Central Australian expedition. After that he had explored the inland regions around Adelaide and had mapped the forbidding areas of salt lakes and seasonal creeks around Lake Eyre.

Stuart left from Adelaide in his first attempt to cross the continent in January 1860 with two other men and 13 horses. He was at Chambers Creek, south of Lake Eyre, by March. The party traveled up the Finke River, crossed the Macdonnell Ranges, and on Sunday April 22 reached the dead center of the continent. Stuart recorded it in his journal: "Today I find from my observations of the sun, 111° 00' 30", that I am now camped in the center of Australia. I have marked a tree and planted the British flag there. There is a high mount about two miles and a half to the north-north-east. I wish it had been in the center; but on it tomorrow I will raise a cone of stones, and plant the flag there, and name it 'Central Mount Sturt'." The name was later changed to Central Mount Stuart in honor of its discoverer.

In the center of the continent Stuart found great stretches of watered and well-grassed country, but as he and his companions pressed on to the north the creeks dried up. Their thirst became overwhelming and at Tennant Creek they ignored gold to dig for the more precious water. At Attack Creek the Aborigines massed with their boomerangs and spears and set the brush on fire in the faces of the explorers. By June 27 the party had covered three quarters of their journey but Stuart wrote in his journal: "I have most reluctantly come to the determination to abandon the attempt to make the Gulf of Carpentaria. Situated as I now am, it would be most imprudent." Supplies were low and his own health was bad. "The days are now become very hot again, and the feed for the horses as dry as if it were the middle of summer. The poor

---

Message, No. 20.

The Governor-in-Chief informs the House of Assembly, in reply to Address No. 12, of the 19th instant, that he has directed to be inserted on the Estimates for the year ending 30th June, 1860, the sum of Two Thousand Pounds (£2,000), as a reward to the first person who shall succeed in crossing through the country lately discovered by Mr. Stuart, to either the north or north-western shores of the Australian Continent, west of the 143° of east longitude, and north of the southern parallel of latitude $23\frac{1}{2}$°.

RICHARD GRAVES MACDONNELL,

Government House, Adelaide, July 26, 1859.   Governor.

Above: the announcement of a government reward for the first south-to-north crossing of the continent. Only two tried for it.

Right: the expedition led by Robert O'Hara Burke in answer to the government's offer. It was one of the most expensively and fully equipped in exploration history.

Left: John Stuart, the second man in the race for the prize. To him goes the honor of being the first to reach the north coast and return, although Burke had been the first to get to the coast.

animals are very much reduced in condition, so much so that I am afraid of their being longer than one night without water." Sick with scurvy and disappointment, he and his men returned to Adelaide. Despite his sufferings he never failed to record his observations of the regions they passed through, noticing a new kind of desert rose, an unfamiliar bird, or the customs of the Aborigines. On the day they headed for home he wrote: "These natives do not deposit their dead

Above: camels were believed to be ideal for crossing the barren interior of Australia because of their desert habitation.

Burke (**below**) and William John Wills (**below right**). A surveyor with some experience of the outback, Wills was second in command.

bodies in the ground, but place them in the trees, and, judging from the number of these corpses which we have passed between this and the large creek, where they made their attack upon us, they must be very numerous."

Stuart had reached as far as the 19th parallel on this trip. In 1861 he tried again and went even farther, reaching the 17th parallel before similar circumstances forced him to turn back again. The burning hot plain and thick scrub proved "as great a barrier as if there had been an inland sea or a wall."

In August 1860 Stuart's rival Burke started out from Melbourne with the best-equipped and most expensive expedition that ever explored any part of Australia. Public contributions and a government subsidy provided ample funds. Twenty-five camels and three drivers were brought from India, and what seemed to be very careful preparations were arranged for a journey from Menindee on the Darling north to the Gulf of Carpentaria. Unfortunately, Burke was not a good leader. Though a man of undoubted courage, he had no knowledge of bushcraft and his impetuosity brought calamity to the expedition. There was quarreling even before the party reached Menindee, where Burke had recruited William Wright to show them a short cut to Cooper's Creek. The original second in command returned to Melbourne with the expedi-

tion's artist, having found Burke's manner unendurable. William Wills, trained as a surveyor and somewhat experienced in the outback, took over as second in command.

Wright guided half the party to Cooper's Creek 400 miles to the northwest and then went back for the others. He was so long in returning that Burke became impatient and began his dash for the north coast. It was December 16. Mounted on his gray horse, he took with him Wills, Charles Gray, and John King, a young former Indian Army soldier. These three rode camels. The expedition's foreman, William Brahe, was left in charge at Cooper's Creek with orders to wait there for three months or until the supplies ran out.

Burke had chosen a better route than Stuart. Much of it skirted the desert and lay on land

269

already occupied by sheep and cattle stations. Sometimes they were obliged to leave the creeks and make their way over sandy ridges, but for the most part they traveled across wide stretches of scrub and grassland watered by occasional rain and flooding from the creeks. The waterholes abounded in ducks and other waterfowl. At first the party made rapid progress, but the rains came and bogged the animals in marshland. It took eight weeks to reach the coast. When the ground became too waterlogged for the camels to move, Burke and Wills went ahead, reaching the estuary of the Flinders River on February 9, 1861. They were within the tidal influence of the river but were unable to see the ocean. It would take another two days to cut their way through the jungle to reach the beach, and it was time they could not afford. They had supplies for only five weeks and the journey would take eight.

It took them nearly 10 weeks, however. They left the coast in a thunderstorm and for the next few days moved in constant rain. All of them

Above: the rescue party that found the bodies of Burke and Wills took them back to Melbourne to be buried with pomp and ceremony.

Opposite: the barren desert of the interior sometimes becomes a swampland of equal harshness.

Left: a sketch of an Aborigine by the artist who sailed with Baudin's expedition. It probably gave Europeans their first view of the inhabitants of Australia.

became ill. Burke and Gray went down with dysentery. Burke's horse died and its flesh was cut up into strips and dried for eating. Four of the six camels also died. On April 17 Gray, who was the strongest man in the group, was the first to die. Four days later, on the evening of April 21, the three weak and emaciated survivors crawled into the camp at Cooper's Creek. It was deserted. Although Brahe had waited six weeks longer than he had been instructed to, he and the rest of the party had left that very morning. Wills recorded his disappointment: "Arrived the depot this evening just in time to find it deserted. A note left in the plant by Brahe communicates the pleasing information that they have started today for the Darling: their camels and horses all well and in good condition."

The next day Burke left a note in the tree at Cooper's Creek saying, "The return party from Carpentaria, consisting of myself, Wills, and King (Gray dead), arrived here last night, and found that the depot party had only started the same day. We proceed on tomorrow slowly down the creek towards Adelaide by Mount Hopeless, and shall endeavour to follow Gregory's track; but we are very weak. The two camels are done up, and we shall not be able to travel faster than

four or five miles a day. Gray died on the road from exhaustion and fatigue. We have all suffered much from hunger. Greatly disappointed at finding the party here gone. Robert O'Hara Burke, Leader. April 22, 1861. P.S. The camels cannot travel and we cannot walk, or we should follow the other party. We shall move very slowly down the creek."

Wills and King argued strongly for following Brahe along their old route to Menindee but Burke insisted on going down the creek because, he said, there was a cattle station at Mount Hopeless 150 miles away. They rested for five days and then set out. Friendly Aborigines gave them some fish and nardoo, the seeds of a cloverlike fern that could be pounded and used like flour for flat cakes, and they learned to find the nardoo for themselves. But their chances of reaching Mount Hopeless, which were already slim, vanished when their last two camels died.

They camped about 50 miles downstream from the Cooper's Creek depot. On May 8 Brahe returned to it after meeting up with Wright who was at last making his way up from Menindee, but the camp looked exactly as he had left it. Burke, Wills, and King had carefully obliterated all signs of their visit so that the Aborigines would not be attracted to the depot and destroy the note they had left behind. Brahe rode away, unaware that his comrades were near death only a few miles from him.

The lives of the three men depended on keeping close to the camp of the kindly Aborigines, but gradually Burke and Wills weakened so much that they were unable to gather nardoo let alone pound it for flour. The Aborigines who

had been giving them fish moved on. For days King looked after the other two, but when he himself began to show signs of weakness, it was decided that he and Burke should leave Wills with eight days' supply of nardoo, water, and firewood and go in search of the Aborigines for help. Burke managed for only two days before he collapsed. King made him a good meal from a crow that he had shot and some pounded nardoo. "I hope you will remain with me here till I am quite dead," Burke said. "It is a comfort to know that someone is by." He died at eight the next morning.

King went back to Wills and found him dead also. The last entry in Wills' diary read: "I am weaker than ever although I have a good appetite and relish the nardoo much, but it seems to give no nutriment. I may live four or five days if the weather continues warm. Starvation on nardoo is by no means very unpleasant but for the weakness one feels and the utter inability to move oneself."

There was nothing left for King to do but to live with the Aborigines. He shot crows and hawks for them, and in return they gave him nardoo and fish and let him sleep in a shelter with the other single men. After three months a rescue party arrived under Alfred Howitt to find King a wasted shadow, hardly to be recognized as a human being. The bodies of the dead leaders, Burke and Wills, were carried back to Melbourne for burial.

To these two goes the honor of being the first to reach the north coast, but the indomitable Stuart led the first party to reach it and return alive. His expedition left Adelaide in December 1861, following the same route as before and not knowing that Burke had reached the north coast the previous April. After seven months they arrived safely at the sea by the mouth of the Adelaide River near present-day Darwin. In his

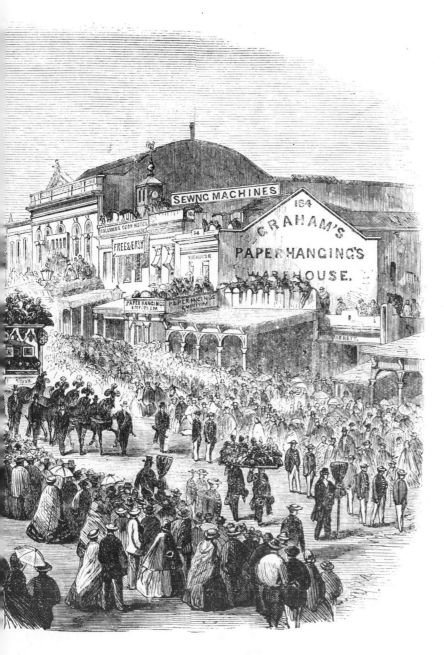

men "leading a string of limping, emaciated horses, came riding slowly, wearily, triumphantly out of the mirage that filled the empty north. The Commander of the South Australia Great North Exploring Expedition, along with his faithful companions, had returned."

Ten years later in 1872 the Overland Telegraph Line connecting Adelaide in the south with Darwin in the north was opened along the trail that Stuart had blazed. Stuart himself had been dead for six years by then. On his return in 1862 he had received £2000 and 1000 square miles of land rent free in the interior, but his health was broken. He returned to England and died there in 1866.

Other crossings still remained to be made, other areas to be discovered. Some explorers brought back news of good grazing land for sheep, others crossed over a wilderness of sand and stones incapable of sustaining life. Still others took a false trail in the desert and vanished. But the goal of proving that the continent could be crossed had been achieved by Stuart, Burke, and Wills.

Terra Australis became no more than a phrase in history books. The only true Terra Australis was the continent of Antarctica, snow-covered, icebound, and inhospitable to all forms of life but a few seals and birds. Already ships were venturing farther and farther south toward its shores. Eventually people would cross that continent as well.

journal Stuart wrote: "I did not inform any of the party that I was so near the sea, as I wished to give them a surprise . . . Thring, who rode in advance of me, called out, 'The Sea!' which so took them all by surprise, and they were so astonished, that he had to repeat the call before they fully understood what was meant. Then they immediately gave three long and hearty cheers." Later Stuart adds: "I dipped my feet, and washed my face and hands in the sea, as I promised the late Governor Sir Richard McDonnell I would do if I reached it."

The 2000 mile return journey in 1862 was the most difficult of all Stuart had made, having spent every ounce of his strength on these great expeditions across the interior. By the time he reached Chambers Creek he was almost blind, was suffering from scurvy, and was living on a little boiled flour which was all he could manage to swallow. When he started to bleed heavily, the others rigged up a litter slung between two horses. Three months later 10 gaunt and ragged

Above: the impressive funeral procession for Burke and Wills in Melbourne. People turned out in force for the two explorers who had become national heroes.

Right: Stuart and his party raising the British flag on reaching the Timor Sea. His journey back was even worse than the one endured in getting there.

Opposite: a sheep farmer driving his flock through the Australian bush. Settlers followed closely on the heels of early explorers like Stuart, Burke, and Wills.

273

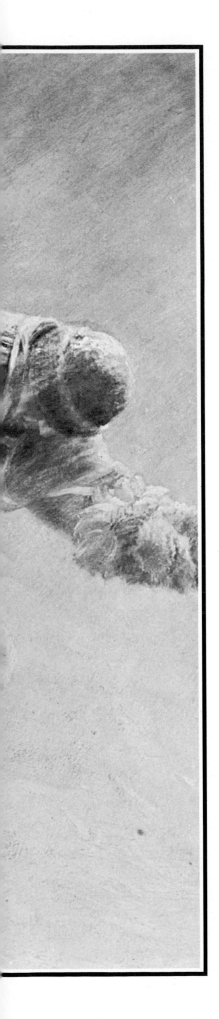

Chapter 10

The Two Poles

Curiosity, ambition, and greed, the three great forces that have driven the human race to the most distant regions of the globe, were also part of the motivation which inspired individual explorers to challenge and conquer the most hostile extremes of the planet. In the modern age, the first mariners to ply the arctic were commissioned by merchant companies eager for a new route to the fabled opulence of the Orient. The quest for the Northeast and Northwest Passages was at the root of western European exploration in northern waters and the Arctic Ocean until the 19th century. Then the search for the geographical pole became increasingly important as an objective which, at the same time, led to the opening up of unknown territory. In the south, exploration concentrated on finding a continent that had appeared on maps for centuries without ever being sighted. The discovery of a southern continent, which was named Antarctica, called forth heroism unparalleled in the history of exploration.

Left: every explorer faced hazards and trials, but perhaps none had to endure as much as those who attempted to travel across the frozen wastes of the two ends of the world – the arctic and the antarctic. This illustration depicts the heroic act of Lawrence Oates in going voluntarily to his death so that his companions – members of Robert Scott's expedition to the South Pole – might have a better chance to survive.

The Polar Regions

The two ends of the earth are areas of diametrically opposite natures. An almost landlocked sea covers the North Pole, a vast island contains the South Pole. In the north the polar region is surrounded by inhabited territories and has been the home of the Eskimo peoples for millenia. The antarctic, unknown until almost two centuries ago, is still uninhabited except for staffs of various national research stations. Its climate is by several degrees harsher than that of the arctic in the north.

The arctic region extends more than a third of the way to the equator. The Arctic Circle at 66° 17′ N is arbitrarily considered to be the southern limit of arctic conditions. However, the weather boundary according to temperature is a wavy line fluctuating with the seasons. It includes most of Greenland, the world's largest island, northern Scandinavia, the northern territories of Soviet Siberia, parts of Alaska, and northern Canada. At the center is the Arctic Ocean, which can be considered a branch of the Atlantic. It is largely icebound throughout the year, but beneath the frozen wastes deep sea currents keep the ice in constant if slow motion. In spite of the region's starkness, a surprising range of animal life is found in it. There are hares, polar bears, gulls, and guillemots as far north as Latitude 88° and zooplankton in all the waters.

The cold loosens its grip only during the brief arctic summer, but throughout the region there is at least one month when temperatures are above freezing. Under the 24-hour daylight of the "midnight sun," temperatures mount and scrubby vegetation springs to life in the seem-

PACIFIC OCEAN

Japa

Sakhalin

Yukon • Anadyr

Mackenzie

Kolyma

ARCTIC OCEAN

Lena

Canada

North Pole

Yenisey

Peary Land

Novaya Zemlya

Greenland

Spitsbergen

USSR

Arctic Circle

Iceland

ATLANTIC OCEAN

Europe

■ Tundra

□ Permanent pack ice

▨ Winter limit of pack ice

Above: this map of the arctic shows that pack ice occurs permanently only inside the Arctic Circle, in the Arctic Ocean.

Left: protective coloration gives the Arctic hare a white coat in winter and a dark one in summer.

Opposite: Greenland in summer gets the sun at midnight because there are 24 hours of daylight. The same is true of the region on the antarctic circle.

ingly barren grounds northwest of Hudson Bay and east of the Mackenzie Basin. The soil is thin and large stretches of bare rock are exposed. Because of the poor drainage, depressions in the terrain become swamps, ponds, and lakes. The summer also reduces the tundra regions of Siberia above the tree line to bogland. However, the flowers of arctic meadows have delighted the eyes of many explorers, and elsewhere in the arctic zone, noticeably in Ellesmere Land and the Yukon, there is so much vegetation that it might be possible to maintain herds of domesticated cattle. The animal life of the southern reaches of the arctic has many fur bearers which were hunted for their pelts since the early 17th century by European settlers, but which had been a mainstay of the Eskimo economy for thousands of generations before. The coming of the European to the arctic, as elsewhere, has meant that some species, such as the Greenland reindeer, the walrus, the hooded seal, and even the polar bear, are endangered.

The adaptation of the Eskimo peoples to their arduous environment is one of the great success stories of the human race. As a matter of fact, the more intelligent of the 19th-century arctic explorers from Europe studied Eskimo survival techniques closely as a way of improving their own chances in the land of ice and snow.

The continent of Antarctica is still being mapped and explored today. It is a land mass of between 5 and 6 million square miles in area, roughly as big as Africa north of the equator. The waters surrounding it are sometimes termed the Antarctic Ocean but are more properly described as the southernmost parts of the Atlantic, Pacific, and Indian Oceans. They are terrible and violent seas, whipped by vicious freezing winds and crowded with drifting ice floes, ice packs, and mountainous icebergs that can reach more than 30 miles long. With such conditions, which can change rapidly, it is not surprising that Antarctica remained unknown for so long.

In shape the continent is roughly circular. It is broken by two seas on opposite sides, the Ross Sea on the Pacific side and the Weddell Sea on the Atlantic side. The full depth of the Ross Sea's indentation is concealed by a massive and permanently frozen ice sheet, the Ross Ice Shelf. This stretches some 400 miles across the vast bay

Right: the old fashioned way of hunting seals. Eskimos once used a hand harpoon and hunted singly, killing only what they needed.

Below: icebergs and pack ice float almost constantly in the seas around Antarctica. Many explorers have found a haunting beauty in the austere frozen scenery of both the polar regions.

Below left: sealskin clothing protects this small Eskimo child from the cold better than any other material could.

and hundreds of miles southward back to the hidden coastline, which is in fact barely 250 miles from the South Pole at its nearest approach. The Ross Ice Shelf, which in places rises a sheer 200 feet from the ocean, is only the largest of a number of similar ice barriers that shield the coastline of the continent at various points. During the summer months open water is found much nearer to the continent on the side of the Weddell Sea, but the hazards of drifting ice are correspondingly greater. Navigation is further complicated by a great current that sweeps around the bay in a clockwise direction, carrying

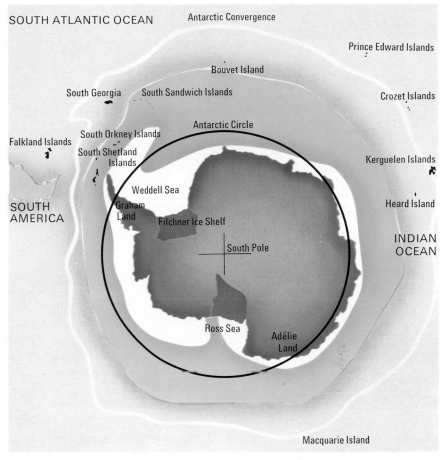

SOUTH ATLANTIC OCEAN   Antarctic Convergence

Prince Edward Islands

Bouvet Island

South Georgia   South Sandwich Islands

Crozet Islands

Antarctic Circle

Falkland Islands   South Orkney Islands

South Shetland Islands

Kerguelen Islands

SOUTH AMERICA

Weddell Sea

Graham Land

Heard Island

Filchner Ice Shelf

South Pole

INDIAN OCEAN

Ross Sea

Adélie Land

Macquarie Island

Above: this map shows how the pack ice is denser and more widespread within the Antarctic Circle than it is around the Arctic Circle.

Right: Nathanial B Palmer, a sealer from the United States, discovered Deception Island. He may have been the first person to actually set foot on Antarctica when he landed on this island on February 7, 1821. Later, having anchored in Hughes Bay, Palmer righly assumed that the land he saw from the bay was a continent.

the ice floes up the coast of a large projection. This is known as the Palmer Peninsula or Graham Land. The name of Palmer Peninsula was given to it on the basis of sightings by the American explorer Nathaniel Palmer in 1820. About 10 years later British explorers, who are said to have mapped the coast more thoroughly, called it Graham Land. The peninsula stretches toward South America, which is about 600 miles away.

Antarctica was long isolated by vast distances as well as dangerous seas from the inhabited regions of the southern hemisphere such as southern Africa, Australia, and New Zealand –

themselves sparsely peopled. Possible settlers were also discouraged by huge belts of pack ice, floating barriers sometimes hundreds of miles wide. These are fed by the glaciers which flow slowly by inches down to the coast, and by iceberg calves, which crack from the main glacier and plunge into the ocean sending spumes of

Above: part of the transarctic expedition led by Wally Herbert in the winter of 1968–69. In spite of the occasional successful use of mechanized equipment such as cars or tractors, the dog team remains the most consistently reliable means of transport across ice.

spray hundreds of feet into the air. The ice shelves conceal some small islands. Larger islands are found off Graham Land – the South Shetlands near its tip and the South Orkneys farther away in the Atlantic being examples.

The surface of the continent proper is almost entirely covered by ice with many hard ridges forced up to heights of more than 50 feet by the conflicting pressures freezing within the ice sheet. Progress across such terrain is difficult even for the largest and most up-to-date tracked vehicles. The most terrifying hazards of polar travel are crevasses, deep cracks in the ice which may reach hundreds of feet deep but are often hidden by treacherous snow-covered ice bridges. These are liable to give way under the weight of a well-laden dog sled, and are an even more serious danger to the ponderous tractors of modern polar travel. Often these tractors are equipped with cumbersome crevasse detectors. Four wooden beams, fitted with large aluminum disks, are pushed ahead of the vehicle. They are linked to detectors that record hollows under the disks and give a warning sound. However, the surest way of finding a crevasse is still the traditional one of a person probing the ground with a metal rod.

The bleak landscape of Antarctica alternates between great ice fields and giant mountain ranges, some with peaks rising over 15,000 feet. The center of the continent is a high plateau hidden under a perpetual ice cap with a thickness at the Pole of some 9000 feet. The average altitude of the whole continent is 6000 feet, almost twice that of any other. In the late 1950s it was estimated that the ice mass that covers it was becoming larger, in contrast to the arctic regions. Being a land mass, Antarctica has a more severe climate than that of the northern polar region. With winter temperatures dropping as low as −70° F and sometimes −80° F, and summer temperatures averaging a good 15° F lower than those in the arctic, the southern

Above: a Sno-cat fitted with a crevasse detector. The disks, which are linked to detectors, record hollows in the ground below and also give a warning sound.

Below: McMurdo Station on Ross Island. This American base is the largest on Antarctica, having a population of 1000 in summer.

continent represents the most hostile environment on the surface of the planet.

Nevertheless, today there are numerous bases in the antarctic. Geological surveys indicate that large reserves of natural resources exist on the continent, though getting to them will pose immense problems. More accessible are the offshore resources of which the chief among them is krill, the protein rich fish food. The huge quantities of krill in antarctic waters make it perhaps the largest untapped source of protein on earth. According to international agreement, Antarctica is a neutral zone; but it remains to be seen whether rivalries over exploitation of resources can be held in balance.

Two Early Maps

In the 16th century very little was known about the polar regions, but map makers nonetheless included them in their atlases. In 1595 Rumold Mercator published the third part of his famous father's atlas. The elder Mercator had died four months before the publication date, and Rumold's picture of the arctic was derived from an

Below: the Mercator map of 1595.

inset which had appeared in his father's world map of some 25 years earlier. This, in its turn, had been based on earlier accounts by seafarers who may have visited both Greenland and America. Inevitably, the Mercator account of the arctic was largely guesswork. It depicts the North Pole or Arctic Pole as a "black and very high rock" rising from the sea. But it was influential because, despite its fantastic geography which shows the Pole surrounded by four islands, it clearly suggested the possibility of Northeast and Northwest Passages from Europe to Asia. Surprisingly it also shows a sea route across the Pole, which is now known to exist.

Ideas about the southern polar region were considerably more speculative, but all theories were dominated by the supposition that there was a vast undiscovered land called Terra Aus-

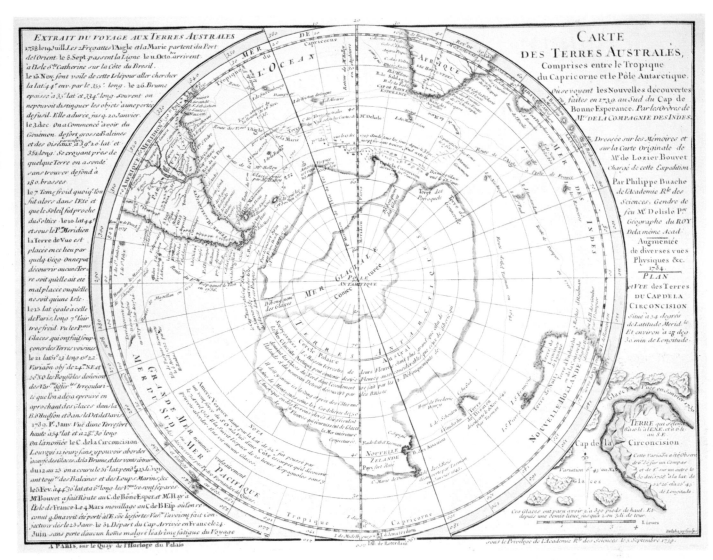

Above: the Buache map of 1739.

tralis. As a result, when New Zealand was discovered it was presumed to be an extension of this great continent. In 1739 the French cartographer Philippe Buache published a map of the earth from the South Pole to the Tropic of Capricorn which shows a huge land mass surrounding the Pole. To satisfy his notions of the proper symmetry of the earth, he supposed that the South Pole, like the North, lay in a frozen sea. So he depicted the continent cut in two by an immense channel. However, Buache annotated his map with his theories and marked his southern "Glacial Sea" as a conjecture. Elsewhere the map is accurate and up-to-date for the period. Not only are the voyages of Magellan, Tasman, and Dampier marked, but also discoveries south of the Cape of Good Hope made in the year of the map's publication. Detailed and authoritative as it seemed to be, the map was made obsolete 40 years later by the voyage of James Cook. Buache had depicted Terra Australis as an immense land stretching as far north as Latitude 30° S at one point. However, Cook circumnavigated the actual continent of Antarctica well within these latitudes without sighting it and was convinced it did not exist.

Right: Adélie penguins sitting out a blizzard. These animals inhabit one of the windiest places on the face of the earth.

Willem Barents ?-1597

Pytheas the Greek, the first European known to have sailed arctic waters, was both a mathematician and explorer. This combination of science and curiosity was often repeated in the saga of polar exploration. Pytheas, however, was searching for the remote northern land of Thule, reported to him by the inhabitants of Britain. On his journey he saw a still greater wonder – the midnight sun – of which, not surprisingly, few believed his description. Eighteen hundred years

later a number of intrepid Europeans penetrated the remotest northern waters, this time in search of wealth. They hoped to discover a northern passage to the fabulous riches of China. The greatest of these navigators, the Dutchman Willem Barents, made his name one of the most revered in the whole history of polar exploration. However, he was not the first of the bold seafarers of the far north.

The history of systematic exploration in the polar regions starts in 1551 with the founding of the London Company of Merchants Adventurers for the Discovery of Regions Unknown. Despite the title, it was strictly a business venture to find a route to China not blocked by the Spaniards and the Portuguese. In May 1553 the company chartered two ships under Hugh Willoughby and Richard Chancellor, an outstanding pilot. Not long after sailing, a fierce storm separated them off northern Norway.

Willoughby was forced into shore where he and his entire crew perished in the harsh northern winter. Chancellor, however, weathered the storm and rounded the northern point of Norway, finally putting in at the mouth of the Dvina River in Russia near the site on which the port of Archangel was to rise some 30 years later. From there, he and his men were enthusiastically escorted to Moscow to be received by Czar Ivan the Terrible.

The search for the northern passage to China then switched to the northwest and in 1576 another Englishman, Martin Frobisher, sailed past the southern tip of Greenland to reach Baffin Island. The island's bay is named Frobisher after him. The Mongoloid features of the Eskimos convinced him that he had reached Asia, and the discovery of rock that glowed gold in fire convinced him that he had found wealth. But the Eskimos he brought back to London died, and the gold turned out to be iron pyrites, now called "fool's gold." His claim to have found the back door to the riches of the East was laughed out of court. Nevertheless, English expeditions continued. Arthur Pet and then John Davis made important contributions. In three voyages made in 1585, 1586, and 1587, Davis clarified much of the geography of the arctic region, discovering Cumberland and sailing through Davis Strait into Baffin Bay. Having

heard that the peoples of Asia were lovers of music, he took four musicians in his crew. This was an unusual approach to the problem of making friends in strange countries at a time when explorers tended to take the Bible if they took anything other than trade goods.

Meanwhile, the merchants of Amsterdam who had been trading in the Archangel region since the 1570s, pushed on with the attempt to discover a Northeast Passage. They were encouraged by the speculations of the Amsterdam geographer Peter Plancius. In 1594 they commissioned Willem Barents to explore north and east of Norway in the sea that still bears his name. In July, from the deck of his little ship the *Mercury*, Barents sighted the coast of Novaya Zemlya. This huge island, today a Soviet nuclear testing site, curves in a 600-mile crescent northward from the Kara Straits which lead into the Kara Sea. The next month Barents probed northward through the ice floes to a promontory on the northwest coast of the island, which he named Cape Nassau, but he failed to round the northern tip of the island in the Kara Sea and returned to Amsterdam.

The following year, 1595, he made an unsuccessful bid to get through the Kara Straits and on May 13, 1596 he set out once more, this time as pilot of an expedition of two ships commanded by Jacob van Heemskerk. The first

Above: Barents' fleet off Novaya Zemlya on his first voyage in 1594.

Below: a map showing the route taken by Barents on his last expedition in 1597.

officer, Gerrit de Veer, kept a journal of the heroic voyage that reached the most northern latitude then touched by Europeans. Hoping to skirt the ice hazards of the Novaya Zemlya coast, Barents set a more northerly course than before. On June 9 they discovered Bear Island and 10 days later sighted West Spitzbergen. This they named New Land, although they thought it to be part of Greenland. They explored its west-

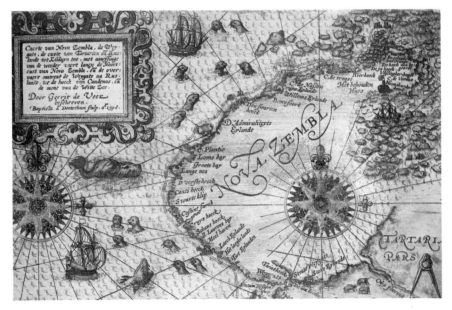

ern coast northward until stopped by pack ice, and then made south again. At Bear Island the second ship headed for home, but van Heemskerk sailed east for Novaya Zemlya.

Late in August the expedition rounded the northernmost point of the island. But the ice was closing in. "It was a terrifying spectacle and the ice moved with the sound of thunder," de Veer wrote. Inexorably it forced the ship upward and out of the water. The timbers were cracked and

Above: an illustration of the bear shooting that saved Barents' expedition during the winter of 1597 when they had to build a hut and stay on Novaya Zemlya.

Below: members of the expedition trying to catch a polar bear while in the water.

the seams loosened. Crew members sought what shelter they could on a hostile shore that they dubbed Ice Haven.

Then there came a winter such as no European had ever experienced before. From the timbers of their wrecked vessel, the Dutchmen built themselves a gabled long house. It had a strange central tower on which perched the ship's crow's nest to be used as a lookout post and, on the advice of the ship's doctor, for Turkish baths. Whether the medical man had seen a Scandinavian sauna or was merely working from good judgment, it is interesting that he should have considered such a bathhouse important. They made the living quarters as comfortable as possible with salvaged bunks and furniture, but it was a life of torment. The sheets froze on their beds, the wine froze in their glasses, and the smoke from the fire all but suffocated them.

With admirable single-mindedness, Barents whiled away the dark days by reading to his men from Juan Gonzales de Mendoza's book *A History and Description of the Great Chinese Empire.* It may not have been every crew member's idea of entertainment, but by reminding them of their ambitious objective, it seemed to help them bear their hardships as a necessary trial in a great enterprise. When the arctic spring came, however, it was obvious that they would have to attempt the return home rather than go on. They faced a 1600 mile journey south to the Kola

peninsula, the nearest mainland. Breaking camp on June 14, they packed what stores they could into the ship's longboats. As they headed away from the shore, Barents turned around so that "he might look on that damned spot, once more." Weakened by the ordeal of the bitter winter, he died after five days in the open boats.

Barents' voyages had established him as one of the great polar explorers of all time. The extent of his explorations and the accuracy of his charts were unprecedented, while the meteorological records he made remain vital data in the history of the polar climate. His companions battled on southward. Sailing, rowing, occasionally dragging their boats overland, they reached the mainland and finally Amsterdam. So ended the great Dutch contribution to polar discovery. Early in the next century, interest in the Northeast Passage to the Far East lapsed as the Netherlands began to exploit the rich whale and sea fisheries in the seas around Spitzbergen. The English also abandoned exploration for a Northeast Passage, having turned toward a search for a passage in the northwest. In the early 17th century, Henry Hudson and William Baffin came near to solving the mystery of the Northwest Passage. Baffin in fact reached the entrance of Lancaster Sound which, had he but known, could have led him through the Beaufort Sea, on to the Bering Straits, and through the Bering Sea to the Pacific Ocean.

Above: the inside of the hut. Although it had beds, some furniture, and a bath, the shelter was miserably cold and extremely difficult to ventilate properly.

Right: instruments found in the hut 275 years after Barents and his companions must have used them. They were among other relics, like cooking utensils and books, that were preserved in the ice.

A dramatic epilogue to the ordeal of Barents and his company was written in 1871. In September of that year a Norwegian expedition discovered the earlier expedition's winter quarters at Ice Haven. Among the equipment still preserved in the snow was the iron clock which had been their companion that hard winter, their cooking caldrons, halberds that they had used in their seal hunts, and even the galoshes of the cabin boy who had died before spring. In one corner of the hut was a chest of religious images which, presumably, were to have been used in the conversion of the Chinese. The Norwegians also found some of the books the Dutch had taken with them. Among these was a translation of the logbook of Arthur Pet. Barents had not been too proud to make use of the experience of his less famous English predecessor. His own records in turn were invaluable to all who came after him.

James Clark Ross 1800-1862

James Clark Ross, a naval officer and nephew of a well-known arctic expedition leader, carved for himself one of the most brilliant careers in modern exploration. He was 18 when in 1818 the British government announced a prize for the discovery of a Northwest Passage. The British interest was political, based on the fact that there had been a Russian settlement in Alaska since 1784. Britain was apprehensive of what it saw as Russian imperialistic ambitions in the Arctic.

The Russian presence in the region had come about through the exploration of Vitus Bering, a Dane commissioned by Czar Peter the Great in 1725 to explore the remote wastes of Siberia. His party made the 6000 mile march from what is now Leningrad to Okhotsk on the North Asian coast. They crossed the Sea of Okhotsk and

Above: a watercolor by John Ross painted during his second voyage in search of the Northwest Passage. His boat *Victory* was caught in the ice at the time.

Left: James Clark Ross, the naval officer and explorer who was the first to reach the North Magnetic Pole. He also tried for the South Magnetic Pole and, although he failed, reached the farthest point south up to his time.

then made their way overland to the east coast of the Kamchatka Peninsula. In 1728 the expedition set sail northward along the shores of what is now called the Bering Sea, entering the Bering Strait before making the long return to Leningrad. Over the next 12 years, Bering and his Russian colleague Aleksey Chirikov mapped vast areas of arctic Siberia in one of the great epics of scientific exploration. In 1741, skirting the Bering Sea and Aleutian Islands, Bering reached the coast of Alaska. He died on the return voyage, but his work was done and the Russian adventure in Alaska was launched.

At the same time, the British were exploring northern Canada, and by 1818 the government decided to protect its position in the arctic. That year, a Royal Navy squadron under Commander John Ross sailed into northern waters. William Edward Parry was his second in command, and his nephew James was one of his junior officers. The ships reached Lancaster Sound in August, but after barely a day's sailing Commander Ross ordered the return. He claimed that he saw a range of mountains closing the western end of the sound. Parry, and virtually everyone else

Right: Edward Parry, who led a polar expedition at the age of 29. His qualities of organization and leadership were outstanding.

288

aboard, saw only clear water merging into banks of mist. In London scandal mongers rumored that Ross had lost his nerve and had made an excuse to run for home. Embarrassed, the navy outfitted a second expedition the following year with Parry in command and the young Ross on the crew.

For the second August in succession, Parry found himself sailing up Lancaster Sound. No mountains barred the way. In fact the channel widened out into a stretch of open water which Parry named Barrow strait. His two ships, *Hecla* and *Griper*, pushed on through the Melville Sound to Melville Island, hundreds of miles farther west than any ship had sailed in those latitudes. There they were stopped by the pack ice and were soon frozen in. Parry kept morale high. A tight program of work and exercise was enlivened with dancing and singing competitions, and the crew even published its own weekly newspaper, the *North Georgia Gazette and Winter Chronicle*. With the return of the sun, the men were ready for a new attempt, but the passage was still blocked by massive ice floes. In the autumn of 1821 Parry sailed for home.

Ross continued to sail in the arctic on expeditions with Parry until 1829 when his uncle was placed in charge of an expedition financed privately. Ross' ship *Victory* had a steam engine which, it was hoped, would manage a drive through the ice. The younger Ross, then nearly 30, was in command of the second ship, the *Erebus*.

Despite the *Victory*'s steam engine, the expedition was icebound for three winters off a region that Commander Ross named the Boothia Peninsula for his patron. He and his nephew made extensive studies of the Eskimo tribes in the region, and he painted a number of watercolours. Captain Ross made several long journeys with Eskimos over the ice to King William Island and made notes on their weatherproof dress and

Above: Parry's ships negotiating narrow channels of water within the packed ice during his third arctic voyage of 1824. One of them was later wrecked.

Below: an earlier painting by John Ross of a strange iceberg he saw in Baffin Bay in 1818.

sledging techniques. On the scientific side, he became the first man to reach and identify the North Magnetic Pole. On May 31, 1831 he computed its location at Latitude $70°$ $51'$ N and Longitude $96°$ $46'$ W. Since his time the pole has shifted several miles northward and is now located in the region of $75°$ N and $101°$ W.

After withstanding three arctic winters, the Rosses realized that they would have to abandon

the ships. The expedition members made their way to Lancaster Sound where they were picked up by a whaling ship and taken back to England. The return was a triumph, John Ross receiving a knighthood from Queen Victoria and James being promoted to a full captaincy in the Royal Navy. For the next three years Captain Ross was busy on a government sponsored magnetic survey of Britain. Then in 1839, his naval reputation and scientific expertise made him the inevitable choice to command Britain's expedition to discover the South Magnetic Pole.

Ross was in a good position to try for the South Pole. His discovery of the North Pole made it possible to speculate with reasonable accuracy the whereabouts of its southern counterpart. In addition, he had at his disposal charts of the southern seas which had been prepared in England by Russia's first antarctic expedition in 1819. Behind him as well was the voyage of James Weddell, a sealer who in search of his quarry had in 1823 reached Latitude 74° 15′ S, the most southern point then recorded. However, Ross faced competition on his venture.

Above; Dumont d'Urville, commander of the French expedition that searched for the South Magnetic Pole. His sighting of Antarctica was only 10 hours behind that of the first person to do so.

Above right: Charles Wilkes who, as the leader of the United States' first expedition to the South Pole, was the first to sight Antarctica. He also made a landing.

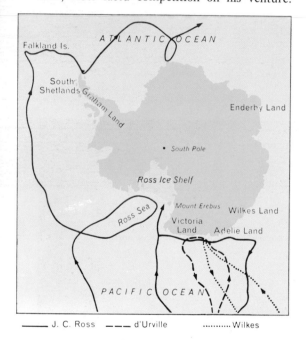

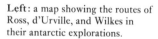

--- J. C. Ross   --- d'Urville   .... Wilkes

Left: a map showing the routes of Ross, d'Urville, and Wilkes in their antarctic explorations.

Below: the Ross Ice Shelf, an ice cliff that is in constant motion. It moves toward the sea at a rate of about five feet a day.

When news of Britain's plans leaked out, France decided to make a race of it. An expedition preparing for a journey to the South Pacific under the command of Dumont d'Urville was ordered into the Antarctic by King Louis Philippe. The United States also decided on Antarctica for its first venture into large-scale exploration.

Although the last to sail, Ross had the advantage that his ships were well adapted to the hostile waters. The French vessels had been chosen for the tropics. Charles Wilkes, the American, commanded a flotilla of warships with gunports through which the icy waters flooded over the decks. His seamen had been issued with clothing that proved to be inadequate and inferior. By contrast, Ross' ships *Erebus* and *Terror*, though clumsy and small, were sturdily built with watertight bulkheads as a precaution against collisions with ice. The crews had been issued with heavy duty winter clothing, and the ships had been provisioned with preserved meat and vegetables.

The earliest officially recognized sightings of Antarctica were made by d'Urville and Wilkes. But, thanks to the superior design of his ships,

Ross was able to push farther south than either of them. By November he was pushing through the iceberg infested waters that had come near to sinking Wilkes. In January 1841 *Erebus* and *Terror* broke through into clear waters that stretched to the horizon. Ross set a course due south.

When at length land was sighted it proved an astonishing landscape. Peaks soared up to 7000 or 10,000 feet above the level of the ocean that was "perfectly covered with eternal snow . . . The glaciers which filled their intervening valleys and which descended from the mountains' summits, projected in many places several miles into the sea." Ross named the territory Victoria Land after Britain's new young queen. The small island on which he landed and to which he laid formal claim he named simply Possession Island. Sailing on, his ships passed latitude 74° 20′ the southernmost record at that time. Then, on the the morning of January 28, the astonished ship's company saw a mountainous island with its peak spewing black smoke and streaks of flame over

Above: an engraving depicting the landing of part of d'Urville's crew on Adélie Land. The original sketch was made by Louis Le Breton, the expedition artist and surgeon.

the frozen landscape. Ross named the volcano Erebus after his ship. Nearby stood an extinct volcano that he named Mount Terror after the second ship.

As they prospected eastward for a southern passage, a new marvel opened up before the explorers. A low white line stretched like a handmade horizon as far as they could see. Approaching cautiously, they at length realized that it was "a perpendicular cliff of ice between 150 and 200 feet above the level of the sea, perfectly flat and level at the top and without any fissures or promontories on its seaward face." It was the edge of what is now called the Ross Ice Shelf – a vast slab of floating ice between 600 and 1000 feet thick.

Ross remained in the antarctic until 1843. He had reached a point south that remained a record for 60 years, but he had to abandon his attempt to reach the South Magnetic Pole. On his return to his birthplace of London, he was honored by a knighthood and in 1847 he published *A Voyage of Discovery and Research in the Southern and Antarctic Regions*. Fifteen years later he died.

Fridtjof Nansen 1861-1930

One of the great names in the history of arctic exploration and one of the outstanding figures of the 20th century, Fridtjof Nansen achieved distinction not only as an explorer but as a scholar, scientist, statesman, and humanitarian. His numerous books include *The First Crossing of Greenland*, *Eskimo Life*, *Russia and Peace*, and *Armenia and the Near East*. He held various academic appointments, became an honored official of the League of Nations, and won the Nobel Peace Prize. But he made his name as an explorer, starting before he was 21 with an arctic voyage as a crew member on a sealer.

Above: the discovery of the dead crew of the *Jeannette*. The ship drifted from Siberia to Greenland in three years after being wrecked. This confirmed Fridtjof Nansen's theory that the arctic was a frozen ocean on which he could drift to reach his goal of the Pole.

Left: Nansen, the polar explorer whose wide interests led him into other paths of achievement too.

Returning to Norway, Nansen embarked on his academic career, being appointed curator of the natural history collection of the Bergen Museum. Six years later, with a party of five companions, he went on an expedition that made the first crossing of the vast island of Greenland. The purpose was primarily scientific, but the journey widened Nansen's interest in and contact with the Eskimo peoples of the region. His knowledge of them gave hints that the arctic ice concealed a great ocean whose currents swept across the polar region. For example, one of his colleagues received from a Greenlander at Godthab a remarkable piece of wood, found among the driftwood on the coast. It was an Eskimo throwing stick, used to propel a short javelinlike "bird-dart," but although found on the west Greenland coast, its design and decoration were unmistakably in the style of the Alaskan Eskimos. Nansen also knew that the Greenland Eskimos built their boats and sledges from driftwood which included logs of Siberian larch. Such evidence was supported in the mid 1880s. A United States Navy expedition in quest of the North Pole, which had sailed from San Francisco in the ship *Jeannette*, was caught in the ice and was finally abandoned by its crew in June 1881 north of the New Siberian Islands. Three years later, wreckage from the *Jeannette* was found on the southwest shore of Greenland. Newspaper reports of this astonishing find fascinated Nansen. His own knowledge of the timber used by the Greenland Eskimos confirmed, for him at least, that the arctic was a frozen ocean with its own currents. He thought it possible that the currents flowed over the North Pole itself, and he conceived the plan of trying to reach the Pole by simply drifting to it on these currents. The theory was ridiculed in many quarters, but Nansen was not deterred.

Satisfied that his theory was sound, Nansen drew up the specifications for his ship. It was to be "just big enough to contain coal and provisions for 12 men for five years." So that it would withstand the pressure of the ice, "the sides should slope sufficiently to prevent the ice from getting a firm hold on the hull. Instead of nipping the ship the ice should raise it up out of the water." Built at government expense, the tough little ship was christened *Fram* (*Forward*). It sailed from Pepperviken, Norway on June 24, 1893. Nansen wrote: "Like an arrow the little boat sped over Lysaker Bay, bearing me on the first stage of a journey on which life itself, if not more, was staked."

The *Fram* sailed east along the northern shores of Russia. About 100 miles short of the New Siberian Islands, Nansen headed due north. By late September, at about Latitude 79°, the boat was firmly locked into the ice. The men were prepared for years of isolation and wandering, but they could not be sure that the *Fram* would behave as the designer planned. Over supper one early December evening, they listened apprehensively to the first gunlike reports of the ice cracking under the pressure that was building up. Before the meal ended, the isolated reports had merged into a continuous roar. Conversation was impossible, but smiles broke out around the table as the company felt the little ship begin to lift slowly. It was not going to be "nipped" in the ice.

The ship seemed safe. Before the end of the month, it had drifted to 82° 30′ N, a record. A more severe test was looming, however. A massive floe seven feet thick had ridden up onto the

surface of the ice in which the *Fram* was held, forcing it and the ship down. Grinding on toward the helpless vessel, it "took her amidships while she was still frozen fast . . . she could hardly have had a tighter squeeze; it was no wonder that she groaned; but she withstood it, broke loose and eased."

The *Fram* had triumphantly demonstrated its iceworthiness, but the drift was painfully slow. At times, wrote Nansen, the boredom "crushed one's very soul. One's life seemed as dark as the winter night outside." Moreover, it was becoming clear that the currents would not take them directly over the Pole. At about 84° N, with the objective 350 miles away, the ship began edging westward. It looked like it would be held fast in the ice for a good long time. Nansen decided on

action. He had calculated that the North Pole could be reached across the ice in 50 days by two men and dogs, with sleds carrying kayaks and food for 100 days. On March 14, 1895 he set out with the young officer Hjalmar Johansen, leaving Captain Sverdrup in charge of the *Fram*.

At first the explorers made good speed over smooth ice, but soon found it forced upward into jagged pressure ridges. By April 6, with 270 miles still to go, Nansen was prepared to abandon the attempt. "Lanes, ridges, and endless rough ice, it looks like an endless moraine of ice blocks; and this continual lifting of the sledges over every irregularity is enough to tire out giants." April 8: "Ridge after ridge . . . stretching as far as the horizon. . . . If there be more such ice between here and land, we shall, indeed, want all the time we have." When they had reached 160 miles further north than any previous explorer, they turned south for the group of islands known as Franz Josef Land. An unexpected hazard was added to the dangers of the terrain. By cruel chance, both men forgot to wind their watches soon after setting their southern course. With no

accurate measure of time, it was virtually impossible to determine their longitude.

With the slow advance of the arctic spring, the ice began to melt patchily. They could make comparatively rapid progress across the open water in their kayaks, but periodic falls in temperature crusted the sea with ice too strong to sail through but not strong enough to bear their weight. They therefore had to make laborious detours by sledge over the stronger ice. Food for men and dogs ran low and on June 9, some 90 days after they had left the *Fram*, they had to kill

Above: Nansen and Johansen carrying kayaks on their sledges for their assault on the Pole.

Below: the boat that Nansen and his companion made from the two kayaks they had spent so much effort in dragging on the sledges.

the remaining three dogs. Then the weather closed in with lashing rain and Nansen, weakened by a severe attack of lumbago, decided on a three day halt. Gradually the going became easier and they were able to supplement their dwindling food with a seal shot by Johansen. On August 7 they found themselves at the edge of the ice with clear water stretching to the horizon. Roping the kayaks together, they rigged a sail and, loading the sledge and the remaining stores, launched the craft.

With a light breeze carrying them to an uncertain destination, a mist closed around the boat. When the mist cleared, they peered ahead to see a group of tiny islands. Almost incredibly it was the northernmost group of Franz Josef Land. They had been navigating for weeks by compass and stars alone. Luck and determination had brought them to their first objective.

By then it was late September 1896. Nansen and Johansen resigned themselves to wintering alone. They found a sheltered spot under a high cliff and built a stone hut roofed with walrus skins. Sea birds, seals, and walrusses at least assured them of their food supply. The sun set on October 15, and not until May were they able to put to sea again. In that same month, after nearly three years, the *Fram* was released from the ice raft. It reached Norway on August 20,

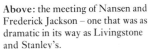

about a week after Nansen and his companion had arrived.

The return of Nansen and Johansen, whom many believed to be dead, bordered on the miraculous. At one point they had nearly lost one of their vital kayaks when a walrus ripped the side open. At another they nearly lost both boats when they broke from their moorings, and worse, Nansen came close to drowning in recovering them. It was while camping temporarily on another of the Franz Josef Land islands that they had heard the distant sound of barking. Eagerly

Nansen had set out to investigate the source of the sound. "It was with a strange feeling that I made my way inland among the numerous hummocks. . . . Suddenly I thought I heard a shout, a strange voice, the first for three years. How my heart beat and the blood rushed to my head as I ran up the hummock and halooed with all the strength of my lungs. Soon I heard another shout and saw a man . . . We approached one another quickly. I waved my hat; he did the same. I heard him speak to the dog, and I listened. It was English."

Above: the meeting of Nansen and Frederick Jackson – one that was as dramatic in its way as Livingstone and Stanley's.

Left: the Aurora Borealis as painted by Nansen. He wrote that the arctic night ". . . is dreamland, painted in the imagination's most delicate tints; it is color etherealized. One shade melts into the other so that you cannot tell where one ends and the other begins."

The man was Frederick Jackson, head of an English expedition that was in Franz Josef Land to confirm its extent and insularity. By an historic coincidence, to which the Norwegians may well have owed their lives, Jackson's party crossed Nansen's route. Jackson peered closely at the unexpected figure. "Aren't you Nansen?" he asked.

The meeting of these arctic explorers ranks with the famous encounter of Stanley and Livingstone in equatorial Africa. On August 7 they embarked on one of the ships of Jackson's expedition. After three years in the most trying terrain in the world, the Norwegian arctic adventurers were home. Their ship was intact and the men were alive and fit. Their 35-year-old leader was a world figure.

Nansen had failed in his bid for the Pole, but the expedition had brought back a wealth of information on oceanography, meteorology, diet, and nutrition which was to be fundamental for all future arctic work. *Farthest North*, Nansen's account of the successful exploit, was published in 1897 and the scientific documentation appeared between 1900 and 1906. The Nansen Fund for scientific research was established in his honor. In 1901 he became director of an international commission to study the sea and in 1908 he was appointed professor of oceanography at what is now the University of Oslo. Between 1910 and 1914 he went back into the field, making a number of scientific journeys in the North Atlantic.

Besides all this, Nansen also embarked on a distinguished career as a statesman. Having been active in the campaign which led to Norway declaring independence from the Swedish crown in 1905, he became his country's first minister to Great Britain the following year. Toward the end of World War I, he again won international respect as a humanitarian for his work in famine stricken Russia and the repatriation of prisoners. In 1921 the League of Nations appointed him High Commissioner for refugees, and the following year he won the Nobel Peace Prize. He was adventurously planning to go north again by airship at the time of his death eight years later.

Vilhjalmur Stefansson 1879-1962

For the Canadian Vihjalmur Stefansson, the arctic region was not merely an arena for adventure and exploration but also the home of one of the most fascinating groups of the human family. Like Fridtjof Nansen, James Clark Ross, and John Rae, Stefansson made a serious study of the Eskimos a central part of his travel in the arctic. Such studies of remote and little known peoples was part of the 19th-century surge of interest in the young science of anthropology, and by 1900 no major arctic explorer discounted the value of gaining knowledge of the Eskimo lifestyle in their hostile environment. But few took this principle as far as Stefansson.

Born in Canada of Icelandic parents in 1879, he had his university education in the United States. In 1906 he enlisted in an Anglo-American expedition to the arctic. Loading his equipment

on the expedition's ship, he himself prepared to trek overland to Herschel Island where he was to meet up with his colleagues. Stefansson doubted whether the ship would reach the rendezvous, and when in fact it failed to do so, his plans were not disrupted. On the contrary. Clad only in lightweight European-style clothing, without supplies or shelter, he looked forward to surviving the cruel winter as a true member of the Eskimo people of the area. "My poverty," he wrote, "was my greatest advantage.

Above left: Vilhjalmur Stefansson, the Canadian explorer who made a lifelong study of the Eskimo people and culture. He was accepted as one of them by the Eskimos.

I was not rich and powerful like the whaling captains or the mounted policemen, so there was no reason why they [the Eskimos] should flatter me or show me deference." From October 1906 to March 1907 he lived as a full and accepted member of the tribe learning their life from the inside rather than studying it from the outside as even the most well-intentioned explorers had done before him.

In May of the following year, Stefansson returned to the delta of the Mackenzie River in the

Opposite: a photograph of the Mackenzie River Eskimos taken by Stefansson during his stay with them in the winter of 1906-07.

Left: a symbolic mask made of wood, used by the Eskimos in one of their dances.

Below right: an Eskimo on a seal hunt, recorded in a photograph by Stefansson.

Point Barrow and, when the important supply was still lacking, wintered there. Stefansson studied the Eskimo language and Anderson made frequent side trips into the mountains to collect zoological specimens.

It was not until August of the next year that Stefansson's party left Point Barrow for Herschel, and not until April of 1910 that he really headed toward the region south of Victoria Island. Anderson, who had been ill, returned to live and work in the Mackenzie delta. Stefansson's aim was to find the "blond" Eskimo tribe he had heard about several years before from a sea captain of the arctic. The area that Stefansson and his Eskimo companions Natkusiak and Tannaumirk entered was believed to be uninhabited, but within a couple of weeks they came upon an Eskimo village. Although Stefansson was the first non-Eskimo the group had ever seen, they did not seem surprised at his blue eyes and light brown hair. This was because their neighbors to

far northwest of Canada. He was supported by the American Museum of Natural History, which financed his study of the Eskimos, and was accompanied by the zoologist Dr Rudolph Martin Anderson, who was also his friend. The two traveled lightly, planning to pick up other supplies at Herschel, particularly the matches that were essential for Arctic exploration.

In mid-August the two men and their Eskimo guides reached Herschel Island, but could not get the vital matches. They decided to make for

Above: a painting by John Ross of an Eskimo village on the Boothia Peninsula. Ross preceded Stefansson to the arctic by 88 years.

the north had these characteristics. Were those neighbors the tribe Stefansson was looking for?

When the Canadian met the Victoria Island peoples, he was struck by their physical resemblance to Europeans in the shape of their head and proportion of their body. He called them the Copper Eskimos, probably because they made simple copper tools and hunting implements, and after living with them for a year, began to believe that they were descended from the Viking colonists of Greenland. His suggestion created a great controversy when he returned to the United States to make his report.

Between 1913 and 1918 Stefansson made the most prolonged polar expedition in history, living for five unbroken years with his Eskimo friends and studying the Copper Eskimos. In later years, he became the arctic consultant at Dartmouth College in New Hampshire, remaining there from 1947 until his death in 1962.

Robert Peary
1856-1920

Late in the afternoon of April 6, 1909, six men stood at the most northern point on the surface of the earth. The leader of the little party was Commander Robert E Peary of the United States Navy. Matthew Henson, his black servant and friend, and four Eskimos were with him. Their success was the culmination of years of preparatory exploration. From the moment he had embarked on the ship *Roosevelt* in the July

Left: Robert E Peary. Taken on the *Roosevelt* after his epic success, the photograph shows his weariness after the 1000-mile sledge journey he had made.

of the previous year, the commander had been determined to succeed. Having already failed twice in attempts financed by private sponsors, it was doubtful whether he would find more backers if he again failed; and he was already 52.

Peary entered the Navy in 1881 after graduating from college as a civil engineer, and was appointed to serve on the survey for the proposed canal route through Nicaragua. The experience seems to have fired his enthusiasm for exploration. Five years later he took part in an expedition that crossed the Greenland ice sheet. From that time on he was absorbed in the study of the arctic and the quest for the North Pole. Fridtjof Nansen, working from brilliant deduction, had

shown that the polar region was a frozen sea and, in the process, came close to reaching the pole. Peary, military style, planned a systematic strategy of conquest. Further exploration of Greenland was the first stage.

In 1891-92 he pushed far to the north by sledge, proving the vast region to be an island. He took important weather measurements and studied Eskimo life closely. Then he spent most of the next five years in the arctic, accompanied on many of his expeditions by his wife. Josephine Peary, who published her *Arctic Journal* in 1893, proclaimed her disdain for the role society expected of women by giving birth to their daughter, Marie, while exploring north of the Arctic Circle. Peary himself consolidated a growing reputation with the discovery of meteorites on his summer voyages of 1896 and 1897, and by the publication of his book *Over the Great Ice* the following year. He was convinced that the Pole could be reached without undue risk to life, and that Greenland was not the best point from which to mount the final assault because the ice flow around the north point of the island and down into the East Greenland Current was unacceptably fast.

Peary, accompanied by Henson, made another survey to find a suitable place for a base of operations in 1898. The bid for the Pole was begun four years later in 1902 from the coast of Grant

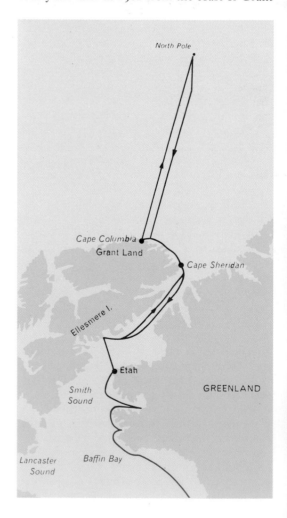

Right: Peary's route to the North Pole in 1908-09 by way of Smith Sound and Cape Columbia.

in furs and hide garments made by the women. Once the bid for the Pole began, it was to be the Eskimos who would break the trail.

The *Roosevelt* forced its way up Smith Sound to Cape Columbia on the northeast coast of Grant Land. Ninety miles ahead was Cape Hecla, the point on the edge of the frozen Arctic Ocean which had been the base camp for Peary's 1902 attempt. The Eskimo advance parties set out in February 1906, but north of Cape Hecla conditions on the frozen wastes turned ever more hostile. Temperatures reached the record low of −60° F, and both the rugged ice surface and the speed and direction of drift were worse than had been expected. To salvage at least something from what looked like another failure, Peary decided to take a small party and a sledge stripped of everything but essentials and push beyond the most northern point yet reached. He turned back at the new high latitude of 87° 6′. Beyond

Land on the northern edge of Ellesmere Island. It ended in failure. There were cruel blizzards, the ice stirred and shifted under the feet of the expedition, and two wide channels or "leads" opened up ahead of them. Peary had to turn back, but this failure had had its rewards. He had done major survey work in Ellesmere Land and had added to his information on the surface and drift of the pack ice.

Back in the United States, Peary plunged into the business of fund raising. His plans required improved sledges that were lighter but broader in order to negotiate the uneven ground and bridge sudden breaks in the ice, and a specially designed ship for better navigation of Smith Sound leading into Baffin Bay. His practical enthusiasm impressed businessmen, and a group of wealthy New Yorkers formed the Peary Arctic Club. By 1904 it was able to commission the building of the ship *Roosevelt* to Peary's specifications. Its captain was Canadian-born Bob Bartlett.

The expedition set sail in July 1905. It was superbly equipped, a dramatic contrast to America's first polar venture under Captain Charles Wilkes 65 years before. But Peary wanted more than first-rate equipment. Twenty years in the arctic had given him a solid respect for the way its native inhabitants adapted, so the *Roosevelt* headed for Greenland to pick up a party of Eskimo men and women and a team of Siberian huskies. The expedition was to live in snow houses built by the Eskimo men and dress

Above: an aerial view of a channel in the ice known as a lead. They are a hazard for polar travelers, often opening at night and carrying everyone away in their sleep.

Right: the *Roosevelt*, designed by Peary for his own use. It was especially strengthened for crashing its way through pack ice. Although it had sails for emergency use, it was powered by steam.

that, 174 miles of untrodden snow lay between him and his life's ambition. His book, *Nearest to the Pole*, recorded many notable achievements, but a final chapter had still to be written.

Peary immediately began preparing for a new expedition, which he managed to get financed. In July 1908 the *Roosevelt*, once again captained by Bartlett, sailed from New York. At Etah, Greenland Peary engaged 50 Eskimos and took on 250 dogs. They cast anchor off Cape Sheridan on the coast of Ellesmere Island early that September, and spent the following months moving supplies laboriously up to the advance base at Cape Columbia.

On February 28, 1909 Bartlett led the first advance party out of the Cape Columbia base. The next morning Peary was ready for his own departure, but there was the kind of gray haze over everything that every experienced arctic traveler knew meant vicious wind. "Some parties would have considered the weather impossible for traveling," Peary wrote in his journal . . . "(but) we were all in our new and perfectly dry fur clothes and could bid defiance to the wind.

"One by one the divisions drew out from the main army of sledges and dog teams, took up Bartlett's trail over the ice, and disappeared in the wind haze."

Peary led the last contingent of 133 dogs, 19 sledges, and 24 men. Their objective lay 420 nautical miles ahead. The assault team was to cover the distance at an average of about 11 miles a day. In that terrain it was a struggle. Time and again the men had to haul the sledges over pressure ridges of ice up to 50 feet high before the dogs could push on. More than once they were halted in their tracks when the ice ahead parted and opened up stretches of water. On the second day out they were stopped by a channel a quarter of a mile wide. In front there was "a dark ominous cloud which always meant open water." The water produced evaporation and the cold air acted as a condenser so that when the wind was in the right direction, it formed a fog "as black as the smoke of a prairie fire." Next

Above: a photograph by Peary of his dog teams walking across the ice hummocks at the beginning of the expedition's march from Cape Columbia.

Below: the front page of the *New York Herald* on September 7, 1909 reporting that Peary had reached the North Pole. It took five months for the news to get back to the United States.

morning the break seemed to be closing. They made the crossing on a succession of floating ice floes that were liable at any moment to capsize a sledge into the sea below.

A little later they were held up for a week waiting for another channel to close. But while one group was held up others pushed on to establish the supply camps, before heading back for the Cape Columbia base. At last, on the morning of April 2, 1909, Peary was poised for the final dash. He and his companions had five sledges and 40 dogs. The North Pole was 133 miles away. Making his farewells to Bartlett, Peary led his party away in the first of the five forced marches that brought them to their goal five days later.

A photograph shows Henson and the Eskimos posing in front of the United States flag, planted triumphantly at the Pole. It was a remarkable flag. Made from taffeta by Josephine Peary, it had been carried by the explorer wrapped around his body. He had planted portions cut from it at various points along the march and, having taken the final photographs, cut a narrow diagonal strip from it and buried it at the Pole. The men

faced the long trek back to their base at Cape Columbia with trepidation, but they had an astonishingly easy return. One of the Eskimos commented: "The devil is asleep or having trouble with his wife, or we should never have come back so easily."

On September 7, 1909 Peary was at last able to announce his achievement to the world. The New York press hailed him enthusiastically, but his victory was marred. Five days earlier Dr Frederick Cook, who had accompanied Peary on one of his previous expeditions and who had returned after a two-year expedition in the north

Above: Peary's photograph of his team standing at the North Pole beneath the flag he had planted. From left to right they are Ooqueah, Ootah, Matthew Henson, Egingwah, and Seegloo. Before starting the return trip, Peary buried a strip cut from the flag.

on September 1, claimed to have discovered the Pole in April 1908 before Peary. The New York Herald reported Cook as saying of Peary: "If he has announced he has reached the farthest north, he has. There is honor enough on it for both of us." Peary immediately challenged Cook who was examined by the geographical societies in the United States and Britain. Peary's own claim was also examined by the experts, and it was Peary who was vindicated in November 1909. The wrangle between Cook's and Peary's supporters continued another 20 years, but few now doubt that Peary was the first at the Pole.

Robert Scott 1868-1912

After the return of James Clark Ross from his last expedition in 1843, exploration in southern polar waters virtually lapsed for half a century. Interest began to revive in the 1890s and by 1911 the South Pole had been reached. This was barely two years after the North Pole had been reached, although arctic exploration had a longer tradition. In the new era of antarctic exploration, Robert Falcon Scott was one of three men who towered over their contemporaries, the others being Roald Amundsen and Ernest Shackleton. A career officer in the British Navy, Scott began

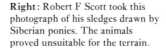

Left: Scott and Edward Wilson taken during the first expedition Scott led from 1901 to 1904.

Right: Robert F Scott took this photograph of his sledges drawn by Siberian ponies. The animals proved unsuitable for the terrain.

his career as an explorer at the age of 33. His tragic death 11 years later was part of perhaps the most famous episode in the whole history of polar exploration.

The first full-scale landing on the antarctic continent, by an Australian expedition, was not made until 1894. Five years later one of its members, Norwegian-born Carsten Borchgrevink, achieved a still more important first. Landing at Cape Adare, he sent his ship the *Southern*

Cross back to New Zealand and spent the winter on the frozen coast. By living through the ordeal, he and his companions demonstrated that people could endure the extremes of this virtually unknown region. The following year Borchgrevink made extensive surveys of the Ross Ice Shelf, also reporting on its flora and fauna.

During the first five years of the 20th century, exploration of the southern polar region accelerated under the impetus of the Berlin Geographical Congress of 1900. This meeting proclaimed an "Antarctic Year," and a series of major national expeditions followed. From 1901 to 1903, a team under Otto Nordenskjold discovered fossil deposits which indicated that tracts of the continent had been covered by lush tropical forests during the Jurassic age about 150 million years ago, and found evidence to suggest that in the remote past Graham Land had been connected to Tasmania.

A German expedition in 1902, after a remarkable epic of endurance in which the participants were icebound for 14 months, discovered Kaiser Wilhelm Land. A Scottish National Antarctic Expedition, led by William Bruce, discovered Coats Land in the same year. In 1903 Jean B. Charcot of France began the important series of

Left: one of the camps set up during Scott's first expedition. It is under the Wild Range.

Right: a painting of Scott's ship *Discovery* at the port of Falmouth, England, made 15 years after the explorer's death.

Bottom: a view of antarctic crevasses covered only with a thin coat of ice. Often a thick coat of snow covers such crevasses, making them invisible. Then the first warning of danger comes when a crack appears under a weight.

surveys which plotted the coast of the continent from Palmer Peninsula to Charcot Land.

It was in 1901 that Scott was given command of the British Antarctic Year expedition, organized jointly by the Royal Geographical Society and the Royal Society. It was fitted out in handsome style. The ship, the *Discovery*, was the latest in a long line of vessels with that name, stretching back to Henry Hudson in the early 1600s. It was equipped with 400 horsepower engines, a specially designed retractable rudder casing, compasses compensated to a fine degree of accuracy to account for the confusion caused when sailing close to the magnetic pole, and many other refinements. The crew's fur clothing, reindeer skin sleeping bags, skis, and sledges were bought from Norwegian factories. The canned foods were purchased only after Scott himself had visited the canneries. All the scientific equipment was of the highest quality and included alcohol thermometers accurate down to − 90° F, a photographic spectrometer, and balloons for reconnaissance. Scott made the first aerial ascent in Antarctica to a height of 790 feet on February 4, 1902.

The expedition returned in 1903 with a mass of meteorological, biological, and oceanographic data and a profusion of other scientific information. It had discovered the territory now known as Edward VII Peninsula, surveyed the coast of Victoria Land, and pushed inland to Latitude 82° 17′, at that time the southernmost point reached. It had developed a British team of immense experience – Ernest Shackleton among them – and had established semipermanent bases in McMurdo Sound and the Bay of Whales.

Such achievements naturally caught public imagination. Scott's book *The Voyage of Discovery* was an immense success. He was promoted to full captain in the Navy. The latest in the Royal Navy's long line of great explorer navigators following after James Cook, Scott

Above: Scott (at front) and, from right to left, Wilson, Oates, and Evans hauling their sledges near the end of their hopeless trek from the South Pole back to their base. Bowers took the photograph.

Right: the wardroom of the *Terra Nova* on December 17, 1910. By then the English knew that they were in a race with Roald Amundsen to reach the South Pole. Scott is seen at the head of the table.

was fired with ambition to be the first man at the South Pole.

In April 1907 he read a news story about Shackleton's plans for a new expedition with apprehension and disappointment. That morning he wrote to Shackleton, informing him of his own intention to try for the Pole in the near future and asking him not to use the bases on McMurdo Sound and the Bay of Whales. Chivalrously, Shackleton complied. When his expedition returned, having failed in its attempt, Scott began to mobilize men and materials. His expedition sailed from London in the ship *Terra*

There was also a film cameraman, the first such technician to go into the region.

The commander of this great enterprise was a man of frail physique and weak lungs who drove himself ruthlessly. Subject to fits of ungovernable temper as a boy, he had mastered himself by the exercise of an iron will. Although a stern disciplinarian with his men, he was able to win their affection as well as their respect and loyalty. His story has become a legend of antarctic exploration.

Scott and his companions were not the only ones with their sights on the South Pole that year. The veteran Norwegian explorer Roald Amundsen was in antarctic waters aboard Nansen's old ship the *Fram*. In October, Scott reached Melbourne, Australia to find a surprising telegram waiting for him from Amundsen. "Beg leave to inform you am proceeding antarctica." The Pole was not mentioned, but the British knew that they had a race on their hands.

Above: one of the motorized sledges being unloaded from the expedition ship. Soon after this picture was taken, the ice gave way and the vehicle disappeared.

Right: a map showing the routes followed by Amundsen, Scott, and Shackleton on their polar journeys.

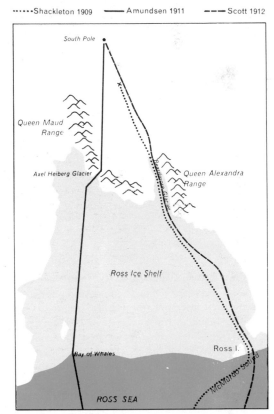

Nova on the first of June 1910.

Britain anticipated its success with confident pride. Its expedition leader was a national hero, and his equipment was the best that modern technology could offer. The *Terra Nova* carried three motor tractors with caterpillar tracks, a major improvement over the wheeled automobile of Shackleton's expedition. Scott's friend, the French explorer Jean Charcot, had helped test them on the snow slopes in the Alps. The expedition included two physicists, two biologists, and three geologists for specialized research of the world's southernmost continent.

It was a race they were not well fitted for. They could be expected to be slowed down by their scientific program and equipment. Their ship, an old whaler, was not built for the kind of dogged progress necessary to get through the hostile ice fields, as the *Fram* was. They had Siberian ponies to do the hauling, even though the superiority of husky dogs was well established by then. Scott recognized this and commented resignedly that Amundsen was "bound to travel fast with dogs." In any case, Scott had a streak of sentimentality that made it impossible for him to exploit dogs to their full practical advantage. To

discipline them ruthlessly, drive them hard, and kill them for meat when their working capacity was drained was not something he could do. Dogs, he insisted, must be treated "humanely."

The *Terra Nova* was quickly beset by trouble. Pack ice slowed its progress to the old base on McMurdo Sound. While the camp was being established, Scott made a reconnaissance along the coast of the Ross Ice Shelf and discovered the Norwegians safely camped by the cliffs of the Bay of Whales, a good 60 miles, perhaps as much as six days, nearer the Pole.

When Amundsen made a start for the Pole on October 19, it was two weeks earlier than the British. With dogs in peak condition and sledges stripped to essentials, Amundsen covered a remarkable 90 miles in the first four days. By contrast, Scott found the going worse than he had expected. On November 5, five days out from the base camp, the crankshaft bearings of the tractors burned out and the vehicles had to be abandoned. Next, the British had to hole up for five days against an early December blizzard. When they were able to continue, they found

that the new blown snow could not bear the ponies' weight. The animals had to be shot, the last being killed on December 9. The unruly dogs had never been of much use to the expedition and the men had to take over the hauling of the sledges themselves. Scott seems to have had this labor in mind, however. To do without dogs, he had once written, "would make the conquest more nobly and splendidly won." He had designed a special harness that fitted around the waist to assist pulling.

On December 22 the British established their base at the head of the Beardmore Glacier, the broad highway that had taken them to the polar plateau. On New Year's Day 1912 Scott's journal reveals that he was in good spirits with "only 170 miles to the Pole and plenty of food." Three days later, he led out the final assault party, which consisted of Dr Edward Wilson, Seaman Edgar Evans, and Army Captain Lawrence Oates. At the last minute and with everything prepared for the final dash, Scott unwisely allowed Lieutenant "Birdie" Bowers to join the team. The decision meant that the tent was desperately overcrowded,

we shall stick it out
to the end but we
are getting weaker of
course and the end
cannot be far.
It seems a pity but
I do not think I can
write more —
R Scott

carefully planned routines were dislocated, and supplies prepared for four men had to be divided among five.

They made barely 10 miles a day through blizzards and soft snow, but on January 15 Scott wrote confidently that two long marches would get them to the Pole. "... the only appalling possibility is the sight of the Norwegian flag forestalling ours," he added. The next day the "appalling possibility" came to pass and the British found the black Norwegian banner near the remains of a camp. "This told us the whole story," Scott wrote. "The Norwegians . . . are

Above: the last page of Scott's diary. Near the end he also wrote several moving letters to people back home.

Below: the expedition hut near McMurdo Station. Beyond it is the cross erected in memory of the unlucky team, whose members became national heroes in Britain.

first at the Pole." The British reached the Pole on January 17, 1912. Glumly they posed for a photograph by the unfurled Union Jack and then prepared for a desperate struggle back to base. "I wonder if we can do it?" wrote their leader.

All five were increasingly troubled with scurvy, frostbite, and mounting exhaustion – and they faced an 800 mile march. They reached the head of the Beardmore Glacier on February 7 in the teeth of blasting winds. Even then they held to their scientific program and collected 30 pounds of rock samples for analysis later. It took them 10 days to fight their way to the foot of the glacier. Shortly afterward, Evans collapsed and died. There was still 430 miles to go and the already bad weather worsened.

On March 15 Captain Oates virtually collapsed and begged the others to leave him behind, but they would not. The next day he made an excuse for going out and, according to Scott's journal, "He went out into the blizzard and we have not seen him since. . . . We knew poor Oates was walking to his death, but though we tried to dissuade him, we knew it was the act of a brave man and an English gentleman. We all hope to meet the end with a similar spirit, and assuredly the end is not far."

The last entry Scott made was on March 29 and it read: ". . . Every day now we have been ready to start for our depot *eleven miles* away, but outside the door of the tent, it remains a scene of whirling drift. I do not think we can hope for any better things now. We shall stick it to the end, but we are getting weaker, of course . . . It seems a pity, but I do not think I can write more. For God's sake look after our people."

Eight months later the three bodies were found. Nearby lay the Beardmore rock samples that they had dutifully carried to the end.

Roald Amundsen 1872-1928

Roald Amundsen, the first man to reach the South Pole, was a veteran of polar exploration at the time of his great triumph. He died in the arctic after a life devoted to adventure and risk in the frozen wastes of the world. Amundsen first trained for a career in medicine, but abandoned his studies to teach himself navigation in order to pursue a boyhood enthusiasm for the arctic which had been fired by reading everything he could find on the ill-fated British expedition of John Franklin.

Commanding the ships *Erebus* and *Terror*, which had served James Clark Ross so well, Franklin sailed from London in May 1845. Nothing more was ever heard of him. In the summer of 1847 the British government offered a large reward for the rescue of the missing expedition, and the following year mounted its own rescue operation. Two ships probed the Northwest Passage from the Bering Straits; an overland team tracked northward from Canada; and Ross led a sea search from the east. Such a concentration of forces had never before been seen in the Arctic; yet nothing was found. Then in 1854 Dr John Rae, an official of the Hudson's Bay Company, recovered utensils bearing Franklin's monogram and crest from the Pelly Bay Eskimos near the Boothia Peninsula. An outstandingly successful explorer, Rae worked as far as possible with the Eskimo peoples of the regions he tra-

Right: Roald Amundsen. Although he did not achieve his ambition of being first at the North Pole, he succeeded in reaching the South Pole first.

Above: John Franklin, leader of the English expedition that was lost in the arctic in 1845.

Left: cutlery bearing Franklin's crest. It was given to John Rae by the Pelly Bay Eskimos on his trip there nine years after Franklin and his team had disappeared.

versed. He was skilled in their techniques of survival and was a fine hunter who could build a snow house in a matter of minutes. He returned with the fullest account of the lost expedition that seemed possible.

Franklin's widow refused to abandon the search, however, and succeeded in finding a private sponsor for another expedition. It sailed in July 1857, and after two years of following up Rae's discoveries, its commander found a message and remains of the Franklin company on King William Island. A record left there showed that Franklin had died on June 11, 1847. The 12-year saga of heroism and determination yielded volumes of data on arctic conditions and held fascination for arctic enthusiasts for years after.

It helped Amundsen decide on a life of arctic exploration, and between the ages of 21 and 25 he became a qualified seaman. After working on a merchant ship in the arctic, he joined the first expedition ever to winter in the antarctic, serving as first mate on the *Belgica* under the command of Adrien de Gerlache. On his return to Norway, Amundsen bought a small ship, the *Gjoa*, and prepared to make his way through the Northwest Passage. In 1906 the *Gjoa* became the first single ship to sail the whole length of the legendary waterway.

Amundsen then set his sights on the Pole itself. He hoped to repeat Nansen's voyage of drift using the same ship, the *Fram*, but support for his proposal was slow in coming. Then, in September 1909, came news of Peary's success. Amundsen nonetheless pressed ahead with his preparations since part of his goal had always been to cross the Pole by Nansen's strategy of drift. In June 1910 Britain's much heralded antarctic expedition sailed from London with Robert Scott in command. In August Amundsen also headed south, and it was presumed that he was going to round Cape Horn into the Pacific and sail up to the Bering Sea to start his drift through the Arctic Ocean. In fact, he was secretly planning to make a race of it with Scott to the South Pole.

The *Fram* carried sledges, dogs, and provisions for a polar journey and a crew that had been preparing for a dash across the ice in the northernmost part of the world. When they reached Funchal in the Madeira Islands on September 9, Amundsen let them into his secret. The next month he cabled his challenge to Scott. The *Fram* made such good speed that the Norwegians were setting up camp in the Bay of

Whales when Scott had only reached his base in McMurdo Sound, 60 miles farther north.

Amundsen left camp with four companions on October 19. They had four sledges and 52 dogs in peak conditions. Their objective was to reach the South Pole, pure and simple, and they traveled much lighter than Scott. Amundsen had ingeniously modified the sledges to reduce their weight and he carried no scientific equipment. Furthermore, his arctic experiences had taught him the superiority of the warm, loose fitting, and lightweight fur garments of the Eskimos, which he and the others wore. By October 23 his party had gone 90 miles across the Ross Ice Shelf, and Amundsen reckoned that he could allow a two day rest at the first food depot. He reached his last advance depot on November 3, which was at Latitude 80° S, and the journey had been virtually free of trouble.

Ahead lay snow fields so smooth that Amundsen and his companions were able to travel by wearing their skis and tying themselves to the sledges to be pulled along by the dogs. "And there I stood," wrote Amundsen, "until we reached 85° 05′ S – 340 miles. Yes, that was a pleasant surprise. We had never dreamed of

Below: Fridtjof Nansen's ship the *Fram*, which Amundsen later used for his successful venture to the South Pole.

Left: Amundsen in his special antarctic clothing. He made many adaptions based on his experiences in the arctic, and they proved effective aids to his success.

well in the pure, clear air and the shining white surroundings. . . . No other moment in the whole trip affected me like this. The tears forced their way to my eyes; by no effort of will could I keep them back." On December 13 he and his companions camped only 15 miles from their goal. They slept fitfully. In his book *South Pole*, Amundsen describes that night as living through the "same feeling that I can remember as a little boy of the night before Christmas Eve – an intense expectation of what was going to happen."

The next day at three o'clock of a sparkling sunny afternoon, their calculations told them that they stood at the South Pole. To be satisfied that they had actually touched the bottom of the world, they made a 12 mile circuit of their camp. It proved them right. They planted the Norwegian flag and celebrated their achievement with double rations. Three days later, they headed back for the *Fram*. The journey was

driving on skis to the Pole." It was the middle of November, barely halfway through the antarctic summer, and the Norwegians, far ahead of their British rivals, had only 270 miles to go. Only when he came to leave the Ross ice fields for the upper Polar plateau did Amundsen encounter any real difficulty. Miles to the east of the broad Beardmore Glacier, they had to fight their way up the narrow and treacherous Axel Heiberg Glacier. Even the dogs could not be sure of their footing there. Amundsen had to turn back time and again because their way was blocked by massive outcrops of ice. Even so, they made a new record for travel south on December 7.

Proudly Amundsen marked the achievement by breaking the flag of Norway over the leading sledge. "It shook itself out, waved and flapped so that the silk rustled; it looked wonderfully

comparatively uneventful and they reached their base on January 25 after a round trip to the South Pole of a mere 99 days.

When the British attempt ended in disaster, some critics in Britain and elsewhere blamed Amundsen for it by saying that he had pushed Scott into a race for which he was neither prepared nor equipped; but the bitterness gradually died away. It was clear that besides luck with the terrain and the weather, concentration on a single objective and tough determination had given the Norwegians their well-deserved triumph. At the same time, nothing could detract from the heroism and devotion to scientific duty of their British rivals.

Below: the planting of the Norwegian flag at the South Pole on December 14, 1911.

Left: the airship *Italia* in 1928. Umberto Nobile, who had flown with Amundsen two years previously, piloted the *Italia* in an attempt to cross the North Pole. When it was feared that he was lost, Amundsen went on a rescue mission to find him. Nobile survived, and it was Amundsen who never came back.

Amundsen's South Pole venture was only the most notable chapter in a brilliant career. Between 1918 and 1920, sailing in the *Maud*, Amundsen navigated the Northeast Passage along the northern coasts of Europe and Asia to Nome, Alaska, becoming the second person in history to make the voyage. His next ambition was to fly over the North Pole. Again he was fated to come second. In 1925 he and the American explorer Lincoln Ellsworth made an unsuccessful attempt in the dirigible *Norge*. The following year, in a perilous flight in the same airship and accompanied by Ellsworth and the Italian aviator Umberto Nobile, he succeeded in crossing from Spitzbergen to Alaska, but they had been beaten by a matter of days by the Americans Richard Byrd and Floyd Bennett. Amundsen's flight, which had crossed previously unexplored territory, added important new information about the arctic, but it ended on a sour note when Nobile, who had designed the *Norge*, claimed that he had not been given due credit for the achievement. Two years later in 1928 Nobile took the *Norge*'s sister ship *Italia* on a second arctic flight. When nothing was heard from the expedition for six weeks, two search parties went out. Amundsen was in one of them, flying in a plane with five others. The second search party found the crashed *Italia*, whose survivors included Nobile. But Amundsen and his rescue team never came back.

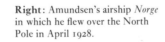

Right: Amundsen's airship *Norge* in which he flew over the North Pole in April 1928.

311

Ernest Shackleton 1874-1922

"The Irish giant," in later years known to his devoted men as "the Boss", Ernest Shackleton had his first experience of the antarctic as a member of Scott's 1901 team on the *Discovery*. He had to be invalided home in 1903 but remained determined to prove himself as an explorer. Over the next 20 years, hero worshiped by the men he led, honored with the dignity of a knighthood by King Edward VII, and absorbed in his own passion for Antarctica, he established himself in the forefront of polar exploration.

Shackleton wanted to be first at the South Pole, but on his return to England in 1903 found neither the British government nor the Royal Navy willing to back him. He finally received an offer of finance from a wealthy industrialist, and in April 1907 made his plans public. His ship, the *Nimrod*, was a 40-year old sealer of 200 tons displacement, equipped with a steam engine. The expedition's supplies included an automobile and a collapsible house some 33 feet long insulated with felt and cork. Shackleton looked on the car as his secret weapon but, since it would be the first such vehicle ever used in polar conditions, it was something of an unknown quantity. It had a 15 horsepower, 4-cylinder, air-cooled engine with an exhaust reheat and was lubricated by a specially developed oil which was effective down to −30° F. The wheels proved to be the principal weakness, despite a variety of ingenious designs evolved by Shackleton himself. Nevertheless, before its loss in a crevasse 11 months after being put to use on the antarctic ice, the machine did valuable work transporting loads of up to 12,000 pounds and reaching average speeds of 22 miles per hour.

Shackleton had plans for a comprehensive program of research as well as exploration. His team included the English-born physicist Douglas Mawson, who had been living in Australia since his boyhood, the geologist T W E David, and other scientists. The expedition reached Antarctica in January 1908. That April Mawson and David climbed to the crater of Mount Erebus, a height of 13,200 feet above sea level. They were able to estimate the approximate depth of the crater at between 800 and 900 feet and its diameter as half a mile. Between September and early February the two scientists, accompanied by a third member of the expedition, made a heroic journey on which they reached the South Magnetic Pole on January 16. The 1200 mile journey had been made entirely on foot, the

Right: Ernest Shackleton. He has been described as a gambler by nature, always ready to take a chance. But he had a particular regard for his crew's safety as well as wide experience as a seaman.

Above: the *Nimrod*, the sealer used by Shackleton on his first expedition. It had a steam engine.

men hauling their own supply sledges and making extensive scientific observations throughout South Victoria Land on their route.

On October 29, 1908, three weeks after their departure, Shackleton led out his assault party for the geographical Pole. Four sledges pulled by the expedition's four remaining ponies carried supplies for 100 days. Crossing the Ross Ice Shelf, the party was the first to see the great ice plateau at the center of the southern ice cap. They negotiated their way upward with comparative ease along the broad sloping glacier that Shackleton named the Beardmore after his financial backer. After a hard march through fierce weather, the party reached Latitude 88° 23′ S. Their ponies all were dead and they had less than half their food in reserve. The Pole lay less than 100 miles distant but Shackleton, whose concern for his men was overriding, ordered the return rather than expose them to possible death. He had failed in his objective, but the expedition had been the training school of some great explorers, chief among them Mawson. Moreover, the scientific results of the venture were immensely important. Shackleton was knighted for his efforts in 1909, the same year in which his book about the expedition, *The Heart of the Antarctic*, appeared.

Some three years later, when Roald Amundsen had won the race for the South Pole and Robert Scott and his companions had met their heroic deaths in that race, it seemed that the great adventures in the antarctic were over. But Shackleton conceived an epic plan. He decided to cross the entire continent from the Weddell

Sea to the Ross Sea over the Pole itself. The strategy called for two expeditions. Shackleton and his party were to land on the Filchner Ice Shelf on the Weddell Sea. The second party was to land on the Ross Ice Shelf and lay a trail of supply depots up the Beardmore Glacier to the polar plateau. These supplies would be used by Shackleton's party in the second stage of their transcontinental trek.

By August 1914 the Imperial Trans-Antarctic Expedition, largely financed by an industrialist, was ready. The *Aurora*, which had once been used by Mawson, was to sail from Tasmania for the Ross Sea. The *Endurance*, specially built to Shackleton's specifications, was to brave the ice of the Weddell Sea. The *Endurance* sailed from London on August 8, four days after the outbreak of World War I and sent on her way with an encouraging message from Winston Churchill, then First Lord of the Admiralty. Polar conditions that year were exceptionally severe. By January 1915 the ice pack closed around the ship, holding it fast. As though to tantalize the

expedition, the ice cracked about two weeks later, opening a channel of clear water near the ship. The men tried to hack a channel toward it, but the water within their ice prison refroze as quickly as they chopped it out. By mid-February, while still 60 miles from the Filchner Ice Shelf, the *Endurance* was hopelessly locked in a slab of ice almost three miles square. It was drifting helplessly away from the expedition's objective, the vast clockwise currents taking the ship northwest.

On August 1, after more than five months in the pack ice, the floe which held the ship cracked in two. The *Endurance* was then exposed to the full pressure of the ice pack, which meant certain destruction. Shackleton held on until the end of October when he gave the order to move all the boats, sledges, and provisions off the ship – and none too soon. As Shackleton described it: "At last, the twisting, grinding floes were working their will on the ship. It was a sickening sensation to feel the decks breaking up under one's feet, the great beams bending and then snapping with

Below: the *Endurance*, caught by the pressure of the ice, keeling over. The ship was destroyed but the expedition members escaped.

a noise like heavy gunfire. . . . The floes, with the force of millions of tons of moving ice behind them, were simply annihilating the ship."

At that point the party was about 350 miles from the nearest land on which they might expect shelter. The great number of icebergs in the sea made it too dangerous for them to consider putting out in the ship's boats. So for the next three and a half months they camped on the drifting floe, supplementing their meager supplies with penguin and seal meat. Early in April, Shackleton

Below: members of Shackleton's expedition on their rescue from Elephant Island. All had survived.

Bottom: the launching of the *James Caird* used by Shackleton for his daring trip to South Georgia to get help for his crew.

judged it possible to try to navigate through the floes. By the end of the month, after a 100-mile voyage through a mass of drifting and colliding bergs, they reached the bleak and hostile shore of Elephant Island. Even to find a landing place took a three-hour search. The wind ripped across the island, shredding the canvas of their tents so that the men had to shelter under the up-turned boats. The chance of rescue was a million to one against. Whalers never passed that way and the nearest manned station was at South Georgia

Island 870 miles away across the stormiest seas in the world. Shackleton decided that someone must try to reach South Georgia and picked five men to sail with him on the desperate voyage.

They were to travel in one of the longboats from the *Endurance*. Twenty-three feet long and six feet wide, its only cover was a crude canvas deck built by the ship's carpenter. They named it *James Caird* in honor of their backer. Furious gales whipped their small boat and accumulated frozen spray iced up the rigging, both threatening to capsize the craft. The men had to chip off the ice while the little boat soared and dived through waves 50 feet high. Toward midnight on May 4, while he took his watch at the tiller, Shackleton saw a "line of clear sky between the south and southwest. I called to the men that the

sky was clearing and then, a moment later, I realized that what I had seen was not a rift in the clouds but the white crest of an enormous wave. ... It was a mighty upheaval of the ocean, a thing quite apart from the big white-capped seas that had been our tireless enemies for many days." The boat was flung forward like a cork, but the men bailed madly with anything that came to hand and somehow the boat came through the wild seething waters.

On May 11 they sighted the coast of South Georgia and landed safely, but on the side opposite to the whaling station which was 150 miles away over steep icy cliffs and deep chasms. Shackleton and two companions, with only a vague idea of the direction on the unexplored island, started out on foot on May 19. After a gruelling journey that included scaling the summit of the glacier, they staggered into the whaling station. A relief party was organized immediately to rescue the three men on the southern shore of the island. As for those on Elephant Island, it took three attempts before they could be taken off. Incredibly, they were still alive and all later recovered fully. The expedition, which had totally failed in its objectives, had nevertheless written another epic chapter in the story of the antarctic.

Shackleton went back to Antarctica in 1921 to map the coast south of the Indian Ocean. Before the expedition actually got under way, the intrepid explorer died of a heart attack. He was buried near the spot where he and his friends had landed on South Georgia Island five years before.

Above: coast of South Georgia. Shackleton had no idea where the station was located and had to go over dangerous uncharted land in search of the aid he needed.

Right: Shackleton's grave on South Georgia, just a few miles from where he had landed on his epic voyage from Elephant Island five years before his death.

The Poles Today

Today Antarctica is governed by international agreements designating that the territory is to be kept free of military use. However, there are numerous rival territorial claims. The largest single area is that of the Australian Antarctic Territory, much of which was explored and claimed for the Commonwealth of Australia by Douglas Mawson, one of the greatest polar explorers. Born in England in 1882, Mawson and his family moved to Australia when he was a child. Having distinguished himself on Shackleton's 1907-08 expedition, he was the natural choice to head the first Australian antarctic expedition. His program was one of both exploration and research.

Mawson's ship, the *Aurora*, set sail in November 1911 during the Scott-Amundsen race for the South Pole. Mawson made his base on Cape Denison in Commonwealth Bay, dubbing it "The Home of the Blizzard" because of the constant winds. The *Aurora* sailed westward with a second group to explore the Shackleton Ice Shelf. The winds that swept Cape Denison were extraordinary even by polar standards. Gusts of up to 200 miles per hour were recorded at the weather hut near the camp, and ceaseless snow storms obscured the starlight. In spite of this, observations were maintained over 10 months. Each trip to the weather hut was hell,

Douglas Mawson (**above**) at the tragic moment when B E S Ninnis (**below**) met his death by falling into a crevasse, and as he looked in later life (**left**).

short as it was. Crawling on hands and knees, head buried against a wind that could lift a tractor 50 yards, a man might find that he had had a finger or a patch of skin on his face frostbitten from just a moment's exposure.

In November 1912 Mawson divided the expedition into five teams. Mawson, accompanied by the English Lieutenant B E S Ninnis and the Swiss Dr Xavier Mertz, headed east to cross the unexplored territory between Cape Denison and Oates Land. By December 14 they were 300 miles from camp and nearing their "farthest east" objective, after which they would turn back to explore inland. They had one sledge loaded with most of their food because one other had been damaged, and Ninnis was bringing up the rear with it. Mertz skiied ahead, searching the route for crevasses, and Mawson was behind him with a lighter sledge. About noon, Mertz gave the warning sign for a crevasse. Mawson gingerly drove his dog team over the danger, but the ice bridge gave way beneath Ninnis' heavily laden sledge and he dropped into the hole.

Peering down into the darkness, Mawson and Mertz saw only two dogs on an ice shelf 150 feet below, one dying and the other dead. For three hours they shouted and waited, but no answer came. Their friend dead, their tent, dog rations, and most of their food lost, they faced a 300 mile trek with only enough food for 10 days and with 15 dogs already weak. They took suicidal risks, worked their dogs to death, and shot the remainder for the stringy meat. On January 1, still 120 miles from base, Mertz collapsed. Mawson had to haul the sledge alone, with his dying companion stretched out on top. A week later, Mertz died.

Discarding everything but the most essential, Mawson sawed away the back half of the sledge to reduce the weight he had to pull. Making about five miles a day on frostbitten feet, he battled on. On January 17, crossing the Mertz Glacier named after his dead friend, he fell into a crevasse and was left dangling at the end of the

sledge rope. Miraculously the sledge stuck in the snow, and after falling back once more, Mawson managed an agonizing inch-by-inch climb up the rope to solid ground. Twelve days later he stumbled on a cairn set up by a search party who left in it a cache of food. Despite his desperate state, Mawson had held accurately to his route. On the morning of February 1, he at last sighted the expedition's headquarters. As he lifted his eyes he saw the *Aurora* steaming out of the bay.

Mawson staggered to safety. Waiting for him at camp were five volunteers who had decided to winter at the base on the slim chance that he would return. They radioed the ship to return, but the captain dared not in the face of a storm. Furthermore, he was on his way to pick up the companion party on the Shackleton Ice Shelf, a group that was not provisioned for the winter. So, despite his long ordeal, Mawson spent another winter in the antarctic. When the *Aurora* returned the following year, Mawson deferred his homecoming long enough to complete some survey work along the coast, showing his dedication to science once more. His homecoming in February 1914 earned him world honor and a knighthood.

Years passed before Mawson recovered fully from his ordeal. During that time he worked as professor of geology at Adelaide University in South Australia. Then in 1929 he took command of the joint British, Australian, and New Zealand antarctic expedition that succeeded in making new territorial and scientific discoveries. Mawson systematically used a small seaplane as an important tool of exploration on that trip. In 1931 he retired from exploration, having claimed 2,225,000 square miles of Antarctica for Australia.

By the early 1930s aerial survey was regularly being used as an aid to mapping. It had started with Scott and Shackleton, who in 1902 made historic balloon ascents in Antarctica. In 1928 the Australian Hubert Wilkins flew the first airplane on the continent, and the following year the American Richard E Byrd made the first bold and hazardous flight across the South Pole. He took off from the large permanent base he called Little America, which his expedition of 1928–1930 built on the coast of the Ross Ice Shelf. It was equipped with electricity, telephones, three radio towers, and airplanes.

In 1933 Byrd led a major scientific expedition to Little America. As part of the program a small weather hut was erected more than 100 miles from the base, and Byrd decided to stay there alone during the seven dark months of the Antarctic winter. After three months his radio transmissions became disturbingly irrational, and his team decided to investigate in spite of his orders to the contrary. They found Byrd too weak to move. Carbon monoxide fumes leaking from the hut's faulty stove had been slowly poisoning him, but he had not asked for help because he did not want to endanger the lives of a rescue mission. It took two months of recuperation before he could be flown back to Little America.

In 1946 Byrd commanded the largest expedition yet sent to Antarctica. Called Operation Highjump, it consisted of 4700 men and 13 ships, which were divided into three groups to cover different regions. They discovered new mountain ranges and islands and mapped and photographed 1400 miles of coastline. During the International Geophysical Year of 1957-58, Byrd headed the program for the United States, which was one of 12 nations that established about 50 scientific bases. The Soviet Union and the United States sent up artificial satellites and high-altitude rockets carrying instruments to study cosmic conditions.

The International Geophysical Year also saw the fulfillment of Ernest Shackleton's dream of crossing the frozen continent from sea to sea. It was achieved by the British Commonwealth Trans-Antarctic expedition under Dr Vivian Fuchs. He started from the Weddell Sea while Edmund Hillary, of Mount Everest fame, was establishing supply bases from the other side. Fuchs made slow progress through fearful con-

ditions, with his heavy new Sno-Cat and Weasel vehicles getting stuck in the snow repeatedly. On the other hand, Hillary made such good progress that he saw the possibility of completing the crossing himself. Early in January 1958 he urged London headquarters to have Fuchs turn back in the face of the coming winter, but it was decided that Fuchs should continue. After an arduous and hazardous trek, he reached his goal on March 2, 1958 – 44 years after Shackleton's attempt.

The following year, 12 nations signed a treaty

Below: Edmund Hillary (center) and Vivian Fuchs (right) of the British Commonwealth expedition meet Rear Admiral George Dufek of the United States naval force in the antarctic during the International Geophysical Year.

Right: a camp pitched by Fuch's team on the way to the South Pole. His party carried out an extensive scientific program.

Left: Richard E Byrd cooking a meal on the stove that almost brought about his death during his lonely vigil in a weather station 123 miles from Little America.

guaranteeing that each of them could perform peaceful or scientific experiments in Antarctica. However, it is open to question how long competition for economic gain can be controlled. It is known that the waters surrounding the frozen continent are rich in krill and food fish, and there is evidence of the existence of coal, oil, and gas on the land. Any exploitation of these natural resources could lead to trouble.

The possibility of settlement and exploitation of resources is even more conceivable in the northernmost part of the globe, where explora-

Above: Wally Herbert, the first man to make a surface crossing of the Arctic Ocean to the North Pole.

Right: members of the Herbert team trying to get their sledge over an ice ridge. The last part of the journey was a race against time before the summer thaw came.

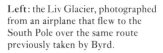

Left: the Liv Glacier, photographed from an airplane that flew to the South Pole over the same route previously taken by Byrd.

tion started much earlier. Yet the first surface crossing of the frozen Arctic Ocean was not made until between February 21, 1968 and April 6, 1969 by a British expedition led by Wally Herbert.

Herbert described the problems of accurately locating the exact position of the North Pole as: "trying to step on the shadow of a bird that was circling overhead. The surface across which we were moving was itself a moving surface on a planet that was spinning about an axis. We were standing approximately on that axis..." Herbert and his team had trekked the 3700 miles from Barrow Point, Alaska to Spitzbergen in 476 days, a decade before the United States nuclear submarine *Nautilus*, sailing on a more direct course, made the journey under the world's ice cap in 96 hours.

In the nuclear age, competition over the arctic among the Soviet Union, the United States, and Canada is intense. The region is strategically critical. The discovery of oil in Alaska adds political and economic factors to the rivalry between Canada and the United States. Nuclear power makes it feasible to consider large permanent settlements and the ancient ecological balance between humans and the icefields is over. The Eskimo peoples have rapidly adapted to modern conditions and are losing their traditional skills. Thanks to generations of explorers, the whole world is now open to technological development. It is to be hoped that their magnificent story will not have an unhappy ending.

Index

Left: Tensing Norgay on the top of
Mount Everest on the morning of
May 29, 1953, as photographed by
Edmund Hillary. In scaling this
formidable Himalaya peak, the two
met one of the last great challenges
of unknown places.

O

P

Picture Credits

Here is the story of the world's great adventures into the unknown, told through the lives of the explorers who dared go where none had gone before. Each chapter deals with an age or area of discovery, from the early Egyptian sea voyages to the modern race for the South Pole. Da Gama and Columbus, Magellan and Hudson, Bering and Cook, Livingstone and Amundsen— these are just some of the most famous of the over 50 explorers in this book. Theirs are now classic tales of sheer courage, strong conviction, and often personal hardship. They filled in the map of the world, first by outlining the coasts and then by penetrating the interiors of Asia, the Americas, Africa, Australasia, the Arctic and the Antarctic. Among the numerous illustrations are old maps that show the world as it was believed to be at the time that various expeditions of discovery were setting out. In all, the book offers an unusual and interesting approach to one of the most fascinating of all human endeavours—the journey into the unknown.